T0192095

Communications in Computer and Information Science 1837

Rationale

The CCIS series is devoted to the publication of proceedings of computer science conferences. Its aim is to efficiently disseminate original research results in informatics in printed and electronic form. While the focus is on publication of peer-reviewed full papers presenting mature work, inclusion of reviewed short papers reporting on work in progress is welcome, too. Besides globally relevant meetings with internationally representative program committees guaranteeing a strict peer-reviewing and paper selection process, conferences run by societies or of high regional or national relevance are also considered for publication.

Topics

The topical scope of CCIS spans the entire spectrum of informatics ranging from foundational topics in the theory of computing to information and communications science and technology and a broad variety of interdisciplinary application fields.

Information for Volume Editors and Authors

Publication in CCIS is free of charge. No royalties are paid, however, we offer registered conference participants temporary free access to the online version of the conference proceedings on SpringerLink (http://link.springer.com) by means of an http referrer from the conference website and/or a number of complimentary printed copies, as specified in the official acceptance email of the event.

CCIS proceedings can be published in time for distribution at conferences or as post-proceedings, and delivered in the form of printed books and/or electronically as USBs and/or e-content licenses for accessing proceedings at SpringerLink. Furthermore, CCIS proceedings are included in the CCIS electronic book series hosted in the SpringerLink digital library at http://link.springer.com/bookseries/7899. Conferences publishing in CCIS are allowed to use Online Conference Service (OCS) for managing the whole proceedings lifecycle (from submission and reviewing to preparing for publication) free of charge.

Publication process

The language of publication is exclusively English. Authors publishing in CCIS have to sign the Springer CCIS copyright transfer form, however, they are free to use their material published in CCIS for substantially changed, more elaborate subsequent publications elsewhere. For the preparation of the camera-ready papers/files, authors have to strictly adhere to the Springer CCIS Authors' Instructions and are strongly encouraged to use the CCIS LaTeX style files or templates.

Abstracting/Indexing

CCIS is abstracted/indexed in DBLP, Google Scholar, EI-Compendex, Mathematical Reviews, SCImago, Scopus. CCIS volumes are also submitted for the inclusion in ISI Proceedings.

How to start

To start the evaluation of your proposal for inclusion in the CCIS series, please send an e-mail to ccis@springer.com.

Juan Antonio Lossio-Ventura ·
Jorge Valverde-Rebaza · Eduardo Díaz ·
Hugo Alatrista-Salas

Editors

Information Management and Big Data

9th Annual International Conference, SIMBig 2022
Lima, Peru, November 16–18, 2022
Proceedings

 Springer

Editors
Juan Antonio Lossio-Ventura ⓘ
National Institutes of Health
Bethesda, MD, USA

Jorge Valverde-Rebaza ⓘ
Visibilia
Sao Carlos, Brazil

Eduardo Díaz ⓘ
Peruvian University of Applied Sciences
Lima, Peru

Hugo Alatrista-Salas ⓘ
Pontifical Catholic University of Peru
Lima, Peru

ISSN 1865-0929   ISSN 1865-0937 (electronic)
Communications in Computer and Information Science
ISBN 978-3-031-35444-1   ISBN 978-3-031-35445-8 (eBook)
https://doi.org/10.1007/978-3-031-35445-8

This Springer imprint is published by the registered company Springer Nature Switzerland AG
The registered company address is: Gewerbestrasse 11, 6330 Cham, Switzerland

Preface

SIMBig 2022[1], the 9th edition of the International Conference on Information Management and Big Data, was held between November 16–18, 2022 at the Facultad de Ingeniería de Sistemas e Informática (FISI)[2], of the Universidad Nacional Mayor de San Marcos[3], Lima, Peru. SIMBig 2022 presented novel methods for the analysis and management of large data, in fields like Artificial Intelligence (AI), Data Science, Machine Learning, Natural Language Processing, Semantic Web, Data-driven Software Engineering, Health Informatics, among others.

The SIMBig conference series aims to promote cooperation between national and international researchers to improve data-driven decision-making by using new technologies dedicated to analyzing data. SIMBig is a convivial place where participants present their scientific contributions in the form of full and short papers. This book contains the papers presented at the 9th edition of SIMBig. After undergoing a double-blind review process, a total of 19 papers were selected for publication in this edition, consisting of 18 long papers and one short paper. The acceptance rate for these papers was 38%.

Keynote Speakers' Resumes

Dr. Monica Lam, from Stanford University, USA, talked about taming neural language models into trustworthy conversational virtual assistants. Dr. Lam started with the question "what if computers can truly converse with us in our native tongue?" Then, she discussed how computers will transform into effective, personalized assistants for everybody. Commercial chatbots today are notoriously brittle as they are hardcoded to handle a few possible choices of user inputs. Recently introduced large language neural models, such as GPT-3, are remarkably fluent, but they are prone to hallucinations, often producing incorrect statements. This talk described how we can tame these neural models into robust, trustworthy, and cost-effective conversational agents.

Dr. Leman Akoglu, from Carnegie Mellon University, USA, talked about unsupervised machine learning for explainable Medicare fraud detection. A major concern in the US federal health care system is overbilling, waste, and fraud by providers, who face incentives to misreport on their claims to receive higher reimbursements. In this talk, focusing on Medicare (the health insurance program for elderly adults and the disabled), Dr. Leman presented data-driven techniques to identify providers with spending patterns consistent with overbilling. Her approach was (i) fully unsupervised, avoiding laborious human labeling and (ii) explainable to end users, guiding the auditing process. Data from the Department of Justice on providers facing anti-fraud lawsuits validated the approach.

---

[1] https://simbig.org/SIMBig2022/.

[2] https://sistemas.unmsm.edu.pe/.

[3] https://unmsm.edu.pe/.

Dr. Jiang Bian, from University of Florida, USA, started his talk with the question: What if AI could utilize real-world data, spanning from prediction to intervention modeling, to address issues of fairness and disparities? The rapid adoption of electronic health record (EHR) systems has made large collections of real-world data (RWD) available for research. These datasets reflect the characteristics and outcomes of patients being treated in real-world settings. The increasing availability of RWD, combined with advancements in AI, especially machine learning and deep learning, offers untapped opportunities to generate real-world evidence for a wide range of biomedical and clinical questions. This talk focused on several applications of AI on real-world data, highlighting the shift from building traditional prediction models to more careful study design that considers "interventional" models. Furthermore, Dr. Bian discussed how the utilization of real-world data and AI can provide opportunities for addressing health disparities and improving health equity, particularly through the inclusion of social determinants of health. However, these advancements also bring challenges in ensuring fairness due to inherent limitations such as structural missingness and data quality issues.

Dr. Andrew Tomkins, from Google, USA, talked about A/B testing for high-quality alternatives. A/B testing is widely used to tune search and recommendation algorithms, to compare product variants as efficiently and effectively as possible, and even to study animal behavior. With ongoing investment, due to diminishing returns, the items produced by the new candidate show smaller and smaller improvement in quality from the items produced by the current system. By formalizing this observation, Dr. Tomkins developed the first closed-form analytical expressions for the sample efficiency of a number of widely used families of slate-based comparison tests. In empirical trials, these theoretical sample complexity results are shown to be predictive of real-world testing efficiency outcomes. These findings offer opportunities for both more cost-effective testing and a better analytical understanding of the problem.

Dr. Wang-Chiew Tan, from Meta AI - Facebook, USA, talked about deep data integration. We have witnessed the widespread adoption of deep learning techniques as avant-garde solutions to different computational problems in recent years. In data integration, the use of deep learning techniques has helped establish several state-of-the-art results in long standing problems, including information extraction, entity matching, data cleaning, and table understanding. In her talk, she reflected on the strengths of deep learning and how that has helped move forward the needle in data integration. Dr. Tan also discussed a few challenges associated with solutions based on deep learning techniques and described some opportunities for future work.

Dr. Yi Guo, from University of Florida, USA, spoke about the use of causal inference in machine learning for actionable healthcare. Machine (deep) learning is increasingly becoming key to precision medicine, from identifying disease risks and taking preventive measures, to making diagnoses and personalizing treatment for individuals. Precision medicine, however, is not only about predicting risks and outcomes, but also about weighing interventions. Interventional clinical predictive models require the correct specification of cause and effect, and the calculation of so-called counterfactual, that is, alternative scenarios. In biomedical research, observational studies are commonly affected by confounding and selection bias. Without robust assumptions, often requiring a priori domain knowledge, causal inference is not feasible. Data-driven prediction models are often mistakenly used to draw causal effects, but neither their parameters nor their predictions necessarily have a causal interpretation. Dr. Guo discussed how target trials, transportability and prediction invariance are linchpins to developing and testing intervention models.

Dr. Rich Caruana, from Microsoft, USA, presented the work "Friends don't Let friends deploy black-box models: glass-box learning to the rescue". Dr. Caruana presented a variety of case studies where glass-box learning methods uncover surprising statistics in data that would make deploying a black-box model trained on that data risky. Fortunately, the high-accuracy glass-box ML methods now available make it possible to detect and correct these problems before deployment, and to protect privacy and reduce bias, too.

Dr. Dilek Hakkani-Tur, from Amazon, USA, presented her work ingesting knowledge from diverse sources to open domain social conversations. Following the recent advancements in language modeling and availability of large natural language datasets, the last decade has seen the flourishing of conversational AI research. The progress also helped emphasize the importance of reasoning over a diverse set of external knowledge and task completion resources for forming relevant, informative, and accurate responses. In her talk, Dr. Hakkani-Tur discussed their recent work on integrating knowledge to conversation responses from such a diverse set of resources, challenges associated with these, and progress they made so far.

Dr. Sanjay Madria, from Missouri University, USA, discussed the negative impact of the COVID-19 pandemic on global health, resulting in a crisis that affected daily life and caused physical, mental, and economic strain. To understand the emotional responses during this crisis, Dr. Madria proposed a neural network model that could detect various emotions at fine-grained levels in COVID-19 tweets. He also used a deep learning model – based on the pre-trained BERT-base – to detect political ideology from tweets and found that using emotion as a feature improved the accuracy of ideology detection. These models could help understand emotional responses during the pandemic and their impact on mental health and socio-economic outcomes.

Juan Antonio Lossio-Ventura
Jorge Valverde-Rebaza
Eduardo Díaz
Hugo Alatrista-Salas

Organization

General Organizers

Juan Antonio Lossio-Ventura   National Institutes of Health, USA
Hugo Alatrista-Salas   Pontificia Universidad Católica del Perú, Peru

Local Organizers

Carlos Navarro Depaz   Universidad Nacional Mayor de San Marcos, Peru
Nora La Serna Palomino   Universidad Nacional Mayor de San Marcos, Peru
Armando Fermín-Pérez   Universidad Nacional Mayor de San Marcos, Peru

SNMAM Track Organizers

Jorge Valverde-Rebaza   Visibilia, Brazil
Alan Demétrius Baria Valejo   Federal University of São Carlos, Brazil
Fabiana Rodrigues de Góes   University of São Paulo, Brazil

DISE Track Organizers

Denisse Muñante-Arzapalo   ENSIIE & Samovar, France
Carlos Gavidia-Calderon   The Open University, UK
Eduardo Díaz   Universidad Peruana de Ciencias Aplicadas, Peru

Program Committee

Nathalie Abadie   LASTIG Lab, Gustave Eiffel University, IGN - ENSG, France
Amine Abdaoui   Huawei Research, France
Pedro Marco Achanccaray Diaz   Technical University of Braunschweig, Germany
Hugo Alatrista-Salas   Pontificia Universidad Católica del Perú, Peru
Marco Alvarez   University of Rhode Island, USA
Sophia Ananiadou   University of Manchester, UK

Erick Antezana	Norwegian University of Science and Technology, Norway
Smith Washington Arauco Canchumuni	Pontifical Catholic University of Rio de Janeiro, Brazil
John Atkinson	Universidad Adolfo Ibañez, Chile
Imon Banerjee	Mayo Clinic, USA
Riza Batista-Navarro	University of Manchester, UK
Guissela Bejarano Nicho	Universidad Peruana Cayetano Heredia (UPCH), Peru
Jesús Bellido Angulo	Universidad de Ingeniería y Tecnología UTEC, Peru
Elena Beretta	Vrije Universiteit Amsterdam, Netherlands
Giacomo Bergami	Newcastle University, UK
Jose David Bermudez Castro	Pontifical Catholic University of Rio de Janeiro, Brazil
Jiang Bian	University of Florida, USA
Vinicius Borges	University of Brasília, Brazil
Carmen Brando	École des hautes études en sciences sociales, France
Sandra Bringay	Paul Valéry University, France
Andrei Broder	Google, USA
Jean-Paul Calbimonte Pérez	University of Applied Sciences and Arts Western Switzerland, Switzerland
Guillermo Calderón-Ruiz	Universidad Católica de Santa María, Peru
Ricardo Campos	Polytechnic Institute of Tomar; INESC TEC, Portugal
Gabriel Carrasco	Universidad Peruana Cayetano Heredia, Peru
Mete Celik	Erciyes Üniversitesi, Turkey
Thierry Charnois	Paris 13 University, France
Qingyu Chen	National Institutes of Health (NLM/NIH), USA
Davide Chicco	University of Toronto, Canada
Andrea Cimmino	Universidad Politécnica de Madrid, Spain
Adrien Coulet	Inria Paris, France
Fabio Crestani	University of Lugano, Switzerland
Erick Cuenca	Yachay Tech University, Ecuador
Jessica Dafflon	National Institutes of Health (NIMH/NIH), USA
Nuno Datia	Instituto Superior de Engenharia de Lisboa (ISEL), Portugal
Dina Demner-Fushman	National Institutes of Health (NLM/NIH), USA
Damiano Distante	University of Rome Unitelma Sapienza, Italy
Marcos Aurélio Domingues	State University of Maringá, Brazil
Martín Ariel Domínguez	Universidad Nacional de Córdoba, Argentina
Alexandre Donizeti Alves	UFABC, Brazil

Antoine Doucet	University of La Rochelle, France
Brett Drury	Liverpool Hope University, UK
Jocelyn Dunstan	University of Chile, Chile
Tome Eftimov	Jožef Stefan Institute, Slovenia
Okyaz Eminaga	Stanford University, USA
Almudena Espin Perez	Stanford Universiry, USA
Jacinto Estima	Department of Informatics Engineering, University of Coimbra, Portugal
Thiago Faleiros	Universidade de São Paulo, Brazil
Karina Figueroa Mora	Universidad Michoacana de San Nicolás de Hidalgo, Mexico
Frédéric Flouvat	Aix-Marseille Université, France
Kimberly Fornace	London School of Hygiene and Tropical Medicine, UK
Diego Furtado Silva	University of São Paulo, Brazil
Ana Paula Galarreta Asian	Pontificia Universidad Católica del Perú, Peru
Daniela Godoy	UNICEN University, ISISTAN Research Institute, Argentina
Cédric Grueau	Setúbal Polytechnic Institute, Portugal
Rafael Giusti	Federal University of Amazonas, Brazil
Jiawei Han	University of Illinois at Urbana-Champaign, USA
Matthias Hagen	Martin-Luther-Universität Halle-Wittenberg, Germany
Patrick Happ	Pontifical Catholic University of Rio de Janeiro, Brazil
Tina Hernandez-Boussard	Stanford University, USA
Pedro Henrique Luz de Araujo	University of Vienna, Austria
David Hicks	Texas A&M University-Kingsville, USA
Pilar Hidalgo-León	Pontificia Universidad Católica del Perú, Peru
Edward Hinojosa	Universidad Nacional de San Agustín, Peru
Ian Horrocks	Oxford University, UK
Sylvia Iasulaitis	Federal University of São Carlos, Brazil
Diana Inkpen	University of Ottawa, Canada
Maulik Kamdar	Elsevier Inc., USA
Eric Kergosien	GERiiCO Lab, University of Lille 3, France
Martin Krallinger	Barcelona Supercomputing Center, Spain
Ravi Kumar	Google, USA
Jose Labra-Gayo	University of Oviedo, Spain
Ka Chun Lam	National Institutes of Health (NIMH/NIH), USA
Juan Lazo Lazo	Universidad del Pacífico, Peru
Florence Le Ber	Université de Strasbourg / ENGEES, France
Alexandre Levada	Federal University of São Carlos, Brazil

Organizing Institutions

Facultad de Ingeniería de Sistemas e Informática (FISI)[4], of the Universidad Nacional Mayor de San Marcos[5], Lima, Peru

Collaborating Institutions

Universidad Peruana de Ciencias Aplicadas, Peru[6]
The North American Chapter of the Association for Computational Linguistics NAACL, USA[7]
Universidad Andina del Cusco, Peru[8]
Visibilia, Brasil[9]

---

[4] https://sistemas.unmsm.edu.pe/.
[5] https://unmsm.edu.pe/.
[6] https://www.upc.edu.pe/.
[7] http://naacl.org/.
[8] https://www.uandina.edu.pe/.
[9] http://visibilia.net.br.

Contents

A Preliminary Analysis of Twitter's LGBTQ+ Discussions

Abu Naweem Khan and Rahat Ibn Rafiq[(⊠)]

Grand Valley State University, Allendale, USA
{khanab,rafiqr}@mail.gvsu.edu

Abstract. Social media platforms play a significant role in the lives of LGBTQ+ (Lesbian, Gay, Bisexual, Transgender, Queer, and others) individuals, where they have to tackle the challenge of managing their sexual and gender identities. In addition, social media have been leveraged as the go-to platform for a significant proportion of LGBTQ+ communities to come out and participate in discussions related to their rights and the discrimination faced. Twitter, in particular, has been analyzed to understand online behaviors towards LGBTQ+ communities, an example being how online Twitter discussions can reveal discriminatory behavior towards them. However, a macro-level analysis of LGBTQ+ tweets since the early days of Twitter has been understudied. In this research, we present a preliminary macro-analysis of users and tweets since 2006 to gather insights into queries such as: What emotions and toxicity levels are more prevalent in LGBTQ+ discussions? Do the emotions and toxicity levels in tweets change over time? What do we know about the users who have frequently been tweeting about LGBTQ+-related topics since 2006? Upon our analyses, we find that emotions such as joy and anger and toxicity such as identity attacks and threats are more prevalent in the negative user-bios and tweets. We also see a significant increase in activity on Twitter over the years for both overall and positive emotions.

Keywords: data-analysis · LGBTQ+ · social networks

1 Introduction

Social media platforms have been changing how people navigate their lives at a breakneck speed, introducing new complicated challenges in balancing public and private lives. It is of particular importance to LGBTQ+ (Lesbian, Gay, Bisexual, Transgender, Queer, and others) individuals who are faced with the task of negotiating how they manage their sexual and gender identities on social media. Social media platforms play a critical role for LGBTQ+ minorities to come out, engage in online discussions, seek help, support, and even validation [11]. Researchers have found that LGBTQ+ communities are more active on social media than cisgender communities [36].

© The Author(s), under exclusive license to Springer Nature Switzerland AG 2023
J. A. Lossio-Ventura et al. (Eds.): SIMBig 2022, CCIS 1837, pp. 1–17, 2023.
https://doi.org/10.1007/978-3-031-35445-8_1

LGBTQ+ individuals are susceptible to unique minority stressors related to their sexual or gender identities that can sometimes negatively affect their self-esteem and emotional health [7]. Although LGBTQ+ identities do not necessitate dysfunction and LGBTQ+ acceptance has improved in many parts of the world, navigating LGBTQ+ identities in hetero- and cisgender-dominant societies can nonetheless result in discrimination and marginalization [19]. However, the online contexts of LGBTQ+ young people have been understudied due to a focus on the experiences of members of dominant groups [3]. Furthermore, research on LGBTQ+ experiences online has often relied on traditional methods like survey data, which provide an indirect and very general picture of participants' online social worlds [22].

Researchers have recently put Twitter under the microscope to understand online behavior toward LGBTQ+ communities. In [15], researchers demonstrate that Twitter online discussions can act as a consistent microcosm to investigate equality of hospital care towards LGBTQ+ individuals. The effect of isolation, lockdown, and Covid-19 on LGBTQ+ communities have also been investigated by analyzing Twitter data [41]. Therefore, we select Twitter social media for our research to understand macro behaviors towards and inside LGBTQ+ communities. We are interested to understand the users who frequently post about issues related to LGBTQ+ issues by mining their metadata statistics and user-bio—a textual section that Twitter users often include to describe themselves. We also investigate the sentiments, emotions, and toxicity levels in the negative tweets that the users share. Note that, throughout this paper, we refer to the collection of tweets related to LGBTQ+ discussions in our dataset as "tweets". Furthermore, we explore the evolution of sentiments and toxicity on Twitter regarding LGBTQ+ topics: have the feelings, emotions, and toxicity levels evolved since the early days of Twitter? If they have, in what way did they develop? In this paper, we compile a dataset of tweets and users; collected by leveraging a set of hashtags and keywords related to LGBTQ+ issues and communities. Note that we define the word "user" as the set of users in our dataset who has posted tweets related to LGBTQ+ topics, not the general Twitter users. Upon completion of compiling the dataset, we perform the following:

– Analyze the bios of the users who post regarding LGBTQ+ topics and issues. We investigate the texts, emotions, and presence of toxicity shared in the bios
– Analyze the user statistics such as the number of tweets posted, number of followers, number of followings, and social media activity
– Analyze the collected tweets' exhibited emotions, sentiments, and toxicity-presence
– Analyze the evolution of sentiments, activities, and toxicities related to LGBTQ+ issues since the early days of Twitter

We organize the rest of the paper as follows. First, we review the related work. Then, in Sect. 3, we provide a description of our dataset. We proceed to present analyses on user metadata and user-posted tweets in Sect. 4 and 5 respectively. Finally, we conclude the paper in Sect. 7 by summarizing our findings and exploring future research directions.

2   Related Work

2.1   Online Social Media Behavior Analysis

Social media are known to provide spaces where marginalized, stigmatized, and prejudiced individuals and communities can express themselves, share their experiences, and seek potential support with less risk of offline harm [5]. Data collected from several social media platforms have been leveraged to provide significant insights into stigmatized experiences in domains such as cyberbullying [29], toxicity [2], drug misuse [12], sexual abuse [4], LGBTQ+ bullying [10] and suicidal behavior [20].

2.2   LGBTQ+ Community on Social Media

Social media often work as platforms for minorities such as LGBTQ+ communities and individuals to engage in online discussions, conversations, and activities, such as seeking out social support, exchanging information, and maintaining social relationships [32, 36]. Recent researches show that LGBTQ+ communities tend to be more active on social media than their cisgender counterparts [36]. Several data analysis studies have focused on the effect of social media usage on the LGBTQ+ population. One recent research identified social media platforms as the primary tool for LGBTQ+ youth to actively come out—viewing the online platforms as a safe place [11]. Furthermore, Researchers have analyzed data from social media to understand the effect of Covid-19 on LGBTQ+ communities [41], mental health [17] and online discussions on hospital care regarding LGBTQ+ individuals [15].

2.3   User, Sentiment and Toxicity Analysis on Social Media

Social media platforms can act as tools to effectively assess human behavior on the web [18]. Keeping this in mind, several online platforms, such as Twitter, Instagram, and TikTok, have been investigated by researchers in recent years to understand better negative human behaviors such as bullying [30, 39], toxicity [26], white nationalist propaganda [42] and religious radicalism [1]. An example of such analysis: In [42], the authors analyzed the Gab social network, analyzing what kind of users it hosts, the main topics of discussions, and to what extent Gab users share toxic postings. In [27], the authors leveraged Google Perspective API to predict toxic interactions on social media Gettr.

3   Dataset Description

This section describes our dataset, collection methodology, and ethical concerns. We begin with an overview of the Twitter APIs used for data collection. Then we describe the API parameters and collection methodology. After that, we explain the data storage and preprocessing techniques employed to generate the final

Table 1. Sample of Hashtags and Keywords used for data collection

Included Hashtags	#pride, #lgbtq, #MeQueer, #loveislove, #gay, #queer, #gayrights, #WorldPride, #antigay, #antilgbt, #antilgbtq, #homophobeandproud, #HomosDNI, #homophobic, #SignsYoSonIsGay, #Gaysmustdie, #Transphobia, #TeamHomophobes, #Biphobia
Included Keywords	Pride month, gay pride, trans pride, pro-gay, gay conversion, homos must die
Excluded Hashtags	#porn, #fuck, #nsfw, #gayporn, #cam, #webcam, #xxx, #porno

dataset of $2,047,292$ users and $8,581,627$ tweets. The dataset is available upon request, and the code is available on[1]. Finally, we discuss the limitations and ethical concerns with the data collection methodology.

3.1 Twitter API

The full description of all the available Twitter APIs is out of the scope of this paper. Therefore, we only briefly discuss the relevant API calls in this section. We leverage Twitter API v2.0 with academic research access that is publicly available [38]. We use the following endpoints for data collection.

Full-Archive Search. This API allows tweet search on the full Twitter database. We use a keyword search for the English language, exclude retweets, and paginate by start and end dates. We start our collection from March 1st, 2006 (Twitter opened in March 2006 [40]) to Dec 31st, 2020. We collect, for every tweet, the tweet id, tweet text, author id, conversation id, like, reply, retweet and quote counts, and tweet creation date.

Users Lookup. This API accepts user id, which we collect by consolidating tweet author ids and returns publicly available metrics of the user. For each user, we collect data such as URL, location, username, creation date, protected status, name, description (i.e., user-bio), profile image URL, and the number of followers, followings, and tweets.

Follows and Friends Lookup. Follows (Friends) API endpoint allows to collect Followers for (users following) a given user-id.

3.2 Collection Methodology

For tweet collection, we use keyword-based archive search from 1st March 2006 to 31st December 2020. We make sure to include Positive, Neutral, and Negative

---

[1] https://github.com/Shuv0Khan/TweetApp.

Hashtags to collect a diversified set of tweets related to the LGBTQ+ community and subjects. At the end of this step, we have a total of 66 positive hashtags, 11 negative hashtags, 5 positive keywords, 1 negative keywords, and 8 excluded keywords. We present a sample of the hashtags and keywords in Table 1. We also include a set of excluded keywords to tackle hashtag-hijacking [24].

We now explain the issues we faced when forming the keywords and hashtags set for the archive search and the methodologies we employed to tackle those.

– As the initial step, we identify several influencers, pro-organizations, and activists. We peruse their public Twitter timeline manually to understand the culture of the LGBTQ+ community better and find out more relevant and diversified hashtags set. In particular, We identify eight highly interactive positive organizations/influencers and one negative influencer to form our positive and negative hashtag sets. We also choose six relevant keywords to ensure we do not miss tweets without hashtags.
– *Hashtag drift* is defined as linguistic changes in how the hashtags are used over time [8]. To tackle this issue, we use Best-Hashtag [6] online service to identify hashtags that occur together. Next, we leverage Hashtagify [14] to identify the stale hashtags; and get more recent hashtags that are used instead of those.

Using the hashtag and keyword set, we collect in total $8,581,627$ tweets. These tweets include the author id, which we use to collect public metrics like followers, followings, tweet counts, user-bios, etc., for $2,047,292$ unique users. Our preliminary analysis shows that 96.28% and 99.21% users in our dataset have at most $10,000$ followers and followings, respectively. The user-bios and tweets we collected are then preprocessed for further analysis. The preprocessing involved lowercasing the user-bios, removing all hyperlinks, user mentions, hashtags, extra whitespaces, and removing all users with empty bios. This preprocessing step resulted in a collection of $1,741,912$ user-bios. We use this set of users for our analysis in later sections.

3.3 Ethical Considerations

The nature of Twitter data has ethical implications. We complied with the Twitter developer agreement and policy in the data collection and analysis. We only collected publicly available data and anonymized the dataset. Further, we only present aggregated results and never interact with users. Regardless, we adopt standard ethical guidelines in our collection, storage, and analysis of the data [31].

4 User Analysis

In this section, we perform initial analysis on the users' profile data collected in Sect. 3.2.

4.1   User Bio Analysis

Table 2. Top 20 hashtags and domains

Hashtags	Users	Domains	Users
#blacklivesmatter	18889	instagram	13996
#blm	15384	youtube	11907
#resist	8171	facebook	11658
#lgbt	4986	twitch	6331
#lgbtq	4880	amazon	5504
#maga	4647	onlyfans	5486
#gay	4475	linktr	4771
#teamfollowback	3604	patreon	3022
#music	2991	ko-fi	3009
#writer	2778	tumblr	2861
#fbr	2767	soundcloud	2442
#theresistance	2728	blogspot	2011
#equality	2451	paypal	1912
#travel	2223	wordpress	1887
#resistance	2218	twitter	1871
#author	2201	apple	1720
#humanrights	2176	etsy	1646
#nsfw	2146	carrd	1634
#mentalhealth	1971	discord	1223
#love	1906	linkedin	1178

First, we perform language analysis on the words and hashtags included by the users in their Twitter Bios. It has been shown in recent research that user-bios can reveal powerful insights about a user's social and political inclinations [27]. To this end, we extract the user-bio texts for

Fig. 1. Wordcloud of User Bios

every user collected in Sect. 3.2 to understand them better. First, we generate a wordcloud in Fig. 1 that shows the most popular words appearing in our dataset's

Table 3. Attributes Definition by Google Perspective API [28]

Attributes	Definition
TOXICITY	rude, disrespectful, or unreasonable comment
SEVERE TOXICITY	very hateful, aggressive, disrespectful comment.
IDENTITY ATTACK	Negative or hateful comments targeting someone's identity.
INSULT	Insulting, inflammatory, or negative comment towards a person or a group of people.
PROFANITY	Swear words, curse words, or other obscene or profane language.
THREAT	Intention to inflict pain, injury, or violence against an individual or group

user-bios. As seen, words such as love, life, music, artist, lover, and gay are the most frequent. Table 2 shows the top 20 hashtags used in the user-bios. In total, we extract 278, 066 unique hashtags from the user-bios. We see that the distribution is dominated by hashtags that are positive towards the LGBTQ+ rights, such as #resist, #lgbt, #lgbtq, #gay, #theresistance, #humanrights, #equality [9] #blacklivesmatter [16]. We also have hashtags such as #maga that are usually associated with supporters of former US president Donald Trump [27] as well as #mentalhealth. The latter hashtag is of particular significance; it has been reported that the LGBTQ+ community is more vulnerable to mental health disorders [23,37].

Next, we perform an emotion analysis of the texts used in the user-bios. As mentioned in Sect. 3.2, after pre-processing, we have 1, 741, 912 user-bios. We then apply DistilBERT, a distilled version of BERT, which is smaller, faster, cheaper, and lighter. DistilBERT model is inspired by the Knowledge Distillation Approach—a compression technique to train a small model to reproduce a larger model's behavior [33]. Using this technique reduces the size of a BERT model by 40% and faster by 60% [33] while keeping 97% of its language capabilities measured on the GLUE benchmark. DistilBERT has been one of the most efficient and accurate models for recognizing emotions in texts [21,25]. The model was trained with Twitter emotion dataset that was tagged with six major human emotions: anger, fear, joy, love, sadness, and surprise [34]. On this dataset, the model achieves an accuracy of 93.8%. We use this model to analyze user-bios. We argue that user-bio and Twitter tweets don't differ much in terms of language. Let $E \in \{anger, fear, joy, love, sadness, surprise\}$, the set of six emotions. The DistilBERT emotion model outputs, for every bio text B in our dataset, a probability score for an emotion e, $P_B(e)$ such that:

$$0 \leq P_B(e) \leq 1 \qquad (1)$$

We assign a user-bio B, an emotion label e_{final}, where,

$$P_B(e_{final}) > \forall_{e \in E - \{e_{final}\}} P_B(e) \qquad (2)$$

Table 4 shows the distribution of the six aforementioned emotion labels in our user-bio dataset. As seen from the table, *joy and anger are the most pervasive emotions expressed in the user-bios, accounting for 87.33% of user-bios.* Next, we separate the user-bios with negative emotions (anger, sadness, fear) to perform toxicity analysis, resulting in a subset of 639,763 user-bios. We leverage Google's Perspective API [28] to measure the negative user-bios in terms of six toxicity attributes: Toxicity, Severe Toxicity, Identity Attack, Insult, Profanity, and Threat. We outline the formal definitions of these attributes in Table 3.

Table 4. Bio Emotion Distribution

Emotions	Frequency	% bios
Anger	529758	**30.4**
Fear	86905	4.9
Joy	991504	**56.9**
Love	60409	3.46
Sadness	63194	3.6
Surprise	10142	0.5
Total	1741912	

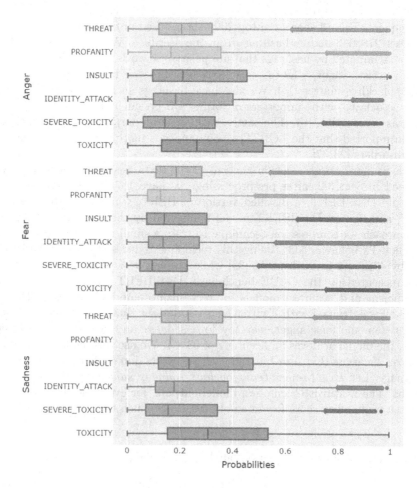

Fig. 2. Boxplot of Perspectives on user bios labeled as Anger, Fear, and Sadness by DistilBERT.

Let $A \in \{toxicity, severe - toxicity, identity - attack, insult, profanity, threat\}$ the set of six toxicity attributes. The Perspective API (Similar to DistilBERT emotion model) outputs, for every negative emotion user-bio text B_N, a score $S_{B_N}(a)$ such that:

$$0 \leq S_{B_N}(a) \leq 1 \tag{3}$$

Similarly, like emotion assignment described in Eq. 2, we assign a user-bio B_N, an attribute a_{final}, where,

$$S_{B_N}(a_{final}) > \forall_{a \in A - \{a_{final}\}} S_{B_N}(a) \tag{4}$$

Figure 2 shows the boxplot of the scores of different toxicity scores of user-bios with Anger, Fear, and Sadness emotions. By aggregating perspective scores on these emotions we observed that most of the bios the Perspective API classified as Threats, Toxicity, and Identity attacks: types of toxicity usually the most differentiating types of toxicity directed towards LGBTQ+ community [13]. Furthermore, Fear has the most outliers across all perspective metrics as shown in Fig. 2. It shows that *there are many user-bio outliers showing severe toxicity, identity attack, profanity, and threats, with scores as high as 0.9.*

4.2   User Statistics Analysis

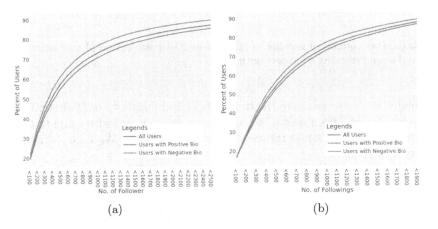

(a)   (b)

Fig. 3. (a)Distribution of number of followers (b) and number of followings for three sets of users with a cutoff of 90%

In addition to the user-bio text, we collect the statistics associated with the user-profiles, such as the number of followers, followings, tweet counts, etc., as delineated in Sect. 3.2. For analysis, we partition our dataset's $1,741,912$ users into three sets: all users, users with positive emotion bio, and users with negative emotion bio. Figure 3 shows the CDF (Cumulative Distribution Function) of the number of followers and followings for the three sets of users. Regarding the number of followers and followings, we see that users with a negative bio are above the overall distribution of all users and users with a positive bio. To be specific, 87.4% and 90.2% of the negative user-bio users have less than 2000 followers and followings, respectively, compared to 82.8% and 88.8% of users with positive emotion user-bio users. Next, we analyze the tweet count for the three sets of users. In Fig. 4a, we depict the CDF of the number of tweet counts for the three sets of users. All three sets of users show the same distribution of tweet counts, as is apparent from the figure.

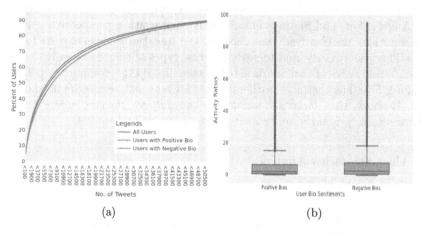

Fig. 4. (a) Distribution of number of total tweets (b) Distribution of user activity for positive-bio and negative-bio users with cutoff at 95%

Finally, we try to compare the three sets of users' activity on Twitter. Let d_u be the number of days a user u has opened an account on Twitter and t_u be the total number of tweets and retweets posted by this user. We then define total activity of user a_u as:

$$a_u = \frac{t_u}{d_u} \tag{5}$$

We acknowledge one limitation of this definition of user activity on Twitter: users on Twitter sometimes deactivate their account on Twitter and reactivate it after some time. However, Eq. 5 includes the period of deactivation because the Twitter API does not provide how long a user has kept their account deactivated. Keeping this in mind, we show the distribution of user activity for the three sets of users in Fig. 4b. We can see from the distribution that both the positive-bio and negative-bio users have similar activity distribution, with the 75th percentile at 6.64 and 8.14, respectively.

5   Tweet Analysis

In this section, we perform analysis on the tweets we collected, as mentioned in Sect. 3.2.

5.1   Timeline of Tweet Activity

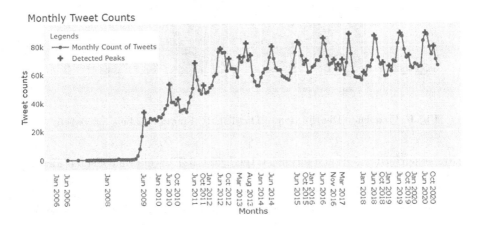

Fig. 5. Monthly LGBTQ+ related tweet counts

We first investigate the monthly tweet count related to LGBTQ+ issues on Twitter—starting from June 2006, the date of the earliest tweet in our dataset. We want to investigate if there are any spikes of activity on Twitter regarding LGBTQ+ issues. Figure 5 shows the distribution of tweet counts every month, with peaks identified on the X-axis. We use Scipy's peak finding algorithm with a threshold of 1000 to identify the peaks [35]. It is evident that *we have significant tweet activity spikes in some months than others, more specifically for June and October, celebrated as Pride and LGBTQ+ history month, respectively.* It is also worth noting that *the activity on Twitter regarding LGBTQ+ issues has risen significantly in the last decade.*

5.2   Sentiment Analysis of Tweets

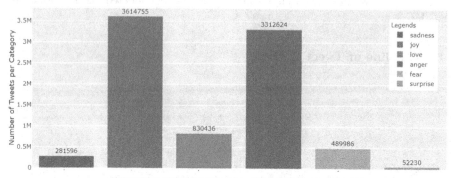

Fig. 6. Frequency Distribution of DistilBERT Emotion Labels for Tweets

Next, we perform emotion analysis on the $8,581,627$ tweets we collected for this study. We also keep the retweets; we argue that retweeting essentially means agreeing and promoting the idea presented in the original tweet. We use Distil-BERT for this task as we did for user-bio emotion analysis in Sect. 4.1. Figure 6 depicts the distribution of emotions of the tweets in our dataset—using the same methodology delineated in Sect. 4.1. We can see that *emotions such as anger and joy is more pervasive than the other four emotions.* This finding is consistent with the emotion distribution we found for the user-bio texts, presented in Table 4.

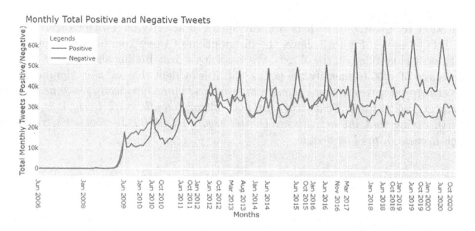

Fig. 7. Monthly LGBTQ+ related tweet counts, with positive and negative emotions

Now, we analyze the emotional distribution of tweets across the timeline they were posted, with the earliest month being June 2006. The positive emotions were joy, love, and surprise and the negative emotions were fear, sadness, and anger—emotions output by DistilBERT. Figure 7 shows the positive and negative emotion tweet counts across time. We see that the recent years, *the pride months (June) have seen significant peaks of positive emotion tweets, accompanied by significant troughs for negative emotion tweets*; examples include June 2020, June 2019, and June 2018, as seen from Fig. 7.

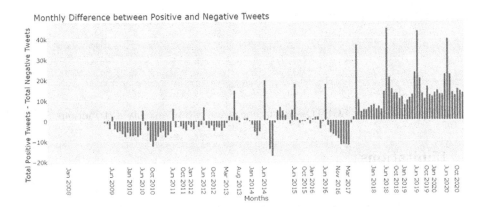

Fig. 8. Diff(= # positive emotion - # negative emotion tweets) across time

Next, we perform a tweet count differentiation analysis for positive and negative emotions across time in Fig. 8. It is fascinating to see that during the initial years (2009–2014), many months had more negative emotion tweets than positive ones. However, the trend has changed in recent years, with significant differentiation in the number of positive tweets. Also, the pride months show a larger difference than the other months in recent years, starting from 2014. *This shows that the overall positive sentiment in tweets related to the LGBTQ+ community has been on the rise in recent years.* For further investigation, we take a sample of 1000 negative tweets for every month since March 2006 and use the Google perspective API to measure the presence of the six types of toxicity in the LGBTQ+ discussions, as mentioned in Sect. 4. Figure 9 depicts the evolution of six toxicity attributes across time. We find that Identity attacks have been consistently more prevalent among the six toxicity attacks and significant troughs across all six toxicity attributes during June of every year due to Pride months. Another interesting finding is that *all six attacks, more or less, have been seeing a diminished level of toxicity since the year 2017, with the peaks not reaching the previous years' highs.*

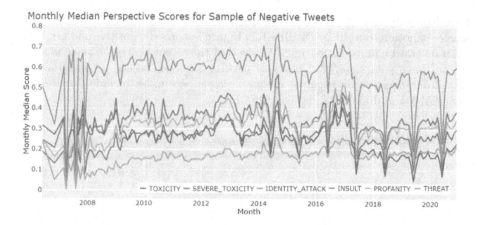

Fig. 9. Monthly LGBTQ+ related negative tweets' toxicity distribution

6   Limitations

Since the data collection relies on the relevant hashtag and keyword identification, our analysis is constrained by the choice of proper hashtags and keywords. As mentioned earlier, finding negative hashtags was challenging and required a manual search. Also, the search API only provides publicly available tweets, so private tweets and users were not included in the dataset. The Twitter API also has a limitation of 1024 characters per request and 200 objects per pagination, in addition to tweet visibility restrictions based on compliance checks. We have also limited our tweet collection to only English tweets to limit the scope of the data collection.

7   Conclusion and Future Works

In this paper, we take a first data-driven macro look at the users and tweets related to LGBTQ+ issues. Analyses performed on the dataset's user-bios, and tweets reveal that emotions such as joy and anger are more pervasive. Moreover, we did not find any significant difference in activity or tweet count regarding users with positive and negative user bios. However, a slight difference exists in follower-following metrics: negative emotion bio users lag their positive emotion bio counterparts by a small margin. Our investigation also detected a significant presence of threat, toxicity, and identity attack in the negative user-bios and negative emotion tweets in our dataset. We also found a significant increase in tweet counts on Twitter, both overall and positive emotion in recent years, with significant spikes in positive emotion tweets in June and October of every year. Furthermore, we found that the overall positivity towards LGBTQ+ issues on Twitter has been on the rise, which was not the case during the early days of Twitter. Our analyses pave the way for several interesting future research directions. First, it would be interesting to explore the topics of the tweets and user-bios with greater granularity. Second, detecting communities on Twitter based on the follower-following relationship and analyzing each community's sentiment towards LGBTQ+ issues separately.

References

1. Albadi, N., Kurdi, M., Mishra, S.: Deradicalizing Youtube: characterization, detection, and personalization of religiously intolerant Arabic videos. arXiv preprint (2022). arxiv:2207.00111
2. Almerekhi, H., Kwak, H., Jansen, B.J., Salminen, J.: Detecting toxicity triggers in online discussions. In: Proceedings of the 30th ACM Conference on Hypertext and Social Media, pp. 291–292 (2019)
3. Alper, M., Katz, V.S., Clark, L.S.: Researching children, intersectionality, and diversity in the digital age. J. Child. Media **10**(1), 107–114 (2016). https://doi.org/10.1080/17482798.2015.1121886
4. Andalibi, N., Haimson, O.L., Choudhury, M.D., Forte, A.: Social support, reciprocity, and anonymity in responses to sexual abuse disclosures on social media. ACM Trans. Comput.-Hum. Interact. (TOCHI) **25**(5), 1–35 (2018)
5. Andalibi, N., Haimson, O.L., De Choudhury, M., Forte, A.: Understanding social media disclosures of sexual abuse through the lenses of support seeking and anonymity. In: Proceedings of the 2016 CHI Conference on Human Factors in Computing Systems, pp. 3906–3918 (2016)
6. Best-Hashtags: Best-hashtags (2022). https://best-hashtags.com/
7. Bond, B.J., Miller, B.: Youtube as my space: the relationships between Youtube, social connectedness, and (collective) self-esteem among LGBTQ individuals. New Media Soc. 14614448211061830 (2021)
8. Booten, K.: Hashtag drift: tracing the evolving uses of political hashtags over time. In: Proceedings of the 2016 CHI Conference on Human Factors in Computing Systems, pp. 2401–2405 (2016)
9. Branson-Potts, H.: L.A. Pride Parade Morphs into ResistMarch, as tens of thousands hit the streets (2022). https://www.latimes.com/local/lanow/la-me-ln-pride-resist-march-20170611-story.html. Accessed 07 Aug 2022
10. Clark, K.A., Cochran, S.D., Maiolatesi, A.J., Pachankis, J.E.: Prevalence of bullying among youth classified as LGBTQ who died by suicide as reported in the national violent death reporting system, 2003–2017. JAMA Pediatr. **174**(12), 1211–1213 (2020)
11. Craig, S.L., McInroy, L.: You can form a part of yourself online: the influence of new media on identity development and coming out for LGBTQ youth. J. Gay Lesbian Mental Health **18**(1), 95–109 (2014)
12. Garg, S., et al.: Detecting risk level in individuals misusing fentanyl utilizing posts from an online community on reddit. Internet Interv. **26**, 100467 (2021)
13. Goyal, N., Kivlichan, I., Rosen, R., Vasserman, L.: Is your toxicity my toxicity? Exploring the impact of rater identity on toxicity annotation. arXiv preprint (2022). arxiv:2205.00501
14. Hashtagify: Hashtagify (2022). https://hashtagify.me/manual/api
15. Hswen, Y., Sewalk, K.C., Alsentzer, E., Tuli, G., Brownstein, J.S., Hawkins, J.B.: Investigating inequities in hospital care among lesbian, gay, bisexual, and transgender (LGBT) individuals using social media. Soc. Sci. Med. **215**, 92–97 (2018)

16. Kai: The deep connections between pride and black lives matter (2022). https://www.nyclu.org/en/news/deep-connections-between-pride-and-black-lives-matter. Accessed 07 Aug 2022

17. Karami, A., Webb, F., Kitzie, V.L.: Characterizing transgender health issues in Twitter. Proc. Assoc. Inf. Sci. Technol. **55**(1), 207–215 (2018)

18. Kwak, H., Lee, C., Park, H., Moon, S.: What is Twitter, a social network or a news media? In: Proceedings of the 19th International Conference on World Wide Web, pp. 591–600 (2010)

19. Lee, C., Ostergard, R.L., Jr.: Restricted access measuring discrimination against LGBTQ people: a cross-national analysis. In: Human Rights Quarterly, vol. 39, pp. 37–72. JHU University Press (2017)

20. Luo, J., Du, J., Tao, C., Xu, H., Zhang, Y.: Exploring temporal suicidal behavior patterns on social media: insight from Twitter analytics. Health Inform. J. **26**(2), 738–752 (2020)

21. Mahmud, M.S., Bonny, A.J., Saha, U., Jahan, M., Tuna, Z.F., Al Marouf, A.: Sentiment analysis from user-generated reviews of ride-sharing mobile applications. In: 2022 6th International Conference on Computing Methodologies and Communication (ICCMC), pp. 738–744. IEEE (2022)

22. McConnell, E., Néray, B., Hogan, B., Korpak, A., Clifford, A., Birkett, M.: "Everybody puts their whole life on Facebook": identity management and the online social networks of LGBTQ youth. Int. J. Environ. Res. Public Health **15**(6), 1078 (2018)

23. McDonald, K.: Social support and mental health in LGBTQ adolescents: a review of the literature. Issues Ment. Health Nurs. **39**(1), 16–29 (2018)

24. Mousavi, P., Ouyang, J.: Detecting hashtag hijacking for hashtag activism. In: Proceedings of the 1st Workshop on NLP for Positive Impact, pp. 82–92 (2021)

25. Nimmi, K., Janet, B., Selvan, A.K., Sivakumaran, N.: Pre-trained ensemble model for identification of emotion during Covid-19 based on emergency response support system dataset. Appl. Soft Comput. **122**, 108842 (2022)

26. Pascual-Ferrá, P., Alperstein, N., Barnett, D.J., Rimal, R.N.: Toxicity and verbal aggression on social media: polarized discourse on wearing face masks during the Covid-19 pandemic. Big Data Soc. **8**(1), 20539517211023532 (2021)

27. Paudel, P., Blackburn, J., Cristofaro, E.D., Zannettou, S., Stringhini, G.: An early look at the Gettr social network. CoRR abs/2108.05876 (2021). https://arxiv.org/abs/2108.05876

28. Perspective: Using machine learning to reduce toxicity online (2022). https://www.perspectiveapi.com/. Accessed 07 Aug 2022

29. Rafiq, R.I., Hosseinmardi, H., Han, R., Lv, Q., Mishra, S.: Identifying differentiating factors for cyberbullying in vine and Instagram. In: Lossio-Ventura, J.A., Valverde-Rebaza, J.C., Díaz, E., Alatrista-Salas, H. (eds.) SIMBig 2020. CCIS, vol. 1410, pp. 348–361. Springer, Cham (2021). https://doi.org/10.1007/978-3-030-76228-5_25

30. Rafiq, R.I., Hosseinmardi, H., Han, R., Lv, Q., Mishra, S., Mattson, S.A.: Careful what you share in six seconds: detecting cyberbullying instances in vine. In: 2015 IEEE/ACM International Conference on Advances in Social Networks Analysis and Mining (ASONAM), pp. 617–622. IEEE (2015)

31. Rivers, C.M., Lewis, B.L.: Ethical research standards in a world of big data. F1000Research **3**(38), 38 (2014)

32. Russell, S.T.: Queer in America: citizenship for sexual minority youth. Appl. Dev. Sci. **6**(4), 258–263 (2002)

33. Sanh, V., Debut, L., Chaumond, J., Wolf, T.: DistilBERT, a distilled version of BERT: smaller, faster, cheaper and lighter. CoRR abs/1910.01108 (2019). https://arxiv.org/abs/1910.01108

34. Saravia, E., Liu, H.C.T., Huang, Y.H., Wu, J., Chen, Y.S.: CARER: contextualized affect representations for emotion recognition. In: Proceedings of the 2018 Conference on Empirical Methods in Natural Language Processing, pp. 3687–3697 (2018)

35. Scipy: Scipy Peak Find (2022). https://docs.scipy.org/doc/scipy/reference/generated/scipy.signal.find_peaks.html. Accessed 07 Aug 2022

36. Steinke, J., Root-Bowman, M., Estabrook, S., Levine, D.S., Kantor, L.M.: Meeting the needs of sexual and gender minority youth: formative research on potential digital health interventions. J. Adolesc. Health **60**(5), 541–548 (2017)

37. Sutter, M., Perrin, P.B.: Discrimination, mental health, and suicidal ideation among LGBTQ people of color. J. Couns. Psychol. **63**(1), 98 (2016)

38. Twitter: Twitter API documentation (2022). https://developer.twitter.com/en/docs/twitter-api

39. Weimann, G., Masri, N.: Research note: spreading hate on Tiktok. Stud. Conflict Terrorism 1–14 (2020)

40. Wikipedia: Twitter Inc. (2022). https://en.wikipedia.org/wiki/Twitter_Inc. Accessed 07 June 2022

41. Yuan, Y., Verma, G., Keller, B., Aledavood, T.: The impact of Covid-19 pandemic on LGBTQ online communitie. arXiv preprint (2022). arxiv:2205.09511

42. Zannettou, S., et al.: What is gab: a bastion of free speech or an alt-right echo chamber. In: Companion Proceedings of the the Web Conference 2018, pp. 1007–1014 (2018)

User-Agnostic Model for Prediction of Retweets Based on Social Neighborhood Information

Pablo Gabriel Celayes[(✉)], Martín Ariel Domínguez, and Damián Barsotti

FaMAF, Universidad Nacional de Córdoba, Córdoba, Argentina
{celayes,mdoming,damian}@famaf.unc.edu.ar

Abstract. Twitter and other social networks have become a fundamental source of information and a powerful tool to spread ideas and opinions. This paper studies the problem of predicting retweets from any user based on the retweeting behavior occurring in their second-degree social neighborhood (followed and followed-by-followed). To do so, a general model is built that can learn from different users in the training phase. The resulting model can then predict both new retweets from known users and retweets from previously unseen users. A simple but effective feature extraction scheme is proposed, to model the neighborhood information in a user-independent fashion. This scheme is then optimized through Bayesian hyperparameter tuning jointly with the hyperparameters of an XGBoost classifier model. The resulting model is trained and evaluated on a large set of 3240 users with 5000 examples of labeled tweets from their social neighborhoods. The general model thus obtained achieves an F_1 score of 83.9%, based purely on aggregated social information, without analyzing the content of the tweets. When this model is applied to a selection of 194 active and central users, an average F_1 score per user of 85.5% is obtained, very close to what was observed in previous works employing multiple single-user models.

Keywords: retweet prediction · Social Network Analysis · Machine Learning · XGBoost

1 Introduction

In the last years, social media platforms have gained massive adoption, becoming a central presence in public discussions, and shaping the way people express themselves, get informed, and influence each other. One of the most prominent of these social networks is Twitter, an online real-time microblogging platform that enables its users to post, read and share short messages of up to 280 characters, known as tweets. Every time a user publishes a tweet, Twitter attaches to it a unique identifier and a creation timestamp. At the core of the social dynamic of these networks lies the "retweet" functionality, which enables users to select tweets from other users and republish them within their own message stream (the

© The Author(s), under exclusive license to Springer Nature Switzerland AG 2023
J. A. Lossio-Ventura et al. (Eds.): SIMBig 2022, CCIS 1837, pp. 18–31, 2023.
https://doi.org/10.1007/978-3-031-35445-8_2

"timeline"). A feature distinguishing Twitter from other popular social networks is that most of the shared content is public by default. Therefore, structured data, both about the way users interact with each other and the content that they share, is easily accessible through the official API. This is perhaps one of the main reasons why most research work of this kind is done on Twitter.

This paper explores the creation of a general machine learning model to predict retweets from users based on the retweet activity happening in their social environment. This model is built upon the ideas from our previous work [5], where social and content-based models were built to predict retweet preferences for specific users. In the present work, the goal is to implement a single user-agnostic model instead of individual models tied to specific central users. This general model will be strongly based on the idea of ranking and grouping neighbours by their activity and network importance, an idea we had already implemented in [15], but in the context of a general prediction of popular tweets. The user-agnostic approach proposed here has several advantages, among them a significant reduction in training times, a more compact representation of data and the possibility of dealing with users not seen during training.

The main contributions of this work are:

- The implementation of a general user-agnostic model that attains a prediction performance comparable to that of individual models, but with added generalization power and less training time.
- A detailed analysis of the prediction performance for both known and unknown users, and comparisons to our previous approach based on single-user models.
- An update of the underlying classification algorithm, replacing the Support Vector Machines from previous works with XGBoost [6] gradient boosted trees to obtain comparable classification performance with much shorter running times.

The rest of this paper is structured as follows: Sect. 2 gives an overview of related works. Section 3 describes how we build the datasets from Twitter for our experiments. Section 4 describes generalized social feature extraction, the tuning and training process of the proposed model and different forms of evaluation. In Sect. 5 the obtained results are summarized and compared to the performance of single-user models. Finally, in Sect. 6 conclusions are presented and possible lines of future research are introduced.

2   Related Work

Along with the increased popularity and impact of social media, the research interest has grown in modeling users' preferences and the distribution of popular content. One exciting line of research on this problem focuses on the interactions and connections between users, regardless of the nature of the shared content.

In [5] we studied the prediction of retweets for a given user, using the behavior of users in their second-degree social neighborhood (followed, and followed by followed) to build a classifier that determines whether or not she will *retweet* a given post. Based purely on social information, these models achieved high predictive performance, with an average F_1 score of 87.6%. In that work, we also explored extending the models with content features for the cases where the purely social models were not performing well. Using a topic modeling algorithm adapted to tweets (TwitterLDA) obtains an average performance improvement of 1.7%. A limitation of this work, which we seek to overcome in the current paper, is given by the fact that it trains a separate model for each user whose preferences we want to predict. This approach can be expensive computationally and lacks generalization power since a model trained on the preferences of a particular user cannot be directly applied to other users.

In [15], we extended the previous work to the problem of predicting popularity within a community of users instead of just individual preferences. The target here was to build classifiers that could identify if a given tweet would become popular or not, based only on the activity that a selected set of *influencers* (i.e., highly central and active users) had on it. This work also explored improvements incorporating embeddings-based features to represent the content and different algorithms for selecting user influencers. Like in the previous work, we first studied the performance of a purely social prediction, obtaining an F_1 score of 79.2%, using only the retweeting behavior of the top 10% most central and active users as influencers. Considering the tweet's content and adding features based on FastText embeddings increased the performance to 86.7%. This second work utilizes a metric of user importance that combines user activity and network centrality. We adapt it to our problem to define a ranking of environment users that will enable us to extract general features. In contrast to the present paper, this work proposes a unified model, but only for predicting collective preferences and cannot predict the retweets of individual users.

In [11] we study the problem of individual retweet prediction and trend prediction based on the evolution in the amount of information available since the creation of the original tweet. The results establish an interesting trade-off between elapsed time and prediction performance, concluding that it is possible to reasonably predict the preference of a user retweet or how massive a publication will be, using only the information available during the first 30–60 min since the creation of a tweet. However, the models in this work are still either user-specific or general models that predict general preferences.

The 2020 and 2021 editions of the RecSys challenge [1] focused on a real-world task of tweet engagement prediction in a dynamic environment. The goal was to predict the probability for different types of engagement (Like, Reply, Retweet, and Retweet with Comment) of a target user for a set of tweets based on heterogeneous input data. It is worth noting that the winning approaches for both editions [8,14] (and other competitors like [16]) make use of the XGBoost algorithm (combined with Deep Learning approaches in the 2021 edition). However, the problem is very different to ours: the predicted target is more generic and even though user and tweet input data are richer than in our problem, there is no explicit information about the graph of followed connections being leveraged. Instead, the predictions are based solely on features about the content of the tweet being predicted, its author and the user for which the engagement prediction is produced.

3   Dataset

This section describes how we build the datasets used in this work. First, we explain how we build the social graph used in the social-based prediction. Second, we describe how we collect a dataset of tweets shared by the users in this graph.

3.1   Social Graph

To perform the experiments in this paper, we reutilize the dataset from our previous work [5], but making a more extensive use of its social interactions since we remove the limitations caused by single-user models. The data consists of Twitter users and the who-follows-whom relation between them.

Back in our previous work, the idea was to create a representative subgraph of Twitter where all users would have a similar amount of social information about their neighborhood of connected users. The decision was to build a homogeneous network where each user would have the same number of followed users. To this end, we performed a two-step process: first, building a large enough *universe graph*, which then was filtered to obtain a smaller but more homogeneous subgraph.

The *universe graph* was built starting with a singleton graph containing just one Twitter user account $\mathcal{U}_0 = \{u_0\}$ and performing 3 iterations of the following procedure: (1) Fetch all users followed by users in $\mathcal{U}_i$; (2) from that group, filter only those having at least 40 followers and following at least 40 accounts; (3) add filtered users and their edges to get an extended $\mathcal{U}_{i+1}$ graph. This process generated a *universe graph* $\mathcal{U} := \mathcal{U}_3$ with $2,926,181$ vertices and $10,144,158$ edges.

For the second step, in order to get a homogeneous network, a subgraph was extracted following the procedure below.

- We started off with a small sample of seed users S, consisting of users in $\mathcal{U}$ having out-degree 50, this is, users following exactly 50 other users.
- For each of those, we added their 50 most socially affine followed users. The affinity between two users was measured as the ratio between the number of users followed by both and the number of users followed by at least one of them.
- We repeated the last step for each newly added user until there were no more new users to add.

This filtering produced the final graph $\mathcal{G}$ with $5,180$ vertices and $229,553$ edges called the homogeneous K-degree closure ($K = 50$ in this case) of S in the universe graph $\mathcal{U}$.

3.2   Content

For each user in the graph $\mathcal{G}$ from the previous section, we fetched their time-lines (i.e., all tweets written or shared) for one month, from August 25th until September 24th, 2015. Finally, we only kept the tweets written in the Spanish language –according to their language tag in the Twitter API results–, resulting in a set $\mathcal{T}$ of $1,636,480$ tweets.

Visible Tweets. Using the Twitter API, we do not have explicit information about whether or not a user saw a given tweet, but we can at least take a universe of *potentially viewed* tweets, which will be used as examples for training and testing our model. This set is the set of all the tweets written or shared by the users followed by u. We exclude from this set those tweets *written* by u herself since our focus is on recognizing interesting external content and not on studying the generation of content from a particular user. Formally this set is defined as: $T(u) := \left(\bigcup_{x \in \{u\} \cup \texttt{followed}(u)} \texttt{timeline}(x) \right) - \{t \in \mathcal{T} | \texttt{author}(t) = u\}$, where $\texttt{followed}(u) := \{x \in \mathcal{G} | (u, x) \in \texttt{follow}\}$, and $\texttt{timeline}(x)$ is the set of all tweets written or shared by x for tweets fetched in $\mathcal{T}$.

Target Retweeted Label. The retweet prediction task is modeled as a binary classification problem where the target for a user u and a tweet $t \in T(u)$ is whether or not t was retweeted in the timeline of u: $y_{u,t} := \texttt{tweet\_in\_tl}(t, u)$. Putting together all values of the target variable for user u and tweets in $T(u) = \{t_1, \ldots, t_m\}$, we obtain the target vector $y_u := [y_{t_i, u}]_{1 \leq i \leq m}$.

Down-Sampling of Negative Examples. For some users, the set $T(u)$ was too large, making experimenting and model training too computationally inten-sive. We decided to prune each $T(u)$ to a maximum of $5,000$ tweets, keeping all positive examples (the minority class) and randomly removing the necessary number of negative examples (non-retweets from u). This dataset still results in a highly imbalanced prediction problem, with only 2.58% of positive examples.

3.3   User Selection

Inactive users will be omitted in this experiment because they are unpredictable by nature. We consider that a user in our dataset is *passive* if she has less than ten retweets in our dataset. Filtering out such users leaves us with a set A of $3,240$ active users in $\mathcal{G}$. We restrict the analysis to those users, removing content shared only by inactive users from $\mathcal{T}$.

3.4   Dataset Partitions

User Level Partition. In our previous work [5], the computational limitations of training one retweet prediction model per user led us to work with a small set U of 194 users, selected as the intersection of the top 1000 most active users (in terms of retweets in their timelines) and the top 1000 most central users (in terms of Katz centrality [10] in $\mathcal{G}$). In the interest of comparing the results of our general model to a good number of those users, we decided to reserve 50% of them for testing, resulting in a random partition of U into sets U_{train} and U_{test}, of 97 users each. For the remaining users in the set $V := A - U$, we randomly select 70% of them for training (V_{train}) and reserve 30% for test (V_{test}).

Tweet Level Partition. For each user $u \in A$ we split her set $T(u)$ of visible tweets as follows:

- $T_{tr}(u) :=$ first 70% of tweets from $T(u)$, ordered by creation date.
- $T_{te}(u) :=$ last 30% remaining tweets.

We extend this notation to denote the combined training or test tweets of any set S of users. For instance $T_{tr}(S) := \bigcup_{u \in S} T_{tr}(u)$.

This split divides the data into 8 pieces, as seen in the table below. Only the two partitions of training users and their training tweets will be used to train the model. The remaining data will be reserved for different types of evaluation (general performance, new tweets by known users, and unknown users) (Fig. 1).

| | | | Tweets | | |
			70% train		30% test
A = active users from closed graph G with timelines (3240)	U = most active and central (194)	50% U_{tr} (97)	$T_{tr}(U_{tr})$		$T_{te}(U_{tr})$
		50% U_{te} (97)	$T_{tr}(U_{te})$		$T_{te}(U_{te})$
	V = A - U (3046)	70% V_{tr} (2111)	$T_{tr}(V_{tr})$		$T_{te}(V_{tr})$
		30% V_{te} (935)	$T_{tr}(V_{te})$		$T_{te}(V_{te})$

Fig. 1. Dataset partitions at user and tweet level. Only highlighted partitions will be used for training. The remaining ones are used for different types of evaluation.

4   Experimental Setup

In this section, we formulate the general user retweet prediction problem and describe in detail the features and model that will be used to solve it, as well as the process of tuning hyperparameters, training, and evaluating against previous models.

4.1 Social Environment

Even though any user u can only see tweets shared by those users she follows, the information about the activity on her extended network can provide more indicators of the degree of interest of a tweet t. This is the reason why we decided to take as a user's environment not only the users she follows but also to continue one more step in the `follow` relation and include the users followed by them. Therefore, we take all users (other than u herself) to 1 or 2 steps forward from u in the directed graph $\mathcal{G}$, formally: $E_u = \left(\bigcup_{x \in \{u\} \cup \texttt{followed}(u)} \texttt{followed}(x) \right) - \{u\}$.

4.2 Raw Environment Features

For any user u and visible tweet $t \in T(u)$, the raw neighborhood features of t relative to u are defined as the boolean features describing which users from the social environment retweeted t. Formally, if we enumerate the neighbors in E_u as $\{u_1, u_2, \dots, u_n\}$, we can define:
$$v_{u,t} := [\texttt{tweet\_in\_tl}(t, u_i)]_{i=1,\dots,n},$$
$$\text{where } \texttt{tweet\_in\_tl}(t, u) := \begin{cases} 1 & t \in \texttt{timeline}(u) \\ 0 & \text{otherwise} \end{cases}$$
The raw dataset assigned to a user u (denoted M_u) is the matrix that contains one row $v_{u,t}$ per tweet $t \in T(u)$ and has one column per user in E_u. Note that each M_u has a dimensionality $|E_u|$, which varies from one user to another.

4.3 General Environment Features

We aim to implement a general model that can learn from multiple users and be applied to any user. In order to do that, we need to transform these neighborhood-dependent features M_u into a fixed-length representation that doesn't depend on the given user.

The proposed transformation will be based on ordering and grouping the neighbors in E_u by an importance metric $m(u)$, as introduced in [15]. This metric is defined as $m(u) := \frac{\texttt{activity}(u) + \texttt{centrality}(u)}{2}$, where $\texttt{activity}(u)$ is given simply by the normalized number of retweets in our dataset ($|\texttt{timeline}(u)|$) and $\texttt{centrality}(u)$ is computed as an average of the normalized centrality metrics computed by the following algorithms: PageRank [12], Betweenness [9], Closeness [13], Eigenvector centrality [3] and Eccentricity [4] included in the `igraph` Python library [7]. We performed a normalization over E_u for both activity and centrality metrics, to guarantee comparable values in the $[0, 1]$ interval.

Let us index the users in E_u sorted by m in decreasing order, that is $E_u = \{u_1, u_2, \dots, u_n\}$, where $m(i) \geq m(j)$ for $i \leq j$. The boolean features for the first k of these neighbors are kept, and for the remaining $n - k$ neighbors, we partition the range of their importance scores in b intervals of equal length $l = \frac{m(u_n) - m(u_{k+1})}{b}$:
$$I_i := [m(u_{k+1}) + (i-1)*l, \; m(u_{k+1}) + i*l) \, i \in [1, b-1]$$
$$I_b := [m(u_{k+1}) + l*(b-1), \; m(u_{k+1}) + l*b]$$

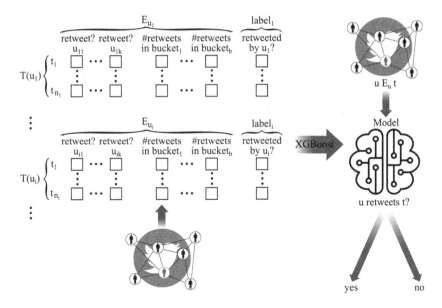

Fig. 2. Schematic of the experimental setup.

We build a feature for each interval, consisting of the number of retweets of the tweet t by users having $m(u)$ in such interval. Formally, we denote with $w_{u,t}^{b,k}$ the vector of neighborhood features of tweet t for user u with selected top-k users and the remaining users grouped in b buckets.

$$w_{u,t}^{b,k}[i] := v_{u,t}[i] \qquad\qquad i \in [1,k] \qquad \text{(top-}k\text{ neighbours)}$$
$$w_{u,t}^{b,k}[k+j] := \sum_{i':m(u_{i'})\in I_j} v_{u,t}[i'] \quad j \in [1,b] \text{ (bucketed neighbours)}$$

Note that this representation gives us a common length of $b + k$ for the feature vector of any u, t pair, independent of the size of E_u. The representation will depend on our choice of the number k of top users and the number b of buckets to group the remaining users. These will be treated as hyperparameters and tuned jointly with other hyperparameters of the chosen classifier model.

In Fig. 2 we show a schematic of the whole experimental setup. On the left hand side of the figure, we synthesized the featurization of the training phase, and on the right hand side, we show how the resulting model is applied.

4.4   Classifier Model

For this work, we chose to use the XGBoost [6] gradient boosted trees classification algorithm, which makes better use of parallelism and is generally faster to train than the Support Vector Machines we used in previous works [5,11,15]. The classification performance of our algorithms will be measured using the F_1 score metric on the positive class, which is suitable for unbalanced problems like this one.

4.5 Hyperparameter Tuning

Since hyperparameter tuning is a computationally expensive process, we chose to perform it on a smaller sample of training tweets, namely the set $T_{tr}(W)$ of training tweets corresponding to a set W of 200 randomly selected training users from $U_{train} \cup V_{train}$. $T_{tr}(W)$ consists of around $700,000$ examples.

We employed the `hyperopt` [2] Python package to perform an efficient bayesian search over the parameter space described by the intervals in Table 1. The process consisted of 20 iterations of 4-fold cross-validation over $T_{tr}(W)$, and the explored parameter space included both hyperparameters for the XGBoost classification algorithm and also `n_topk` and `n_buckets` for the representation of environment features. The best CV F_1 score was 0.864, and it was obtained for the hyperparameter configuration detailed in the right column of Table 1 below:

Table 1. Intervals of hyperparameter values explored with `hyperopt` Bayesian search. This includes both hyperparameters for XGBoost classifier and (k, b) for our neighborhood feature transformations.

hyperparameter	search interval	best configuration
`colsample_bytree`	[0.5, 1]	0.8
`eta`	[0.025, 0.5]	0.275
`gamma`	[0.5, 1]	0.8
`max_depth`	[1, 13]	11
`min_child_weight`	[1, 6]	6.0
`n_estimators`	[50, 1000)	380
`subsample`	[0.5, 1]	0.75
`n_buckets`	[0, 50]	5
`n_topk`	[5, 50]	6

4.6 Model Training

The model was trained using the training tweets from all training users, that is, the set $T_{tr}(U_{tr} \cup V_{tr})$, which consists of $7,535,386$ labeled (user, tweet) pairs. We will denote this trained general model with M_{gen}. In the next section, we will perform a variety of evaluations of M_{gen} that reflect its performance under specific scenarios (known users, unknown users, comparison to individual models).

5 Results

We describe next the performance metrics obtained by our general retweet prediction model M_{gen}. We will perform the following evaluations:

- General F_1 score metrics over all test data.
- Comparison to the performance of single-user models.
- Evaluation over known vs. unknown users and how the performance is affected by users' activity level.

5.1   General Evaluation

To get a general metric of the classification performance of M_{gen}, we evaluate it over all the data not seen during training, that is $D_{test} := T_{te}(U_{tr}) \cup T_{tr}(U_{te}) \cup T_{te}(U_{te}) \cup T_{te}(V_{tr}) \cup T_{tr}(V_{te}) \cup T_{te}(V_{te})$. This dataset consists of $8,170,959$ samples, with $217,624$ positive labels (2.66%). The metrics obtained are `precision` $= 99.5\%$, `recall` $= 72.5\%$ and F_1 `score` $= 83.9\%$.

5.2   Comparison to Single User Models

We now proceed to compare the model to the performance of single-user models [5]. To this end, we consider all users in the selected set of active and central users U for which we built individual SVC classifier models in our previous works. The metrics obtained by M_{gen} over the combined set $T_{te}(U)$ of test tweets on all these users are: `precision` $= 99.9\%$, `recall` $= 77.4\%$ and F_1 `score` $= 87.3\%$.

For any user $u \in A$, we will denote with $F_1^{gen}(u)$ the F_1 score of the M_{gen} model over $T_{te}(u)$. Additionally, if $u \in U$, we denote with $F_1^{ind}(u)$ the F_1 score over $T_{te}(u)$ of the individual SVC model of u. The distributions of scores over U can be seen here (Fig. 3):

	F_1^{gen}	F_1^{ind}
mean	85.5%	87.7%
std	0.155	0.109
$Q1$	79.7%	82.4%
median	89.2%	88.5%
$Q3$	95.9%	95.9%

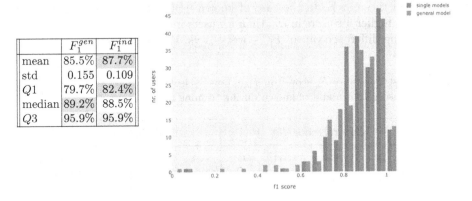

Fig. 3. Distribution of F_1 scores of general vs. individual models over selected 194 active and centrals users in U.

We observe that the mean F_1 score per user is 2.2% less for the general model, but if we look at the median and upper quartile $Q3$, M_{gen} has similar scores to those of single-user models. For more difficult-to-learn users with lower scores (see lower quartile $Q1$), single-user models still perform better (2.7% higher at $Q1$). It is also interesting to mention that M_{gen} achieved better scores than single-user models for 52 of the test users and 32 of the train users, which accounts for 43% of all the users in U.

5.3   Performance on General Users

We now turn away from the limitation to users in U imposed by individual models and analyze the performance of the M_{gen} model on more general users in V. We start by computing performance metrics over the combined set of samples of users from V not used during training; this is $D_{test}^V := T_{te}(V_{tr}) \cup T_{tr}(V_{te}) \cup T_{te}(V_{te})$ The metrics obtained by M_{gen} over D_{test}^V are: precision = 99.4%, recall = 70.7% and F_1 score = 82.6%.

5.4   Performance on Known Vs. Unknown Users

To better understand the generalization power of the M_{gen} model, we compare its performance for users known during training versus previously unseen test users. In Fig. 4 we see a comparison of the distributions of F_1^{gen} scores for known and unknown users in the set of selected users U. In Fig. 5 we can see a similar analysis for the set of regular users V. In Table 2 we can see a summary of these distributions, extending the comparison to individual model performance for users in U.

We generally do not observe better performance for users known during training, which indicates that M_{gen} generalizes well to previously unseen users. However, we observe that M_{gen} performs better for users in U, more active and central than those in V. In the case of known users, the mean F_1^{gen} score per user is 9.4% higher for users in U_{tr} than for users in V_{tr}. For unknown users, the corresponding difference (mean F_1^{gen} over U_{te} vs. V_{te}) is 10.3%.

Table 2. Distribution of F_1 scores on $T_{te}(u)$ over selected (U) and regular users (V), grouped by users known and unknown during training of M_{gen}.

	General model (M_{gen})				Individual models			
	Q1	mean	median	Q3	Q1	mean	median	Q3
U_{tr}	79.5%	84.8%	89.2%	95.7%	83.1%	88.6%	91.8%	96.4%
U_{te}	80.0%	86.2%	89.4%	95.9%	82.1%	86.7%	87.3%	95.7%
V_{tr}	66.7%	75.4%	82.4%	93.7%				
V_{te}	66.7%	75.9%	83.6%	94.7%				

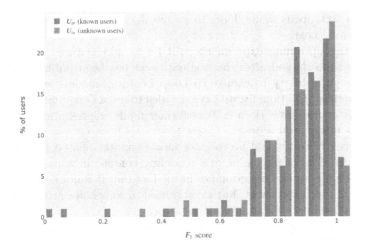

Fig. 4. Distribution of F_1 scores of M_{gen} over known vs. unknown selected users (U).

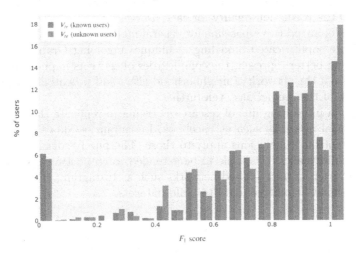

Fig. 5. Distribution of F_1 scores of M_{gen} over known vs. unknown regular users (V).

6   Conclusions and Future Work

As a general conclusion, we observe that modelling social environments in a standardized way across users achieves good predictive performance. The implemented model is much faster to train and generalizable than single-user models, at the expense of only a 2.2% drop in the mean F_1 score per user. Furthermore, the general model proved able to keep the same prediction quality for the best performing half of the evaluated single-user models. We also conclude that XGBoost is a suitable classification algorithm for this type of problem, improving the training times over SVM without harming model accuracy.

This research opens many doors to evolve the model. The most relevant to us are described next.

One of the upcoming experiments will be to add features that take into account the time elapsed after the original tweet has been published. Another line of research is to try to change to Deep Learning models and replace the XGBoost models. Additionally, we have the idea to use a Long Short-Term Memory (LSTM) neural network or a Transformer model representing the activity on tweets as a temporal series.

Another extension would be to incorporate content related features to the general model. The challenge here is modeling content in a user-independent way. The difficulty of this direction lies in the fact that it is not enough to model the content of the target tweet, but we also need to somehow encode the content preferences of the user we are predicting for.

Even though the introduced general model is able to handle previously unseen users, we still observe that the prediction quality is higher for more experienced users. So it would be interesting to explore better ways of dealing with cold start users, and also better understand the relation between the amount of past activity and the prediction quality for each user.

This model introduces a baseline for general modeling of neighborhood information. More sophisticated modeling techniques involving Graph Neural Networks [17] can better represent the complexities of retweets happening in different positions of the network of neighborhood users and potentially improve the performance of the predictions even further.

Finally, an interesting line of research is trying to replicate the experiments for other social networks such as Facebook, Instagram or Sina Weibo, and see to what extent our conclusions apply to those. The purely social nature of the proposed model makes it suitable to be extended to any network of users sharing content, even in image-based networks such as Instagram. However, we are limited by the availability of data to build datasets.

References

1. Recsys challenge. https://recsys.acm.org/challenges/
2. Bergstra, J., Komer, B., Eliasmith, C., Yamins, D., Cox, D.D.: Hyperopt: a python library for model selection and hyperparameter optimization. Comput. Sci. Discov. **8**(1), 014008 (2015). https://stacks.iop.org/1749-4699/8/i=1/a=014008
3. Bryan, K., Leise, T.: The \$25,000,000,000 eigenvector: the linear algebra behind google. SIAM Rev. **48**, 569–581 (2006)
4. Buckley, F., Harary, F.: Distance in Graphs. Addison-Wesley (1990)
5. Celayes, P.G., Domínguez, M.A.: Prediction of user retweets based on social neighborhood information and topic modelling. In: Castro, F., Miranda-Jiménez, S., González-Mendoza, M. (eds.) MICAI 2017. LNCS (LNAI), vol. 10633, pp. 146–157. Springer, Cham (2018). https://doi.org/10.1007/978-3-030-02840-4_12
6. Chen, T., Guestrin, C.: XGBoost: a scalable tree boosting system. In: Proceedings of the 22nd ACM SIGKDD International Conference on Knowledge Discovery and Data Mining, KDD 2016, pp. 785–794. ACM, New York (2016). https://doi.org/10.1145/2939672.2939785

7. Csardi, G., Nepusz, T.: The igraph software package for complex network research. InterJournal Comp. Syst. **1695** (2006). https://igraph.org/python/
8. Deotte, C., Liu, B., Schifferer, B., Titericz, G.: GPU accelerated boosted trees and deep neural networks for better recommender systems. In: Proceedings of the Recommender Systems Challenge, RecSysChallenge 2021, pp. 7–14. Association for Computing Machinery, New York (2021). https://doi.org/10.1145/3487572.3487605
9. Freeman, L.C.: A set of measures of centrality based on betweenness. Sociometry **40**(1) (1977)
10. Katz, L.: A new status index derived from sociometric analysis. Psychometrika **18**(1), 39–43 (1953)
11. Meriles, E., Domínguez, M.A., Celayes, P.G.: Twitter early prediction of preferences and tendencies based in neighborhood behavior. In: Lossio-Ventura, J.A., Valverde-Rebaza, J.C., Díaz, E., Alatrista-Salas, H. (eds.) SIMBig 2020. CCIS, vol. 1410, pp. 29–44. Springer, Cham (2021). https://doi.org/10.1007/978-3-030-76228-5_3
12. Page, L., Brin, S., Motwani, R., Winograd, T.: The pagerank citation ranking: bringing order to the web. Stanford University, Technical report (1999)
13. Sabidussi, G.: The centrality index of a graph. Psychometrika **31**(4) (1966)
14. Schifferer, B., et al.: GPU accelerated feature engineering and training for recommender systems. In: Proceedings of the Recommender Systems Challenge, RecSysChallenge 2020, pp. 16–23. Association for Computing Machinery, New York (2020). https://doi.org/10.1145/3415959.3415996
15. Silva, M.G., Domínguez, M.A., Celayes, P.G.: Analyzing the retweeting behavior of influencers to predict popular tweets, with and without considering their content. In: Lossio-Ventura, J.A., Muñante, D., Alatrista-Salas, H. (eds.) SIMBig 2018. CCIS, vol. 898, pp. 75–90. Springer, Cham (2019). https://doi.org/10.1007/978-3-030-11680-4_9 ISBN 978-3-030-02840-4
16. Volkovs, M., et al.: User engagement modeling with deep learning and language models. In: Proceedings of the Recommender Systems Challenge 2021, RecSysChallenge 2021, pp. 22–27. Association for Computing Machinery, New York (2021). https://doi.org/10.1145/3487572.3487604
17. Zhou, J., Cui, G., Zhang, Z., Yang, C., Liu, Z., Sun, M.: Graph neural networks: a review of methods and applications (2018). https://arxiv.org/abs/1812.08434

Segmentation and Classification of Pages for Digitized Documents of the Public Prosecutor's Office

Kevin Rivera[1,2,3]([✉]) [iD], Diana Quintanilla[1,3]([✉]) [iD], and Ángel Espezua[3]([✉]) [iD]

[1] National University of San Marcos, Lima, Peru
kevin.rivera1@unmsm.edu.pe
[2] National University Santiago Antunez de Mayolo, Huaraz, Peru
[3] Public Prosecutor's Office, Lima, Peru
qpdiam@gmail.com, jimyespc@gmail.com

Abstract. The digitization of physical documents is a common objective in the process of digital transformation of public organizations in Peru, however this process has a particular task that consumes a lot of time and resources: the segmentation and classification of pages in digitized documents, that is, determine where one document ends and the next begins, as well as naming each classified document. To this end, in this article we present a solution that uses machine learning and regular expressions for the automatic segmentation of pages in digitized documents of the Public Prosecutor's Office and their classification. Our solution achieved an accuracy of 93% using Random Forest for page segmentation and high accuracy in the classification of document types above 90% accuracy using regular expressions based on rules.

Keywords: Machine learning · Regular expressions · Page classification · Page segmentation · Digitized documents

1 Introduction

The digitization of documents is a very common activity today in public organizations in Peru, which is carried out mainly to facilitate the administration and access to information of the documents, it is also a way of safeguarding said documents.

Now, for organizations focused on investigation, as is the case of the Public Prosecutor's Office, there is a context in which large batches of documents have to be scanned, which, for example, in the Public Prosecutor's Office are handled through fiscal folders and each fiscal folder handles several documents and each document on average contains about 200 pages, within these 200 pages there is a mixture of various individual legal documents such as official letters, reports,

Supported by Public Prosecutor's Office.

declarations, notifications, among other documents that are usually part of a tax investigation.

The idea is to obtain an independent typified document that corresponds to the prosecutor's file, but this implies investing a lot of time and resources, which are not available in the Public Prosecutor's Office due to the excessive workload that the staff of the prosecutor's offices usually handle. However, in an ideal scenario in which there is sufficient staff to perform this task, obtaining a manually typed independent document is more prone to error due to a large number of batches of digitized documents.

A document flow is a list of successive scanned pages, representing several documents without explicit separation marks between them [1]. Documents are scanned as a continuous stream, losing the original version and producing a single output that includes all scanned documents. [9]. It is very common for documents to include pages that bear little resemblance to each other and for documents of different types to include similar pages [2]. Managing this information flow manually by classifying documents is time consuming, costly and error prone [4]. A simple solution is to put legible marks between pages to facilitate document identification. However, in a large flow of pages, this would be very costly and error-prone [6]. When the flow is scanned, it may lose the way that it was initially structured, and which corresponds to the document's boundaries. These boundaries are of importance to be able to group pages from a document and put them in the same file or folder [7].

Thus, many works seek to solve the segmentation of the page flow and the classification of each identified segment. This work used different models from rules to deep learning models on public datasets and only Fabricio Ataides Braz and Nilton Correia [11] used legal documents but not in documents types focused on folder fiscal and consider the outlines generation multilevel. Therefore in this study, we focused on the legal domain, especially in documents corresponding to fiscal folder of Public Prosecutor's Office. This research addresses the problem of how the use of machine learning algorithms and regular expressions contribute to the segmentation and classification of digitized documents in the Public Prosecutor's Office, being this a great option to optimize this activity and thus add to the effort to further modernize the processes of the Public Prosecutor's Office.

This paper organized as follows: In Sect. 2, the Related Works. Then, in Sect. 3, segmentation and classification of pages. Section 4 the contributions of our research are detailed and Sect. 5 will give a conclusion and some perspectives.

2   Related Work

There are different works carried out for page segmentation and classification, which over time have used different methods and techniques to address the problem and using different data sources.

For example in the 2009 [1] uses Multi-gram models applied to a database containing 356 documents distributed in 719 pages, which contain invoices of different type and language. Four years later [2] he presents an approach that leans towards the over segmentation of documents, for which they used a database of 7203 documents with 70,000 pages, containing 13 different semantic classes of documents (invoices, tax forms, contracts, property records, etc.). He also in the 2014 [3] year presents a work in which he analyzes heterogeneous documents (invoices, insurance, etc.) for which the images are subjected to an OCR process, empty words are removed and each page is presented in XML format for these experiments using four databases, the same databases are used [4] where a generic approach is proposed for the segmentation of a heterogeneous flow of documents.

An automated mechanism for segmentation and classification of large quantity of documents, can be useful in providing optimization in terms of both segmentation/classification accuracy and processing time [5], in this 2016 research they use deep neural networks for page segmentation and classification, for their experiments they use 576053 pages in image format, The images were saved using the RGB color model, then have been resampled and resized to 256×256. The database is divided into 224 different types of documents (identity documents, payroll, contracts, etc.). On the other hand tity of documents, can be useful in providing optimization in terms of both segmentation/classification accuracy and processing time [7] proposes a comparison of a rule-based approach with a machine learning method based on Doc2Vec, for this they use a corpus of more than 4,000 real administrative documents composed of more than 8,000 pages, obtaining that the machine learning method offers better results on multi-page documents, while the rule-based method works better with single-page documents.

There are also other works such as [8] from 2018 in which they use an approach that segments PDF documents into sections semantically applied to XML-based training data. Very similar to [6] that also uses structural analysis of pages, mentioning that 9 descriptors is enough for the identification and breaking of pages and obtaining very good results being its main disadvantage the costly of the process. Following similar methodologies [9] bases its method on contextual and design descriptors intended to specify the relationship between each pair of consecutive pages, to steal it they use a database composed of 4068 documents with 7000 pages.

In more current research such as [10] of 2019 in which convolutional neural networks are used but with the particularity that the visual information of the scanned images is combined with the semantic information of the texts, thus demonstrating that a multi-modal classification of features in a single classification architecture allows significant improvements for the optimal separation of documents; in order to apply these techniques they used 2 public datasets of documents Archive26k and Tobacco800. Following the line of combining visual and textual information in 2022 [10] proposes the use of a multimodal binary classification network that incorporates textual and image aspects of the pages of digital documents, obtaining very good results. In order to test their model, they use the same databases as in Heyer [10]. Finally in 2022 we also find a research [13] that performs segmentation and classification through a focused task such as a semantic analysis of the relationships between pages and proposes an end-to-end approach to feature extraction inspired by the dependency analysis literature.

Table 1 below summarizes the results obtained in the previous research reviewed.

Table 1. Summary of the discussed methods. S = Segmentation, C = classification, L = Labelled, T = Textual features, V = Visual Features.

N°	Authors(s)	Method	Features	Best model	Result
Summary of the discussed methods					
1	Fabricio Ataides et al. Ref. [11]	S,C and L	T	EfficientNet (ANN)	95.3 % F1
2	Th. Meilender, A. Belaïd [1]	S	T	K-means	82 % F1
3	Gordo, Albert et al. Ref. [2]	C and S	T and V	Probabilistic approach	
4	Daher, Hani et al. Ref. [3]	S and C	T	Incremental classifier	93 % Accuracy
5	Hani Daher and Abdel Belaïd. [4]	S	T	Multilayer Perceptron	94 % F1
6	Gallo, Ignazio et al. Ref. [5]	S and C	V	CNN + DNN	97.01 % F1
7	Karpinski, Romain and Belaïd, Abdel [6]	S	T	Factual descriptors	96.17 % Precision
8	Hamdi, Ahmed (2017) et al. Ref. [7]	S	T and V	Doc2Vec	67 % Accuracy
9	Jan Oevermann [8]	S	T	semantic text properties	81.7 % Accuracy
10	Hamdi, Ahmed (2018) et al. Ref. [9]	S	T	contextual and layout descriptors	91.5 % Accuracy
12	Wiedemann, G., Heyer, G. [10]	S	T and V	Multi-modal CNN	93 % Accuracy
13	Guha, Abhiji et al. Ref. [12]	S	T and V	multi-modal binary classification network	97.37 and 97.15% F1
14	Demirtaş, Mehmet Arif et al. Ref. [13]	S and C	T and V	Semantic Parsing	

3   Methodology

The methodology used in this research to develop the page segmentation and classification algorithms was CRISP-DM, an acronym that stands for Cross Industry Standard Process for Data Mining, which is a process model used as a basis for data science projects [14]. Within this methodology, 6 points are considered, which are detailed below based on the research:

3.1   Business Understanding

We focused on the digitalization of tax documents in the Public Prosecutor's Office, identifying the need for the segmentation and classification of pages to be done automatically, contributing to the reduction of time and cost, and ensuring accuracy in the segmentation and classification of pages.

3.2   Data Understanding

Being part of the electronic fiscal folder team, we were granted access to digitized fiscal case files, from which we identified the design and text characteristics, needed to generate a dataset from the documents provided.

3.3   Data Preparation

To apply the page segmentation algorithms, it was necessary to create a dataset based on the text and design characteristics of the digitized documents, with the final result detailed in Table 2. For page classification, a dictionary of regular expressions was defined as shown in Fig. 2.

3.4   Modeling

For page segmentation, tests were made with 9 machine learning algorithms, the algorithms used are detailed in Table 3, and for page classification, rules were defined based on the analysis of the contents of the documents, these rules are shown in Fig. 2.

3.5   Evaluation

The models used for page segmentation were evaluated based on 3 metrics (Accuracy, Sensitivity, and Precision), the results obtained can be seen in Table 3. For page classification, manual experiments were performed, evaluating the accuracy of the classification algorithm based on rules, these results can be seen in Fig. 3.

3.6   Deployment

The deployment of the algorithms for page segmentation and classification is designed to be used through a desktop application that allows reading the digitized files and gives as a result the segmentation and classification of the documents as shown in Fig. 4.

4   Segmentation and Classification of Pages

The process begins with the digitization of physical documents through scanners with OCR technology, the latter so that it is easy for us to read the information of the documents and thus be able to make the segmentation of the pages, which consists of identifying the breaks in the document, which in this case our segmentation algorithm analyzes whether a page is the beginning of a document or otherwise is part of a document, resulting in several documents contained in the initial document. Once we obtain the segmentation of the pages, we proceed to the classification, i.e. the classification of each identified document, which in the context of the research can be dispositions, notifications, minutes, requirements, official letters, among other types of documents that are automatically classified. This is visually detailed in Fig. 1.

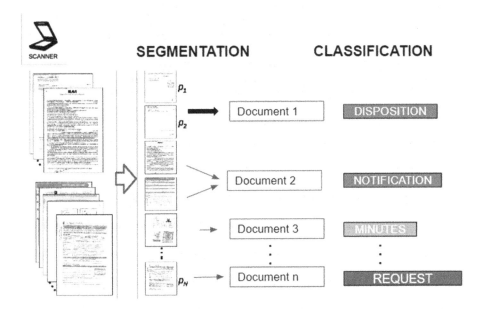

Fig. 1. The flow of the process of segmentation and classification of digitized pages of the Public Prosecutor's Office.

4.1   Segmentation of Page

In order to obtain an algorithm that can perform an automatic segmentation of pages, in our case to identify whether a page is part of a document or the beginning of a new document, we first proceeded to generate a dataset based on existing documents of the tax capitals in order to train and test predictive algorithms in order to obtain the best segmentation algorithm.

Dataset Generation. For our research, a dataset of 18 features and 1 target was generated from the analysis of over 1000 pages of 5 tax cases. In total, we managed to have 1071 records, one record for each page processed, each of which contained all the characteristics of a page, as defined in Table 2, where it can be seen that the design and text characteristics were considered and translated into sums, averages, standard deviation, and quantities, which were generated taking

Table 2. Long table caption.

Details of dataset features

N°	variable	Type	Description
1	text_has_regex_doc	Text	1 if the content of the page text matches some of the key words of the representative documents of the tax cases, e.g.: oficio, disposición, notificación; otherwise 0
2	layout_std_1_size	Layout	Standard deviation of the number of first empty spaces per line at the top of the page
3	layout_std_2_size	Layout	Standard deviation of the number of non-empty spaces per line in the middle of the page
4	layout_std_3_size	Layout	Standard deviation of the number of non-empty spaces per line at the bottom of the page
5	layout_mean_1_size	Layout	Average number of non-empty spaces per line of the initial part of the page
6	layout_mean_size	Layout	Average number of non-empty spaces per line across the page
7	layout_sum_1_size	Layout	Sum of the number of non-empty spaces per line at the top of the page
8	layout_sum_2_size	Layout	Sum of the number of non-empty spaces per line in the middle of the page
9	layout_empty_avg_1_group		Average number of blank spaces of the lines at the top of the page
10	layout_empty_avg_2_group	Layout	Average number of blank spaces of the lines in the central part of the page
11	layout_empty_avg_3_group	Layout	Average number of blank spaces of the lines at the bottom of the page
12	layout_first15_sum_size	Layout	Sum of the number of non-empty spaces per line of the first 15 lines of the page
13	text_numeral	Text	Number of numbering signs in the text, e.g.: Nro, N°, Numero:, N:
14	layout_sum_space	Layout	Sum of the number of empty spaces per line of the entire page
15	layout_size	Layout	Page text content size
16	text_n_keywords	Text	Number of keywords
17	text_n_words	Text	Number of words in the page
18	layout_std_space	Layout	Standard deviation of the number of the first empty spaces per line of the whole page
19	label	Target	Represents whether a page is part of a document or the start of a new document

into account the previous literature review and as a product of the analysis of the researchers, knowledgeable about the context and the processes of the Public Prosecutor's Office concerning the digitization of prosecutorial cases. Once the database was generated, we used it to test several predictive models that allow us to automatically segment whether a page is the beginning or part of a document.

Algorithms for Page Segmentation: Once the data set was obtained, tests were performed with supervised machine learning algorithms, for this research Random Forest, Logistic Regression, Support Vector Machine and k nearest neighbors were tested. In order to be able to apply and perform experiments with the mentioned models, the dataset of 1071 rows was divided into test and training data, allocating 30% for testing and 70% for training the model. The metrics obtained for each model for the test data are shown below.

Table 3. Machine learning algorithms used.

Summary of the discussed methods			
N°	Machine learning algorithms	Accuracy	Sensitivity	Precision
1	Logistic regression by gradient of descent	0.92	0.95	0.92
2	Random Forest	0.93	0.95	0.93
3	Random Forest with GridSearch	0.93	0.94	0.94
4	KNN	0.77	0.80	0.81
5	KNN (standard scale)	0.89	0.92	0.88
6	KNN (MinMax scale)	0.91	0.96	0.90
7	KNN (GridSearch)	0.92	0.97	0.91
8	Support Vector Machine with linear kernel	0.89	0.91	0.91
9	Support Vector Machine with radial kernel	0.76	0.88	0.76

The algorithms that obtain the best results and exceed 90% accuracy are 4: Random Forest, Random Forest with GridSearch, KNN (MinMax scale), and KNN(GridSearch). Of the 4 we chose to work with Random Forest which is the one that gives us the best result with 93% accuracy.

Unlike other research that use neural networks or deep learning, such as [5] or [10], in our case, for this stage of the application under development, due to the available resources and to seek an application as light as possible, it was decided not to use these algorithms, since they represent a greater investment of computational resources.

4.2   Classification of Page

To classify the segmented pages, we use regular expressions, which are rule-based algorithms for which we first identify all possible document types that may exist in a fiscal folder and based on them generate the rules that result in the document type.

Regular Expressions: The regular expressions used for classification are mainly composed of the text of each page and the keywords contained in the text of each type of document, as detailed in the following table.

Code	Regular expression	Document type
	Regular expression	
a	['(EXP(\.|\s)|Cargo\s*.*.ngreso.*Exped.ente|E.PEDIENTE)']	FILE
b	['RESOLUC.ON.*(JUDI)*|(Resoluci.n\s*(NO|Nro))']	RESOLUTION
c	['(Oficio N°)|(F[I||1|I]C.O|OF[I||1|I]C.*)\s*(N.|\d+|-|O)*']	OFFICIAL
d	['.ISSE.*E.* NOT.*FICACI|.AVIS.* DE NOTIFI|(.*mprimir.*)*Outlook(.|\n)*notifica|(AVISO\s*FISCAL|.REA.*NOTI|NOTIFICA CION\s*N|(ANEXO.*)*(C.NSTANC.A|CEDU.*)\s*(DE)*(.|\n)*(NOT.F|noti))']	NOTIFICATION
f	['(CERTIFICADO|C.R.*TF.*ICADO|CONSTANCIA)\s*(M.DICO|.*DOSA|.*POS|.*ENTRE)']	CERTIFICATE
g	['(Esc..T0|Escrito|ESC...o|ESCRITO|Cargo\s*.*Ingreso.*Escrito)\s*(:|;|N)*']	WRIT
h	['((?i)(consulta)).*REN']	RENIEC
h1	['HOJA.*DATO.*IDENTIFICA']	FINGERPRINT
i	['MANIFESTAC.*|PECIA.RACI.NDEL|(Iu:C1.ARAC1.N|[^0-	DECLARATION
w	['(INFORME POL.C.AL|REGPOI|REGPO.|CITACION\s*POLI)']	POLICE REPORT
j	['(PR.*D.L.GENC.AS	DISPOSITION
k	['A[C|L|I|1]TA']	MINUTES
l	['ARPETA FISCALN°|.*CO.*PROBANTE.*.AGO|.onsulta.*aso.*iscal|(EI.*suscri|Asunto|SUMILLA|[sS]umilla|ASUNTO|SUM:)\s*(:|;)*|.onsulta.*aso.*iscal']	OTHER
m	['PROVIDENCIA']	PROVIDENCE
n	['FICHA']	FICHA
r	['(S.DP.L|.*sistemas\.policia\.gob)']	SIDPOL
s	['CAR.*TA.*(AUXILIAR|PRINC.|F.S)']	FOLDER
t	['CERTIFI.*(\n|\s).*PENALES']	CRIMINAL CERTIFICATE
u	['CONSTANCIA.*(CONCUR|.*LLAMA)']	CONSTANCE
v	['TOMO']	VOLUME
y	['.argo.*ngreso.*aso|CARGO\s*.*INGRESO.*(CARPETA|CAR)*']	POSITION INGRESS
p	['[I1]N...ME|MINUT.*']	REPORT
e	['(AVISODENOT.F.CAC.ÓNJUDICIAL|AV.SO DE NOT.F.CACI.N JUDICIAL)']	NOTIFICATION NOTICE
z	['CONTR.*O']	CONTRACT
w2	['CA.TURA.*PANTA.*A']	SCREEN CAPTURE
w3	['CADENA.*CUSTODIA']	CHAIN OF CUSTODY
w4	['REQUERIMIENTO|SENOR JUEZ']	REQUEST

Fig. 2. Regular expression.

The results obtained are very favorable and have a high degree of accuracy when typing the segmented pages, as shown below, which details the results obtained when performing the experiments with two tax case files, the first of 135 pages and the second of 89 pages. These experiments were performed manually by the researchers themselves as part of the validation of the classification algorithm, which is then applied to execute the page segmentation.

Experiments with the page classification algorithm									
Splits	File 1 (135 sheet file, weight 19.68 MB)					File 2 (file of 89 sheets, weight 33.32 MB)				
	Documents generated	Classification				Documents generated	Classification			
		Correct	Incorrect	Accuracy (%)	Error(%)		Correct	Incorrect	Accuracy (%)	Error(%)
Split 1	84	73	11	87%	13%	37	29	8	78%	22%
Split 2	84	78	6	93%	7%	37	29	8	78%	22%
Split 3	84	79	5	94%	6%	37	30	7	81%	19%
Split 4	84	80	4	95%	5%	37	30	7	81%	19%
Split 5	84	79	5	94%	6%	37	30	7	81%	19%

Fig. 3. Result of the experiments with the page classification algorithm.

5   Contributions and Results

The input to our solution to generate the database and create the model for the automatic segmentation of documents is delivered by an OCR engine, which is the source of information from the digitized pages that after a process of data analysis and preprocessing we obtain quite detailed design and text features as shown in Table 2, in total 1071 records were obtained with 18 features and one target, this guaranteed the high accuracy of the algorithms used.

Nine machine learning algorithms were evaluated, see Table 3, based on the measurement of 3 metrics Accuracy Sensitivity, Precision. As a result, 5 of the evaluated algorithms exceeded 90% in the 3 metrics, being the Random Forest algorithms the ones that obtained the best result with 93% of Accuracy, a quite high result when we are dealing with machine learning algorithms.

Within the classification of document types, we mainly used the text of the pages and their keywords, from which a rule-based algorithm was generated (see Fig. 2) to identify the types of documents generated in the segmentation of the pages, obtaining results with a high percentage of accuracy as can be seen in Fig. 3, which details the results obtained in the experiments carried out concerning the classification of pages.

[1] obtained an accuracy of 75%, making use of multigrams, where to digitize the documents they also used OCR and identified 19 features, in our case in the same way OCR was used to digitize the documents, with this it was possible to generate 18 base features (see Table 2) and from these features a total of 42 features were generated, which guaranteed an accuracy of 93% in page segmentation and 90% accuracy in classification.

It is worth mentioning that in [2], supervised learning was used in a large dataset of 7 203 documents with 70 000 pages, which include 13 types of documents, obtaining initial results, a dataset much larger than the one used in our research, however, we were able to work with 27 types of documents as shown in Fig. 2.

[11] The results show that the methods that combine text and image, with an accuracy of 91%, are best. However, they mention that although this is indeed a remarkable result, it requires excessive computational resources, so they opt to use a labeling system, achieving the same result with fewer computational resources; In our research, we also evaluated the possibility of tagging at the time of digitizing pages, however, it requires investing more man-hours in a public ministry overloaded with the workload, so we opted to continue with the use of text and design features along with the use of regular expressions, also achieving very good results in accuracy; in addition to the model will be deployed as a service ensuring that it can operate with minimal computational resources.

Based on the initial tests running the automatic segmentation and classification of digitized documents, the test was performed with a fiscal folder of 89 pages, of which our application was able to perform the process in 23 s and generated 37 documents, this result is shown in Fig. 3.

Fig. 4. Result of the segmentation and classification of an 89-page tax case.

6 Conclusion and Future Works

With the generation of an adequate dataset, it is possible to obtain very favorable results by applying machine learning algorithms that allow automatic segmentation and classification.

The best machine learning algorithms for automatic page segmentation, in our particular case to identify whether a page is the beginning or part of a document, are the Random Forest algorithms, with which we obtained a high Accuracy of 93%.for page type classification, using algorithms with well-defined regular expressions results in high accuracy in page typing. Thus, the implementation of our solution in the Public Prosecutor's Office is timely and necessary.

Initial tests show that the time of segmentation and automatic classification of digitized documents is quite short and acceptable, which leads us to infer that its implementation guarantees the reduction of time and costs and ensures a high accuracy in the results. It is expected to continue with the development and continuous improvement of the application in order to promote its massive use in the Public Prosecutor's Office, for a more efficient administration of the digitized fiscal folders.

Although there are indeed previous works that use neural networks and have obtained very good results, in our case, due to the limited initial amount of data used for training and testing, we consider that it is not convenient to use them, so we decided not to test algorithms related to neural networks, however, we do not rule out their use in the future as long as we have access to a larger amount of training and testing data.

Acknowledgment. We thank the executing unit of the Public Prosecutor's Office for allowing us to be part of the project and thus be able to carry out this research. This project is part of the electronic prosecutor's folder, a project financed by the Inter-American Development Bank (BID).

References

1. Meilender, T., Belaïd, A.: Segmentation of continuous document flow by a modified backward-forward algorithm. In: Kathrin Berkner and Laurence Likforman-Sulem, F. (eds.) International Society for Optics and Photonics, vol. 7247, pp. 27–36. SPIE (2009). https://doi.org/10.1117/12.805646
2. Gordo, A., Rusinol, M., Karatzas, D., Bagdanov, A.D.: Document classification and page stream segmentation for digital mailroom application. In: 2013 12th International Conference on Document Analysis and Recognition, pp. 621–625 (2013). https://doi.org/10.1109/ICDAR.2013.128
3. Daher, H., Bouguelia, M.R., Belaid, A., d'Andecy, V.P.: Multipage administrative document stream segmentation. In: 2014 22nd International Conference on Pattern Recognition, pp. 966–971 (2014). https://doi.org/10.1109/ICPR.2014.176
4. Daher, H., Belaïd, A.: Document flow segmentation for business applications. In: Document Recognition and Retrieval XXI, Bertrand Coüasnon and Eric K. Ringger, pp. 135–145. SPIE (2014). https://doi.org/10.1117/12.2043141
5. Gallo, I., Noce, L., Zamberletti, A., Calefati, A.: Deep neural networks for page stream segmentation and classification. In: 2016 International Conference on Digital Image Computing: Techniques and Applications (DICTA), pp. 1–7. DICTA (2016). https://doi.org/10.1117/12.805646
6. Karpinski, R., Belaïd, A.: Combination of structural and factual descriptors for document stream segmentation. In: 2016 12th IAPR Workshop on Document Analysis Systems (DAS), pp. 221–226. DAS (2016). https://doi.org/10.1109/DAS.2016.21
7. Hamdi, A., Voerman, J., Coustaty, M., Joseph, A., d'Andecy, V.P., Ogier, J.M.: Machine learning vs deterministic rule-based system for document stream segmentation. In: 2017 14th IAPR International Conference on Document Analysis and Recognition (ICDAR), vol. 05, pp. 77–82. ICDAR (2017). https://doi.org/10.1109/ICDAR.2017.332
8. Oevermann, J.: Semantic PDF segmentation for legacy documents in technical documentation. Procedia Comput. Sci. **137**, 55–65 (2018). https://doi.org/10.1016/j.procs.2018.09.006

9. Hamdi, A., Coustaty, M., Joseph, A., d'Andecy, V.P., Doucet, A., Ogier, J.M.: Feature selection for document flow segmentation. In: 2018 13th IAPR International Workshop on Document Analysis Systems (DAS), pp. 245–250. DAS (2017). https://doi.org/10.1109/DAS.2018.66

10. Wiedemann, G., Heyer, G.: Multi-modal page stream segmentation with convolutional neural networks. Lang Resour. Eval. **55**, 127–150 (2021). https://doi.org/10.1007/s10579-019-09476-2

11. Braz, F.A., da Silva, N.C., Lima, J.A.S.: Leveraging effectiveness and efficiency in page stream deep segmentation. Eng. Appl. Artif. Intell. **105**, 104–394 (2021). https://doi.org/10.1016/j.engappai.2021.104394

12. Guha, A., Alahmadi, A., Samanta, D., Khan, M.Z., Alahmadi, A.H.: A multimodal approach to digital document stream segmentation for title insurance domain. IEEE Access **10**, 11341–11353 (2022). https://doi.org/10.1109/ACCESS.2022.3144185

13. Demirts, M.A., Oral, B., Akpinar, M.Y., Deniz, O.: Semantic Parsing of Interpage Relations. arXiv (2022). https://doi.org/10.48550/ARXIV.2205.13530

14. What is CRISP DM?. https://www.datascience-pm.com/crisp-dm-2/. Accessed 09 Oct 2022

A Semantic Query Engine for Knowledge Rich Legal Digital Libraries

Hasan M. Jamil$^{(\boxtimes)}$ [iD]

Department of Computer Science,
University of Idaho,
Moscow, ID, USA
jamil@uidaho.edu

Abstract. Contemporary legal digital libraries such as Lexis Nexis and WestLaw allow users to search case laws using sophisticated search tools. The sophistication of these legal search tools, however, vary widely between commercial and non-commercial libraries, and by user groups. At its core, various forms of keyword search and indexing are used to find documents of interest. While newer search engines leveraging semantic technologies such as knowledgebases, natural language processing, and knowledge graphs are becoming available, legal databases are yet to take advantage of them fully. Even more scarce is any search engine able to support reasoning to identify legal documents based on legal precedent matching. In this paper, we introduce an experimental legal document search engine, called *Prism*, that is capable of supporting legal argument based search to support legal claims. We use a document engineering method to embed legal premise graphs, called the AND-OR graph, in the document to facilitate semantic match. A prototype implementation of Prism as a component of a document management system, called *VOiC*, is also discussed.

Keywords: Document Engineering · Story Understanding · Premise Graph · Knowledge Graphs · Graph Matching · Natural Language Processing

1 Introduction

Search is a basic function supported in all digital archives of information. While search techniques have evolved in structured and unstructured databases, it is still an ongoing research issue in digital libraries and document databases [14], in stark contrast with other types of digital libraries such as music [8], mathematics [18], judicial [6], etc. in terms of techniques and applications. Among the search techniques currently in use, some form of keyword search [20,24,25] or text mining based association search [1,13,19] are prevalent. In recent research, however, an emerging trend of searching digital libraries using knowledge graphs (KG) is gaining popularity [10] with the goal to improve semantic matching [12,21].

J. A. Lossio-Ventura et al. (Eds.): SIMBig 2022, CCIS 1837, pp. 45–60, 2023.
https://doi.org/10.1007/978-3-031-35445-8_4

It is not uncommon in digital library search for users to land on useful documents almost by accident [17]. This is because most of the search engines do not allow queries that make sense semantically. For example, the following legal query

Q_1: *"List case laws where parents retained jurisdiction in Virginia despite the opposing parent having the home state jurisdiction in another state under UCCJEA."*

is unlikely to return any case laws that meet the exact legal criteria expressed in the query. Most likely a keyword search will return all Michigan cases under UCCJEA mentioning home state and nothing much. To appreciate the complexities inherent in this query, it is important that we briefly understand the structure of legal brief, and the UCCJEA law in the USA.

1.1 Structure of Case Laws

Roughly, there are two types of laws – black letter law, or the articles of the constitution and case laws, or the adjudicated proceedings of the cases in the courts of law. Case laws are specific litigation in which black letter laws and other case laws, called legal precedents, are applied and the legal merits of opposing arguments are decided by the courts. In the USA, we have a three tier court system – 1) trial court where litigation first starts, merit is decided based on facts, and logic of the arguments by direct application of the laws; 2) appeals court where constitutionality of decisions made by trial courts is challenged and decided relative to the case at hand; and finally 3) the supreme court which adjudicates any misinterpretation of the laws by the lower courts.

With respect to digital representation of judicial documents, counsels of the parties involved in a litigation submit legal briefs, courts rule on the briefs, and produce another document called ruling or judgment. These rulings become legal precedents and enter the database as case laws. A ruling has roughly four parts: 1) court, party, counsel details, and case details such as case number, dates and jurisdiction. 2) a preamble that states the overall description of the litigation and applicable case laws. 3) facts that lay out the "truth" about the case as seen by each party which can be established by evidence. 4) legal argument why or why not the facts lead to legal conclusions supported by case laws. Finally, 5) relief sought or final opinion of the courts after deliberations and argument.

1.2 Article UCCJEA

UCCJEA stands for Uniform Child Custody Jurisdiction and Enforcement Act, which is an article of USA federal constitution dealing with jurisdiction of litigating parents or custodians of minor children residing in distinct court jurisdictions, often in multiple states. Some versions of the UCCJEA act has been adopted by all 50 states.

Essence of UCCJEA. Two of the main purposes of the article were to (i) stop competing jurisdictions from abusing their power and forcing families to needlessly waste resources in multiple states by usurping the jurisdiction from a state having a legitimate claim on the jurisdiction, and (ii) prevent parents from seeking a more convenient forum across state boundaries to make it difficult for the other parent to seek relief from a rightful jurisdiction or to frustrate them. The article does so in many ways but mainly by (i) removing the use of "best interest of the child" argument from the clauses of UCCJA (the predecessor of UCCJEA), (ii) prioritizing the jurisdictional bases in a tie proof hierarchy so that a state/court at a higher strata can assume jurisdiction, (iii) allowing a state at a higher strata exercise jurisdiction without any regard for a court in a competing jurisdiction at a lower strata in the absence of an exclusive continuing jurisdiction by another court, (this sounds confusing) (iv) requiring the courts to evaluate their jurisdictional authority anew (even if the court has exclusive continuing jurisdiction) every single time a new cause is brought before them by recognizing the fact that jurisdiction of any court is not permanent and may change primarily due to the mobility of the child, and (v) giving the home state the absolute priority and preemptive jurisdiction over all courts again in the absence of exclusive continuing jurisdiction by another court.

UCCJEA Provisions. Virginia UCCJEA [5] (as well as the Federal UCC-JEA which was adopted by all 50 US states) essentially recognizes the following provisions:

1. Initial child custody jurisdiction: A court in Virginia can exercise jurisdiction to make an initial custody determination only if the state is the home state of the child. Home state is a state where the child lived at least 183 days prior to the commencement of the proceeding, or the maximum number of days between the two competing states at the time of the commencement of the proceeding, no other state(s) has/have jurisdiction, or has/have declined to exercise jurisdiction.
2. Exclusive, continuing jurisdiction: A court in Virginia which has legally made a custody determination will have exclusive continuing jurisdiction as long as the child or the custodial parent continues to live in this state. Also, a Virginia court that has made a child custody determination and does not have exclusive, continuing jurisdiction under (UCCJEA?) may modify that determination only if it has jurisdiction to make an initial determination.
3. Jurisdiction to modify determination: Virginia may not modify a child custody determination made by another state unless it has jurisdiction to make an initial determination, and the other state determines that it no longer has exclusive, continuing jurisdiction or that Virginia would be a more convenient forum, or Virginia or the other state determines that neither a parent, nor the child presently resides in the other state.

1.3   Use Case

Abebi and Pierre had a child named Fiia when they divorced in a Mississippi court at which time they agreed to joint custody of Fiia. Subsequently, both Abebi and Pierre moved to Virginia and Michigan respectively, and Fiia moved to Michigan according to the terms of the Mississippi court order which granted each parent a two year primary rotational custodianship. However, upon moving to Virginia, Abebi filed for sole primary custody in Virginia and a jurisdictional litigation ensued involving three different states. The primary question being debated was which court has jurisdiction over Fiia, and where this custody matter will be decided.

On pleading with Virginia by Abebi, the court assumed jurisdiction despite objection that Michigan was Fiia's home state and Virginia did not have jurisdiction to make an initial determination. Furthermore, Mississippi still had exclusive continuing jurisdiction and did not decline to exercise jurisdiction. Michigan, on the other hand, deferred to Virginia stating "since" Virginia is exercising jurisdiction, it (MI) cannot despite having home state jurisdiction, and despite the UCCJEA stating that Michigan is not required to extend full faith and credit to Virginia court because they did not have the jurisdiction in the first place.

With the intention of appealing the two decisions in Virginia as well as Michigan courts, Pierre is looking for case laws that show precedent supporting Virginia's stance, and then researching if that erroneous decision was reversed by superior courts in Virginia. In fact, there are plenty of case laws that refute the Virginia and Michigan position in the case of Abebi v Pierre in favor of Pierre that existing legal search engines cannot find or link multiple case laws to offer a more complete picture.

For example, the Janet Miller-Jenkins v. Lisa Miller-Jenkins, Virginia (2006)[1] case is almost exactly identical to Abebi v. Pierre and supports Pierre's position, which was denied by both Virginia and Michigan, Janet and Lisa lived together in Virginia in the 1990's where Lisa gave birth to their daughter IMJ in April 2002. Soon after in August 2002 they moved to Vermont and entered into a civil union. Unfortunately, in September 2003, the parties ended their relationship and Lisa moved to Virginia with IMJ while Janet remained in Vermont.

Lisa asked a court in Vermont to dissolve their union in November 2003 and sought legal and physical custody of IMJ. In June 2004, Vermont issued a temporary order awarding Lisa primary custody. On July 1, 2004 Lisa filed for sole custody with sole parental rights in Virginia upon Virginia's affirmation of Marriage Affirmation Act. Upon learning the Virginia action, the Vermont court on July 19, 2004, exercised its exclusive continuing jurisdiction, stating that it will not defer to Virginia and ordered that its previous custody order be followed. When the Virginia courts proceeded with the litigation in Virginia, the court of Vermont forcefully ignored all Virginia orders holding that Virginia lacked subject matter jurisdiction and retained its (Vermont's) right to exercise jurisdiction. The Vermont Supreme court held that the state acted according

---

[1] http://www.courts.state.va.us/opinions/opncavwp/2654044.pdf.

to its established law, had jurisdiction to do so and that Parental Kidnapping Prevention Act (PKPA) afforded preemptive jurisdiction to Vermont and denied full faith and credit to Virginia orders that contradicted those entered by the Vermont court. On appeal in Virginia, the Virginia court of appeals affirmed and upheld Vermont's position.

Both Vermont and Virginia appeals court's positions have been affirmed in several other similar courts such as in Rogers v. Rogers, Alaska (1995)[2], Swalef v. Anderson, Virginia (2007)[3], Key v. Key, Virginia (2004)[4], and in numerous other cases. In particular, in Markle v. Markle, Michigan (2007)[5], the Michigan court of appeals denied to extend full faith and credit to Texas court's custody order citing Texas court's lack of subject matter jurisdiction. In Johnson v. Johnson, Michigan (2005)[6], the Michigan court of appeals reversed the Michigan trial court's order that denied Michigan jurisdiction in favor of Idaho without determining that Michigan was an inconvenient forum by simply determining that Michigan lacked jurisdiction under a scenario similar to that of Abebi v. Pierre case even though Michigan was the home state.

The critical point is that none of these cases were systematically discovered using existing search engines in law libraries; rather, they were accidentally discovered [17] on the internet by Pierre. The research issue we are addressing is designing a search engine to help find cases that support or refute the position of a plaintiff or defendant given the case facts as the user sees it. We call the reasoning a user uses to establish a claim a *premise graph*. The task the search engine assumes is to find the cases that at least partially match the edges in the premise graph, and possibly all the edges to render a conclusion. We lay out our experimental model in the sections to follow.

2 Document Understanding Using *Prism*

Abebi v. Pierre illustrates a complex system of information structure that most likely will not lend itself to traditional query engines such as keyword search, layered indexing, and other techniques discussed earlier, to produce the documents these litigants seek. More novel approaches based on knowledge graphs [7,9,15,22] or knowledge driven querying of digital documents [2–4,16] were not shown to be effective in the type of search we are interested in. We therefore propose a document authoring and engineering model to enrich legal documents with meta-information at creation time so that improved semantic search becomes possible. Our goal is to make the enrichment steps as user transparent as possible.

---

[2] http://touchngo.com/sp/html/sp-4293.htm.

[3] http://www.courts.state.va.us/opinions/opncavwp/2510061.pdf.

[4] http://www.courts.state.va.us/opinions/opncavwp/1079041.pdf.

[5] https://www.michbar.org/opinions/appeals/2007/081407/36789.pdf.

[6] http://www.michbar.org/opinions/appeals/2005/030105/26467.pdf.

A careful examination of the UCCJEA black letter law suggests a premise-conclusion relationship in the form a logic structure $\alpha \leftarrow \beta_1, \wedge, \ldots, \wedge \beta_m$, where β_is are the conjuncts in the antecedent and α is the consequent of a logical implication. For example, for the following facts,

> resident(pierre,fiia,michigan).
> jurisdiction(Cust,Subject,State,homestate) ← resident(Cust,Subject,State),
>   ¬ jurisdiction(Cust,Subject,State,exclusivecontinuing).
> jurisdiction(Cust,Subject,State, homestate) ← resident(Cust,Subject,State),
>   jurisdiction(Cust,Subject,State,exclusivecontinuing),
>   declined(Cust,Subject,State,exclusivecontinuing).
> jurisdiction(Cust,Subject,State, convenientforum) ←
>   resident(Cust,Subject,State), deferred(Cust,Subject,State,ExState)
>   jurisdiction(Cust,Subject,ExState,exclusivecontinuing).

the above rules codifying Home State jurisdiction under UCCJEA will determine that Pierre, as a custodian of Fiia, has home state jurisdiction in Michigan. However, if we add this fact to the database,

> jurisdiction(pierre,fiia,mississippi,exclusivecontinuing).

Pierre will not gain home state jurisdiction in Michigan. This rule base then can act as a recommendation system to suggest Pierre to seek a convenient forum determination, or home state deferral by the state of Mississippi.

Some of the facts claimed in the legal briefs or pleadings are subject to dispute, and a ruling is necessary. For example, in Miller-Jenkins v. Miller-Jenkins, Virginia (2006), as well as in Abebi v. Pierre, Michigan (2009), both Lisa and Abebi claimed home state jurisdiction. In Lisa's case, home state was obvious since IMJ lived with Lisa in Virgina for more than six months. Lisa could not exercise the home state jurisdiction because Vermont was exercising its exclusive continuing jurisdiction, which takes precedent under UCCJEA. However, for Abebi, Fiia lived in Virginia for two weeks, after moving from Mississippi, and then lived with Pierre for more than four months at the time Abebi filed for custody. In such cases, both parties need to state why they believe their respective states have jurisdiction. A judge then decides the correct status based on case laws, which is clearly spelled out in the UCCJEA article. We can capture the premises for residency as the following set of rules.

> resident(Cust,Subject,State) ← livedin(Cust,Subject,State,From,To),
>   duration(Days,From,To), filed(Date), Date=To, Days>183.
> resident(Cust1,Subject,State1) ← livedin(Cust1,Subject,State1,From1,To1),
>   livedin(Cust2,Subject,State2,From2,To2), priorto(To2,From1),
>   duration(Days1,From1,To1), duration(Days2,From2,To2), filed(Date),
>   Date=To1, Days1>Days2.

The rules above say that on the date of filing the case, a custodian gains residency in a state if the child lived in that state six months or more continuously until the date of filing, or if the child lived in that state the most compared to the state she lived immediately prior. Note that both cannot simultaneously hold true. Now given the following facts, Pierre is certain to gain residency, i.e., home state residency.

livedin(abebi,fiia,virginia,1/1/2007,1/14/2007).
livedin(pierre,fiia,michigan,1/15/2007,5/20/2007).

The duration predicate above can be implemented as a computable function that will return the difference between two dates in number of days, and priorto as a Boolean function that returns true or false given two dates To and From if To is prior to From.

The technical issue now is, how do we arrive at these logical conclusions from a search of the available digital documents? One way to accomplish this is to design a text understanding system in ways similar to [9, 22] that is capable of deriving fact predicates, e.g., livedin or resident, from the case laws, and applying these rules to decide if a document is relevant and meets the query conditions. In this approach, no additional manipulation of the documents will be necessary except the knowledge extraction engine. However, we can expect the search cost to be high because all documents will need to be understood and mined first for discovering the predicates. An alternative is to create these knowledge at the time of document authoring. We adopt the latter approach because it is efficient, even though slightly demanding and intrusive for users authoring the documents. We, however, contend that our document engineering approach is efficient for both creating documents, and processing queries.

2.1 Document Authoring

The main idea is to design an HTML WYSIWYG legal document editor that will transparently embed a premise graph into the document as a searchable meta-data, which will not be rendered, yet the authors of the document will be able to view and edit it. To help authors embed the graph, we design a type-ahead searchable legal terms such as *resident, exclusive continued jurisdiction, convenient forum,* etc. from which authors are able to pick node descriptions for a premise graph along with the required parameters. For example, they will be able to construct a node "Mississippi" has "exclusive continuing jurisdiction" over "Fiia" as a triple ⟨Fiia, Mississippi, Exclusive Continuing⟩ that we call *c-term,* or complex term. Subsequently, with a click of a mouse, this c-term can be added to an edge as a node, and stored as the document meta-data. Figure 1 shows the editor in use by the attorney of Pierre filing the objection to Abebi's attempt to retain jurisdiction in Virginia.

AND/OR Graphs. The major reasons question answering systems or legal search engines such as Lexis Nexis or WestLaw fail to respond to queries such as Q_1 is because they require causal reasoning or causality determination [11, 23] which none of these contemporary digital libraries support. Since such causalities

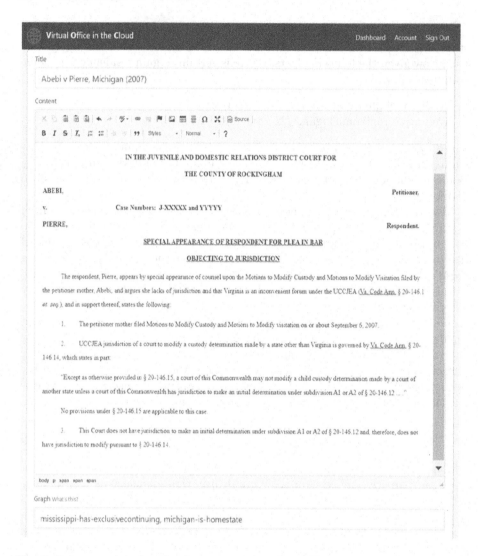

Fig. 1. Prism user interface for document engineering with premise graph embedding.

are application specific and orthogonal to document authoring, we believe they need to be addressed separately. Current approaches to such discoveries tend to be based on learning models, are quite involved and computationally expensive, in systems that support something of similar nature. In Prism, we seek to find a cheaper and more direct solution using the concept of directed AND/OR graphs that was exploited in past research [26].

The process we have adopted to capture the premise graphs in Prism exploits the AND/OR graph representation. For example, the jurisdiction/4 rule[7] can be

---

[7] jurisdiction/4 means the predicate jurisdiction has four arguments.

represented in the form of a modified AND/OR graph as shown in Fig. 2(b). In this modified AND/OR graph, the nodes are pre-processed and made grounded, and unlike the logic rules discussed in Sect. 2, there are no variables. In other words, the rules are instantiated with ground facts. Users select these facts from a fixed set of terms which come with predefined slots to be filled in. For example, when the term resident is selected, the interface asks for two values, one, the name of the child, another, the state, and once supplied, generates the c-term. In order to support more complex premise graphs, Prism also allows expressing premise graphs in the form of RDF-like triples, node1-edgename-node2 type of edges, as shown in Fig. 1 with the document rendered and in Fig. 2(c) as the HTML document representation. Note that the premise graph is not visible to readers, yet remains visible to the author during editing.

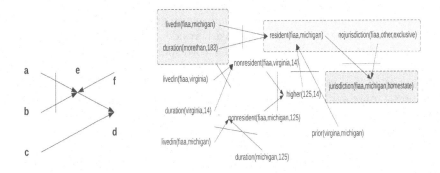

(a) Causal net in the form (b) jurisdiction/4 (home state) rules captured using
of AND/OR graphs.   AND/OR graph.

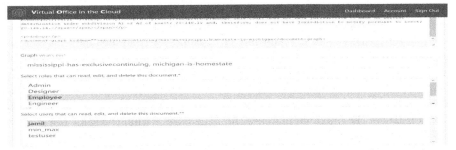

(c) Premise graphs are embedded in the document using a non-rendering mode.

Fig. 2. Representing Premise graphs in Prism. (Color figure online)

Users are also able to visualize the premise graph before they save the document. Prism allows validation functions to check if the premise graph is legally valid, and semantically accurate. It reports mistakes using color coding of the edges. All semantically and legally accurate edges are shown in green, and the others in red. Edges being edited or not validated are shown in black.

Semantic Search Using Premise Graphs. Usually, a legal researcher will try to find case laws that support even part of their claims. In other words, it is usually difficult to find case laws that have the exact circumstances that will warrant identical outcomes in the court of law. Given that a large percentage of cases are decided on erroneous premises and often get redressed in appeals or in supreme courts, it is not unlikely to find contradictory case laws. Therefore, case laws need to be interlinked so that the whole decision process is clear. Consequently, counsels can piece together their legal claims by citing cases that support parts of their arguments in the premise graphs, with the hope of finding such support for every part of their premise graph.

We, therefore, support a maximal constrained subgraph isomorphic matching search of the premise graphs of case laws in a systematic way. To understand the process, let us consider another case, Michelle v. Maxwell, 2002 (Nebraska) over the custody of Elli. In her case, let us assume that the case law contains the purple, yellow and green shaded parts of the premise graph shown in Fig. 2(b) with the following details: livedin(elli,nebraska), resident(elli,nebraska) and nojurisdiction(elli,other,exclusive) replacing the corresponding nodes in the premise graph. A search by Pierre's attorney with the entire premise graph in Fig. 2(b) which he intends to prove as his whole case, will match with Elli's case law since it supports "maximally" his argument that Michigan has jurisdiction over Fiia. This is because circumstances are identical to Fiia's with the only substitution being of Nebraska for Michigan, an isomorph.

On the other hand, if Prism can find another case law that supports the other branch of Pierre's premise graph, namely the non-shaded branches, Prism will include that case law as well, which only strengthens his argument even though one support is logically sufficient. In reality, Prism will list all such matches. The important issue to note here is that Prism will also find partial matches. For example, consider a case in which Prism could only find support (matching) for the purple branch, and nothing else. In that event, Prism will list this case as a possible partial match if and only if it could not find any more case laws to support the yellow or the green shaded portions (i.e., it did not find Elli's case). This is called the maximal constrained subgraph isomorphic search – i.e., Prism always searches for maximum possible matches. Technically, Prism breaks down every AND and OR into individual subgraphs to match isomorphically, then constructs the maximal matches from the parts within the same document, and discards a match the moment a relatively more maximal match is found.

2.2 Premise Graph Embedding

We have implemented Prism within a virtual legal office environment, called *VOiC*, in which documents are created, routed and shared across an enterprise. While AND/OR graphs can be included in any VOiC documents as a set of edges in the form of triples, or in the database as a set of predicates (as shown in Figs. 1 and 2(c)), they are often difficult to conceive, and tedious to express correctly by non-technical users, such as law clerks or even counselors. To help users capture the premise graphs precisely, VOiC includes a user initiated premise

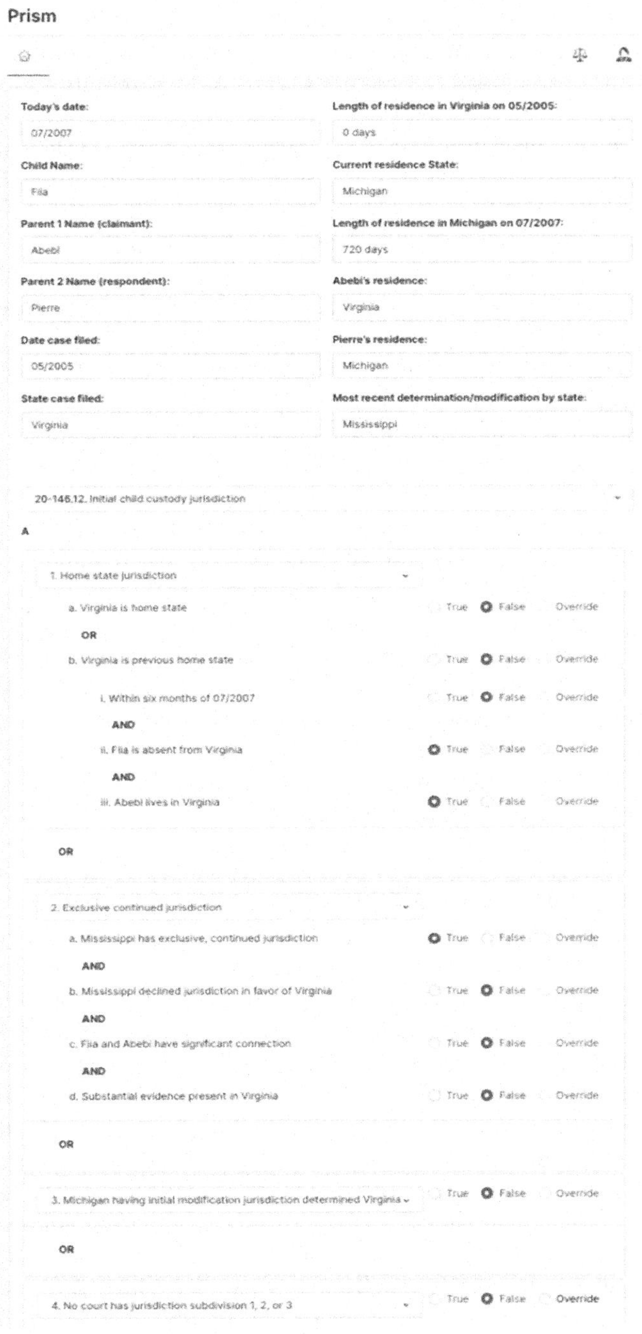

Fig. 3. Dialogue box for Premise graph generation. (Color figure online)

graph selection and description tool, a dialogue box, as shown in Fig. 3. Users can activate the Prism dialogue box from the document authoring interface shown in Fig. 1, and once the dialogue is completed, the generated graph can be included in the document, or the set of predicates representing the case facts can be transferred to the database.

To generate a premise graph, users first choose an article of the law. In Fig. 3, Virginia UCCJEA article § 20-*146.12 Initial child custody jurisdiction* is selected. Once it is selected, the form to collect case specific information is displayed, e.g., child's name (Fiia), state the litigation filed (Virginia), and so on. As the entries are added, the graph entries with case specific details are initialized in the AND/OR template below the entry form. Users are then required to select one of three options – True, False, or **Override** (if the user is a judge) – for each of the pre-conditions that must be satisfied under the article selected. The graph in general is a forest of AND/OR trees. Every time a truth value of a node becomes true, the node is highlighted in green, otherwise, it stays red. As expected, if a conjunct is false, its consequent is also false (red).

For example, to make Section A.1 (home state jurisdiction) true (green) under article § 20-146.12, we must choose either A.1.a true, OR, A.1.b true, and to make A.1.b true, we must choose all three, A.1.b.i, A.1.b.ii and A.1.b.iii, true. Finally, to make Section A (initial child custody jurisdiction) true, we must find A.1, A.2, A.3 or A.4 true. Once the premise tree is constructed, it can be easily converted into an AND/OR graph and embedded into the Prism document.

This Prism premise graph interface dual both in a counselor authoring mode (counselor icon), and as a judge decision mode (justice icon). In the counselor authoring mode, the override button stays inactive. In the judge authoring mode, it becomes active and allows the judge to express that she disagreed with this specific claim by the counselors of one or both parties.

3   Implementation of Prism as a Virtual Office Environment on the Cloud

In VOiC, document privacy and controlled sharing are our top priorities. We have used Flask for the implementation of VOiC for its well-known support for web applications, using its two core components Werkzeug for web server functions and Jinja for HTML templating. Flask is extendable by virtue of its support for many extensions, and it also works with the majority of third-party Python libraries, which we have used as well. In addition to several other extensions of Flask, we have used the flask_ckeditor extension. CKEditor is an embeddable rich text editor with full support for HTML editing. This extension allows a core feature of Prism-HTML editing and embedding of graphs directly into documents. Bootstrap 4 open source front-end framework was used for creating platform-agnostic and responsive websites using its wide range of CSS styling options. For data management, SQLAlchemy was used to seamlessly convert data from a SQLite relational database into Python objects.

VOiC provides a comprehensive document management system – a Virtual Office in the Cloud. It consists of four main processes: storing, sharing, searching, and rendering. Storage includes the holding of users, roles, and documents in a relation database. Sharing relates to access control, and allowing users to access pertinent documents through their username and role. Searching serves users with a tool for data discovery with documents searchable by their search graph, title, and content. Rendering forms the front-end portion of VOiC. Together, these elements form a robust solution for document management in a virtual setting.

VOiC has two document sharing capabilities. First, users must sign in to authenticate their account before accessing or creating any documents. During document creation, the creator chooses which roles and individual users will have access to her document. This selection is done through two multi-select input fields. By default, all users have the "Employee" role. Therefore, sharing a document with this role shares it with all system users. After creation, the added users and roles can then edit these permissions as desired. Each user then sees documents they have access to on their dashboard. We generate this list of documents by filtering out each document that does not have the active user in its list of users or any intersection between the document and user roles.

VOiC has two search options – keyword or substring search, and graph search. On submitting the keywords, a SQLAlchemy query then executes and retrieves all documents in which the search query keywords are a substring in the title or content. The graph search uses the maximal isomorphic search as described earlier, and is thus a more powerful search. However, the graph search is substantially slower than text search.

4   Discussion

Both Prism and VOiC are ongoing research and implemented as a test prototype with bare bone functionalities. The main purpose of this paper is to introduce a novel search engine for legal documents each of which are very large. To our knowledge, no comparable search engine for legal documents exists that can find case laws based on the arguments used to decide the merit of the cases. However, there are several improvements we can contemplate over the current prototype. We now highlight a few of these improvements planned for the future.

First, we plan to improve user experience by including a natural language processing, or a knowledge graph based premise graph construction system that will obviate the need for manual premise graph authoring and embedding. Such an automated generation of premise graphs will also eliminate the need for validation. Recall that authoring a premise graph is different than using one for searching. For searching, authoring one will still be required.

Second, in the current edition of Prism, we do not support interlinking of case laws across court hierarchies to support tracking of any reversal of decisions. This can be achieved by developing a document representation system with case IDs, and using them to link up. An indexing system can also be developed to help expedite the search.

A tagging and highlighting scheme and system can be designed to link the nodes and edges in the embedded premise graph with the sections and articles of the law or the case laws to better visualize the relevance of the sections and the importance of the premise graphs. While these are more advanced features to improve usability and user experience, the core novelty is already implemented in Prism - the semantic search engine that fundamentally changes the way legal documents are searched. Finally, while in this paper, we have primarily discussed a premise graph based search engine, our future plan includes a logic template based search engine as well and to compare the efficacy of both approaches.

5   Conclusion

Both VOiC and Prism are ongoing research projects to support experimentation on a new approach to document authoring, sharing and searching, and collecting enough usage data to understand the usefulness of this new digital office environment. We feel that the approach and the technology can also be used across other scientific domains including ecology, computational biology, and network science to search for scholarly documents to discover interacting entities, such as cause-effect relationship in nature, gene regulatory networks, and so on. However, more research will be necessary to understand how the effectiveness of our system in other scientific disciplines. In particular, the document matching using subgraph isomorph discussed in Sect. 2.1, and the premise graph induction tool described in Sect. 2.2, require further research.

Acknowledgement. This publication was partially made possible by an Institutional Development Award (IDeA) from the National Institute of General Medical Sciences of the National Institutes of Health under Grant #P20GM103408. We acknowledge that Hayden Carroll, Austin Kugler, and Kallol Naha helped build parts of first edition of the VOiC and the Prism systems as a class research project.

References

1. Asiri, Y.: Short text mining for classifying educational objectives and outcomes. Comput. Syst. Sci. Eng. **41**(1), 35–50 (2022)
2. Aso, T., Amagasa, T., Kitagawa, H.: A method for searching documents using knowledge bases. In: Pardede, E., Indrawan-Santiago, M., Haghighi, P.D., Steinbauer, M., Khalil, I., Kotsis, G. (eds.) iiWAS2021: The 23rd International Conference on Information Integration and Web Intelligence, Linz, Austria, 29 November 2021–1 December 2021, pp. 250–258. ACM (2021)
3. Cavallo, G., Mauro, F.D., Pasteris, P., Sapino, M.L., Candan, K.S.: Crowd sourced semantic enrichment (CroSSE) for knowledge driven querying of digital resources. J. Intell. Inf. Syst. **53**(3), 453–480 (2019)
4. Charalampous, A., Knoth, P.: Classifying document types to enhance search and recommendations in digital libraries. In: Kamps, J., Tsakonas, G., Manolopoulos, Y., Iliadis, L., Karydis, I. (eds.) TPDL 2017. LNCS, vol. 10450, pp. 181–192. Springer, Cham (2017). https://doi.org/10.1007/978-3-319-67008-9_15

5. V. Constitution. Uniform child custody jurisdiction and enforcement act. https://law.lis.virginia.gov/vacode/title20/chapter7.1/. Accessed 18 Aug 2022

6. de Lourdes da Silveira, M., Ribeiro-Neto, B., de Freitas Vale, R., Tôrres Assumpção, R.: Vertical searching in juridical digital libraries. In: Sebastiani, F. (ed.) ECIR 2003. LNCS, vol. 2633, pp. 491–501. Springer, Heidelberg (2003). https://doi.org/10.1007/3-540-36618-0_35

7. Dhani, J.S., Bhatt, R., Ganesan, B., Sirohi, P., Bhatnagar, V.: Similar cases recommendation using legal knowledge graphs. CoRR, abs/2107.04771 (2021)

8. Duggan, B., O'Shea, B.: Tunepal: searching a digital library of traditional music scores. OCLC Syst. Serv. **27**(4), 284–297 (2011)

9. Filtz, E.: Building and processing a knowledge-graph for legal data. In: Blomqvist, E., Maynard, D., Gangemi, A., Hoekstra, R., Hitzler, P., Hartig, O. (eds.) ESWC 2017. LNCS, vol. 10250, pp. 184–194. Springer, Cham (2017). https://doi.org/10.1007/978-3-319-58451-5_13

10. Heidari, G., Ramadan, A., Stocker, M., Auer, S.: Leveraging a federation of knowledge graphs to improve faceted search in digital libraries. In: Berget, G., Hall, M.M., Brenn, D., Kumpulainen, S. (eds.) TPDL 2021. LNCS, vol. 12866, pp. 141–152. Springer, Cham (2021). https://doi.org/10.1007/978-3-030-86324-1_18

11. Hompes, B.F.A., Maaradji, A., La Rosa, M., Dumas, M., Buijs, J.C.A.M., van der Aalst, W.M.P.: Discovering causal factors explaining business process performance variation. In: Dubois, E., Pohl, K. (eds.) CAiSE 2017. LNCS, vol. 10253, pp. 177–192. Springer, Cham (2017). https://doi.org/10.1007/978-3-319-59536-8_12

12. Huynh, T.T., Do, N.V., Pham, T.N., Tran, N.T.: A semantic document retrieval system with semantic search technique based on knowledge base and graph representation. In: Fujita, H., Herrera-Viedma, E. (eds.) New Trends in Intelligent Software Methodologies, Tools and Techniques - Proceedings of the 17th International Conference SoMeT_18, Granada, Spain, 26–28 September 2018. Frontiers in Artificial Intelligence and Applications, vol. 303, pp. 870–882. IOS Press (2018)

13. Ignaczak, L., Goldschmidt, G., da Costa, C.A., da Rosa Righi, R.: Text mining in cybersecurity: a systematic literature review. ACM Comput. Surv. **54**(7),140:1–140:36 (2022)

14. Ipeirotis, P.G.: Searching digital libraries. In: Liu, L., Özsu, M.T. (eds.) Encyclopedia of Database Systems, 2nd edn., pp. 2518–2521. Springer, Boston (2018). https://doi.org/10.1007/978-0-387-39940-9_327

15. Crotti Junior, A., et al.: Knowledge graph-based legal search over German court cases. In: Harth, A., et al. (eds.) ESWC 2020. LNCS, vol. 12124, pp. 293–297. Springer, Cham (2020). https://doi.org/10.1007/978-3-030-62327-2_44

16. Bloehdorn, S., et al.: Ontology-based question answering for digital libraries. In: Kovács, L., Fuhr, N., Meghini, C. (eds.) ECDL 2007. LNCS, vol. 4675, pp. 14–25. Springer, Heidelberg (2007). https://doi.org/10.1007/978-3-540-74851-9_2

17. Kumpulainen, S.W., Kautonen, H.: Accidentally successful searching: users' perceptions of a digital library. In: Nordlie, R., Pharo, N., Freund, L., Larsen, B., Russel, D. (eds.) Proceedings of the 2017 Conference on Conference Human Information Interaction and Retrieval, CHIIR 2017, Oslo, Norway, 7–11 March 2017, pp. 257–260. ACM (2017)

18. Oviedo, A., Kasioumis, N., Aberer, K.: $5e^{\{x+y\}}$: searching over mathematical content in digital libraries. In: Bogen, P.L., II., et al. (eds.) Proceedings of the 15th ACM/IEEE-CE Joint Conference on Digital Libraries, Knoxville, TN, USA, 21–25 June 2015, pp. 283–284. ACM (2015)

19. Roychowdhury, D., Gupta, S., Qin, X., Arighi, C.N., Vijay-Shanker, K.: emiRIT: a text-mining-based resource for microRNA information. Database J. Biol. Databases Curation **2021** (2021)
20. Sarode, R.P., Sachdeva, S., Chu, W., Bhalla, S.: Segment-search vs knowledge graphs: making a key-word search engine for web documents. In: Madria, S., Fournier-Viger, P., Chaudhary, S., Reddy, P.K. (eds.) BDA 2019. LNCS, vol. 11932, pp. 88–107. Springer, Cham (2019). https://doi.org/10.1007/978-3-030-37188-3_6
21. Sarrafzadeh, B., Vechtomova, O.: Combining document retrieval with knowledge graphs for exploratory search. In: Elsweiler, D., Ludwig, B., Azzopardi, L., Wilson, M.L. (eds.) Fifth Information Interaction in Context Symposium, IIiX 2014, Regensburg, Germany, 26–29 August 2014, pp. 345–347. ACM (2014)
22. Sovrano, F., Palmirani, M., Vitali, F.: Legal knowledge extraction for knowledge graph based question-answering. In: Villata, S., Harasta, J., Kremen, P. (eds.) Legal Knowledge and Information Systems, JURIX 2020: The Thirty-Third Annual Conference, Brno, Czech Republic, 9–11 December 2020. Frontiers in Artificial Intelligence and Applications, vol. 334, pp. 143–153. IOS Press (2020)
23. Thagard, P.: Causal inference in legal decision making: explanatory coherence vs. Bayesian networks. Appl. Artif. Intell. **18**(3–4), 231–249 (2004)
24. Xu, W., Chen, H., Huan, Y., Hu, X., Nong, G.: Full-text search engine with suffix index for massive heterogeneous data. Inf. Syst. **104**, 101893 (2022)
25. Yellepeddi, V., Manimegalai, P., Suvanam, S.B.: Accurate approach towards efficiency of searching agents in digital libraries using keywords. J. Medical Syst. **43**(6), 164:1–164:6 (2019)
26. Yu, H., Zhou, Q., Liu, M.: A dynamic composite web services selection method with QoS-aware based on AND/OR graph. Int. J. Comput. Intell. Syst. **7**(4), 660–675 (2014)

Getting Quechua Closer to Final Users Through Knowledge Graphs

Elwin Huaman[1(✉)] ⬤, Jorge Luis Huaman[2], and Wendi Huaman[2]

[1] University of Innsbruck, Innsbruck, Austria
Elwin.Huaman@uibk.ac.at
[2] National University of the Altiplano of Puno, Puno, Peru

Abstract. Quechua language and Quechua knowledge gather millions of people around the world, especially in several countries in South America. Unfortunately, there are only a few resources available to Quechua communities, and they are mainly stored in unstructured format. In this paper, the Quechua Knowledge Graph is envisioned and generated as an effort to get Quechua language and knowledge closer to the Quechua communities, researchers, and technology developers. The process model for building the Quechua Knowledge Graph involved its creation, hosting, curation, and deployment phases. Currently, there are 553,636 triples stored in the Quechua Knowledge Graph, which is accessible on the Web, retrievable by machines, and curated by users. To showcase the deployment of the Quechua Knowledge Graph, use cases and future work are described.

Keywords: Quechua Knowledge Graph · Wikibase · Linguistic Knowledge Graph

1 Introduction

The availability of interoperable linguistics resources is nowadays more urgent in order to save and help under-resourced languages, and their communities. Despite the efforts of the linguistic community, not all languages are represented, nor made accessible in a structured format. For instance, there are only a few resources available for the Quechua language, and they are mostly in unstructured format.

In the literature, and to the best of our knowledge, most knowledge bases constructed recently are in well-spread languages and for well-established communities, like English or Spanish, as they take up an overwhelming majority on the Web, while under-resourced languages or indigenous communities receive less attention, for example, there is no structured knowledge graph dedicated to the Quechua community.

In order to overcome these limitations, in this paper, we propose the Quechua Knowledge Graph, which aims to support a harmonization process of the Quechua language and knowledge. To do it, we are following a process model for

J. A. Lossio-Ventura et al. (Eds.): SIMBig 2022, CCIS 1837, pp. 61–69, 2023.
https://doi.org/10.1007/978-3-031-35445-8_5

knowledge graph generation [3], which involves i) knowledge creation, ii) knowledge hosting, iii) knowledge curation, and iv) knowledge deployment phases. To date, the Quechua Knowledge Graph contains 553,636 triples, which are accessible on the Web, retrievable by machines, and curated by the Quechua community.

The remainder of the paper is organized as follows. In Sect. 2 the related work is presented, Sect. 3 describes the Quechua Knowledge Graph, and the feasibility of it is discussed in Sect. 4. Furthermore, in Sect. 5 we list use cases where the Quechua Knowledge Graph may be used. Finally, we conclude with Sect. 6, providing some remarks and future work plans.

2   Related Work

Knowledge graphs are semantic nets that represent knowledge about certain domains from integrating heterogeneous sources [3]. They have shown to be very useful for applications such as personal assistants (e.g. Alexa), question-answering systems (e.g. WolframAlpha), and search engines (e.g. Google) [2]. Content in knowledge graphs can be either open or proprietary, and they can be classified according to those criteria. Open knowledge graphs can be manually curated by humans (e.g., community-driven) or semi-automatically curated based on authoritative knowledge sources. By contrast, proprietary knowledge graphs are restricted to be accessed, therefore the curation process is mostly unknown. There are various well-known and widely used knowledge graphs that represent general-purpose knowledge, for instance, DBpedia[1] and Wikidata[2].

In the context of the Quechua language and knowledge, to the best of our knowledge, there is no dedicated knowledge graph for it. The most approximate knowledge graph to be considered on this matter may be Wikidata, which represents multilingual knowledge in a structured format. Furthermore, it is important to mention Wiktionary[3] as a database for the Quechua language. We compare those approaches in Table 1.

3   Quechua Knowledge Graph

In this section, we describe the workflow followed to build the Quechua Knowledge Graph, which is available at https://qichwa.wikibase.cloud/. This includes the creation, hosting, curation, and deployment phases.

3.1   Knowledge Creation

It describes the process of acquiring different sources, modelling them, and applying the models to incoming knowledge. It can be described as follows:

---

[1] https://www.dbpedia.org/.

[2] https://wikidata.org/.

[3] https://qu.wiktionary.org/.

Table 1. Comparing approaches built for the Quechua language and knowledge.

Description	Wiktionary	Wikidata	The Quechua Knowledge Graph
RDF support	No	Yes	Yes
Reuse of ontologies	No	Yes	Yes
Scalability	Wiktionary server	Wikibase	Wikibase
Learning curve	User should learn code templates	User selects classes and properties	User selects classes and properties
Anyone can edit	Yes	Yes	Yes
Search	Yes	Yes	Yes
Track changes	Yes	Yes	Yes
Community-driven	Yes	Yes	Yes
Fixed structure of entries	No	Yes	Yes
Automatic (Bots)	Yes, restricted	Yes, restricted	Yes
Use-oriented	Human	Human, machine	Human, machine
Covers	Quechua language	Quechua language and knowledge	Quechua language and knowledge

- **Identifying sources**. In the Quechua Knowledge Graph, we first identify sources, like Quechua dictionaries, vocabularies, and so on. One of the sources we started to work with was the Runasimi Vocabulary[4], which contains 22,866 Quechua words described in different languages.
- **Defining domain specifications**. Domain specifications model what properties or features must be described for each type of instance in the Quechua Knowledge Graph, for instance, a lexeme type should be described with language category (e.g., Quechua), lexical category (e.g., noun), described in (e.g., the source it comes from), usage example (e.g., text and a reference link where the text comes from), senses, forms. See Fig. 1 and Fig. 2. The domain specifications defined for lexicographical data are supported by the WikibaseLexeme[5] model and OntoLex[6] vocabularies. Furthermore, vocabularies such as Schema.org[7] will be used for creating domain specification for general purpose Quechua knowledge (e.g., biographies, places, etc.).

It is important to note that for ingesting the Runasimi vocabulary into the Quechua Knowledge Graph, we customized a Wikibase Integrator[8], which is a Python package[9].

---

[4] https://runasimi.de/.
[5] https://www.mediawiki.org/wiki/Extension:WikibaseLexeme/Data_Model.
[6] https://www.w3.org/community/ontolex/.
[7] https://schema.org/.
[8] https://github.com/LeMyst/WikibaseIntegrator.
[9] https://www.python.org/.

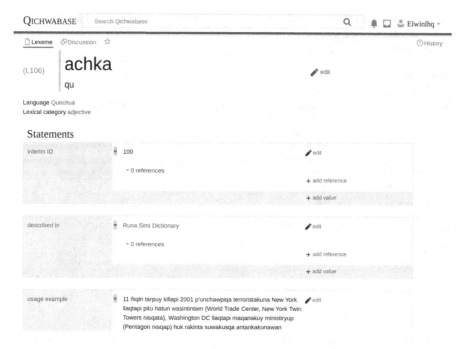

Fig. 1. Quechua Knowledge Graph interface (I).

3.2   Knowledge Hosting

The Wikibase Cloud[10] hosts the Quechua Knowledge Graph we build. Furthermore, the Wikibase infrastructure provides various components, for instance, some of them are:

- **MediaWiki**, it allows installing extensions to customize Wikibase instances.
- **Wikibase**, allows knowledge to be represented as a structured data repository. For instance, Wikibase provides tools like the WikibaseIntegrator[11], which is a Python library used for automatizing tasks or creating bots for inserting or editing data.
- **MariaDB**[12] **database** that allows data, user, and permission management.
- **SPARQL**[13] **endpoint** for querying and exploiting the knowledge.

Entering data is done by a bot, which inserts data into the Quechua Knowledge Graph based on identified sources and defined models (see Sect. 3.1). Currently, there are 553,636 triples contained in the Quechua Knowledge Graph.

---

[10] https://www.wikibase.cloud/.
[11] https://github.com/LeMyst/WikibaseIntegrator.
[12] https://mariadb.com/.
[13] https://www.w3.org/TR/sparql11-overview/.

Fig. 2. Quechua Knowledge Graph interface (II).

3.3 Knowledge Curation

To build a high-quality Quechua Knowledge Graph, it is important to curate the knowledge contained in it. A manual curation is not recommended due to the large size of knowledge graphs. Therefore, there are some tools that can automatize the curation tasks and can be used or configured in the Quechua Knowledge Graph. Those tools are:

- **OpenRefine**[14], it is very useful for cleaning and normalizing data, furthermore, it can also handle different formats, as well as, it provides an entity linking feature between the Quechua Knowledge Graph and Wikidata.
- **WikibaseImport**[15], it allows importing data from Wikidata into the Quechua Knowledge Graph.
- **EntitySchema**[16], it allows storing domain specifications (in the form of Shape Expression[17] Schemas) on wiki pages, and use them for knowledge valildation.

---

[14] https://openrefine.org/.
[15] https://github.com/Wikidata/WikibaseImport.
[16] https://www.mediawiki.org/wiki/Extension:EntitySchema.
[17] https://shex.io/.

3.4   Knowledge Deployment

We have built the Quechua Knowledge Graph, which provides various ways of being easily consumable or deployed:

- **An Enhanced GUI**, which allows users to edit faster and more productive, for instance, by adding and editing statements in the form of triples into the Quechua Knowledge Graph, as shown above in Fig. 1 and Fig. 2.
- **A SPARQL endpoint**, it is the standard query service of the Quechua Knowledge Graph, and it is available at https://qichwa.wikibase.cloud/ query/. A screenshot of a query[18] is displayed in Fig. 3.
- **Exporting**, the knowledge contained in the Quechua Knowledge Graph can be queried and then exported in various formats (JSON, CSV, HTML, ...).

Fig. 3. Query displaying lexemes that have multilingual sense descriptions, usage examples, and their source references.

4   Feasibility

In order to validate the feasibility of the Quechua Knowledge Graph, we analyse it from a technological, social, and organizational point of view.

---

[18] The query can be executed here: https://tinyurl.com/2laryjez.

4.1 Technological Risks

There are several factors that may compromise the success of the Quechua Knowledge Graph. First of all, is likely to fail without dedicated tools to support tasks, such as i) schema modelling, ii) population of modelled schemas, iii) Knowledge assessment, and iv) knowledge querying. Currently, what is used in the Quechua Knowledge Graph are the built-in features of Wikibase[19], which allows one to specify the classes, properties, and constraints at the terminological level (TBox). Furthermore, the initialization and completion of those tasks are done by the community. For instance, defining classes for describing linguistic concepts (verbs, nouns, etc.). Similarly, tools are needed for the curation [4] of the instance level (ABox) of the Quechua Knowledge Graph, which meanly addresses the assessment, cleaning, and enrichment of the knowledge graph. For instance, evaluating the correctness and completeness is not a straightforward task. Currently, Wikibase integrates OpenRefine[20] for data cleaning and reconciliation. Furthermore, it is necessary to scale up the tools so that they can handle a large Quechua Knowledge Graph.

Fig. 4. Quechua community event in Nuñoa (Peru), where the Quechua Knowledge Graph is presented and discussed.

4.2 Social and Organizational Risks

From a social and organizational point of view, there is one main factor that may endanger the success of the Quechua Knowledge Graph. Without a Quechua community, the initiative would certainly fail. However, participation in the

---

[19] https://wikiba.se/.
[20] https://openrefine.org/.

Quechua Knowledge Graph is a rewarding and self-promoting activity. It means that Quechua speakers and users are better off if they participate and contribute so i) a high quality knowledge base can be built and used for developing applications, and ii) a collaborative mentality can be achieved throughout the community, see Fig. 4.

5   Use Cases

The Quechua Knowledge Graph, as described in Sect. 3, aims to get the Quechua language and knowledge closer to end-users. For that, a knowledge graph generation lifecycle has been followed. In order to leverage the usefulness of the Quechua Knowledge Graph, we list some use cases where it can be used:

- **Question Answering.** The Quechua Knowledge Graph may be used as an interface to answer simple queries, which are equivalent to triples (Subject, Predicate, Object), e.g., (Peru, capital city, Lima). However, complex queries would need different approaches.
- **Dialogue Systems.** They provide a more natural and friendly interaction with final users than question answering systems. In this context, a dialogue system can take advantage of the explicit semantics declared in the Quechua Knowledge Graph for performing reasoning and creating language models.
- **Entity linking.** It allows identifying the same resource across various knowledge bases. For instance, the entities contained in the Quechua Knowledge Graph might be linked to Wikidata and Wikipedia articles, so the representation of entities is richer.
- **Knowledge Validation.** It is a critical task that verifies statements (or facts) against a knowledge base [5], in this context the Quechua Knowledge Graph aims to represent knowledge about persons, organizations, places, publications, etc., so the Quechua Knowledge Graph can be used for validating or supporting the semantic correctness of statements.
- **Collaborative Community.** In scattered communities, the mentality might be competitive rather than collaborative [1], e.g., "if another Quechua variant wins, then my Quechua variant loses." Or "if I make my dataset available to others, then others will profit from my dataset, and I risk that they may outperform me." However, the Quechua Knowledge Graph allows everyone to contribute and make fruitful discussions about the representation of an entity (e.g., Places, Words, etc.) and the historical discussions and arguments are saved and made accessible to anyone.

There are more possible use cases where the Quechua Knowledge Graph is applicable. Here, we presented some of them to give an idea about how useful and necessary it is to have a Knowledge Graph for the Quechua community.

6   Conclusion and Future Work

In this paper, we have described our effort for building the Quechua Knowledge Graph from scratch. First, we identified relevant sources and defined models (or domain specifications). Second, we set up a Wikibase instance and programmed a bot for ingesting data. Then, we take advantage of Wikibase features for addressing curation tasks. Finally, we provide various ways of consuming the stored knowledge. Moreover, we also validate the Quechua Knowledge Graph by presenting it to the Quechua community, and by analysing its technological, social, and organizational feasibility. Last but not least, we listed use cases where the Quechua Knowledge Graph can be used.

The limitations of our approach are for example the dependence of the Quechua Knowledge Graph on external services and features. However, Wikibase offers various services that might be very convenient for deploying the Quechua Knowledge Graph. Finding sources in the Quechua language is still a complex process, but we are building and engaging the Quechua community to help to tackle this limitation.

As a next step, we will define more domain specifications (e.g., person and place domains) that can be used for ingesting knowledge about various domains. Furthermore, we will develop applications (e.g., chatbots) powered by the Quechua Knowledge Graph. Besides that, we are planning to evaluate the Quechua Knowledge Graph by conducting surveys from domain experts, the Quechua community, and knowledge graph researchers to evaluate and improve the quality of the Quechua Knowledge Graph.

Acknowledgements. We would like to thank: David Lindemann, Valeria Caruso, and Ibai Guillen for their fruitful collaboration and technical contribution to this work. Furthermore, the research leading to these results has been supported by the NexusLinguarum COST Action CA18209.

References

1. Benjamins, V.R., Fensel, D., Gómez-Pérez, A.: Knowledge management through ontologies. In: Reimer, U. (ed.) PAKM 98, Practical Aspects of Knowledge Management, Proceedings of the Second International Conference, Basel, Switzerland, 29–30 October 1998. CEUR Workshop Proceedings, vol. 13. CEUR-WS.org (1998). https://ceur-ws.org/Vol-13/paper5.ps
2. Fensel, D., et al.: How to use a knowledge graph. In: Knowledge Graphs, pp. 69–93. Springer, Cham (2020). https://doi.org/10.1007/978-3-030-37439-6_3
3. Fensel, D., et al.: Knowledge Graphs - Methodology, Tools and Selected Use Cases. Springer, Cham (2020). https://doi.org/10.1007/978-3-030-37439-6
4. Huaman, E., Fensel, D.: Knowledge graph curation: a practical framework. In: IJCKG'21: The 10th International Joint Conference on Knowledge Graphs, Virtual Event, Thailand, 6–8 December 2021, pp. 166–171. ACM (2021). https://doi.org/10.1145/3502223.3502247
5. Huaman, E., Kärle, E., Fensel, D.: Knowledge graph validation. CoRR abs/2005.01389 (2020). https://arxiv.org/abs/2005.01389

Using Features Based on Elongation to Enhance Sentiment Analysis

Abderrahim Rafae[1]([✉]), Mohammed Erritali[1], Youness Madani[1][iD],
and Mathieu Roche[2,3][iD]

[1] Data4earth Laboratory, Sultan Moulay Slimane University, Beni Mellal, Morocco
`rafae.abderrahim@gmail.com, m.erritali@usms.ma`
[2] CIRAD, UMR TETIS, 34398 Montpellier, France
`mathieu.roche@cirad.fr`
[3] TETIS, Univ Montpellier, AgroParisTech, CIRAD, CNRS, INRAE,
Montpellier, France

Abstract. Elongated words such as "heellloo" or "heyyy" are a frequent feature of oral communication and are often used to underline or exaggerate the hidden message of the root word. Although elongated words are rarely found in written languages and dictionaries, they are common in social networks. They can be considered in the analysis of users' sentiments. In this paper, we analyze the impact of elongation on the classification of sentiments, in addition to an in-depth study at the level of lexical forms of elongation. In this work we present a method to improve the accuracy of sentiment classification based on elongations of features. Experimental results conducted on Twitter data show that our model achieves an accuracy of 0.79 in 7-fold cross-validation experiments.

Keywords: Elongations · Sentiment analysis · Textual features

1 Introduction

The main purpose of this paper is to study the impact of elongation on increasing the precision of sentiment analysis, since elongation is now more presentable on social networks and throughout the publications of teenagers. Therefore, we thought to study their impact on the famous subject of social networks, which is sentiment analysis, but in this study we took a deeper look into the analysis of the lexical forms of elongation that have a significant impact on the precision of the sentiment analysis, to extract the features that have the most impact on sentiment analysis.

Currently, social networks are in full bloom, thus generating a huge amount of data. Millions of people share their opinions daily over social networks, and because they contain short and simple expressions that make it an increasingly key application area for natural language processing (NLP), we are faced with a language that differs significantly from many other reference corpora.

J. A. Lossio-Ventura et al. (Eds.): SIMBig 2022, CCIS 1837, pp. 70–81, 2023.
https://doi.org/10.1007/978-3-031-35445-8_6

These datasets can be useful in studies where, for example, it is possible to extract the sentiments expressed in the opinions shared by social network visitors. Sentiment analysis, which is an approach to (NLP) that identifies the emotion behind posts, has become a popular way to classify opinions.

This is very useful for companies who want to obtain feedback on their product brands or for customers who want to determine what others think about a product before deciding to buy it.

If you browse through the Twitter publications, you may find tweets that look like the following example "cooool i loooooooveeee twiiiiiitter". The elongation of vowels and consonants (called gemination) is a characteristic of certain languages and may change a term, as well as its significance [1]. Elongated words, as in the previous example, sometimes called stretched words, have also become an integral component of many languages, especially in spoken language. Rather than altering the word's meaning entirely, however, this elongation, also called word stretching, expressive lengthening, or the use of letter repetition, is usually employed to modify the meaning of the original word somehow, to reinforce meaning (e.g., "huuuuuuuge"), involve sarcasm (e.g., "suuuuuure"), show excitement (e.g., "yeeeessss"), or communicate danger (e.g., "noooooooooooooooooo"). We shall refer to words that lend themselves to such elongation as "stretch words".

Despite the fact that they are a basic feature of spoken language, however, these words are rarely present in both lexicons and literature: The Oxford English Dictionary has no "hahahahahahahahahaha" [2]. Their presence in books is few, so they are only actually present in fictional dialogs [3]. However with the rise and spread of social networks, stretch words have finally taken their place in large-scale written texts.

However, with increasing work on social networks, the preprocessing and analysis of elongation has become a challenge to achieve more accurate results, especially in sentiment analysis because it disturbs the polarity calculation (positive, negative, neutral); it does not manage to be classified, although sometimes this word has a major expression of the writer's sentiment in the tweet.

Our work aims to study this type of writing and determine whether it has an impact on the classification of sentiments, as well as looking for a method to use word elongation in social networks to improve the accuracy of sentiment classification.

Our paper will be organized as follows: First, we present the literature on elongations and their relationship with the classification of sentiments. Section 3 presents the methodology and the steps of our study. Then, in Sect. 4, we show the results of our analysis on the impact of elongation in the classification of sentiments. The article is concluded in Sect. 5.

2 Related Work

The growing use of social media is associated with rich datasets of a linguistic nature, offering science an opportunity to study the everyday linguistic patterns of society in an unprecedented way. For example, in recent years, several papers have been released using data from social media platforms such as Twitter, to study different aspects of language. Eisenstein cited stretched words such as one of the several kinds of "bad language" on social networks that cause issues in attempting to process text and discussed some of the issues related to the proposed current methods of normalizing and adjusting domains to assist in language processing [4].

Brody and Diakopoulos studied stretched words on a small set of Twitter data and discovered that they are fairly plentiful and that there is a high match between stretched words and words that give a feeling. They also suggested a method to find and automatically classify the new sentiment words using this connection [5]. Other research has also studied stretched words in connection with sentiment analysis in a text.

Pandarachalil and al. in [6] proposed an unsupervised method for analyzing tweet sentiments. The polarity of tweets is evaluated by using three sentiment lexicons-SenticNet, SentiWordNet, and SentislangNet. To prepare the tweets for the classification, the authors used a number of preprocessing methods: removing links/URL and hashtags, replacing words with contractions, explicit negation handling, WordNet lemmatizing, and elongation replacer that consists of removing repeating characters (such as 'looooooove') until no more characters are removed or recognized by WordNet. In addition, the method is implemented and tested in a parallel Python framework and is shown to scale well with a large volume of data on multiple cores.

Researchers of [7] tried to improve the results of sentiment analysis of Arabic tweets using new deep learning algorithms. For that, they used an ensemble model, combining convolutional neural network (CNN) and long short-term memory (LSTM) models, to predict the sentiment of Arabic tweets. In addition, for the phase of pretreatment of tweets authors use a lot of methods where elongation is among them. As experimental results, the proposed model achieves an F1-score of 64.46%, which outperforms the state-of-the-art deep learning model's F1-score of 53.6%, on the Arabic Sentiment Tweets Dataset (ASTD).

El-Beltagy and al. [8] presented a set of features that were integrated with a machine learning-based sentiment analysis model and applied to Egyptian, Saudi, Levantine, and Modern Standard Arabic (MSA) social media datasets to extract sentiments and opinions. The authors in this work use a set of features from the input text to improve the accuracy of the analysis such as character normalization, emoticons detection and replacement, mention normalization, named entities tagging, stemming, and elongation removal (for example "yesssssss" will be transformed to "yes"). Experimental results show that the presented features have resulted in an increased accuracy across six of the seven datasets they have experimented with and that are all benchmarked.

In [9] researchers proposed a work that addresses the analysis of user senti-ments in the Telecom domain. For the classification, a novel idea based on the cosine similarity measure is proposed for classifying the sentiment expressed by a user's comment into a five-point scale of −2 (highly negative) to +2 (highly positive). Before classification, the authors applied a number of preprocessing methods such as elongation removal and stop word removal. The proposed cosine similarity-based classifier gives 82% accuracy for the 2-class problem of identi-fying positive and negative sentiments. It outperforms all other classifiers by a considerable margin in the 5-class sentiment classification problem with an accuracy of 71.5%.

The authors of [10] proposed a new tool called HILATSA which is a hybrid approach that combines both lexicon based and machine learning approaches to identify tweets sentiment polarities. Before classification using the proposed approach, the authors apply some preprocessing methods such as: detecting and removing URLs, detecting whether the tweet has hashtags or not, removing non-Arabic words and numbers, detecting negation, removing elongation, etc. As experimental results, the proposed approach achieved an accuracy of 73.7% for the 3-class classification problem and 83.7% for the 2-class classification problem. The semiautomatic learning component proved to be effective as it improved the accuracy by 17.5%.

3   Methodology

The methodological needs of this work can be taken up in the following process. We will start by extracting tweets containing the stretched words to build our corpus of elongations. Then, we compare texts in corpora with and without elongations, with the aim of determining if there is an impact of elongations on the accuracy of sentiment classifiers. We finish our analysis with a deep study on the lexical forms of elongation, to extract features that can improve the classification of sentiments. The process of our study is summarized in Fig. 1.

As shown in Fig. 1, we start by extracting the publications and storing them in our database. Then, we proceed to preprocess these data to detect those words that contain an elongation of letters to build a corpus of elongation that will be the subject of this analysis.

3.1   Corpus with Elongations

The best data we can use for a social application-especially for the purpose of detecting elongation in a text, are data from applications that deal with the same subject such as Facebook and Twitter. Below we will give some information about the datasets used. Sentiment 140: The dataset is a CSV file, where each line is a tweet. It contains 1,600,000 tweets extracted using the Twitter API. The tweets have been annotated (0 = negative, 4 = positive), and they can be used to detect sentiments [11].

To build our elongation corpus, we extract the publications that contain stretched words to obtain a database based only on the elongated publications.

Fig. 1. Methodological architecture

3.2 Data Cleaning

Data preprocessing (see Fig. 2) is an important step in the analysis of tweets; in our case the preprocessing function that we create and use follows a number of steps giving importance to the semantics of the tweets that we have just collected. Our preprocessing function can be summarized in the next step.

To prepare each tweet for treatment, we will start by going through some steps. We will start by removing the unwanted characters, and proceed to the treatment of the Nan values, followed by converting sentences to lower case. We finish our pretreatment with a check if the string consists only of alphabetics characters.

3.3 Elongation Detection

We can summarize this part in the following process. First, each tweet is tokenized. We check if it contains a repetition of the characters. If it does, we will add this word to an elongation list. At the end to check if the tweets contain the elongation or not, it is enough to see if the length of the elongation list is greater than or equal to 1, and then elongation is detected on tweet text. The proposed architecture for detecting elongation based on tweet text is presented in Fig. 3.

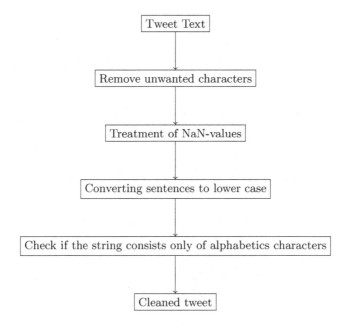

Fig. 2. Data Cleaning

3.4 Impact of Elongation on Sentiment Classification

To study the impact of elongation on the classification of sentiments, we use two corpora labeled with the polarity of sentiments: (i) the first one is the elongation corpus, which we created in the 1st phase, and (ii) the second one is the corpus without elongation.

For the comparison stage, we need methods to test the impact of elongation on the classification. Sentiment classification techniques can be divided into three main categories: machine learning, lexicon-based approaches, and hybrid approaches.

In this analysis, we will use only machine learning (ML) approaches that which apply well-known ML algorithms and linguistic features. The most popular algorithms of sentiment classification used in this study are illustrated in Fig. 4 and Table 1.

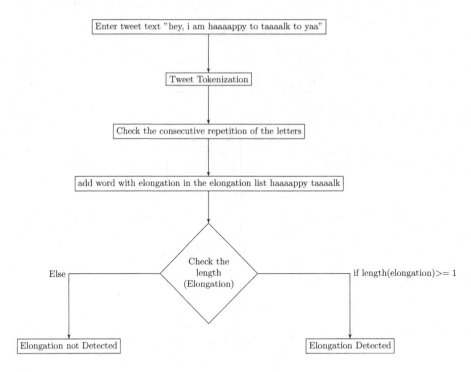

Fig. 3. Process of elongation detection

Table 1. Abbreviation of name of machine learning algorithms

Abbreviation	Name of algorithms
SVM	Support Vector Machine
KNN	K-Nearest Neighbors
LR	Logistic Regression
RF	Random Forest
DT	Decision Tree
MNB	Multinomial Naive Bayes
BNB	Bernouili Naive Bayes

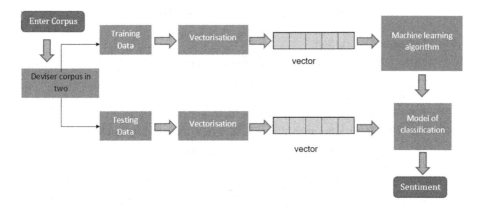

Fig. 4. Process to analyse the impact of elongation

3.5 Feature Extraction

We have decided to launch a deeper study, except that this time our target will be the analysis of the features within the words that have been elongated. We will do this by extracting a set of these features, as shown in Table 2.

4 Experiments

In this section, we present all the results we have achieved thus far. Hence, we will start by presenting the corpus of elongation we managed to create, which is composed of 100,000 lines divided into two polarities (positive and negative), as shown in Fig. 5. This corpus is the basis of our study.

1²₃ Sentiment Polarity	▾	A⁸_C Text	▾	✗✓ Elongation	▾
	0	awww i soo wish i was there to see you finally im sad that i missed it			TRUE
	0	our duck and chicken are taking wayyy too long to hatch			TRUE
	0	i have a sad feeling that dallas is not going to show up i gotta say think...			TRUE
	0	i saw the failwhale alllll day			TRUE
	0	sooo they killed off kutner on house whyyyyyyyy			TRUE
	4	upload di indowebster dong banggggg			TRUE
	4	awww pookie feel pray for bag the nurse up			TRUE
	4	today is our two month i love you sooooooo much omg you dont even...			TRUE
	4	wait to see ur hot ass in woot annnd love the bob with i went the royal...			TRUE
	4	failed physics what a keeen for the holidays days to			TRUE

Fig. 5. Elongation corpus

Table 2. Description of elongation features

Features	Description
NCR	This feature aims to return the number of consecutive repetitions for a repeated character
NWR	Return number of words containing elongation
VR	Return number of vowels that have been stretched
CR	Return number of consonants that have been stretched
IR	Return number of '?' that have been stretched
ER	Return number of '!' that have been repeated
Adj	Return number of adjectives containing elongation
Nouns	Return number of nouns containing elongation
PWR	Returned the proportion of words with elongation over the total number of words in each tweet
PCR	Returned the proportion of characters with elongation over the total number of characters in each tweet
PVR	Return the proportion of vowels s with elongation over the total number of vowels in each tweet
PC	Return the proportion of consonants with elongation over the total number of consonants in each tweet

We built two models, with and without elongation, to compare them. The objective of this study is to evaluate the impact of elongation on sentiment analysis (i.e. sentiment classification).

In this context, two corpora were constructed following the different steps summarized in Fig. 5. To evaluate the results, we adopted the following protocol, which starts by dividing each corpus into 7 subsets and trains on 6 one of those subsets. We hold the last subset for testing. Then, we performed a vectorization to (i.e. bag-of-words), where we used TF-IDF (term frequency - inverse document frequency), which aims to determine the importance of a feature so that the classifier does not miss less frequent but important features [12]. Next, we applied different (ML) algorithms to perform the comparison between tweets with and without elongation.

In our case, the key factor for evaluating the results of those algorithms will be that the cross-validation value is set to 7 i.e., 'cv = 7'

- The 'cv = 7' will partition the data into 7 parts.
- Then it will use the 'first' part as the 'test set' and others as the 'training set'.
- Next, it will use the 'second' part as the 'test set' and others as the 'training set' and so on.
- In this way, each sample will be in the test dataset exactly one time.
- Additionally, in this method, we have more training and testing data.
- Last, we need not split the data manually in the cross-validation method.

Table 3. Results of comparisons between corpora with and without elongation

Accuracy	Without elongation	With elongation
SVM	0.756	**0.771**
KNN	0.543	0.679
LR	0.754	**0.771**
RF	0.746	0.759
DT	0.693	0.702
MNB	0.749	0.766
BNB	0.750	0.768

Following the application of the different machine learning algorithms on both corpora with and without elongation as the bag-of-words (BOW) approach, we obtained that the elongation has a positive impact on the improvement of the accuracy of sentiment classification. This behavior is highlighted in Table 3, which presents the results of different ML algorithms.

Bag-of-words is a statistical linguistic model used to analyze texts and documents according to their number of words. This model is not based on the order of the words in a document. The BOW model could be implemented as a Python dictionary where each key corresponds to a word and every value to the number of occurrences of this word in a text.

In the second part of our analysis, we evaluate the impact of features of elongations on the classification of sentiments. We started by extracting them and testing each one on its own with BOW by using two machine learning algorithms (i.e. LR and SVM) that have good behavior (see Table 4).

A support vector machine (SVM) is a supervised machine learning algorithm that divides data into two classes. It is trained with a collection of data already classified into two categories, building the model as it is initially trained. The task of an SVM is to identify which category a new data point belongs to. This turns SVM into a kind of nonbinary linear classifier.

Logistic regression (LR) is a statistical analysis approach for making predictions about a binary result, such as yes or no, based on prior observations of a dataset. A logistic regression model predicts a dependent data item based on an analysis of the relation between one or more existing independent variables.

Following these results, we found that these features improve the accuracy of the classification of sentiments, hence we thought of making combinations with some features.

As shown in Table 5 we obtain an accuracy of 0.790 and 0.794 in 7-fold cross-validation experiments using the combination of BOW, Nouns, and Adj with LR and SVM as classifiers.

Table 5 highlights that elongation criteria have a positive impact on sentiment classification results with the best ML algorithms (i.e. LR and SVM - see Table 3), specifically by integrating two elongation features **Nouns** and **Adj**,

Table 4. Accuracy results obtained with Bag-Of-Words (BOW) with elongation features using LR and SVM

BOW + Features	Accuracy (LR)	Accuracy (SVM)
NCR	0.785	0.787
NWR	0.787	0.787
VR	0.783	0.788
CR	0.791	0.787
IR	0.788	0.791
ER	0.782	0.786
Adj	0.788	0.791
Nouns	0.788	0.791
PWR	0.789	0.792
PCR	0.783	0.789
PVR	0.784	0.786
PC	0.787	0.790

Table 5. Result of combination of elongation's features with BOW

	BOW	BOW + IR + ER	BOW + Nouns + Adj	BOW + NWR + PWR
Accuracy (LR)	0.771	0.787	**0.790**	0.791
Accuracy (SVM)	0.771	0.793	**0.794**	0.792

with the **SVM** algorithm. The results of other combinations are presented in the Annex section.

5   Conclusion and Future Work

In this paper, we have carried out a study that aims to improve the classification of sentiments. Hence, we focused on a part that is becoming increasingly usable on our social networks, namely the elongation of words, and then we studied the impact of this on the accuracy of the classification of sentiments.

During our analysis we found that elongation has an important role in the classification of sentiments, and furthermore, we discovered that there are features of elongation that have given promising results for improving the sentiment classification patterns of tweets containing elongation, especially as stretched words began to appear in written forms of communication and, more importantly, in social networks.

The results obtained in this study are promising, so we will continue the work to improve it by using the BERT (bidirectional encoder representations from transformers) and word embedding approaches [13] with the elongation features in order to build a powerful classification model. For this work, we plan to identify textual features (i.e. words) that have an elongation to construct a specific textual context associated with these dedicated features. These contexts will be used for enriching both the BOW and elongation features used in this paper.

Acknowledgements. This study was partially funded by EU grant 874850 MOOD and is catalogued as MOOD011. The contents of this publication are the sole responsibility of the authors and do not necessarily reflect the views of the European Commission.

References

1. Gray, T.J., Danforth, C.M., Dodds, P.S.: Hahahahaha, Duuuuude, Yeeessss!: a two-parameter characterization of stretchable words and the dynamics of mistypings and misspellings. PLoS One **15**(5), e0232938 (2020)
2. Weiner, E.S.C., Simpson, J.P.: The Oxford English dictionary. Oxford **21989**, 65 (1989)
3. McCulloch, G.: Because Internet: Understanding the New Rules of Language. Riverhead Books (2020)
4. Eisenstein, J.: What to do about bad language on the internet. In: Proceedings of the 2013 Conference of the North American Chapter of the Association for Computational Linguistics: Human Language Technologies, pp. 359–369 (2013)
5. Brody, S., Diakopoulos, N.: Cooooooooooooooollllllllllllllll!!!!!!!!!!!!!! Using word lengthening to detect sentiment in microblogs. In: Proceedings of the 2011 Conference on Empirical Methods in Natural Language Processing, pp. 562–570 (2011)
6. Pandarachalil, R., Sendhilkumar, S., Mahalakshmi, G.S.: Twitter sentiment analysis for large-scale data: an unsupervised approach. Cogn. Comput. **7**(2), 254–262 (2015). https://doi.org/10.1007/s12559-014-9310-z
7. Heikal, M., Torki, M., El-Makky, N.: Sentiment analysis of arabic tweets using deep learning. In: The 4th International Conference on Arabic Computational Linguistics (ACLing 2018), 17–19 November 2018, Dubai, United Arab Emirates (2018)
8. El-Beltagy, S.R., Khalil, T., Halaby, A., Hammad, M.: Combining lexical features and a supervised learning approach for Arabic sentiment analysis. In: Gelbukh, A. (ed.) CICLing 2016. LNCS, vol. 9624, pp. 307–319. Springer, Cham (2018). https://doi.org/10.1007/978-3-319-75487-1_24
9. Bhattacharjee, S., Das, A., Bhattacharya, U., Parui, S.K., Roy, S.: Sentiment analysis using cosine similarity measure. In: 2015 IEEE 2nd International Conference on Recent Trends in Information Systems (ReTIS) (2015). https://doi.org/10.1109/ReTIS.2015.7232847
10. Elshakankery, K., Ahmed, M.F.: HILATSA: a hybrid incremental learning approach for Arabic tweets sentiment analysis. Egypt. Inform. J. **20**(3), 163–171 (2019)
11. https://www.kaggle.com/kazanova/sentiment140
12. Eshan, S.C., Hasan, M.S.: An application of machine learning to detect abusive Bengali text. In: 2017 20th International Conference of Computer and Information Technology (ICCIT), pp. 1–6. IEEE (2017)
13. Torregrossa, F., Allesiardo, R., Claveau, V., Kooli, N., Gravier, G.: A survey on training and evaluation of word embeddings. Int. J. Data Sci. Anal. **11**(2), 85–103 (2021). https://doi.org/10.1007/s41060-021-00242-8

Image Generation from Sketches and Text-Guided Attribute Edition

Dennis Marcell Sumiri Fernandez$^{(\boxtimes)}$ and José Ochoa-Luna$^{(\boxtimes)}$ ⓘD

Department of Computer Science, Universidad Católica San Pablo, Arequipa, Peru
{dennis.sumiri,jeochoa}@ucsp.edu.pe

Abstract. Every day new Artificial Intelligence models are created, and existing ones are modified or combined to extend their range of applications and tasks they can solve. This paper presents a novel approach that combines Natural Language Processing and generative networks to generate images from sketches and descriptions in natural language. We present a pipeline that was followed to recondition the generative network. It includes the processed text that will give the context to the sketch used for the generation. Finally, the model and the generated images are evaluated and compared using benchmark data sets, and promising results are reported.

Keywords: GAN · Transformer · Text-guided · Image generation · Deep Learning

1 Introduction

Generating realistic images that match semantically given a text description is a challenging problem that has many applications in different fields such as image editions, video games, and even computer-assisted design [16]. Modern approaches based on Machine Learning for text-to-image synthesis started with generative models capable of generating novel visual scenes. Also, it was shown that using generative adversarial networks instead of a recurrent auto-encoder variation improves the image quality and fidelity [16]. On the other hand, this kind of system can not just generate objects with recognizable features but can generalize Zero-shot learning. This is a setup for machine learning problems where at the time of testing, samples from classes are observed that were not observed previously during training, and it is needed to predict the class where they belong [15].

Through the years many problems have been addressed by using a combination of models and algorithms to solve different tasks. These could include an improvement to generative model architecture making changes as multi-scale generators which add loss functions to take advantage of additional source information of conditioning beyond the text.

However, many generative networks used for different tasks could be uncontrollable. For example, the output of the generator could be significantly different from

© The Author(s), under exclusive license to Springer Nature Switzerland AG 2023
J. A. Lossio-Ventura et al. (Eds.): SIMBig 2022, CCIS 1837, pp. 82–95, 2023.
https://doi.org/10.1007/978-3-031-35445-8_7

the image generated using the original text if you want to change a word in the initial description [9]. Furthermore, most models just focus on solving one task for a generation and it is difficult to combine model features to achieve better control over the output image. This is not desirable when it comes to real-world applications where users want to make a specific image or change attributes in a new image.

Thus, we propose a novel approach to control image generation using a natural language description. Most generative models use real images to obtain the context when you want to generate new images from sketches. However, in our proposed model the context is obtained from a natural language description, to do so a transformer model is used. The new image is generated from a generative model which processes the sketch with a processed text. Then, the discriminator decides whether the image is accepted or not.

The results obtained are promising, however, it is still necessary to adjust the parameters of the network and take care of the generation process. Some generated images are defective due to the overlapping of some characteristics in the training phase of the generative networks. The paper is organized as follows. Section 2, background regarding concepts on the generative adversarial net and transformer models is given. Related works are presented in Sect. 3. Our proposed model is presented in Sect. 4. In Sect. 5, results obtained from this model are reported and, in Sect. 6, conclusions are given.

2 Background

The field of Artificial Intelligence has evolved notably. The presence of new technologies such as Transformer models and Generative Adversarial Networks has led to the development of many models which can easily generate realistic images. In this section, we are going to review recent models that combine natural language processing and image generation.

2.1 Generative Adversarial Networks

Generative Adversarial Networks (GANs) have become popular because of their capacity to solve image processing problems and computer vision. Many of them are designed and parameterized to solve a specific task. However, the architecture remains almost unchanged, i.e., it is formed of two networks, one generator, and one discriminator. Each one has a different function. In the case of the generator, it replicates new images using real image data sets. On the other hand, the discriminator decides whether one image generated is real or fake. Moreover, these networks improve themselves until the generator overcomes the discriminator [5].

These models are easy to apply when they are made up of several layers of Perceptrons. To define the distribution p_g over a data set x, a previous noise is defined for input variables $p_z(z)$. Then a data space map is represented as $G(z; \theta_g)$ where G is a differentiable function portrayed as a multi-layer Perceptron with parameters θ_g. Moreover, a second multi-layer Perceptron $D(x; \theta_d)$ is defined that generates a unique scalar. $D(x)$ denotes the probability that x comes from input data instead of p_g. To maximize the probability of assigning the correct label for both training samples and G samples we train D. Simultaneously, G is trained to minimize $(1 - D(G(z)))$. So, G and D play a two-player min-max game with function $V(G, D)$.

$$\min_{G}\max_{D}V(D, G) = E_{x\sim p_{data}(x)}[logD(x)] + E_{z\sim p_z(z)}[log(1 - D(G(z)))] \quad (1)$$

In practice, it is implemented using a numeric iterative approach. Optimizing D in the inner training loop until the end could be computationally expensive and, in some cases with finite data sets, this could result in overfitting. On the other hand, to optimize D it is alternated into k steps and one step to optimize G. This results in D staying closer to its optimal solution, while G will change slowly. This strategy is analogous to the way SML/PCD[1] training maintains samples of a Markov chain from one learning step to the next to avoid burning into a Markov chain as part of the inner learning loop [4]. Moreover, the Eq. 1 may not provide enough gradient to make G learns well. In early learning stages when G is still weak, D could reject samples with high confidence because they are clearly different from the training data and $log(1 - D(G(z)))$ saturates [5].

A graphical representation of the architecture for this model is shown in Fig. 1. The complete network allows the generation of images from sketches. In this case, we can observe that the generator is fed with a data set of real images defined by z. Then, a lineal layer remodels the input using five convolution layers with a kernel size of 5. In this example, it also has a batch normalization layer after each convolution layer except the last one aimed to accelerate the training and stabilize learning.

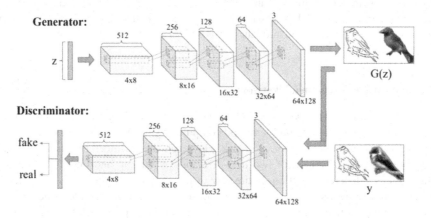

Fig. 1. Generative adversarial network architecture. Taken from Generative adversarial Nets [5]

---

[1] Stochastic Maximum Likelihood or Persistent Contrastive Divergence. Models that can learn a probability distribution over its set of inputs.

2.2   Contextual GAN

GANs have shown a great performance to generate images from a set of real images. However, generating images from sketches is challenging and has been approached in many ways. This difficulty is due to the lack of context we can get from a sketch, where the models try to follow the edges because of the harsh condition imposed by the process of image-to-image translation. Because of that, contextual GANs are proposed since they use the sketches as a weak constraint where the output edges do not necessarily follow the input edges. The objective of this network is to learn the mixed distribution between the sketches and the corresponding image by using joint images [11].

This model has two stages, the first one for training and the other for completion. The training stage is the same as the traditional GANs except that the training samples are joint images. After training, generative network G manages to produce the distribution of joint image data, this means mapping samples from the noise distribution p_z to the data distribution p_{data}.

Actual freehand real sketches exhibit a wide variety of styles and can be quite different from synthetic sketches generated automatically from images. To improve the generality of the network and avoid overfitting to any particular sketch image pair, we increase the training data using multiple sketch styles as a training set. A detector of edges XDoG [22] and a filter FDoG [8] are used to produce those styles.

Generator. The generator takes as input a pair of a sketch and a ground truth image. The contextual loss is kept from the base model to measure the similarity between the corrupt part that is generated and the reconstructed sketch. This loss is defined in the Eq. 2.

$$\mathcal{L}_{contextual}(z) = D_{KL}(M \odot y, M \odot G(z)) \tag{2}$$

where M is a binary mask from the joint corrupted image and $\odot$ is the Hadamard production. It also uses a KL divergence to measure the similarity between two sketches that tend to produce a better alignment of the sketches [14].

A perceptual loss is also used to keep the semantic content from the predicted image and is defined in Eq. 3.

$$\mathcal{L}_{perceptual}(z) = log(1 - D(G(z))) \tag{3}$$

The objective function for this network $\hat{z}$ is the weighted sum of the two losses and is shown in Eq. 4

$$\hat{z} = \underset{z}{argmin}(\mathcal{L}_{contextual}(z) + \lambda \mathcal{L}_{perceptual}(z)) \tag{4}$$

What we want to achieve is a set of automated image synthesis processes that allow us to generate natural images based on an input sketch and a ground truth image that gives us the context to generate new images.

Discriminator. The discriminator uses a set of images with dimension 64×64 pixels and four convolutional layers where the map dimension for features is cut in half and the number of channels is doubled with respect to the previous layers.

2.3   Natural Language Processing

In the beginning, autoencoders were the approach to translate text. They are a particular type of neural network which is designed to encode the input in meaningful compressed representation and then decode it so that the reconstructed input is as close to the original as possible. The ones used for guided-text image generation are text encoders. Given a phrase S, text encoders are responsible for encoding it in a sentence function $s \in R^D$ with dimension D that describe the entire phrase and word features $w \in R^{DxL}$ with length L and dimension D [1].

On the other hand, we have transformer models which have become popular nowadays due to a large number of problems solved efficiently [21]. Most of the competing models of sequence transduction have an encoder-decoder structure. The encoder assigns a sequence of symbols representation $(x_1, ..., x_n)$ to a sequence of continuous representations $z = (z_1, ..., z_n)$. Given z, the decoder generates an output sequence of symbols $(y_1, ..., y_m)$, one element at a time. Each step of the model is retrogressive, consuming the previously generated symbols as additional input when generating the next one. The transformer uses an architecture fully connected point-to-point and self-attending stacked layers for encoder and decoder [21].

The encoder has a stack of $N = 6$ identical layers. Each layer has two sub-layers where the first one is a multi-headed self-attention mechanism while the latter is a simple, fully positionally connected feedback network. We use a residual connection around each of the two sub-layers, followed by a normalization of the layers. That is, the output of each sub-layer is $LayerNorm(x + Sublayer(x))$, where $sublayer(x)$ is a function implemented by the sub-layer itself [21].

The decoder is also made up of a stack of $N = 6$ identical layers. Besides the two sub-layers for each layer, it introduces a third sub-layer, which performs the attention of several heads on the output of the encoder stack. Similar to the encoder, we employ residual connections around each of the sub-layers, followed by layer normalization. We also modify the self-attention sub-layer in the decoder stack to prevent positions from paying attention to subsequent positions. This can be seen in Fig. 2 [21].

3   Related Work

3.1   Dall-E

Modern approaches of machine learning for synthesis from text to image started with the task of generating images from subtitles with attention [12]. In that work it is shown that the generative model DRAW [6] when extended to the condition of photo tags, can also generate novel visual scenes. It is also shown that using a GAN can improve the fidelity of the images generated [16].

The main goal of that work is to train a transformer to auto-regressively model the text and image tokens as a single data stream. However, using pixels directly as image tokens requires an inordinate amount of memory for high-resolution images [15].

Likelihood goals tend to prioritize modeling short-range dependencies between pixels, most of the modeling capacity would be spent capturing high-frequency detail rather than the low-frequency structure that makes objects visually recognizable [15].

This problem is addressed by making a two-stage procedure:

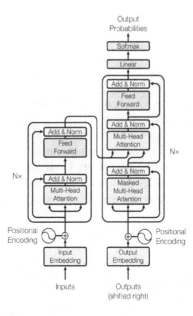

Fig. 2. Transformer architecture. Taken from Attention is all you need [21]

1. An autoencoder is trained with a discrete variation to compress images of 256×256 RGB in image tokens from an image mesh of 32×32. Each element can take 8192 possible values. This reduces the context size of the transformer without affecting the image quality.
2. Up to 256 tokens from the encoded text are concatenated in BPE [13]² with the tokens of image size $32 \times 32 = 1024$. An autoregressive transformer is trained to model the joint distribution of the tokens.

3.2 Cycle Text-to-Image GAN with BERT

The goal of text to image translation task is to generate realistic images given a natural language text description. This problem has many possible applications from computer-assisted design to art generation. In addition, a multi-modal problem is an important and interesting task in natural language understanding because it connects the language with the understanding of the visual world.

The problem is decomposed into two parts: embedding the text in a feature representation that captures the relevant visual information, and using that feature representation that captures the relevant visual information to generate a realistic image that corresponds to the text.

To solve this, a combination of two generative models with a transformer is used. The first of them is the AttnGAN [23] which uses the attention that first inserts the label

---

² Byte Pair Encoding which keeps the most frequent word intact while splitting the multiple ones into multiple tokens.

and executes it through an LSTM, generating vectors of words and sentences. With the conditioning augmentation first proposed in StackGAN [24], a mean and variance are created from the inserted sentence through a fully connected layer. These values are used to parameterize a normal distribution from which a sample of the sentence is generated to be passed to the GAN. This is used for regularization and to promote multiple smoothness. In addition, the Gaussian noise is concatenated to this new sentence insertion sample and passed to the generator.

On the other hand, BERT[3] is used for the parameterization of the text in vectors of words to obtain the context and send it to the generative network. These vectors are a common component in many of the NLP models. Until recently, however, one limitation of these word vectors was that they only allowed context-independent insertion [20]. BERT avoids this, using a bidirectional transformer instead of bidirectional LSTM.

3.3 High-Resolution Image Synthesis with Latent Diffusion Models

Stable Diffusion [17] is the most recent model which has become popular in the text-to-image translation field. It decomposes image generation into a sequential application of automatic denoising encoders. In addition, its formulation allows a guidance mechanism to control the image generation process without retraining. Diffusion models achieve synthesis results that are close to those of the current state of the art.

The model separates the generative compressive phase from the generative learning phase which is an automatic coding model. It learns a space that is perceptually equivalent to the image space but offers significantly reduced computational complexity. This approach has several advantages but the most significant is that the model is more efficient because sampling is done in a low-dimensional space. It takes advantage of the inductive bias from diffusion models to inherit from its UNet architecture [18]. This makes them particularly effective for spatially structured data and alleviates the need for aggressive quality-reducing comprehension levels [3]. To deal with the computational complexity of training diffusion models the explicit separation of the comprehensive from the generative learning phase is performed. An automatic coding model is used to achieve this. It learns a space that is perceptibly equivalent to the image space offering reduced complexity.

Finally, with the trainer perceptual compression models, we have a low-dimensional latent space in which high-frequency and imperceptible details are abstracted. The space is more suitable for likelihood-based generative models than high-dimensional pixel space. Thus, models can focus on the important semantic bits of the data and train in a lower dimensional but computationally much more efficient space.

3.4 Midjourney

Midjjourney[4] is an independent research lab that has produced a proprietary artificial intelligence that creates images from natural language descriptions, similar to DALL-E,

---

[3] Bidirectional Encoder Representations from Transformers is a transformer-based machine learning technique for natural language processing. It was developed by Google.

[4] https://www.midjourney.com/home/.

and stable diffusion [2]. This tool has recently become open beta. The maximum scale for pictures is 3 megapixels. It has some parameters which control resolution and size. Moreover, we can define how strong of "stylization" the images have[5].

4   Proposed Model

We propose a new model that combines both, generative adversarial networks and transformers model to generate images from sketches and a text description in natural language. The pipeline is shown in Fig. 3. First, the natural language text description is processed, then it is passed to the generative network with a ground truth image and its corresponding sketch. Then the generative network starts training to generate new images given the processed text description and the sketches and real images. An example of what is intended to get as a result of this model is shown in Fig. 4.

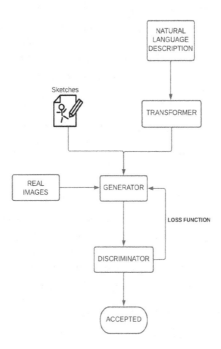

Fig. 3. Proposal Pipeline

Fig. 4. Expected result

4.1 Text Processing

First, we need to process the natural language statement that contains the context which is required for the image we want to generate. For that, we use a transformer model which is going to translate the input from natural language words to a feature vector. Thus, we convert the input into a feature vector which will then be sent as input along with a sketch to the generator network. This transformer will handle the tokenization of the chain of words and obtain only those that are the most relevant and those that will be used to form a coherent context to generate an image.

The transformer takes the natural language text which is processed in parallel using all the words that are part of the description at the same time. For that, all words are mapped to a point in the space where the words with similar meanings are close to each other. This has the name of embedding space which can be trained. However, to save time and resources we used a pre-trained embedding space. On the other hand, the position of each word from the sentence that is processed could change its meaning. To solve this, a positional encoder is used which uses a function that will generate a context vector for each word that is being processed according to its position in the given description. The output of the transformer model is a vector that contains the relevant features which are going to be used in the training of the generative network.

4.2 Generator

The next step is to put the feature vector obtained from the transformer together with the image sketches. They are used to being very abstract with low visual content and in many cases, they could be poorly drawn. To give these sketches more context we are going to use the processed natural language description alongside ground truth images and the drawings thus, we can generate realistic images. The training stage takes a pair from the data set with their corresponding sketch and from the other set that is the description processed. The output of the generative network is sent to the discriminator as the input.

In this stage, the generator processes the sketches as a vector called a tensor, then we introduce the feature vector from the transformer. It will give the context to generate a new image. To predict new pixels and to control the face generation, we take the feature vector and combine it with the sketch tensor to produce a new vector which will produce our output. We should be careful about the features that are being used to generate an image because they can overlap with another feature which can give us miss match images as a result. For that, we block the zones in the image that should not be modified after they get the context in a previous step.

4.3   Discriminator

In this step we will handle the evaluation of the images that come from the generative network—this network receives a pair as an input. It is composed of a ground truth image and the generated image and both of them are compared. If the synthetic image manages to circumvent the discriminator, it will pass to the accepted state, on the other hand, if it is rejected, a response will be sent to the generator. Thus, we will apply a loss function to the generator in order to produce new images. In this sense, it continues training and produces better results.

5   Experiments and Results

For the experiments, we use a dataset of faces CelebA which contains a large-scale facial attribute with over 200,000 celebrity images [10]. Additionally, we use an algorithm that will handle the edge recognition of these images to extract sketches from them.

On the other hand, we use natural language descriptions which are processed by the transformer. We can use the descriptions along the image to train the network to generate new images from the sketch and the description which gives the context to the image to be generated.

In order to evaluate, we use quantitative metrics: Inception Score (IS) [19] and Frechet Inception Distance (FID) [7]. These metrics are suitable to evaluate and judge both the model and the images generated. The first of them takes an image list and returns a single float value, the score which is a measure of how realistic is the output of the GAN. It measures two things simultaneously, the variety of the images and whether each image clearly resembles something, and is an automatic alternative to users rating the quality of the images. The second one does not just evaluate the generated images' current distribution but also compares the distribution of the generated images with the distribution of the current images used to train the generator.

The dataset we used has more than 200000 in images of celebrity faces whose edges were extracted to be used as sketches in the generation of new images. We divide the dataset for training and testing in a proportion of 70% and 30% respectively. In addition, we used descriptions that control the context of the image that is generated from the sketch. The results are shown in Table 2, where we can observe the description and the sketch used to generate the face. However, the control of the effects of the attributes in the generation stage still has to be improved, since images can be produced that do not match the description given and the sketch used. The generated images have the dimension of 64×64 pixels. In addition, as the control of the description over the generation still needs to be improved, some results are obtained that do not coincide with the sketch or the description given to them, this can be seen in Table 1.

The result for a batch of images generated is shown in Fig. 5. It is observed different results are obtained for different face generations after a thousand of training epochs for a generation. It is also shown that some images have overlapping features. The model still produces some images that miss match the given description, even though, we block the zones that have been already modified with a feature.

Table 1. Face generation which do not match the description

Description	Result	Description	Result
Female, Big_Lips, Heavy_Makeup, Wear-ing_Lipstick		Female, Big_Lips, Heavy_Makeup, Wear-ing_Lipstick	
Male, Big_Nose, Glasses		Male, Big_Nose, Chubby, Double_chin	
Male, Big_Nose, Mouth_Open, Smiling, Double_Chin		Female, Heavy_Makeup, Pointy_Nose, Big_Mouth, Open_Eyes	

Table 2. Face generation from sketch and natural language description

Description	Result	Description	Result
Female, Heavy_Makeup, pointy_nose, Smiling		Male, Open_Mouth, Pointy_Nose	
Female, Smiling, No_Shadow, Open_eyes, No_glasses		Female, Heavy_Makeup, Open_Mouth, Smiling	
Male, Chubby, Open_Eyes, Open_mouth, Smiling		Female, No_Makeup, Pointy_Nose, Close_Mouth, Big_Lips	

As explained before, there are two quantitative metrics to judge the images that are generated. These metrics measure the distribution of the generated images and the images used to train the model, to simulate a subjective evaluation made by a human. The results obtained after applying these metrics are compared with the scores obtained by other generative models using the same dataset that was used for this research work. The scores are shown in Table 3 where we can see that the score for IS obtained from the model is lower compared to the others. On the other hand, the score for FID in our proposed model is averaged when compared to other generative models for faces.

Fig. 5. Last Iteration for face generation

Table 3. Values obtained from quantitative metrics with other generative models

Models	Inception Score	Frechet Inception Distance
Proposed Model	1.584	2.154
U-Net GAN	3.33	2.03
COCO-GAN	4.15	5.74
CR-GAN	1.87	16.97
SS-GAN	–	24.36
QSNGAN	2.249	29.417
PA-GAN	–	15.4

6 Conclusion

We have presented a novel model capable of generating images of faces from sketches and natural language descriptions. Generative models have proven to be versatile when adding a component or adding an extra step to the generation process. For instance, the addition of a transformer component to process the description in natural language can be useful to generate realistic images of faces. The proposed method is separated from the conventional contextual generative models, where real images are used to give context to the sketches to generate new images. This part has been replaced by a description in natural language that provides context when generating an image of a face.

We evaluate our model with quantitative metrics (IS and FID) which are suitable metrics to judge the images obtained and simulate a subjective human evaluation. The proposed model, in terms of IS, obtains a score that is below some generative models that use the same data set. While in terms of FID, it remains within the mean of other models that also use the same images to generate realistic images of faces.

References

1. Bank, D., Koenigstein, N., Giryes, R.: Autoencoders. arXiv preprint arXiv:2003.05991 (2020)
2. Borji, A.: Generated faces in the wild: quantitative comparison of stable diffusion, midjourney and DALL-E 2. arXiv preprint arXiv:2210.00586 (2022)
3. Frans, K., Soros, L.B., Witkowski, O.: CLIPDraw: exploring text-to-drawing synthesis through language-image encoders. arXiv preprint arXiv:2106.14843 (2021)
4. Geyer, C.J.: Practical Markov chain Monte Carlo. Stat. Sci. 473–483 (1992)
5. Goodfellow, I., et al.: Generative adversarial nets. Advances in Neural Inf. Process. Syst. **27** (2014)
6. Gregor, K., Danihelka, I., Graves, A., Rezende, D., Wierstra, D.: DRAW: a recurrent neural network for image generation. In: International Conference on Machine Learning, pp. 1462–1471. PMLR (2015)
7. Heusel, M., Ramsauer, H., Unterthiner, T., Nessler, B., Hochreiter, S.: GANs trained by a two time-scale update rule converge to a local nash equilibrium. Adv. Neural Inf. Process. Syst. **30** (2017)
8. Kang, H., Lee, S., Chui, C.K.: Coherent line drawing. In: Proceedings of the 5th International Symposium on Non-photorealistic Animation and Rendering, pp. 43–50 (2007)
9. Li, B., Qi, X., Lukasiewicz, T., Torr, P.: Controllable text-to-image generation. Adv. Neural Inf. Process. Syst. **32** (2019)
10. Liu, Z., Luo, P., Wang, X., Tang, X.: Deep learning face attributes in the wild. In: Proceedings of International Conference on Computer Vision (ICCV) (2015)
11. Lu, Y., Wu, S., Tai, Y.W., Tang, C.K.: Image generation from sketch constraint using contextual GAN. In: Proceedings of the European conference on computer vision (ECCV), pp. 205–220 (2018)
12. Mansimov, E., Parisotto, E., Ba, J.L., Salakhutdinov, R.: Generating images from captions with attention. arXiv preprint arXiv:1511.02793 (2015)
13. Provilkov, I., Emelianenko, D., Voita, E.: BPE-dropout: simple and effective subword regularization. In: Proceedings of the 58th Annual Meeting of the Association for Computational Linguistics, pp. 1882–1892. Association for Computational Linguistics, Online (2020). https://doi.org/10.18653/v1/2020.acl-main.170, https://aclanthology.org/2020.acl-main.170
14. Radford, A., Metz, L., Chintala, S.: Unsupervised representation learning with deep convolutional generative adversarial networks. arXiv preprint arXiv:1511.06434 (2015)
15. Ramesh, A., et al.: Zero-shot text-to-image generation. In: International Conference on Machine Learning, pp. 8821–8831. PMLR (2021)
16. Reed, S., Akata, Z., Yan, X., Logeswaran, L., Schiele, B., Lee, H.: Generative adversarial text to image synthesis. In: International Conference on Machine Learning, pp. 1060–1069. PMLR (2016)
17. Rombach, R., Blattmann, A., Lorenz, D., Esser, P., Ommer, B.: High-resolution image synthesis with latent diffusion models (2021)

18. Ronneberger, O., Fischer, P., Brox, T.: U-net: convolutional networks for biomedical image segmentation. In: Navab, N., Hornegger, J., Wells, W.M., Frangi, A.F. (eds.) MICCAI 2015. LNCS, vol. 9351, pp. 234–241. Springer, Cham (2015). https://doi.org/10.1007/978-3-319-24574-4_28

19. Salimans, T., Goodfellow, I., Zaremba, W., Cheung, V., Radford, A., Chen, X.: Improved techniques for training GANs. Adv. Neural Inf. Process. Syst. **29** (2016)

20. Sarzynska-Wawer, J., et al.: Detecting formal thought disorder by deep contextualized word representations. Psychiatry Res. **304**, 114135 (2021)

21. Vaswani, A., et al.: Attention is all you need. Adv. Neural Inf. Process. Syst. **30** (2017)

22. Winnemöller, H., Kyprianidis, J.E., Olsen, S.C.: XDoG: an extended difference-of-gaussians compendium including advanced image stylization. Comput. Graph. **36**(6), 740–753 (2012)

23. Xu, T., et al.: AttnGAN: fine-grained text to image generation with attentional generative adversarial networks. In: Proceedings of the IEEE Conference on Computer Vision and Pattern Recognition, pp. 1316–1324 (2018)

24. Zhang, H., et al.: StackGAN: text to photo-realistic image synthesis with stacked generative adversarial networks. In: Proceedings of the IEEE International Conference on Computer Vision, pp. 5907–5915 (2017)

ADRAS: Airborne Disease Risk Assessment System for Closed Environments

Wilber Rojas[1]([✉]) [iD], Edwin Salcedo[1] [iD], and Guillermo Sahonero[1,2] [iD]

[1] Department of Mechatronics Engineering, Universidad Católica Boliviana "San Pablo", La Paz, Bolivia
{wrojas,esalcedo}@ucb.edu.bo
[2] Institute for Biological and Medical Engineering, Pontificia Universidad Católica de Chile, Santiago, Chile
gsahonero@uc.cl
https://www.ucb.edu.bo/

Abstract. Airborne diseases are easy to spread in any population. The advent of COVID-19 showed us that we are not prepared to control them. The pandemic has drastically posed challenges to the daily functioning of public and private establishments. In general, while there have been several approaches to reduce the potential risk of spreading the virus, many of them rely on the commitment that people make, which - unfortunately - cannot be constant, for example, wearing a facemask in closed environment at all times or social distancing. In this work, we propose a computer vision system to determine the risk of airborne disease spread in closed environments. We modify and implement the Wells-Riley epidemiological equation. We also evaluate and implement models for facemask and person detection from OpenVino. For mask detection, we applied transfer learning and obtained the best performance for a model based on MobileNetV2. The generated data from several devices is visible in a web platform to monitor multiple areas and locations. Finally, an OAK-D camera and a Jetson device are embedded in a end device meant to monitor a closed environment and send spread risk data continually to the web platform. Our results are promising as we obtained up to 88% of accuracy for the person detection task and up to 57% of mAP for the facemask task. We expect this paper to be beneficial for developing new control measurements and prevention tools to prevent airborne contagion.

Keywords: Airborne Disease · Risk Assessment · Stereo Vision · Edge Computing

1 Introduction

In the past few years, society has become more conscious of airborne diseases due to the disruption caused by the COVID-19 pandemic. This aiborne disease,

This research was supported by the OpenCV Foundation through an award provided at the OpenCV AI Competition 2021.

also known as COVID-19, is caused by the SARS-CoV-2 virus and has different symptoms such as fever, breathing difficulties, fatigue, tiredness, cough, and loss of taste and smell [1]. Different from other illnesses transmitted between people, viruses or bacteria of airborne diseases can stay in the air mixed with dust particles and respiratory droplets for longer times [1]. Then, these particles are eventually inhaled by other people and cause a spread of the disease. Airborne diseases comprise Measle, Tuberculosis, Chickenpox, Influenza, Pertussis, SARS-CoV-1, and SARS-CoV-2, among others. Even though the contagious rate and symptoms vary between them, their control and prevention are similar and consist mainly of the installation of isolation rooms for infected people, use of protective clothes such as Personal Protective Equipment (PPE), facemasks, and gloves, better ventilation for closed environments, and stricter practices of sanitation and hygiene. In-depth investigations on SARS-CoV-2 spread proved that the closer or denser a group of people, the higher the risk of airborne disease contagion [1].

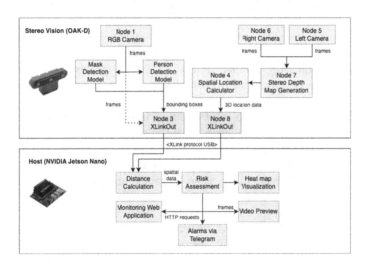

Fig. 1. End device architecture

The current research aims to propose a computer vision-based system to monitor the spread risk of an airborne disease. We considered Coronavirus disease 2019 as a study case for the investigation. So far, it has spread through 591 million people and caused 6.4 million deaths worldwide as of August 19, 2022 according to [2]. This disease has completely disrupted the entire world unexpectedly, consequently, there is a constant research need of new control and prevention methods for new airborne viruses or variants since a rapid increase of infected people can collapse any healthcare system. In the current investigation, we present a real-time hardware and software system that calculates the risk of airborne diseases in one or multiple closed environments. The architecture of the monitoring end device is illustrated in Fig. 1. The model we use for assessing the risk is based on the number of people, compliance with the correct use of masks, and compliance with social distancing and exposure time as variables.

The rest of the paper is structured as follows. We first review some related works in Sect. 2. Then, we adapt an epidemiological model by considering several concepts from Wells-Riley estimation model in Sect. 3. Later, we explain the details of the computer vision models for person and mask detection in Sect. 4 which is complemented with the description of the distance estimation in Sect. 5. Moreover, we explain how the monitoring system works in Sect. 6 and present our results discussing their implications in Sect. 7. Finally, we conclude the paper in Sect. 8.

2 Related Works

By the end of 2019, the initial breakthrough of the SARS-CoV-2 virus led to a massive number of deaths and the declaration of a worldwide pandemic. This encouraged many computer vision developers and researchers to collaborate towards the development of new ideas to prevent the virus spread. Since keeping physical distance of at least one meter from others has proved to be one of the most effective measure against SARS-CoV-2 [2], extensive research has been carried out for the development of Visual Social Distance Monitoring Systems (VSDMS) [3]. In addition, other projects complemented the distance measuring idea with face masks detection, or face-hand interaction [4–6] to control that people comply with measures against a contagion.

The state-of-the-art proposals to measure physical contact among people can be classified as either 2D based or 3D based. The former commonly uses a sequence of methods to recognize people: a) image processing; b) image segmentation; c) shape extraction; d) object recognition. This last step might vary from classical computer vision-methods [7] to deep learning-based methods [4–6,8,9]. Focusing on deep learning methods, researchers usually implement person detectors based on Convolutional Neural Networks (CNNs) such as YOLOv4, Yolov5, MobileNet, SSD, or R-CNN [10]. Then, the investigations regularly calculate the pairwise Euclidean distances among the centroids of the detected bounding boxes [3,4]. These models are commonly applied to video frames given that monitoring an environment requires continuous surveillance. Consequently, recent proposals combine person detectors with object tracking algorithms such as DeepSORT, SORT, or StrongSort [11,12].

Even though camera-based surveillance systems have been developed up to the point of becoming commercialized solutions [13–15], this brief literature review let us note that 3D vision has been less explored despite its higher accuracy for distance calculation. To the authors' best knowledge, researchers in [16] have been the first to publish about the application of stereo vision in a VSDMS in April 2022. Not only did they combine stereo and monocular cameras for person detection, but also conclude that stereo vision cameras were superior than monocular cameras. Specifically, they use a Zed M Camera and an MSI laptop equipped with NVIDIA GTX 1060 3GB GPU, with which they stream videos and obtain depth maps to measure the distance among people. Beyond the published work in indexed venues, developers in [17] and [18] applied stereo-vision cameras for social distance monitoring in September 2020 and January 2021, respectively.

Beyond social distancing, only a few works explore further implications and contagion risk assessment by leveraging the extracted visual information of the protective measures compliance. For instance, investigators in [12] contributed with a remarkable online infection risk assessment scheme for open environments named DeepSocial, which considers people's moving trajectories and the rate of social distancing violations to calculate the contagion risk. Moving on, researchers in [19] propose BEV-NET to assess social distancing compliance and probability of infection in closed environments using a monocular camera from a top perspective. Furthermore, this investigation proposes the COVID-19 infection risk assessment for each individual present in a scene and a general risk assessment for the complete ambient. In both projects, the closer or denser a group of people is, the higher the risk of contagion [12, 19].

In contrast to COVID-19, the infection risk quantification of other airborne diseases by recognising visually the protective rule's compliance is less investigated, however, their risk monitoring can also be implemented using the approaches proposed for COVID-19. The multiple waves of SARS-CoV-2 have taught us that airborne diseases can severely affect the economy and normal functioning of an entire country, therefore, there is a shortage of research to have better tools that monitor and inform the risk of contagion in an ambient. All these to provide confidence to citizens and users in outdoor and indoor environments.

3   Epidemiological Model

This section describes the definition of the equation for estimating the spread risk of a airborne disease in a closed environment. We know that the classification of risk prediction models can be split into Wells-Riley based and Dose-Response based models [20]. We analyze the first one and modify it so that the implementation is feasible in a computer vision monitoring environment.

Wells developed an equation to estimate the risk of infection in a close environment [21]. Riley proposed an improvement to the equation, considering the ventilation of the room as a parameter [22]. The Wells-Riley equation generalizes the infectivity of pathogens with a new infectious dose unit called *quanta*. A *quanta* is the number of infectious particles required to infect a person [23]. So a *quanta* of influenza would infect the same number of people as a *quanta* of tuberculosis or COVID-19. If the disease is more contagious, the infected person would have a higher *quanta* emission rate.

The Wells-Riley equation is defined by Eq. 1:

$$P_i = 1 - exp\left(\frac{I * q * p * t}{Q}\right) \tag{1}$$

where, P_i is the probability of infection, I is the number of infected people, q is the quanta emission rate, p is the pulmonary ventilation rate of a person, t is the exposure time, and Q is the ventilation rate of the room [23]. For this investigation, each of these parameters were obtained as follows:

- Number of infected people (I):
  Wells-Riley estimates the risk of infection based on a certain number of infected people [23], however, we cannot know this information with entire certainty. We calculate the probability of infected people based on the population percentage of cases in a region:

$$p_c = \frac{c}{P_r} \tag{2}$$

where, p_c is the percentage of cases, c is the number of cases in a region, and P_r is the total population of the region. If we multiply the percentage of cases by the number of people in a room, we obtain the probability of infected people in that room. So, our value for I is:

$$I = N * p_c \tag{3}$$

where N is the number of people.
- Quanta emission rate (q):
  The quanta generation rate is the only parameter that contains the infectivity of the virus [11,23], so each pathogen has its own value of q. Mikszewski et al. [24], analyzed the quanta generation rate for the most common airborne diseases, including SARS-CoV-1, SARS-CoV-2, MERS, Tuberculosis, and Influenza. These values are constants in the monitoring system and are described in Table 1.

Table 1. Quanta emission rate values $[q * h^{-1}]$ [24].

Pathogen	Resting, oral breathing	Standing, Speaking	Light activity, speaking loudly
SARS-CoV-1	0.008	0.042	0.71
MERS	0.011	0.056	0.96
Tuberculosis (On Treatment)	0.020	0.098	1.70
Influenza	0.035	0.17	3.00
Coxsackievirus	0.062	0.31	5.20
Rhinovirus	0.210	1.00	18.00
SARS-CoV-2	0.550	2.70	46.00
Tuberculosis (Untreated)	0.62	3.1	52.00
Adenovirus	0.780	3.90	66.0
Measles	3.100	15.00	260.00

Li et al. determined that the viral load, therefore also the quanta, is almost the same between presymptomatic, asymptomatic, and symptomatic subjects [25]. In the case of the advent of a new airborne disease or actual disease variant, the value of q should be calculated using Eq. 4:

$$q = c_v * c_i * p * v_d \tag{4}$$

where, c_v is the viral load, c_i is a conversion factor between a quanta and the infectious dose, p is the inhalation rate, and v_d is the volume of droplets expelled by a person [26].
- Pulmonary ventilation rate (p):
Adams [27], conducted a study where he empirically determined the average person inhalation rate for different activities. Table 2 shows the values obtained from this study, which are used in Eq. 1.

Table 2. Inhalation rate values [27].

Activity	Inhalation Rate [$m^3\ h^{-1}$]
laying down	0.49
stand	0.54
very light exercise	0.72
light exercise	1.38
moderate exercise	2.35
heavy exercise	3.30

- Ventilation rate of the room (Q):
It refers to the ACH (Air Changes per Hour) value of a close environment. To obtain this parameter, first we determined the air flow rate.

$$A_{FR} = w * A_v \tag{5}$$

In Eq. 5, A_{FR} is the air flow rate, w is the window area, and A_v is the air velocity. Finally, the ACH is the Air flow rate divided by room volume (V_R) [28].

$$ACH = \frac{A_{FR}}{V_R} \tag{6}$$

In case of having artificial ventilation, the ACH value can be obtained from the specifications of the machine, and should be added to the natural ventilation calculated in the Eq. 6.
- Exposure time (t):
This parameter refers to the time that "I" number of infected people will remain in the closed environment. Note that the Wells-Riley formula requires the total exposure time as a parameter. And, in this research, the objective

is to implement it in a monitoring system, so the number of infected people for a specific time is variable and will be calculated in real time.

We can represent the Wells-Riley equation with the use of integrals for the time variation:

$$P_i = 1 - exp\left(\int_0^\infty \frac{I * q * p}{Q} dt\right) \tag{7}$$

– Facemask detection:

Wells-Riley does not consider if people wear facemasks, which is required for estimating the spread of a disease in a closed environment. Therefore, we implement an additional parameter to the equation considering that we will monitor the presence of facemasks on the detected people's faces.

It is well-known that the worst type of facemasks are made of cloth, so we consider it as the default type of facemask used by everybody detected in a scene. It is worth noting that the use of cloth facemask reduces the contagion risk of an airborne disease by half [29]. From the Wells-Riley equation, we know that if we double the ventilation rate, we also halve the risk of spread. Consequently, the final equation is:

$$P_i = 1 - exp\left(\int_0^\infty \frac{I * q * p}{Q * (1 + M)} dt\right) \tag{8}$$

where M is the percentage, in range $[0, 1]$, of people wearing a mask in a closed environment. To conclude the equation requires setting the ventilation of the room (Q), the pulmonary ventilation rate (p) and the Quanta generation rate (q) as constants before monitoring. The exposure time (t), the estimated number of infected people (I), and the percentage of masks (M) will be calculated in real time by computer vision. Equation 8 is the Risk Assessment block in Fig. 1.

4   Person and Mask Detection

In the proposed system, two CNN-based object detection models localize person and facemask appearances in the frames coming from the OAK-D camera. The collected datasets, the object detection models, and most importantly, the used metrics are presented in the following subsections.

4.1   Dataset and Preprocessing

We collected the dataset of person and mask instances separately through three different means: web scrapping, video processing, and public datasets. First, we developed a Python script to download images from Google images. The terms used to find people images were: "pedestrians", "people in room", and "meeting". Once we obtained 377 images, we needed to review their quality due to some unrelated images downloaded by mistake. Second, we used the Computer

Vision Annotation Tool (CVAT) [30] to obtain image samples of people and face-masks independently by labelling video frames. This let us get 1,084 instances of people and 337 instances of facemasks. Finally, we obtained 756 images by combining public datasets [31]. All these subsets were sorted to create two sub-sets: one with instances of people without facemasks, and another with images with facemask instances. Since the subsets were small, we needed to implement data augmentation techniques, such as horizontal flip, brightness change, and grayscale, by using the Roboflow platform [32].

Table 3. Datasets

Subset	Collected	Augmented	Total
Person Instances	1084	2277	3361
Facemask Instances	337	606	943

4.2 Object Detection

First, instead of creating and training object detection models from scratch, the person detection models that we tried were based on pre-trained architectures provided by Intel OpenVino [33]. Specifically, we tested the models 106, 200, 201, 202, 203, 301, 302, and 303 to achieve a good performance with our col-lected dataset. In addition, it is worth mentioning that OpenVino models can be easily deployed on OAK-D devices by using the MiryiadX Blob Converter [34], which made us decide to use them. Secondly, for facemask detection, we applied transfer learning to re-train the models Mobilenet v2, which had been previously trained with bigger datasets. It is important to note that several developers who worked with OAK-D devices defined Mobilenetv2-based models as the best object detectors to deploy on them [33].

4.3 Metrics

Intersection over Union: The main tool to evaluate the human and facemask detection models with respect to each localized bounding box was Intersection Over Union (IoU). This metric, also known as the Jacquard Index, measures the overlap area between the ground-truth bounding boxes and the predicted bounding boxes, and ranges between 0 and 1. For object detection tasks, it is recommended to set a confidence threshold to filter good-quality detected bounding boxes. In the current project, we used 50% as threshold confidence because it gave us good experimental results.

Confusion Matrix: We calculated a confusion matrix per image where the pixels under the area of the detected objects were classified as 1; otherwise, they were classified as 0. Consequently, both predicted and ground truth masks let us quantify the well and wrong classified pixels as True Positive (TP), True Negative (TN), False Positive (FP), or False Negative (FN). Then, the matrix let us calculate the Matthew's Correlation Coefficient, F1 score, Sensitivity (Recall), Specificity, Accuracy, Negative Predictive Value (NPV), False Positive Rate (FPR), and False Negative Rate (FNR) according to Eqs. 18, 17, 10, 11, 9, 12, 13, and 14, respectively. Among them, Precision shows the percentage of correct predictions among all the positive-predicted pixels in the images while Sensitivity describes the percentage of actual positives that were identified correctly.

$$\text{Accuracy} = \frac{\text{TP} + \text{TN}}{\text{TP} + \text{FP} + \text{TN} + \text{FN}} \quad (9) \qquad \text{Sensitivity} = \frac{\text{TP}}{\text{TP} + \text{FN}} \quad (10)$$

$$\text{Specificity} = \frac{\text{TN}}{\text{TN} + \text{FP}} \quad (11) \qquad \text{NPV} = \frac{\text{TN}}{\text{TN} + \text{FN}} \quad (12)$$

$$\text{FPR} = \frac{\text{FP}}{\text{FP} + \text{TN}} \quad (13) \qquad \text{FNR} = \frac{\text{FN}}{\text{FN} + \text{TP}} \quad (14)$$

Mean Average Precision: Commonly, precision and sensitivity (recall) can be plotted against each other to obtain the precision-recall curve, and the Average Precision will be the area under this curve. This metric is defined in Eq. 15, where r represents recall, p represents precision as a function of r. Therefore, $p(r)$ means "precision at recall r".

$$AP = \int_0^1 p(r) \, dr \quad (15)$$

Given that the person and facemask detection models were applied separately, Mean Average Precision (mAP) in our case is the same as Average Precision (AP). However, it is worth mentioning that mAP is the mean of Average Precisions of all individual classes for multi-class detection tasks and should be calculated as in Eq. 16.

$$mAP = \frac{1}{N} \sum_{i=1}^{N} AP_i \quad (16)$$

Here, mAP is Mean Average Precision, N is the number of class labels, and AP_i is the Average Precision for the ith class. We evaluated and calculated mean average precision for different IoU thresholds: mAP@50% IoU, mAP@75% IoU, mAP@50%:5%:95% IoU. However, we finally kept 50% as confidence threshold.

F1 Score: Both precision and recall were used to calculate the F1 Score metric provided in Eq. 17. The benefit of this metric is that it considers the number of prediction errors that the model makes and also the type of errors that are made.

$$F1Score = \frac{2 * TP}{2 * TP + FP + FN} \tag{17}$$

Matthews Correlation Coefficient: Finally, the Matthews Correlation Coefficient (MCC) was used as a measure of the quality of binary classifications of bounding boxes. This is defined in Eq. 18.

$$MCC = \frac{TP * TN - FP * FN}{\sqrt{(TP + FP) * (TP + FN) * (TN + FP) * (TN + FN)}} \tag{18}$$

5   Distance Estimation

To calculate the distance among people, we need to estimate the relative position of the objects detected with respect of the camera. Stereo vision helped us estimate these distances and positions by obtaining a three-dimensional view of a scene through the OAK-D camera and its binocular vision. Stereo vision can be applied to calculate the depth of an object by making use of the angle of convergence.

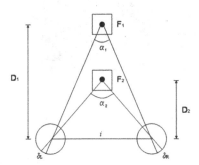

Fig. 2. Stereo vision definition, where α is the convergence angle, D is the distance between the camera and the detected object, and i is the distance between cameras. F_1 and F_2 are different objects, which have different distances, and therefore, different angles [16].

As shown in the Fig. 2, the convergence angle α_2 is in the middle of the two monocular cameras that capture an object located on the front [16]. Also, this angle varies depending on the distance of the object detected, this allows a precise approximation of its real distance. We used the OAK-D device built-in functions to calculate this distance. Specifically, the function used was "Spatial Location Calculator" [35]. In order to control social distancing, we calculated the Euclidean distance between each person, defined by Eq. 19, where d is the distance between person p_1 and person p_2, and x, y, z refers to the positions in the three dimensional plane.

$$d(p_1, p_2) = \sqrt{(x_1 - x_2)^2 + (y_1 - y_2)^2 + (z_1 - z_2)^2} \tag{19}$$

6   Monitoring System

Combining the result of Wells-Riley equation and the positions of the people determined by the stereo camera, we can analyze the sectors with the highest risk of infection in the monitoring area. We implement a Gaussian analysis to distribute the concentration of infectious particles. The Fig. 3 shows an example analysis of a room monitoring COVID-19. This analysis can only be displayed in square or rectangular shapes. And the unit of the axes is centimeters.

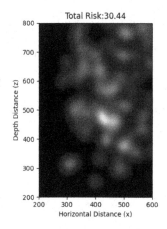

Fig. 3. Gaussian analysis of quanta concentration

In Fig. 3, a heatmap shows the sectors where people remained for the longest time. Additionally, we send the data to an online monitoring system shown in Fig. 4. This system was developed as a web application and was deployed on a cloud server, which collected the airborne spread risk calculated from multiple end devices. If the risk in an environment exceeded a threshold, the system sent notifications via Telegram to alert the authorities. Specifically, Fig. 4(a) shows an example of the interface in which a bank can register multiple areas for real-time surveillance. The system was developed to monitor multiple areas by collecting data from end in several public places. For instance, the interface shown in Fig. 4(b) was the detail view that helped us monitor a specific closed environment every 30 s.

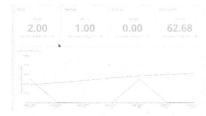

(a) Web application to monitor multiple places.

(b) Detail view of a closed environment.

Fig. 4. Online Monitoring System.

About the end device, this was designed using SolidWorks, assembled with 3D printing and installed to monitor a closed environment continually. Internally, the device consisted of a Jetson Nano computer and an OAK-D camera. The final design is shown in Fig. 5. The device has a screen that shows the risk of spread, as well as, activates an alert when the calculated risk exceeds a safety threshold.

Fig. 5. Monitoring Device

7   Results and Discussion

In the validation our Wells-Riley model, we collected data from similar studies and used them as input to the Eq. 8. The results, in Table 4, show that our equation obtains a value close to that reported in these studies, with an average error of 4.29%. These values were expected because the equation was essentially unchanged, and the structure was only slightly modified to allow for different input values. We can conclude that the small differences between the results are due to the fact that each study proposes new parameters to consider.

Table 4. Evaluation of the modified Wells Riley equation

Input					Output			Reference
I	M	q	p	t (min)	Q	P_i	Expected P_i	
1	1	10	0.54	60	12.00	9.88	10.00	F. Velarde et al. [36]
1	1	30	0.54	4	3.86	2.76	2.50	Z. Liu et al. [37]
1	1	100	0.36	60	15.00	21.34	21.20	Y. Guo et al. [38]
1	1	14	0.35	60	0.56	1.44	1.40	Z. Wang et al. [39]
1	1	14	0.35	420	0.56	10.30	9.70	Z. Wang et al. [39]

Regarding person detection model, we evaluated several pretrained models provided by OpenVino on its Github repository [33]. These tests were performed with the total subset named "Person Instances", described in Table 3. As mentioned above, we mainly used these models because they were already trained with bigger datasets for person detection, in consequence, the obtained results were better than implementing detection models from scratch. The resulting metrics are shown in Table 5, which shows the models' code in the first row. Note that all models in [33] have the term "person-detection-0" as the prefix name and a unique code as an identifier. In addition, each model has three versions that vary in their weights' precision: "float point 16" (FP16), "float point 16 - int 8" (FP16-INT8), and "float point 32" (FP32). We focused on testing the FP16 version of the models for better memory usage when deployed in the OAK-D device. Based on the evaluation results, the model person-detection-0106 obtained the best results according to the MCC, IoU and Accuracy metrics. The final evaluation results are presented in Table 5, where the row "Complexity"

Table 5. Evaluation results for the tested models for person detection [33]. Complexity row is in GFLOPS. Size row is in MParams. IoU, Accuracy, mAP, F1 Score, Sensitivity, Specificity, NPV, FPR, and FNR are in the [0; 1] interval. MCC is in the [−1; 1] interval.

Metric/Model	106	200	201	202	203	301	302	303
Complexity	**404.264**	0.786	1.768	3.143	6.519	79318.216	370.208	24.758
Size	**71.565**	1.817	1.817	1.817	2.394	55.557	51.164	3.630
IoU	**0.829**	0.605	0.605	0.605	0.716	0.632	0.657	0.657
mAP	**0.737**	0.021	0.021	0.021	0.545	0.335	0.370	0.376
MCC	**0.630**	−0.001	−0.001	−0.001	0.366	0.131	0.172	0.186
Accuracy	**0.884**	0.706	0.706	0.706	0.816	0.749	0.770	0.768
F1 Score	**0.884**	0.706	0.706	0.706	0.816	0.749	0.770	0.769
Sensitivity	**0.683**	0.001	0.001	0.001	0.510	0.385	0.371	0.428
Specificity	**0.962**	0.999	0.999	0.999	0.864	0.742	0.801	0.757
NPV	**0.869**	0.706	0.706	0.706	0.817	0.796	0.788	0.801
FPR	**0.045**	0.001	0.001	0.001	0.135	0.258	0.197	0.242
FNR	**0.316**	0.999	0.999	0.999	0.490	0.615	0.629	0.572

defines the number of computational operations to pass a frame through the model, and the row "Size" defines the memory footprint needed for each model.

Finally, for mask detection, we trained a transfer learning-based model with Tensorflow using the subset "Facemask Instances". This task was performed using the training instructions for the OAK-D camera provided by Luxonis [40], and the selected base model was MobileNetV2. From training, we obtained 57.98% of mAP result with IoU 0.50. Finally, the facemask model and the best person detection models were deployed on the OAK-D camera. A sample of detection results using both models can be seen in Fig. 6.

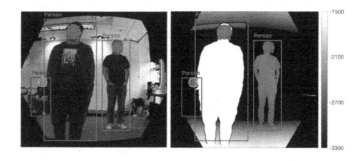

Fig. 6. Object Detection Inferences

8   Conclusions

In this paper, we proposed the implementation of epidemiological models in computer vision systems, with the aim of reducing the spread of airborne diseases. We adapted the Wells-Riley equation to be able to calculate the risk of infection in real time. We use object detection models to determine the number of people in an environment, as well as the number of people wearing masks. We implement stereo-cameras and Gaussian mathematical models to obtain a Heatmap of the sections with the highest risk of infection. All information is sent to an online monitoring system, with which multiple environments can be monitored. Our results, although preliminary, are promising and contribute by bridging the gap between computer vision, health care and spread modeling. As future work, the facemask detector requires to be more robust. Another important limitation is that our percentage of infected (I) is an estimate and it cannot be guaranteed that it is the real value of infected in the environment. An oversize can be added to this value in order to prevent false security values. Something to consider, is that no ethical protocol is needed. Although the system monitors people, no private data or video recording is saved, only general data, such as the number of people and how many have a mask.

References

1. Park, S.E.: Epidemiology, virology, and clinical features of severe acute respiratory syndrome -coronavirus-2 (SARS-CoV-2; Coronavirus Disease-19). Clin. Exp. Pediatr. **63**(4), 119–124 (2020). https://pubmed.ncbi.nlm.nih.gov/32252141
2. WHO: Coronavirus (COVID-19) Statistics. https://covid19.who.int/
3. Himeur, Y., et al.: Deep visual social distancing monitoring to combat COVID-19: a comprehensive survey. Sustain. Cities Soc. **85**, 104064 (2022). https://www.sciencedirect.com/science/article/pii/S2210670722003821
4. Ahmed, I., Ahmad, M., Rodrigues, J.J.P.C., Jeon, G., Din, S.: A deep learning-based social distance monitoring framework for COVID-19. Sustain. Cities Soc. **65**, 102571 (2021). https://www.sciencedirect.com/science/article/pii/S2210670720307897
5. Razavi, M., Alikhani, H., Janfaza, V., Sadeghi, B., Alikhani, E.: An automatic system to monitor the physical distance and face mask wearing of construction workers in COVID-19 pandemic. CoRR, vol. abs/2101.0 (2021). https://arxiv.org/abs/2101.01373
6. Eyiokur, F.I., Ekenel, H.K., Waibel, A.: A computer vision system to help prevent the transmission of COVID-19. Undefined (2021)
7. Petrovic, N., Kocić, D.: IoT-based system for COVID-19 indoor safety monitoring (2020)
8. Degadwala, S., Vyas, D., Dave, H., Mahajan, A.: Visual social distance alert system using computer vision deep learning. In: Proceedings of the 4th International Conference on Electronics, Communication and Aerospace Technology, ICECA 2020, pp. 1512–1516 (2020)
9. Yang, D., Yurtsever, E., Renganathan, V., Redmill, K.A., Özgüner, Ü.: A vision-based social distancing and critical density detection system for COVID-19. Sensors **21**(13), 4608 (2021). https://www.mdpi.com/1424-8220/21/13/4608/htm
10. Karaman, O., Alhudhaif, A., Polat, K.: Development of smart camera systems based on artificial intelligence network for social distance detection to fight against COVID-19. Appl. Soft Comput. **110**, 107610 (2021)
11. Li, J., Wu, Z.: The application of yolov4 and a new pedestrian clustering algorithm to implement social distance monitoring during the COVID-19 pandemic. J. Phys.: Conf. Ser. **1865**(4) (2021). https://doi.org/10.1088/1742-6596/1865/4/042019
12. Rezaei, M., Azarmi, M.: DeepSOCIAL: social distancing monitoring and infection risk assessment in COVID-19 pandemic. Appl. Sci. **10**(21) (2020). https://www.mdpi.com/2076-3417/10/21/7514
13. Kamalasanan, V., Sester, M.: Living with rules: an AR approach. In: Adjunct Proceedings of the 2020 IEEE International Symposium on Mixed and Augmented Reality, ISMAR-Adjunct 2020, pp. 213–216 (2020)
14. Delta variant: 8 things you should know | Coronavirus | UC Davis Health. https://health.ucdavis.edu/coronavirus/covid-19-information/delta-variant.html
15. COVID-19 vaccine tracker: View vaccinations by country. https://edition.cnn.com/interactive/2021/health/global-covid-vaccinations/
16. Li, M., Varble, N., Turkbey, B., Xu, S., Wood, B.J.: Camera-based distance detection and contact tracing to monitor potential spread of COVID-19. In: Mello-Thoms, C.R., Taylor-Phillips, S. (eds.) Medical Imaging 2022: Image Perception, Observer Performance, and Technology Assessment, vol. 12035, p. 120351D. International Society for Optics and Photonics. SPIE (2022). https://doi.org/10.1117/12.2612846

17. ibaiGorordo: Ibaigorordo/social-distance-feedback-for-the-blind: a social distancing feedback system for the blind using the oak-d camera. https://github.com/ibaiGorordo/Social-Distance-Feedback-For-The-Blind

18. Kanjee, R.: Social distance detection system - using raspberry pi and OpenCV AI kit. https://medium.com/augmented-startups/social-distance-detection-system-using-raspberry-pi-and-opencv-ai-kit-97fd68ff8dd4

19. Dai, Z., Jiang, Y., Li, Y., Liu, B., Chan, A.B., Vasconcelos, N.: BEV-net: assessing social distancing compliance by joint people localization and geometric reasoning. In: 2021 IEEE/CVF International Conference on Computer Vision (ICCV), pp. 5381–5391 (2021)

20. Mittal, R., Meneveau, C., Wu, W.: A mathematical framework for estimating risk of airborne transmission of COVID-19 with application to face mask use and social distancing. Phys. Fluids **32**, 101903 (2020)

21. Wells, W.: Airborne Contagion and Air Hygiene. An Ecological Study of Droplet Infections. Cambridge, MA (1955)

22. Riley, E., Murphy, G., Riley, R.: Airborne spread of measles in a suburban elementary school. Am. J. Epidemiol. **107**, 421–432 (1978)

23. To, G.N.S., Chao, C.Y.H.: Review and comparison between the wells-riley and dose-response approaches to risk assessment of infectious respiratory diseases. Indoor Air **20**, 2 (2010)

24. Mikszewski, A., Stabile, L., Buonanno, G., Morawska, L.: The airborne contagiousness of respiratory viruses: a comparative analysis and implications for mitigation. Geosci. Front. **13**, 101285 (2021)

25. Li, J., et al.: Evaluation of infection risk for SARS-CoV-2 transmission on university campuses. Sci. Technol. Built Environ. **27**, 1165–1180 (2021)

26. Buonanno, G., Morawska, L., Stabile, L.: Quantitative assessment of the risk of airborne transmission of SARS-CoV-2 infection: prospective and retrospective applications. Environ. Int. **145**, 106112 (2020)

27. Adams, W.: Measurement of breathing rate and volume in routinely performed daily activities (1993)

28. Teppner, R., Langensteiner, B., Meile, W., Brenn, G., Kerschbaumer, S.: Air change rates driven by the flow around and through a building storey with fully open or tilted windows: an experimental and numerical study. Energy Build. **80**, 570–583 (2014)

29. Eikenberry, S.E., et al.: To mask or not to mask: modeling the potential for face mask use by the general public to curtail the COVID-19 pandemic. Infect. Dis. Modell. **5** (2020)

30. Computer Vision Annotation Tool (2022). https://cvat.org/

31. GotG: How to train an object detector using mobilenet SSD V2 (2020). https://github.com/GotG/test_object_detection_demo/tree/master/data/medmask_voc

32. Roboflow (2022). https://roboflow.com/

33. Overview of OpenVINO^{TM} Toolkit Intel's Pre-trained Models (2022). https://docs.openvino.ai/latest/omz_models_group_intel.html

34. Luxonis: Luxonis mytiadx blob converter. http://blobconverter.luxonis.com

35. Luxonis: Spatial location calculator. https://docs.luxonis.com/projects/api/en/latest/components/nodes/spatial_location_calculator/

36. Velarde, F., Rub, R., Mamani-Paco, R., Andrade-Flores, M.: Estimation of the probability of contagion of COVID-19 by aerosols in closed environments: applications to cases in the city of La Paz, Bolivia, vol. 37, pp. 22–30 (2020) http://www.scielo.org.bo/scielo.php?script=sci_arttext&pid=S1562-38232020000200004&lng=es&nrm=iso

37. Liu, Z., et al.: Potential infection risk assessment of improper bioaerosol experiment operation in one BSL-3 laboratory based on the improved wells-riley method. Build. Environ. **201**, 107974 (2021)
38. Guo, Y., et al.: Assessing and controlling infection risk with wells-riley model and spatial flow impact factor (SFIF). Sustain. Cities Soc. **67**, 102719 (2021)
39. Wang, Z., Galea, E.R., Grandison, A., Ewer, J., Jia, F.: A coupled computational fluid dynamics and wells-riley model to predict COVID-19 infection probability for passengers on long-distance trains. Saf. Sci. **147**, 105572 (2022)
40. GotG: How to train an object detector using mobilenet SSD V2 (2020). https://github.com/GotG/test_object_detection_demo

Predictive Sentiment Analysis Model Regarding the Variation of the Dollar Exchange Rate

Joaquin Bernabe-Polo$^{(\boxtimes)}$, Yudi Guzmán-Monteza ,
and Elizabeth Puelles-Bulnes

National University of San Marcos, University City - Av. Germán Amézaga, Lima, Perú
{joaquin.bernabe,yudi.guzman,mpuellesb}@unmsm.edu.pe

Abstract. The benefits of sentiment analysis have become a topic of enormous interest in recent years. Obtaining information about this massive bank of social networks is essential. The dollar exchange rate for Peru, as well as for any country, is one of the most important economic indicators. Investment decisions made by national or international companies, as well as by governments, are based on the exchange rate. Exchange rate prediction is essential for future investors and companies. Twitter is the frequent mean by which people indicate their points of view about a specific topic. Therefore, in the present investigation, the proposal is described to analyze the trend of Twitter users for the dollar variation using open banking data and data from social networks as pillars. In the first phase, NB and RF were used and obtained an accuracy of 90% for both models' four (04) combinations. For the results of the second phase of the research, better results were obtained with the SVM algorithm, achieving a percentage of accuracy of 92.82% to predict the variation of the dollar exchange rate.

Keywords: Dollar Exchange Rate · Machine Learning · Sentiment Analysis · Social media

1 Introduction

Today it is of great interest to extract information from all documentary sources in which people express their opinions and interests for economic, political, or social purposes [1]. Sentiment analysis, also known as opinion mining, is instrumental in monitoring social networks as it allows us to get an idea of public opinion on specific topics [2].

Small, open economies like Peru's are constantly exposed to external and internal shocks. Given these circumstances, proper management of exchange rate policy plays an essential role in assimilating these shocks [3]. The exchange rate for Peru, as well as for any country, is one of the most important economic indicators. Investment decisions made by national or international companies, as well as by governments, are based on the exchange rate. So, exchange rate prediction is essential for future investors and companies.

Therefore, being such a relevant issue in the economic situation in Peru, social networks such as Twitter are a frequent medium in which people indicate their points

J. A. Lossio-Ventura et al. (Eds.): SIMBig 2022, CCIS 1837, pp. 113–125, 2023.
https://doi.org/10.1007/978-3-031-35445-8_9

of view about this issue. "Twitter is a platform that allows participating in the global conversation of varied audiences; due to the chronological transmission and the ability to follow tweets outside its network through a label (#Hashtag), keyword or username, it allows the audience to follow the media, political actors and other members of the public" [4].

Previously, data mining has been used to know the trends of voters and thus effectively carry out political campaigns in presidential elections. An example of the good results of its use is evidenced in the article by Cellan-Jones [5] on the presidential elections in the United States, the case of Donald Trump.

According to Ranjit S. et al. (2018) [6], two kinds of analysis are mainly used to predict the exchange rate: technical and fundamental. Technical analysis, in theory, is that a person can look at historical price movements and determine that history tends to repeat itself, and then-current trading reflects old age. It mainly looks for similar patterns that formed in the past and forms trade ideas believing that price will act the same way it did before. Fundamental analysis deals with economic and social forces that may cause deflection on current market rates. In the line of Ranjit S. et al. (2018) [6], Muhammad Y. et al. (2019) [7] considered a fundamental analysis because they analyze sensitives factors like social and political events, gold and crude oil prices that could impact the currency market and incorporated a sentiment analysis for local and foreign affairs to enhance the accuracy of the exchange rate. In this research, only a technical study was applied by collecting data on the dollar variation through the social network Twitter and banking data from the Central Reserve Bank (BCR) of Peru for the year 2021. This data shows the dollar's upward trend in Peru in the run-up to the second round of presidential elections, reflecting the influence of factors such as political uncertainty and the start of the economic slowdown.

Also, if you make financial trades at the right time with the right approach, you can profit, but an unknowing transaction can cause huge losses. Therefore, predicting the movement of the financial market has become challenging. In the present investigation, the proposal to carry out a predictive model is described, analyzing the trend of Twitter users concerning the variation of the dollar to know the movement of the dollar exchange rate in Peru during the year 2021. The phases are the related work reviewing, dataset, methodology, experimental setup, results, discussions, and finally, the conclusions.

2 Background and Related Works

Batra et al. [8] used Apple's sentiment data (Tweets) extracted from StockTwits. Three hundred thousand tweets were removed as a JSON object. JSON data was converted to CSV file format. In addition, Apple stock data is extracted from Yahoo Finance from 2010 to 2017. The SVM model suggests whether a person should buy or sell a stock. Two SVM models were created, i.e., one for sentiment analysis of stock tweets and one model for predicting stock movement. For the SVM Sentiment model, the achieved test accuracy is 63.5%, and for the SVM Stock model, the completed test accuracy is 76.68%.

In Kordonis' research, [9] it is emphasized that measuring public sentiment by retrieving online information from Twitter can be valuable in forming business strategies. The correct prediction of the fluctuation of stock prices depends on many factors and arguably includes public opinion. The work is based on two datasets, the first contains the costs of the shares obtained with Yahoo! Finance API, and the second includes a collection of tweets using the Twitter Search API divided by days. This project examines two classifiers used for text classification: Naive Bayes and Support Vector Machines (SVM). To successfully use Twitter sentiment scores to predict stock market movements, each classifier was trained and tested on a particular subset of our tweet corpus using 7-fold cross-validation. Finally, with SVM, an average accuracy of 87% was obtained for the correct stock movement prediction.

Mankar's [10] research details that any positive or negative public sentiment related to a particular company can ripple affect its share prices. The work focuses on the tweet's time and text for a more detailed analysis. Two classifiers were mainly examined: Naïve Bayes and Support Vector Machine. The same features were extracted from the tweets for each classifier to classify them. Based on the comparative study that was carried out, the Support Vector Machine proved to be the most efficient and feasible model to predict the movement of the stock price in favor of the sentiments of the tweets with an accuracy of 64.10%.

Yasir [7] is based on a data set that provides information on the exchange rate of currencies from April 2018 to January 2019. The article proposes a deep learning-based currency exchange rate prediction technique using Linear Regression, Support Vector Regression, and ANN. The results show that the foreign exchange market is highly dependent on socio-political factors, problems, and greater accuracy can only be achieved if these events, known sentiments in this study, are considered when predicting the exchange rate.

Zaidi [11] in the work he, used 76 think tanks that actively operated Twitter accounts. On the other hand, for the OC (oil crude) dataset, the relevant oil companies and associations listed 52 oil companies and associations that operated active Twitter accounts, thus obtaining the most recent 3,200 tweets from each username. Support Vector Machine (SVM), Naïve Bayes, and multilayer perception (ML) were used, whose number of layers and neurons was initially tuned.

"Sentiment analysis, also known as opinion mining, is instrumental in monitoring social networks as it allows us to get an idea of public opinion on certain topics" [2].

"Twitter is a platform that allows participating in the global conversation of varied audiences, due to the chronological transmission and the ability to follow tweets outside its network through a label (#hashtag), keyword or username, allows the audience follow the media, political actors and other members of the public" [4].

Machine learning, machine learning has become one of the pillars of information technology and, with it, a reasonably central, although usually hidden, part of our lives. With the ever-increasing amount of data available, intelligent data analytics will become even more ubiquitous as a necessary ingredient for technological progress. [12].

Therefore, the general architecture adopted for the prediction is based on phases using three classifiers: Random Forest (RF), Naive Bayes (NB), and Support Vector Machine (SVM). In the first phase, RF and NB will be used to predict the trend of Twitter users, and in the second phase, the output of the first phase will be used as input, RF, and SVM to predict the value of the final exchange rate.

3   Dataset

In the present investigation regarding the variation of the dollar exchange rate, we will work with two datasets stored in ".csv" files.

The Twitter dataset is compiled using the Python Snscrape library on the Twitter social network, considering the Keyword: 'dollar.' In addition, the time range of the tweets will be limited from January 1, 2021, to December 31, 2021, Twitter metadata collection was monthly, and data analysis was daily in the indicated range. The results for Peru will be filtered. We obtained a total of 20736 tweets.

The banking dataset is obtained from the BCRP data for the dollar exchange rate. The numerical values were discretized; all discretized values were compared with the previous day's opening and closing prices to predict the value of the next day's dollar exchange rate.

Regarding the spatiality of the data obtained, it was filtered using the Twitter metadata, specifically with the 'user.location' feature of the Snscrape library, to get records from the locality of Lima and Peru.

4   Methodology

As mentioned before, first, we extracted a total of 20736 tweets. Second, because the social network data present inconsistencies, emoticons, unnecessary data, etc., the preprocessing and treatment of these were carried out.

As shown in Fig. 1, the data from social networks will be processed, for which different pre-processing techniques were used.

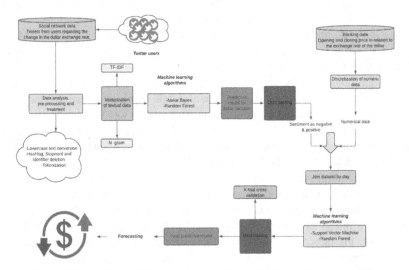

Fig. 1. Methodology. Note. Adaptation of [13, 14], Own elaboration (2021)

This is done because tweets contain unwanted elements, such as user mentions, hashtags, etc., so performing this phase before feature extraction is essential. The applied preprocessing techniques were:

- Converting text to lowercase. – This will be done to reduce the dictionary of words so as not to recognize words that are essentially the same (case difference) as different.
- Elimination of hashtags and Identifiers. – Both features are widely used by Twitter users but do not add value to the analysis.
- Elimination of Stopwords. – These words do not add value to the analysis.
- Tokenization. – They will segment tweets into independent words.
- Stemming. – Aims to eliminate affixes and inflectional extensions to obtain the word's root.

As shown in Fig. 5, the next step is vectorizing the text, for which N-gram and TF-IDF will be used. TF-IDF will be used to evaluate the weights of the words in the document. This investigation used unigrams and bigrams; the data were processed word by word and in pairs.

Once the processed data was obtained, the models were implemented. In the first phase, the Random Forest Classifier and Multinomial Naive Bayes (MNB) models provided by the Python library 'sklearn' were used. The first phase is the classification stage, in which the RF and NB algorithms will be used to predict the trend of the previously classified tweets. Ranjit S. et al. (2018) applied sentiment analysis using Naïve Bayes and lexicon strategies to perform the sentiment analysis of different traders to classify the tweets as positive or negative [6]. Both models will be trained and tested according to the percentage partitions of 70-30, 75-25, and 80-20 for each dataset resulting from the text's vectorization (unigrams and bigrams). These results were the input for the second phase, in which the banking dataset was used together with the output of the first phase, joining the information per day to predict the Dollar Exchange Rate's value. Finally, forecasting will be made on the Dollar Exchange Rate.

In the second phase, the RF and SVM models were used. They used a procedure analogous to the first phase. The Random Forest Regressor and SVM (SVR) models, also offered by the same library, were used for the second phase.

Figure 2 depicts an example of tweet preprocessing, having the raw tweet as input, and the result of applying the techniques described above. As a first step, we perform the tokenization of the tweets; once the tokens are obtained, the hashtags, user mentions, punctuation marks, the "URL," numbers, and emoticons are eliminated. In addition, the tokens that are part of the Python NLTK stopwords for the Spanish language will be removed. Finally, the Stemming was carried out.

5   Experimental Setup.

Vectorization of the Text
Term Frequency – Inverse Document Frequency (TF-IDF)
Stands for term frequency times inverse document frequency. It is term frequency over document frequency, which depicts how often this word occurs in the document compared to how usually it appears in the entire body of documents [15].

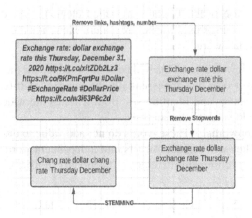

Fig. 2. Tweet pre-processing Example

The TF-IDF algorithm is a quantitative metric mainly used to determine the importance of a word or term and assign the value based on the number of occurrences within a document.

To calculate these weights, the formulas in Fig. 3 and Fig. 4 are used to find the TF and IDF, respectively, according to the term or document numbers.

$$TF(f) = \frac{(The\ amount\ of\ occasions\ the\ term\ t\ is\ seen\ in\ the\ document)}{(Total\ number\ of\ terms\ in\ the\ document)}$$

$$TF(f) = \frac{(The\ amount\ of\ occasions\ the\ term\ t\ is\ seen\ in\ the\ document)}{(Total\ number\ of\ terms\ in\ the\ document)}$$

Fig. 3. Term frequency. Note. Taken from [15].

$$IDF(t) = \log\frac{(Total\ number\ of\ documents)}{(Number\ of\ documents\ with\ term\ t\ in\ it)}$$

$$TFIDF(t) = TF(t) * IDF(t)$$

$$IDF(t) = \log\frac{(Total\ number\ of\ documents)}{(Number\ of\ documents\ with\ term\ t\ in\ it)}$$

$$TFIDF(t) = TF(t) * IDF(t)$$

Fig. 4. TF-IDF. Note. Taken from [15].

N-gram

It is the collection of n elements of a document. N-gram features indicate a specific number of tokens that help to understand the meaning of the token considering its context. Depending on the objective, the preceding word in an N-gram sentence is a negation or could be unigram, bigram, or n-gram, which can understand the context of each document element [16].

Machine Learning Algorithms

Support Vector Machine (SVM)

The SVM can be defined as a vector space-based method that establishes a decision boundary between two classes by calculating the maximum distance between the hyperplane and its closest random points. The goal is to design a hyperplane in N-dimensional space (N - the number of features) that classifies the training vectors of the two classes [17, 18].

The graphic representation is exemplified in Fig. 5, where the maximum margin in the hyperplane is sought, thus obtaining the optimal hyperplane.

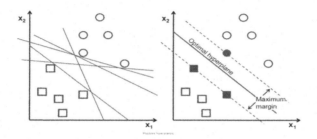

Fig. 5. Support Vector Machines. Note. Taken from [18].

Naive Bayes

They are based on the principles of conditional probability as given by Bayes' Theorem. It is mainly used to classify text that includes a high-dimensional data set.

Nave Bayes classifier is a predictive model, which is easier to apply. Let X = x, x, x, ...X be the sample set, and C, C, C,...C be the set of classes [17].

Detailing the Naive Bayes formula shown in Fig. 6, we have:

- P (c|x) is the posterior probability
- P (c) is the class prior probability.
- P (x|c) is the probability of the given class of the predictor.
- P (x) is the prior probability of the predictor.

$$P(c|x) = \frac{P(x|c)P(c)}{P(x)}$$

$$P(c|x) = P(x_1|c)\,x\,P(x_2|c)\,x\,\ldots\,x\,P(x_n|c)\,x\,P(c)$$

$$P(c|x) = \frac{P(x|c)P(c)}{P(x)}$$

$P(c|x) = P(x_1|c) \times P(x_2|c) \times \ldots \times P(x_n|c) \times P(c)$

Fig. 6. Naïve Bayes. Note. Taken from [19].

Random Forest

Random forest (RF) is a supervised learning algorithm. RF is an ensemble of decision trees on various sub-samples of the dataset that combine tree predictors. Each tree depends on the values of a random vector with a uniform distribution for all trees in the forest [20].

Likewise, the research uses the Python GridSearchCV library to estimate the best hyperparameters for the RF (Classifier and Regressor) and SVM models, leaving the default parameters for the MNB model. Table 1 shows the parameters evaluated for the RF Classifier model, which estimation result gives the following values as the best parameters: N_Estimators: 100, Max_features: "sqrt.", Max_depth: None, Criterion: "Gini."

Table 1. Parameters evaluated for RF Classifier

N_Estimators	Max_features	Max_depth	Criterion
100	"sqrt"	None	"gini"
200	"log2"	2	"entropy"
300		4	"log_loss"
400		6	
500		8	

Table 2 shows the parameters evaluated for the RF Regressor model, whose estimation result gives the following values as the best parameters: N_Estimators: 100, Max_features: "sqrt," Max_depth: 6, Criterion: "squared_error".

Table 3 shows the parameters evaluated for the SVM model and whose estimation result is obtained as the best parameters in the following values: C: 10000, Epsilon: 0.0000006 (1e-06), Gamma: 0.001.

Once the parameters of the models have been obtained, they will pass to the training stage, as shown in Fig. 5. The RF model will be trained and tested according to the percentage partitions of 70–30, 75–25, and 80–20. And for the SVM model will be carried out under a cross-validation of K = 5 (K-folds cross-validation) that divides the total data into K parts, selecting one piece for testing and the rest for training. After this, the forecasting of the variation of the exchange rate will be carried out.

Table 2. Parameters evaluated for the RF Regressor model

N_Estimators	Max_features	Max_depth	Criterion
100	"sqrt"	None	"squared_error"
200	"log2"	2	"absolute_error"
300		4	"Poisson"
400		6	
500		8	

Table 3. Parameters evaluated for the SVM model

C	Épsilon	Gamma
0.0001	0.000001	0.000001
0.01	0.00001	0.00001
0.1	0.0001	0.0001
1	0.001	0.001
10	0.01	0.01
100	0.1	0.1
1000	1	1
10000	10	10
100000	100	100
1000000	1000	1000
10000000	10000	10000

6 Results and Discussion

The tweets were classified in the first phase to have an adequate model for determining the daily trend using the Naive Bayes and Random Forest algorithms. The best accuracy was obtained by dividing the dataset by 75% for train and 25% for testing.

Precision, Recall, F1_Score, and Accuracy were applied to measure the algorithms' performance. The results of each model using Unigrams and Bigrams are shown in Table 4:

Table 4 shows the results of the first phase of the investigation. Unigram and bigram datasets were applied, obtaining similar results for the models according to different percentage partitions like 70% and 30% for train and test, respectively; 75% and 25% for train and test, respectively; 80% and 20% for train and test respectively. However, when comparing the results with the different percentage partitions, better results are obtained when the models are trained with 75% of the data, highlighting that an increase in the percentage of data used for training does not increase the accuracy of the models, on the contrary, they are reduced.

Table 4. Results of the models with the percentage partition 75-25

Algorithms	Precision	Recall	F1_Score	Accuracy
NaiveBayes - Unigram	0.901459854	0.901459854	0.901459854	0.901459854
NaiveBayes - Bigram	0.901459854	0.901459854	0.901459854	0.901459854
RandomForest - Unigram	0.901459854	0.901459854	0.901459854	0.901459854
RandomForest - Bigram	0.901459854	0.901459854	0.901459854	0.901459854

Figure 7 and Fig. 8 show a line and bar chart, respectively, to represent the actual versus predicted values using a 75% and 25% partition for training and testing data, respectively. It is evident that there is no significant difference between the actual and predicted values for the month of January 2022.

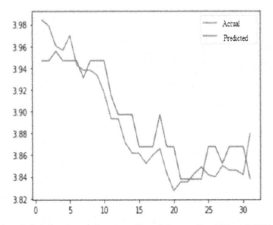

Fig. 7. Lineal Graph of actual vs. predicted data using RF and SVM models.

Table 5 shows the result of the SVM algorithm using cross-validation. We obtain 0.009605179 and 0.000232213 for the MAE and MSE metrics, respectively. It is evident that in the second phase of the research, better results of the percentage of correctness are obtained with the SVM algorithmic technique.

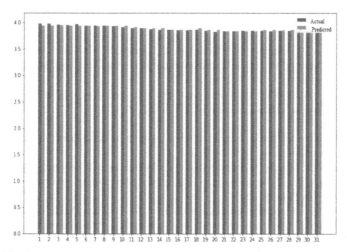

Fig. 8. Bar Graph of actual vs. predicted data using RF and SVM models

Table 5. SVM model results using cross-validation

Algorithm	Score Mean	MAE (Mean Absolute Error)	MSE (Mean Squared Error)
SVM	0.928261809	0.009605179	0.000232213

7 Conclusions

This research analyzes the productivity of the algorithms used in the two (02) phases. In the first phase, NB and RF are used with the selected evaluation metrics such as Accuracy, Recall, F1 Score, and Accuracy, thus obtaining a better result using the percentage partition of 75% and 25% for training and testing, respectively, having an accuracy of 90% for the four (04) combinations of both models.

For the results of the second phase of the research, better results are obtained with the SVM algorithm, achieving a percentage of accuracy of 92.82% to predict the variation of the dollar exchange rate and with an approximation of 2×10^{-4} as the minimum error rate using MSE.

In sentiment analysis, the efficiency of ML models such as Naïve Bayes and Random Forest was demonstrated. It is also shown that for the predictive model, the SVM technique yields favorable results for predicting the percentage of success concerning the change in the daily dollar exchange rate. However, in any case, and with any other market, a prediction tool cannot guarantee success in predicting the dollar exchange rate on all occasions.

There needs to be more research on Twitter's sentiment analysis of the economic context in Peru. Investors, politicians, financial analysts, data scientists, and researchers can take advantage of the utility of our model, which performs a sentiment analysis and predicts the variation of the Dollar Exchange Rate as a significant economic indicator for our country.

References

1. Soto, B., Vega, H., Guzmán, Y., Rodriguez, C., Quinto, D.: Classification algorithm based on machine learning to optimize athletes talent detection. Test Eng. Manage. **83**(13464), 13464–13471 (2020)

2. Bannister, K.: Análisis de sentimiento: qué es y para qué se usa I Brandwatch, 10 Febrero 2015. https://www.brandwatch.com/es/blog/analisis-de-sentimiento/. Accessed 10 Octubre 2021

3. Ribeiro, J.: El rol del tipo de cambio en Perú: ¿Amortiguador o fuente de choques? Revista de análisis económico **33**(2), 79–89 (2018)

4. McGregor, S.C., Mourão, R.R., Molyneux, L.: Twitter as a tool for and object of political and electoral activity: considering electoral context and variance among actors. J. Inform. Technol. Politics 154–167 (2017)

5. Cellan-Jones, R.: Elecciones en Estados Unidos: ¿fue Facebook la clave para el triunfo de Donald Trump?, 11 Noviembre 2016. https://www.bbc.com/mundo/noticias-internacional-37946548

6. Ranjit, S., Shrestha, S., Subedi, S., Shakya, S.: Foreign rate exchange prediction using neural network and sentiment analysis. In: IEEE 2018 International Conference on Advances in Computing, Communication Control and Networking, Greater Noida, 2018

7. Yasir, M., et al.: An intelligent event-sentiment-based daily foreign exchange rate forecasting system. Appl. Sci. (2019)

8. Batra, R., Daudpota, S.M.: Integrating StockTwits with sentiment analysis for better prediction of stock price movement. iCoMET, pp. 1–5 (2018)

9. Kordonis, J., Symeonidis, S., Arampatzis, A.: Stock price forecasting via sentiment analysis on Twitter. In: ACM International Conference Proceeding Series (2016)

10. Mankar, T., Hotchandani, T., Madhwani, M., Chidrawar, A., Lifna, C.S.: Stock market prediction based on social sentiments using machine learning. In: 2018 International Conference on Smart City and Emerging Technology (2018)

11. Zaidi, A., Oussalah, M.: Forecasting weekly crude oil using twitter sentiment of U.S. foreign policy and oil companies data. In: 2018 IEEE 19th International Conference on Information Reuse and Integration for Data Science, Salt Lake City (2018)

12. Osisanwo, F.Y., Akinsola, J.E.T., Awodele, O., Hinmikaiye, J.O., Olakanmi, O., Akinjobi, J.:Supervised machine learning algorithms: classification and comparison. Int. J. Comput. Trends Technol. 128–138 (2017)

13. Khedr, A.E., Salama, S.E., Yaseen, N.: Predicting stock market behavior using data mining technique and news sentiment analysis. Int. J. Intell. Syst. Appl. 22–30 (2017)

14. Chen, S., Gao, T., He, Y., Jin, Y.: Predicting the stock price movement by social media analysis. J. Data Anal. Inform. Process. 295–305 (2019)

15. Pimpalkar, A.P., Raj, R.J.R.: Influence of pre-processing strategies on the performance of ML classifiers exploiting TF-IDF and BOW Features. ADCAIJ: Adv. Distrib. Comput. Artific. Intell. J. 49–68 (2020)

16. Wan, Y., Gao, Q.: An ensemble sentiment classification system of twitter data for airline services analysis. In: 15th IEEE International Conference on Data Mining Workshop, Atlantic City (2016)

17. Basarslan, M.S., Kayaalp, F.: Sentiment analysis with machine learning methods on social media. ADCAIJ 5–15 (2020)

18. Gandhi, R.: Support Vector Machine—Introduction to Machine Learning Algorithms" 07 Junio 2018. https://towardsdatascience.com/support-vector-machine-introduction-to-machine-learning-algorithms-934a444fca47

19. Ray, S.: Commonly Used Machine Learning Algorithms | Data Science, 09 Setiembre 2017. https://www.analyticsvidhya.com/blog/2017/09/common-machine-learning-algorithms/
20. Vicente, S.: El uso de dispositivos inteligentes y "machine learning" para la predicción de enfermedades, Universidad de Sevilla, pp. 1–29, 03 Setiembre 2019

Maximising Influence Spread in Complex Networks by Utilising Community-Based Driver Nodes as Seeds

Abida Sadaf[1]($\boxtimes$), Luke Mathieson[1], Piotr Bródka[2], and Katarzyna Musial[1]

[1] Complex Adaptive Systems Lab, School of Computer Science,
University of Technology Sydney, Sydney, Australia
`abida.sadaf@student.uts.edu.au`
[2] Department of Artificial Intelligence, Wroclaw University of Science
and Technology, Wroclaw, Poland
`http://www.uts.edu.au`, `https://pwr.edu.pl/`

Abstract. Finding a small subset of influential nodes to maximise influence spread in a complex network is an active area of research. Different methods have been proposed in the past to identify a set of seed nodes that can help achieve a faster spread of influence in the network. This paper combines driver node selection methods from the field of network control, with the divide-and-conquer approach of using community structure to guide the selection of candidate seed nodes from the driver nodes of the communities.

The use of driver nodes in communities as seed nodes is a comparatively new idea. We identify communities of synthetic (i.e., Random, Small-World and Scale-Free) networks as well as twenty-two real-world social networks. Driver nodes from those communities are then ranked according to a range of common centrality measures. We compare the influence spreading power of these seed sets to the results of selecting driver nodes at a global level. We show that in both synthetic and real networks, exploiting community structure enhances the power of the resulting seed sets.

Keywords: Influence · Complex Network · Social Networks · Seed Selection Methods · Driver Nodes · Communities

1 Introduction

Due to the prevailing use of online social networking sites, social networks are very much a hot topic in network science. Nowadays, we have a good understanding of network structures and attention has shifted more towards their prediction, influence, and control. Full control of social networks is very hard to achieve due to their varying structures, dynamics, and the complexities of human behaviour. This study looks into how driver nodes, which enable complex network control, can be used in the context of influence spread in the social network space. We use driver nodes at both the local and community level to 'divide and conquer' the

© The Author(s), under exclusive license to Springer Nature Switzerland AG 2023
J. A. Lossio-Ventura et al. (Eds.): SIMBig 2022, CCIS 1837, pp. 126–141, 2023.
https://doi.org/10.1007/978-3-031-35445-8_10

time-consuming problem of driver node identification. Until recently, we did not know if and how the structure of social networks correlated with the number of driver nodes required to control the network [21]. As driver nodes play a key role in achieving control of a complex network, identifying them and studying their correlation with network structure measures can bring valuable insights, such as what network structures are easier to control, and how we can alter the structure in our favour to achieve the maximum control over the network. Our previous work [21] determines the relationship between some global network structure measures and the number of driver nodes. This study builds an understanding of how global network profiles of synthetic (random, small-world, scale-free) and real social networks influence the number of driver nodes needed for control. It focuses on global structural measures such as network density and how it can play an important role in determining the size of a suitable set of driver nodes. Our results show that as density increases in networks with structures exhibited by random, small world and scale free networks, the number of driver nodes tends to decrease. In this work we explore the potential that exploiting local structures (in this study we focus on communities) can offer in developing control of, and influencing, the network. Finding communities in a social network is itself a difficult task due to both dynamic and combinatorial factors [24].

This study explores the possibility of using community structure in social networks to reduce the cost of identifying driver nodes, and whether this remains a feasible approach for network control and influence spread methods.

Our main research questions for this work are stated as follows:

1. How can we rank driver nodes within communities to identify an optimal subset of driver nodes for use as seed nodes?
2. How quickly does influence spread from seed nodes chosen using driver node selection methods at the community level?
3. Does the percentage of influenced nodes increases or decreases when using driver node based seed selection methods in communities as compared to driver node based seed selection methods in the network as a whole, for both synthetic and real data?
4. How does the network structure (of synthetic or real networks) impact the percentage of nodes influenced with each method?

This paper contains the following sections: Sect. 2 describes related work and the main research challenge that is the focus of this study. Sections 3 and 4 describe (i) the research methodology in detail and (ii) include results and analysis of the experiments performed respectively. Finally, the conclusions drawn from the experiments and future work are discussed in Sect. 5.

2 Related Work

The Influence Maximisation problem aims at discovering an influential set of nodes that can influence the highest number of nodes in social networks in the shortest possible time. A set of these nodes can be used to propagate influence in terms of social media news, advertising, etc. Several algorithms have been proposed to solve the influence maximisation problem that identify a set of nodes that is highly influential as compared to other nodes. For example Basic Greedy [13], CELF [14], CELF++ [10], Static Greedy [5], Nguyen's Method [20], Brog et al.'s Method [1], SKIM [6], TIM+ [26], IMM [25], Stop and Stare [18], Zohu et al.'s Method [28] and BCT [19] are some of those algorithms. Many algorithms have high run times when identifying a set of nodes to diffuse the influence through a social network, therefore there is a need to work on exploring different types of nodes if those can work towards achieving the high influence [12]. The problem of influence maximisation has high relevancy to the spreading of information on networks. The two most common network-based models are Independent Cascade model [13] and Threshold models [11]. In one of the previously proposed framework, the possible seed set has been identified by analysing the properties of the community structures in the networks. The CIM algorithm (i.e. Community-Based Influence Maximisation), utilises hierarchical clustering to detect communities from the networks and then uses the information of community structures to identify the possible seed nodes candidates, and at the end the final seed set is selected from the candidate seed nodes [4]. From the previous work such as [4] and [12], we can see, that by detecting communities and then selecting seed nodes from those communities can be an effective strategy to maximise influence.

From previous study [21], following main results were achieved, which are the basis for further new experiments in this current research work.

- Correlation between network density and number of driver nodes: For this purpose, network densities and number of driver nodes in those networks are plotted against each other to see the increase/decrease in number of driver nodes with the increase/decrease in the densities of the networks.
- Structural measures and density of driver nodes: In this step a comparison of structural measures like (Betweenness Centrality, Closeness Centrality, Nodes, Edges, Eigenvector Centrality and Clustering Coefficient) is presented with the density of number of driver nodes. Density of number of driver nodes is defined as total number of driver nodes divided by total number of nodes in the network.

In our proposed methods, we utilise driver nodes within the communities of networks for the influence spread using Linear Threshold Model. To make the driver nodes more influential, we propose different ranking mechanisms to see the number of nodes influenced after a certain time with a certain percentage of seed nodes in synthetic as well as real networks. The detail of network datasets has been presented in the later sections. We explain our method to select seed nodes from the communities in the next section.

3 Methodology

This work springs from the question, whether network control methods, in particular driver node selection, can be used to improve seed selection in influence models.

This prompts two possible approaches: (i) using driver nodes selected from the network as a whole, and (ii) using driver nodes selected at the community level as seeds. For all experiments, we used the Linear Threshold Model to model influence propagation. We used a set threshold of 0.5 for the network diffusion model. We have previously observed that a threshold value of at least 0.4 accelerates influence propagation [4].

3.1   Datasets Description

To enable comprehensive and robust testing of the proposed approaches, both generated and real-world social networks have been used. Following is a brief description of networks used in the experiments.

1. Generated Networks: we generated random, small-world and scale free networks from network size of (100, 200, 300, 400, 500) nodes. For each network size (from 100 to 500), we generated networks with increasing density, to the maximum density of 1. A total of 720 networks were generated [21].
2. Social Networks: we use 22 real-world social networks of varying size, the number of nodes and number of edges are presented in Table 2. The networks are available for download at SNAP[1].

3.2   Influence Spread Using Global Driver Nodes as Seeds

The first experiment focuses on the seed selection process from the global perspective. Driver nodes are selected from the network as a whole, ranked, and finally used as seeds in the influence process. The below described approach has been proposed in [22]. As it outperforms other state-of-the art ranking methods, it serves in this study as a benchmark to show a difference between global- and local-level seed selection methods. The steps are as follows:

1. Minimum Dominating Set method [17] has been used to identify the number of driver nodes from the networks. More detail of this process can be found in [21]. DMS has been found by using greedy algorithm. At start, the dominating set is empty. Then in each iteration of the algorithm, a vertex is added to the set such that it covers the maximum number of previously uncovered vertices. Then, if more than one vertex fulfils this criteria, the vertex is added randomly among the set of nominated vertices [23].
2. We ranked the nodes using different ranking mechanisms. The goal was to achieve an efficient set of nodes as seeds that can achieve maximum or full influence more quickly. The ranking mechanisms used are: Random, Degree Centrality, Closeness Centrality, Betweenness Centrality, Kempe Ranking, Degree-Closeness-Betweenness. We tested various seed set sizes: 1%, 10%, 20%, 30%, 40% and 50% of all detected driver nodes ranked these methods. In each of the methods, the driver nodes are ranked based on the following measures:

---

[1] http://snap.stanford.edu/.

– In Random (Driver Random – DR) we ranked the driver nodes randomly.
– In Degree seed selection (DD) we ranked the driver nodes based on their degree in descending order.
– For Closeness Centrality based seed selection method (Driver Closeness – DC), we ranked the nodes on the basis of their closeness centrality in descending order.
– For Betweenness Centrality based seed selection method (Driver Betweenness – DB), we ranked the nodes on the basis of their betweenness centrality in descending order.
– For Degree-Closeness-Betweenness method (Driver Degree Closeness Betweenness – DDCB), we ranked (in descending order) the driver nodes on the basis of the average of degree, closeness and betweenness centralities of each driver nodes.
– For Kempe ranking (Driver Kempe – DK), we start by spreading influence through all the driver nodes as seed nodes. So we calculate the total number of nodes influenced by each driver node already in the seed set, and then rank them in descending order. After ranking, we select a percentage of nodes that are required for a seed set.
– Linear Threshold Model (LTM) has been implemented for influence spread process. In LTM the idea is that a node becomes active if a sufficient part of its neighbourhood is active. Each node u has a threshold $t \in [0, 1]$. The threshold represents the fraction of neighbours of u that must be active in order for u to become active. At the beginning of the process, a small percentage of nodes (seeds) is set as active in order to start the process. In the next steps a node becomes active if the fraction of its active neighbours is greater than its threshold, and the whole process stops when no node is activated in the current step [7].

3.3   Influence Spread Using Local Driver Nodes as Seeds

The second experiment employs a new strategy: first identify communities in the network, and then identify driver nodes on a per-community basis.

Once driver nodes for each community are identified, they are then ranked using the same ranking mechanisms as in the first experiment, with seed sets chosen to cover all communities (detailed below). In detail, the approach is as follows:

1. Firstly, communities are identified in the network. This was done using Girvan-Newman algorithm [9]. The Girvan-Newman algorithm detects communities by progressively removing edges from the original graph in order of the highest betweenness centrality.
2. Within each community, candidate driver nodes were identified using the Minimum Dominating Set [17] approach as used with the whole network. Correlation between community densities and number of driver nodes is found by obtaining densities of the communities and identifying number of driver nodes in those communities by MDS method. Difference (Diff.) between total

number of driver nodes identified in overall networks (NDN) as compared to
the number of driver nodes found in communities of those networks (NDNC)
is also obtained. The Diff. tells us, the significance of identifying driver nodes
within communities, like following a divide and conquer approach.

3. To rank the nodes, we introduce a multi-round selection process. This process
effectively ranks driver nodes within each community according to the ranking criterion, then selects one node per community per round, in the order
given by the ranking, until the total percentage to be chosen is reached. This
is perhaps better explained by the following example, illustrated in Fig. 1.
Consider a network with 1,000 nodes and 6 communities. Select a ranking
method, in this case the node degree. Choose a target percentage of nodes to
use as seed nodes, 1% in the example. Now, in order to choose 10 nodes from
the driver nodes detected in the communities, we select 6 nodes at first – the
highest degree node from each community, marked in yellow in the figure.
In the second round, we can select at most 4 nodes to reach the target of
10 – from each community, we take the node with the second-highest node
degree and rank these nodes according to their degrees and take the 4 nodes
with the highest degree. We choose the same ranking mechanism for all the
community based driver nodes seed selection methods i.e., the highest node
degree, apart from the original ranking that is different in each technique as
explained previously.

4. Influence spread in the overall network using Driver Based Seed Selection
Methods is done by following a series of steps. Starting from identification of
driver nodes from the networks, ranking of driver nodes based upon Random,
Node Degree, Closeness Centrality, Betweenness Centrality, Kempe Ranking,
Degree-Closeness-Betweenness Centralities combined. After ranking of driver
nodes, we selected our seed set on the basis of percentage of nodes from that
set. We run our LTM for different seed sets, namely for example 1%, 10%,
20%, 30%, 40% and 50%.

5. Influence spread through Driver Nodes in communities of Networks is done
by identifying driver nodes in communities. However, there was a challenge of
getting the ultimate seed set that has representation from all the communities
of the network. For this purpose, we devised our ranking approach that makes
sure that at least one driver node is selected from each community of the
network to make sure that the nodes in those communities can also be part
of the influence process. For each of the driver based seed selection methods,
we used one unified approach to further rank the nodes so that we are able
to select at least one node from each of the communities.

4   Results and Analysis

Six novel network level seed selection methods (i.e. Driver-Random (DR),
Driver-Degree (DD), Driver-Closeness (DC), Driver-Betweenness (DB), Driver-
Kempe (DK) and Driver-Degree-Closeness-Betweenness (DDCB)) have been
proposed and tested on synthetic and real world networks before in [22] and

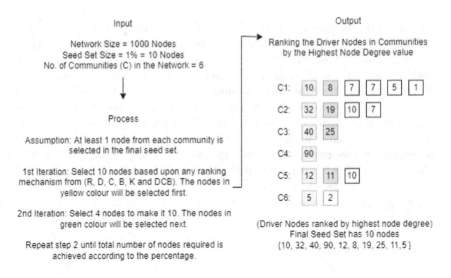

Fig. 1. An example showing the process for selecting seed nodes set from the driver nodes identified in network communities

the results show that those methods outperform their non-driver based counterparts. In this study, we use those methods but instead of selecting driver nodes from the global network, we propose a local approach where driver nodes are identified within the networks' communities. We name the new methods by adding C (for community) to the previously proposed methods (i.e., DRC - Driver-Random-Community, DDC - Driver-Degree-Community, DCC - Driver-Closeness-Community, DBC - Driver-Betweenness-Community, DKC - Driver-Kempe-Community and DDCBC - Driver-Degree-Closeness-Betweenness-Community). Below, we compare community based driver seed selection methods to network based driver seed selection methods.

4.1   Results from Generated Networks

This section covers the results and analysis of the experiments performed on generated networks.

What is the Speed and Reach of the Influence Spread? First, we compare the percentage of nodes influenced for global-level driver based seed selection methods and local-level (community) driver based seed selection methods. We perform the analysis iteration by iteration to see which seed selection methods enable to achieve the highest coverage the fastest.

In Fig. 2, we can see trend-lines for all the seed selection methods (when seed set size is 1% of all the driver nodes) for random, small-world and scale-free networks. DDCBC method outperforms other methods in almost all the experimented cases. We can see a 'head-start' in the trend-line of DDCBC (represented

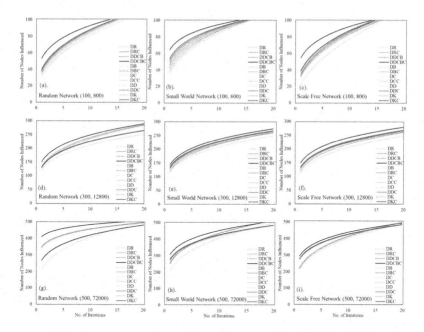

Fig. 2. Number of Nodes Influenced in Random, Small-World and Scale-Free Networks: when the number of nodes (N) is 100 and the number of edges (E) is 800 (Figures a, b and c); when N is 300 and E is 12800 (Figures d, e and f); when N is 500 and E is 72000 (Figures g, h and i). A Comparison of all methods for 20 iterations when the seed size is 1% is presented.

in black colour) for all the networks when number of nodes in the network is 100 and number of edges is 800. This means that in only few iterations, DDCBC enables to influence more nodes than in the case of other seed selection methods.

Results in Fig. 3 show that when the network is of small size, and density is approximately equal to 0.6, the influence spreads faster when using driver-community based seed selection methods than when the global-level driver based methods are employed. If we look at Fig. 3, the network of smaller densities (i.e. 0.4), where number of nodes is 300 and number of edges is 2,800, the difference between the global-level driver based methods and community-level driver based methods is not so big. But we do see a gap between DDCBC method and other methods. Which tells us that, so far, DDCBC ranking of driver nodes in communities is working better than when we are using driver nodes of communities as seed nodes.

Although the comparison is done on a very small size of seed set (1% of all driver nodes), in DDCBC, we still achieve more influence earlier in the spreading process when using community-level driver based methods. It also gives us another insight regarding larger networks, their structures and densities, and how those are connected to spreading influence. We see that the spread is faster when density is higher than 0.5 as in the case of networks presented in the Fig. 2

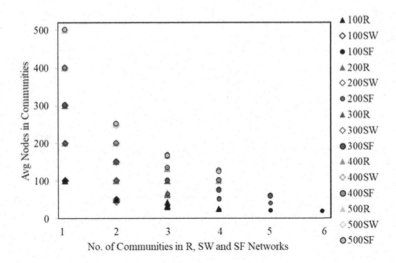

Fig. 3. Average Number of Nodes in Communities of Random, Small-World and Scale-Free Networks versus number of communities in those networks. Legend shows the Number of Nodes in communities of generated networks i.e. Random (R), Small-World (SW) and Scale-Free (SF).

(network with 500 nodes and 72,000 edges). We can see that in those cases, the driver-community based method DRC, DDC, DBC, DKC and DDCBC outperforms their counterpart methods DR, DD, DB, DK and DDCB.

Based upon these observations, we conclude it does not matter which type of network it is, as long as its density is higher than 0.5 it will respond to the community-based seed selection methods better and the spread will be faster. Also, regardless of the network density, community-based method – DDCBC – outperforms all other methods Fig. 2(a–f). This holds true for all the other settings as well. As when we have different edges for 100, 200, 300, 400 and 500 nodes networks.

How Much Advantage Do Community-Level Driver Based Seed Selection Methods Give? Given a number of iterations n and a method X, let $N_n^{infl}(X)$ denote the number of nodes influenced using the method X after n iterations. The Percentage Gain of method A over method B after n iterations is then given by:

$$\frac{N_n^{infl}(A) - N_n^{infl}(B)}{N} \times 100 \tag{1}$$

where N is the number of nodes in the network.

Table 1 shows the percentage gain of the DDCBC method over the global-level driver based methods. We represent only driver based methods (i.e. DR, DB, DC, DD, DK and DDCB), as the gain is higher over these methods as compared to other driver-community based methods (i.e. DRC, DBC, DCC, DDC and DKC) as well as they are our baseline for this study. Percentage gain is calculated by knowing the maximum number of nodes influenced after 20 iterations when seed size is 1%.

From Table 1 we can see the maximum gain in when the average density of the communities of the network is greater than 0.5. When the density reaches 1 all the methods perform very similar as spread in fully connected network behaves in a very similar way regardless of applied seed selection method. This highlights our previous point that density of network plays an important part in how effective a network is going to respond to the influence spread process. We can see the highest gain for DDCBC method in random networks, but DDCBC outperforms all global-level driver based methods in all the networks, except for the networks with densities equal or very close to 1.

From Fig. 3, we can see the number of average nodes in communities versus the total number of communities in Random, Small-World and Scale-Free networks. The denser the network, the fewer communities we have, and those communities are denser than the previous ones. Hence, due to increase in community density, we see the higher percent gain in DDCBC method. The number of nodes influenced by DDCBC method increases, when there are fewer communities. Because when number of communities are less, they tend to be denser, hence the increase in number of nodes influenced. We see the difference in number of nodes influenced in DDCBC method which is bigger than compared to other methods.

4.2   Results from Social Networks

The observation that real-world social networks tend to contain dense communities suggests that community based driver node selection would have a significant advantage over global selection. This relationship with density is also apparent in the generated networks. To verify whether this intuition is correct, we conduct similar analysis to this performed on generated networks. First, we analyse the percentage of nodes influenced by each method over 100 iterations with a seed set size of 20% of driver nodes. We have run the experiments for the seed set sizes from 1%, 10%, 20%, 30%, 40% and 50%. We show the comparison in case of 20% seed size, as it is the lowest seed set level to reach maximum influence in at most 100 iterations. We note however that there is also improvements at smaller seed set sizes.

What is the Speed and Reach of the Influence Spread? Figures 4, 5 and 6 show a comparison between global-level driver based seed selection methods and community-level driver based seed selection methods. We grouped the networks on the basis of their sizes and densities to analyse the results effectively. From Fig. 4, we see a higher density of networks. The densities of these networks are: FB (0.01), Z (0.13), LC (0.003), LF (0.003), PF (0.007), FbG (0.003), FbP (0.002), FbPF (0.001) and FbT (0.002). Overall comparison tells us that, in these networks, there is less difference between the percentage of number of nodes influenced after 100 iterations. Which indicates that when the network's

Table 1. A percentage gain table shows the percentage gain of DDCBC method over other seed selection methods in influencing the nodes in Random, Small-World and Scale-Free networks when the seed set size is 1% after 20 iterations. N is number of nodes, E is number of edges, C is number of communities and CD is average community density.

N	E	C	CD Avg ± SD	Random Networks						Small-World Networks						Scale-Free Networks					
				DR	DB	DC	DD	DK	DDCB	DR	DB	DC	DD	DK	DDCB	DR	DB	DC	DD	DK	DDCB
100	800	6	0.16±0.01	2	2	2	2	2	1	3	2	3	3	3	2	4	2	2	3	3	2
	1600	5	0.3±0.03	3	2	3	3	2	2	3	2	2	2	2	2	4	2	3	3	3	2
	2400	4	0.44±0.06	3	2	2	3	2	2	3	2	3	3	2	2	4	2	2	3	3	2
	3200	3	0.58±0.12	2	2	2	2	2	1	4	3	3	3	3	3	3	2	2	2	2	1
	4000	2	0.73±0.14	4	2	3	3	2	2	3	2	2	2	2	2	4	3	3	3	3	2
	4800	1	0.88±0.15	2	1	1	2	1	1	0	0	1	1	0	0	2	1	1	1	1	1
	4950	1	0.96±0.07	0	0	0	0	0	0	0	0	0	0	0	0	0	0	0	0	0	0
200	2400	5	0.12±0.01	4	4	4	5	4	4	5	5	5	5	5	4	5	4	4	4	4	4
	4800	4	0.23±0.02	3	2	2	3	2	2	3	2	2	3	2	2	5	4	4	4	4	3
	7200	4	0.36±0.01	8	7	7	7	7	6	8	7	7	7	7	7	9	8	8	8	8	8
	9600	4	0.48±0.02	6	6	6	6	6	5	6	5	6	6	6	5	7	6	6	6	6	5
	12000	3	0.56±0.07	6	5	5	5	5	4	7	7	7	7	7	6	7	6	6	6	6	6
	14400	2	0.67±0.09	3	3	3	3	3	2	4	3	4	4	3	3	4	3	3	3	3	2
	16800	1	0.78±0.11	2	1	1	1	1	0	2	1	2	2	2	1	3	1	1	2	1	1
	19200	1	0.9±0.1	1	0	0	0	0	0	2	0	1	1	0	0	1	1	1	1	1	0
	19900	1	0.97±0.06	0	0	0	0	0	0	0	0	0	0	0	0	0	0	0	0	0	0
300	12800	5	0.31±0.03	4	3	3	3	3	2	4	3	3	3	3	2	5	3	3	4	4	3
	19200	5	0.41±0.03	4	3	3	3	2	2	3	2	3	3	3	2	4	3	3	3	3	3
	22400	4	0.46±0.06	4	3	3	3	2	2	4	3	3	3	3	2	5	3	3	4	3	3
	25600	4	0.53±0.08	4	2	2	3	2	2	3	2	3	3	3	2	4	3	3	3	3	2
	28800	3	0.58±0.1	3	2	2	3	2	2	2	2	2	2	2	1	3	2	2	2	2	2
	32000	2	0.63±0.17	6	4	4	4	4	3	4	3	3	3	3	3	5	4	4	4	4	3
	35200	1	0.69±0.16	10	8	8	8	8	4	5	5	5	5	5	4	6	5	5	5	5	4
	38400	1	0.76±0.17	13	6	7	7	7	7	10	3	3	3	3	2	13	4	4	4	4	4
	41600	1	0.83±0.17	0	0	0	0	0	0	0	0	0	0	0	1	0	2	2	2	2	1
	44850	1	0.91±0.15	0	0	0	0	0	0	0	0	0	0	0	0	0	0	0	0	0	0
400	40000	4	0.43±0.12	23	21	21	22	21	21	5	4	4	4	4	4	5	4	4	4	4	3
	44000	4	0.48±0.12	25	22	22	22	22	22	4	4	4	4	4	3	6	4	4	5	4	4
	48000	4	0.53±0.12	25	21	21	21	21	21	9	8	8	8	8	7	10	8	8	9	8	8
	52000	4	0.58±0.12	22	12	12	13	12	12	12	11	11	11	11	11	13	11	12	12	12	11
	60000	3	0.67±0.14	18	12	12	12	12	12	10	9	9	10	10	9	12	10	10	11	11	10
	64000	2	0.76±0.07	13	8	9	9	8	9	7	7	7	7	7	6	8	7	7	7	7	7
	68000	1	0.83±0.03	8	6	6	6	6	6	5	4	4	4	4	4	7	5	6	6	6	5
	72000	1	0.88±0.03	4	1	1	2	1	1	5	4	4	4	4	4	4	3	3	3	3	3
	76000	1	0.93±0.03	1	0	0	0	0	0	1	1	1	1	1	0	1	2	2	3	2	2
	98000	1	0.98±0.03	0	0	0	0	0	0	0	0	0	0	0	0	0	0	0	0	0	0
500	72000	4	0.52±0.1	23	15	15	16	16	15	11	6	6	6	6	6	12	11	11	11	11	10
	76800	3	0.56±0.1	21	16	16	16	16	16	11	6	7	7	6	6	7	6	6	6	6	6
	81600	4	0.6±0.09	19	13	14	14	13	13	10	7	8	8	8	7	8	7	7	7	7	6
	86400	3	0.69±0.01	19	13	13	13	13	13	10	2	2	2	2	2	9	8	8	8	8	7
	91200	3	0.73±0.01	15	14	14	14	14	14	7	3	3	3	3	3	3	2	2	2	2	1
	96000	3	0.76±0.01	12	10	10	10	10	10	7	2	2	2	2	1	5	3	3	4	4	3
	100800	1	0.81±0.01	8	8	8	9	9	8	7	1	1	2	1	1	4	3	3	3	3	2
	105200	1	0.84±0	3	4	5	5	5	5	3	0	1	1	0	0	2	1	1	1	1	0
	110000	2	0.88±0	0	3	3	4	4	3	0	0	0	0	0	0	0	1	1	1	1	0
	124750	2	0.97±0.06	0	0	0	0	0	0	0	0	0	0	0	0	0	0	0	0	0	0

densities are higher, then there is more chance that seed selection methods are able to achieve influence faster. If we look at the Fb network in Fig. 4, its network density is 0.01 which is greater than the rest of the networks except the network

Table 2. A percentage gain table shows the percentage gain of DDCBC method over other seed selection methods in influencing the nodes of the social networks. Average Community Densities of the networks are as follows: FB (0.06 ± 0.02), ZKC (0.32 ± 0.4), Twitter (0.00029 ± 0.05), Diggs (0.00008 ± 0.007), Youtube (0.000012 ± 0.04), Ego (0.00034 ± 0.05), LC (0.007 ± 0.032), LF (0.0073 ± 0.09), PF (0.015 ± 0.54), MFb (0.001 ± 0.43), DHR (0.00085 ± 0.21), DRO (0.0005 ± 0.4), DHU (0.0004 ± 0.63), MG (0.0011 ± 0.03), L (0.0019 ± 0.54), FbAR (0.0014 ± 0.03), FbA (0.0015 ± 0.09), FbG (0.0075 ± 0.05), FbN (0.0013 ± 0.003), FbP (0.0049 ± 0.003), FbPF (0.004 ± 0.032) and Fbt (0.0051 ± 0.05)

N	E	C	Networks	Seed Selection Methods (20% of all nodes)										
				DR	DD	DC	DB	DDCB	DK	DRC	DDC	DCC	DBC	DKC
4039	88234	180	FB	28.68	25.03	24.94	25.94	25.15	24.59	21.59	21.59	22.19	22.28	21.14
34	78	2	ZKC	12.18	4.00	2.82	2.09	1.95	1.73	1.18	1.18	1.27	1.00	1
23371	32832	350	Twitter	37.81	27.83	26.80	26.78	20.16	26.77	23.81	23.80	23.74	23.06	21.22
1924000	3298475	156432	Diggs	42.49	39.05	36.76	36.47	38.37	39.21	20.11	18.89	17.67	16.53	19.85
1134891	2987625	54983	Youtube	42.00	38.02	35.12	32.79	32.59	33.92	3.51	2.71	1.91	1.11	6.45
23629	39195	75	Ego	24.83	15.34	14.33	14.33	17.15	21.81	9.64	10.62	11.14	9.05	8.89
4658	33116	517	LC	33.84	26.62	25.61	25.61	25.52	31.81	22.40	23.23	23.98	21.65	22.06
874	1309	97	LF	19.29	10.62	9.56	9.34	9.25	9.33	8.38	9.35	10.20	7.86	9.11
1858	12534	206	PF	10.62	6.66	5.43	5.21	5.13	5.25	2.94	3.78	4.64	2.60	2.71
22470	171002	2643	MFb	25.44	22.16	21.11	21.11	21.10	21.11	15.07	15.80	22.70	20.43	16.8
54574	498202	6420	DHR	39.77	35.42	33.21	32.00	31.90	34.2	6.78	7.26	7.73	5.21	6.01
41774	125826	4914	DRO	42.43	35.74	36.42	34.22	34.12	34.45	13.50	13.40	13.13	12.94	34.18
47539	222887	5592	DHU	45.40	35.77	34.52	34.33	34.13	38.85	26.35	27.02	25.84	25.61	25.33
37700	289003	4435	MG	30.54	27.43	26.07	26.25	26.07	26.34	16.14	15.49	16.05	10.35	14.86
7624	27806	759	L	26.55	25.25	24.04	23.82	23.79	23.81	18.34	18.11	17.75	17.71	17.70
50516	819306	5943	FbAR	39.97	32.40	31.18	30.95	30.93	31.30	29.43	29.14	30.85	28.56	29.28
13867	86858	1383	FbA	47.29	32.45	31.05	30.55	40.87	45.89	32.28	31.83	33.28	30.46	32.01
7058	89455	784	FbG	21.95	20.22	18.93	18.71	19.18	19.20	13.97	13.75	15.39	13.13	13.68
27918	206259	3284	FbN	33.82	23.03	22.00	21.95	21.96	22.01	12.85	12.64	12.18	12.10	12.40
5909	41729	562	FbP	31.73	22.90	21.76	21.40	21.87	21.89	15.89	15.47	15.15	14.90	15.31
11566	67114	1051	FbPF	39.61	32.21	30.85	30.57	30.39	30.48	26.30	26.12	25.85	25.21	26.21
3893	17262	387	FbT	25.93	22.84	24.70	24.29	17.73	17.77	19.37	18.46	13.71	13.36	17.63

Z which has the highest density of 0.14. If we compare the plots, we see that DDCBC method also works exceptionally better in most networks as compared to the rest of the methods. From Fig. 5, we see the networks with densities ranging from 0.0001 to 0.0009. Densities of these networks are: MFb (0.0006), DHR (0.0003), DRO (0.0001), DHU (0.0001), MG (0.0004), L (0.0009), FbAR (0.0006) and FbA (0.0009). With the lower density networks, we can see that the gain in driver community based methods is more prominent as compared to driver based methods. It means density of the network does play an important role to determine the total number of nodes influenced. From Fig. 6, we see the networks with the lowest densities ranging from 0.000002 to 0.0001. Densities of these networks are: Youtube (0.000004), Twitter (0.00012), Diggs (0.000002) and Ego (0.00014). In these networks, we see a huge gap between DDCBC method and the rest of the methods. Which means, even in the lowest density networks, when we locally construct communities, the density tend to increase as we can see from Table 2. Average community density of Youtube was calculated to be

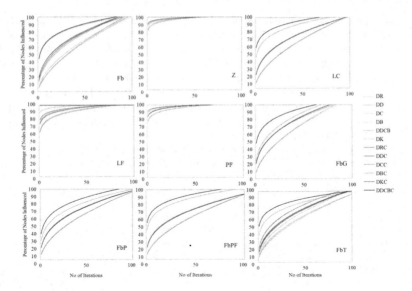

Fig. 4. Percentage of Number of Nodes Influenced in FB, Z, LC, LF, PF, FbG, FbP, FbPF and FbT Networks. A Comparison of all methods for 100 iterations.

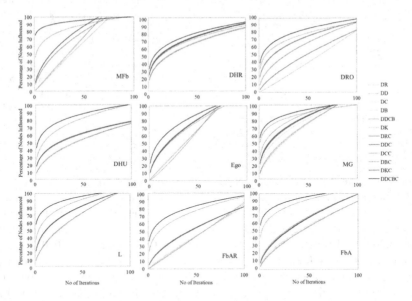

Fig. 5. Percentage of Number of Nodes Influenced in MFb, DHR, DRO, DHU, MG, L, FbAR and FbA Networks. A Comparison of all methods for 100 iterations.

0.000012 ± 0.04, which means if we compare it to the overall network density of 0.000004, it is notably denser. That is why, even in these networks, driver-community based methods specially DDCBC method outperforms the driver based methods.

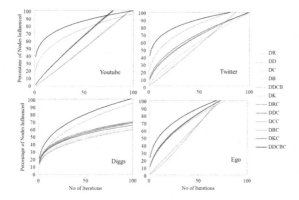

Fig. 6. Percentage of Number of Nodes Influenced in Youtube, Twitter, Diggs and Ego Networks. A Comparison of all methods for 100 iterations.

How Much Advantage Do Community-Level Driver Based Seed Selection Methods Give? From Table 2, we see the percentage of gain that DDCBC has over other seed selection methods in terms of number of nodes influenced after 100 iterations when seed size is 20%. We can see from the table that DDCBC outperforms all methods, but the gain is bigger in terms of global-level driver based methods than the community-level driver based methods. We see this difference in gain mainly because of locally selected and then ranked driver nodes. Also, community creation plays an important role as, the communities are denser than the overall network. From Table 2 we can see that the biggest gain is achieved by DDCBC method over DK method which is 45.89% in FbA network. And the lowest gain is achieved by DDCBC method over DK method in ZKC network. The reason for lowest or lower gain is that ZKC has the highest network density and smallest size. In denser networks, we tend to see the less gain in DDCBC method. Which precisely can mean that, if we locally identify communities, those have denser structures as compared to the overall network. That is why community-driver based methods combined with ranking of DCB works better than the rest of the methods.

5   Conclusion and Future Work

An idea of bringing the methods from control and influence fields together has been proposed in this research. In fact, we played with a research dimension that is at the intersection of both fields and fulfils the objectives of many research questions from both domains. We proposed, implemented and compared a list of new and novel seed selection methods with the traditional seed selection methods from influence domain and driver seed selection methods from influence meets control field. In this work, we introduced new seed selection methods, by utilising driver nodes in communities of the networks. The new methods outperformed the old ones. This opens up an avenue in the already existing research of control methods in complex networks. Our community-driver based methods show that, we can achieve maximum influence in fewer number of iterations and with a comparatively less seed set size. Also, if we use ranking mechanisms based upon the centrality measures combining degree, betweenness and closeness, the driver nodes selected as seed nodes perform much better in that case as compared to when we rank them on the basis of individual centrality measures.

Work remains to be done in the context of ranking of driver nodes by using different other algorithms for example, Page Rank, Leader Rank, cluster Rank and K-Shell Decomposition. E.g., Page Rank [2], Leader Rank [16], Cluster Rank [3] and K-Shell Decomposition [15]. New methods such as Preferential Matching [27] can be used to identify driver nodes to improve the efficiency of the seed selection process. Another avenue for exploration is the effects of differing influence models, such as the Independent Cascade Model [8].

Acknowledgement. This work was supported in part by the Polish National Science Centre, under Grant no. 2016/21/D/ST6/02408, and in part by the Australian Research Council, Dynamics and Control of Complex Social Networks, under Grant DP190101087.

References

1. Borgs, C., Brautbar, M., Chayes, J., Lucier, B.: Maximizing social influence in nearly optimal time. In: Proceedings of the Twenty-Fifth Annual ACM-SIAM Symposium on Discrete Algorithms, pp. 946–957. SIAM (2014)
2. Brin, S., Page, L.: The anatomy of a large-scale hypertextual web search engine. Comput. Netw. ISDN Syst. **30**(1–7), 107–117 (1998)
3. Chen, D.B., Gao, H., Lü, L., Zhou, T.: Identifying influential nodes in large-scale directed networks: the role of clustering. PLoS ONE **8**(10), e77455 (2013)
4. Chen, Y.C., Zhu, W.Y., Peng, W.C., Lee, W.C., Lee, S.Y.: CIM: community-based influence maximization in social networks. ACM Trans. Intell. Syst. Technol. (TIST) **5**(2), 1–31 (2014)
5. Cheng, S., Shen, H., Huang, J., Zhang, G., Cheng, X.: StaticGreedy: solving the scalability-accuracy dilemma in influence maximization. In: Proceedings of the 22nd ACM International Conference on Information & Knowledge Management, pp. 509–518 (2013)
6. Cohen, E., Delling, D., Pajor, T., Werneck, R.F.: Sketch-based influence maximization and computation: scaling up with guarantees. In: Proceedings of the 23rd ACM International Conference on Conference on Information and Knowledge Management, pp. 629–638 (2014)
7. D'Angelo, G., Severini, L., Velaj, Y.: Influence maximization in the independent cascade model. In: ICTCS, pp. 269–274 (2016)
8. Duan, W., Gu, B., Whinston, A.B.: Informational cascades and software adoption on the internet: an empirical investigation. MIS Q. 23–48 (2009)
9. Girvan, M., Newman, M.E.: Community structure in social and biological networks. Proc. Natl. Acad. Sci. **99**(12), 7821–7826 (2002)
10. Goyal, A., Lu, W., Lakshmanan, L.V.: CELF++ optimizing the greedy algorithm for influence maximization in social networks. In: Proceedings of the 20th International Conference Companion on World Wide Web, pp. 47–48 (2011)

11. Granovetter, M.: Threshold models of collective behavior. Am. J. Sociol. **83**(6), 1420–1443 (1978)
12. Kazemzadeh, F., Safaei, A.A., Mirzarezaee, M.: Influence maximization in social networks using effective community detection. Phys. A **598**, 127314 (2022)
13. Kempe, D., Kleinberg, J., Tardos, É.: Maximizing the spread of influence through a social network. In: Proceedings of the ninth ACM SIGKDD International Conference on Knowledge Discovery and Data Mining, pp. 137–146 (2003)
14. Leskovec, J., Kleinberg, J., Faloutsos, C.: Graphs over time: densification laws, shrinking diameters and possible explanations. In: Proceedings of the eleventh ACM SIGKDD International Conference on Knowledge Discovery in Data Mining, pp. 177–187 (2005)
15. Liu, Y., Tang, M., Zhou, T., Do, Y.: Improving the accuracy of the k-shell method by removing redundant links: from a perspective of spreading dynamics. Sci. Rep. **5**(1), 1–11 (2015)
16. Lü, L., Zhang, Y.C., Yeung, C.H., Zhou, T.: Leaders in social networks, the delicious case. PLoS ONE **6**(6), e21202 (2011)
17. Nacher, J.C., Akutsu, T.: Dominating scale-free networks with variable scaling exponent: heterogeneous networks are not difficult to control. New J. Phys. **14**(7), 073005 (2012)
18. Nguyen, H.T., Thai, M.T., Dinh, T.N.: Stop-and-stare: optimal sampling algorithms for viral marketing in billion-scale networks. In: Proceedings of the 2016 International Conference on Management of Data, pp. 695–710 (2016)
19. Nguyen, H.T., Thai, M.T., Dinh, T.N.: A billion-scale approximation algorithm for maximizing benefit in viral marketing. IEEE/ACM Trans. Netw. **25**(4), 2419–2429 (2017)
20. Nguyen, H., Zheng, R.: On budgeted influence maximization in social networks. IEEE J. Sel. Areas Commun. **31**(6), 1084–1094 (2013)
21. Sadaf, A., Mathieson, L., Musial, K.: An insight into network structure measures and number of driver nodes. In: Proceedings of the 2021 IEEE/ACM International Conference on Advances in Social Networks Analysis and Mining, pp. 471–478 (2021)
22. Sadaf, Mathieson, B., Musial: A bridge between influence models and control methods [manuscript submitted for publication]. IEEE Trans. Netw. Sci. Eng. (2022)
23. Sanchis, L.A.: Experimental analysis of heuristic algorithms for the dominating set problem. Algorithmica **33**(1), 3–18 (2002)
24. Sathiyakumari, K., Vijaya, M.S.: Community detection based on Girvan Newman algorithm and link analysis of social media. In: Subramanian, S., Nadarajan, R., Rao, S., Sheen, S. (eds.) CSI 2016. CCIS, vol. 679, pp. 223–234. Springer, Singapore (2016). https://doi.org/10.1007/978-981-10-3274-5_18
25. Tang, Y., Shi, Y., Xiao, X.: Influence maximization in near-linear time: a martingale approach. In: Proceedings of the 2015 ACM SIGMOD International Conference on Management of Data, pp. 1539–1554 (2015)
26. Tang, Y., Xiao, X., Shi, Y.: Influence maximization: Near-optimal time complexity meets practical efficiency. In: Proceedings of the 2014 ACM SIGMOD International Conference on Management of Data, pp. 75–86 (2014)
27. Zhang, X., Lv, T., Yang, X., Zhang, B.: Structural controllability of complex networks based on preferential matching. PLoS ONE **9**(11), e112039 (2014)
28. Zhu, J., Wang, B., Wu, B., Zhang, W.: Emotional community detection in social network. IEICE Trans. Inf. Syst. **100**(10), 2515–2525 (2017)

Peak Anomaly Detection from Environmental Sensor-Generated Watershed Time Series Data

Byung Suk Lee[✉], John Clay Kaufmann, Donna M. Rizzo, and Ijaz Ul Haq

University of Vermont, Burlington, VT 05405, USA
{bslee,jckaufma,drizzo,ihaq}@uvm.edu

Abstract. Time series data generated by environmental sensors are typically "messy," with unexpected anomalies that must be corrected prior to extracting useful information. This paper addresses automatic detection of such anomalies and discusses two lines of study for achieving efficient and accurate detection using AI techniques with a focus on *peak* anomalies. One study uses the classic knowledge-engineering process and the other uses a deep-learning method to mimic how a trained watershed scientist detects anomalies. These two approaches were applied to time series data collected from a research watershed in Vermont, U.S.A., and their performances were assessed with respect to detection accuracy and computational efficiency. The two approaches had different anomaly detection accuracy depending on the peak type. The knowledge engineering approach was readily tunable to achieve competitive or better detection accuracy while computationally far more efficient than the deep learning approach. Results indicate the advantage of using the two approaches in combination, while a more general study involving other watersheds' time series data would be needed.

Keywords: Peak anomaly detection · sensor-generated data · time series data · knowledge engineering · deep learning

1 Introduction

Background and Motivation. Anomaly detection from sensor-generated time series data is an important problem in many real-world applications for manufacturing, monitoring, and management of resources. Often associated with the Internet-of-Things, there has been a large body of work conducted in this area (see the surveys by Cook et al. 2019 [1] and Sgueglia et al. 2022 [2]). Publications show a substantial focus on environmental sensor-generated time series data such as temperature, humidity, etc. (e.g., Hill and Minker 2010 [3], Jae-Myoung et al. 2020 [4], Conde 2011 [5], Hayes and Capretz 2014 [6], Hill and Minker 2006 [7], Russo et al. 2020 [8]).

This paper focuses on a data-driven approach to anomaly detection using watershed environment sensor-generated time series data. These time series data are typically "messy", with unexpected phenomena. At the present time, watershed scientists rely on manual examination of the time series data, their domain expertise in having observed a variety of anomaly types, and field notes during on-site sensor maintenance

J. A. Lossio-Ventura et al. (Eds.): SIMBig 2022, CCIS 1837, pp. 142–157, 2023.
https://doi.org/10.1007/978-3-031-35445-8_11

to detect anomalies. Recently there has been increasing attention in the environmental science community in replacing human effort with a more automated process (e.g., Jones et al. 2021 [9]). This is a challenging endeavor because of the "messiness" of data; but successful automation has the potential to bring great scientific and societal benefits.

Objectives. Our primary objective is to develop an automatic mechanism for detecting anomalies in time series data for a hydrological and biogeochemical study. A secondary objective is to build an inventory of common anomaly types for domain scientists (e.g., hydrologists) and study the performance for different anomaly types.

Methodology. The performance study employs classification-based anomaly detection, which is a supervised machine-learning task and requires labeled anomaly data for training and tuning. Two machine-learning approaches are used: knowledge-engineering and deep-learning. Knowledge engineering is a process that identifies parameters based on the domain expert to solve the problem at hand (i.e., detecting anomalies). The deep-learning fits a model, i.e., a neural network trained using expert labeled data. Knowledge engineering specializes in a fixed set of anomaly types (i.e., patterns) and uses a small number of "hand-crafted" parameters (e.g., 2 to 5 for each anomaly type) to characterize the patterns. Deep learning, on the other hand, generalizes to a variety of anomaly types (i.e., patterns) and uses millions of neural-network parameters (or coefficients) to characterize the patterns at different levels of the network. Naturally, knowledge engineering incurs much lower computing cost (in terms of both computation time and the memory consumption) to tune the parameters, and it may perform better or worse than deep learning depending on the complexity of the pattern.

Outcome Summary. The deep learning approach and the knowledge engineering approach had different performances. They achieved different detection accuracies depending on the peak type, while overall accuracy was comparable. Besides, there were contrasting relative accuracies between the different time series data (fDOM and turbidity). The knowledge engineering was significantly more efficient computationally (i.e., training time and memory usage) for all peak types. Using both the knowledge engineering and the deep learning approaches in combination would take advantage of the different performances of the two approaches.

Contributions. The contributions of our work can be summarized as follows.

- It introduces peak anomalies as an important anomaly type and identifies a set of peak types of practical importance in hydrological watershed science.
- It implements classification-based peak anomaly detection using supervised learning techniques via knowledge engineering and deep learning approaches and compares the resulting performances.
- It identifies and labels the peak types in hydrological time series data collected from a watershed.

2 Related Work

There are different anomaly types handled by anomaly detection methods, categorized into *point* anomaly, *pattern* anomaly, and *system* anomaly (Lai et al. 2021 [10]), (Chandola et al. 2009 [11]). A point refers to a single time series sample data; a pattern is identified over a sequence of time series samples that exhibit a given characteristic (e.g., statistic, shape) or behavior (e.g., trend, change); and a system refers to a group of systems (e.g., multivariate time series patterns) where one of many systems is in an abnormal state.

Most of the existing work on anomaly detection addresses *point* anomalies (Cho et al. 2015 [12], (Enikeeva et al. 2019 [13]), (Fearnhead et al. 2010 [14]), (Fryzlewicz and Piotr 2014 [15]), (Tveten et al. 2020 [16]). Pang et al. 2021 [17] mentioned that the methods for detecting point anomalies cannot be applied to group anomalies as they have entirely distinct characteristics. Group anomalies refer to a subset of anomalous data instances, which has the same definition as pattern anomalies used in our work. The peak anomalies in our watershed data are a type of pattern anomaly identified by the shapes of time series sample sequences.

There are some works on pattern anomaly detection from hydrological watershed sensor-generated time series data, mainly focused on detecting pattern deviations. Yu et al. 2020 [18] used a distance-based approach to extract the trend and mean feature of time series segments of equal size, for which they proposed two algorithms called the Trend Feature Symbolic Aggregate approximation (TFSAX) and weighted Probabilistic Suffix Tree (wPST). Sun et al. 2017 [19]'s work also depends on significant feature points in which the time series is separated into numerous patterns; the system then calculates the pattern features using a density-based anomaly detection algorithm. Qin et al. 2019 [20] proposed the iForest algorithm to extract anomalous patterns using an adaptive segmentation algorithm based on key feature points; the pattern features of each time series segment are then translated to a k-dimensional space, i.e., restricted to a space with k orthogonal axes. The nearest neighbor distance is then used to extract top-K patterns and the K patterns with the highest anomaly scores are output. However, the pattern anomalies detected by these algorithms are not the peak anomalies handled in our work.

We find works closer to the peak anomaly detection in our time series data in other application domains, such as ECG anomaly detection (Lin et al. 2018 [21]), (Li et al. 2020 [22]). These ECG datasets are annotated with codes that indicate whether segments are normal or abnormal at each R peak location. However, to the best of our knowledge, there is nothing similar in hydrological watershed time series data.

3 Time Series Data and Peak Anomaly Types

3.1 Time Series Data

This study uses experimental sensor time series data collected over nine years at a small forested research watershed in Vermont, U.S.A.[1] The researchers measure stream stage, from which stream discharge is computed, at a 5-min interval. They measure turbidity and fluorescent Dissolved Organic Matter (fDOM) at a 15-min interval, using optical Turner Designs Cyclops sensors (see Fig. 1). The sensors are positioned below the depth of ice formation and are operated year-round. The data are used to estimate stream fluxes of dissolved and particulate organic carbon (DOC and POC). Turbidity in the

---

[1] The watershed name is not mentioned due to a data management policy of the agency that owns the datasets.

water interferes with light transmission needed for the fDOM measurement, so fDOM values are corrected based on the turbidity values. Fluorescence is temperature sensitive, so fDOM values are also adjusted using concurrent water temperature measurements. The stage time series has 231,465 samples, and the turbidity and fDOM time series have 229,620 samples each.

Fig. 1. Turbidity/fDOM sensor mounted on a board immersed in the water. The image in the corner is a Turner Designs Cyclops-7 submersible sensor.

Stage is already corrected and used as reference data; so, in this study, anomalies are defined and detected for fDOM and turbidity. The actual anomalies in the fDOM and turbidity data sets have been labeled through a visual examination and have been vetted by a domain scientist. We refer to these labeled datasets as the "ground truth" in this study. Figure 2 shows the three time-series (stage, fDOM, turbidity) segments with normal peaks.

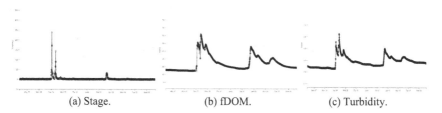

(a) Stage.   (b) fDOM.   (c) Turbidity.

Fig. 2. The watershed time series data (from May 27–June 6, 2012) containing normal peaks.

3.2 Peak Anomaly Types

The focus is on "peak anomaly" types in this study. Five main anomaly types have been identified: skyrocketing peaks (SKP), plummeting peaks (PLP), flat plateau (FPT), flat sinks (FSK), and phantom peaks (PHP). Normal (i.e., non-anomalous) peaks (NAP) are of another peak type. See Fig. 3 for illustrations. A skyrocketing peak is an upward spike or a narrow peak (with a short base width), and a plummeting peak is a downward spike; both may be caused by electronic sensor noise. A plummeting peak is observed in fDOM only and its detection requires that there is no preceding rise in the turbidity (which triggers a drop in fDOM). A flat plateau and a flat sink are characterized by near-constant signal amplitude near the top (plateau) and the bottom (sink); they may be caused by sediment deposition near or around the sensors. Flat sinks are observed in fDOM only. A phantom peak appears as a normal peak but has no preceding stage rise that triggers the peak; it may be caused by a non-hydrological event like animal activity in the water near the sensor. Note that detecting a phantom peak and a plummeting peak requires identifying causal relationships between two data time series, whereas the other peak types require only one data time series.

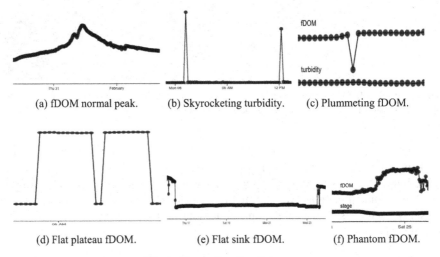

(a) fDOM normal peak.   (b) Skyrocketing turbidity.   (c) Plummeting fDOM.

(d) Flat plateau fDOM.   (e) Flat sink fDOM.   (f) Phantom fDOM.

Fig. 3. Examples of peak types.

4 Computational Methods

4.1 Knowledge Engineering

As mentioned earlier, the knowledge engineering in this study is a process to emulate what a domain expert does to identify and detect anomalies. The knowledge gained from our expert hydrologist has been formalized into the definition of each anomalous peak type. The detection mechanism of anomaly instances according to the definition of an anomalous peak type and the associated threshold parameters are summarized below. The threshold parameters are tuned against the labeled

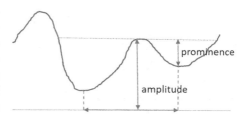

Fig. 4. Terms used in defining a peak

anomaly instances in the ground truth time series. Figure 4 summarizes some key terms used in the definition of peak anomalies, where base width is the interval (number of data points) between the start time and end time of a peak; amplitude is the maximum rise above baseline among all values between the start and end times of the peak; and prominence is the amplitude of a peak measured relative to the amplitudes of the neighboring peaks.

Definition of Peak Anomaly Types

The intuitive meaning, detection mechanism, and the associated threshold parameters are defined below for each anomalous peak type.

Skyrocketing Peak (SKP) is an upward peak for which the base width is smaller than a threshold number δ_{SPBW} (e.g., 10) of data points and the prominence is larger than a threshold unit δ_{SPA} (e.g., 10 units). A probable cause is the sensor impulse noise.

Plummeting Peak (PLP) (for fDOM only) is a downward peak (decrease) for which the base width is smaller than a threshold number δ_{PLPFBW} (e.g., 4) of points and the negative prominence (decrease from baseline) is larger than a threshold unit δ_{PLPFA} (e.g., 4 units), and there is no abrupt rise or elevated level of turbidity more than δ_{PLPTI} NTU (e.g. 100 NTU) within the preceding threshold time interval δ_{PLPFI} (e.g., 1 h). Here, NTU stands for "Nephelometric Turbidity Units." A probable cause of a plummeting peak is the sensor impulse noise.

Flat Plateau (FPT) denotes consecutive samples between an abrupt rise and an abrupt drop where the rise amplitude is more than a threshold value δ_{FPA} (e.g., 300) and the values within the plateau portion remain near-constant. Here, "near-constant" means (max − min)/max ratio of the sample amplitudes is less than a threshold ratio δ_{FPR} (e.g., 20%), and "abrupt" rise/drop is defined as a rise/drop of more than 10 units over the course of four points in the time series, before and after the ends of the plateau. A flat plateau may be caused by a sensor partially buried under sediment.

Flat Sink (FSK) denotes consecutive samples between an abrupt drop and an abrupt rise where the drop amplitude is more than a threshold value δ_{FSA} (e.g., 2) and the amplitude within the drop portion is near-constant. Here, "near-constant" and "abrupt" are defined the same as those for the flat plateau (FPT). A flat sink may be caused by a sensor buried under sediment partially or completely.

Phantom Peak (PHP) is an upward peak that is not preceded by a rise in stage within a threshold interval δ_{PHPI-F} for fDOM, δ_{PHPI-T} for turbidity (e.g., 0.5 h) (and, hence, is not a real peak). There are additional conditions to account for exceptional cases specific to either fDOM or turbidity:

- For a phantom peak in fDOM, the period of Sep-15 to Oct-31 is not considered. This additional condition during the foliage season in Vermont accounts for fluorescent DOC released from fallen leaves in the stream channel, which may cause in increase in fDOM without a hydrological driver. (For phantom peaks in fDOM, the fDOM time series is smoothed prior to this detection in order to keep locally fluctuating small peaks from being detected as phantom peaks.)
- For a phantom peak in turbidity, the prominence of the peak is above a threshold δ_{PHPTA} and there is no turbidity interference evident in fDOM. True turbidity (values above 100 NTU) causes a drop in fDOM by more than a threshold ratio in an otherwise rising fDOM trajectory; and this phenomenon indicates that the turbidity peak is a real peak.

Figure 5 illustrates fDOM phantom peaks in relation to the stage time series. Figure 6 illustrates turbidity phantom peaks in relation to the stage time series (subfigure a) and the fDOM time series (subfigure b).

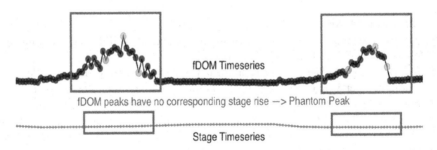

Fig. 5. fDOM phantom peaks.

Precedence Among Peak Anomaly Types. There are peaks that fit the definitions of two or more peak anomaly types. In this study, only one anomaly type is chosen according to a predefined precedence rule. Specifically, for fDOM, in order of highest to lowest precedence, skyrocketing peaks, phantom peaks, plummeting peaks, flat plateaus, flat sinks, non-anomaly peaks. For turbidity, the order is skyrocketing peaks, phantom peaks, flat plateaus, and non-anomaly peaks.

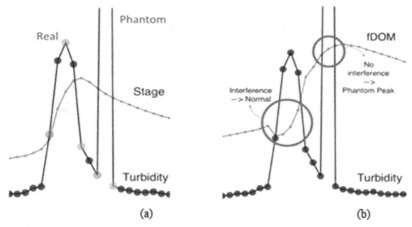

Fig. 6. Turbidity phantom peaks. In the subfigure (a), the first peak following a stage rise is real, and the second peak is phantom. In the subfigure (b), the first peak causing a turbidity-interference in fDOM is real, and the second which does not is phantom.

4.2 Deep Learning

We have chosen ResNet as the deep learning model for its proven ability to avoid the vanishing gradient issue, thereby achieving outstanding classification accuracy. Specifically, we use a 1-D time-series ResNet-50 implementation, with the PyTorch model code obtained from the repository of Hong et al. 2020 [23]. It showed the best performance in a review by Fawaz et al. 2019 [24] for univariate time series classification among the current state-of-the-art deep learning-based time series classification algorithms.

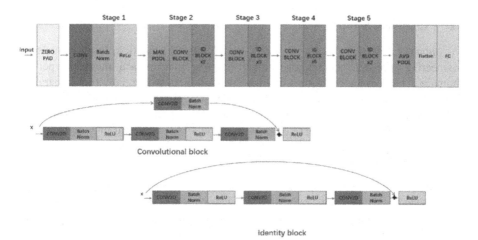

Fig. 7. Time series 1-D ResNet-50 architecture.

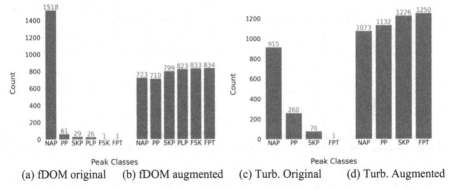

Fig. 8. Class sizes of fDOM peaks and turbidity peaks before and after augmentation.

Figure 7 shows the network architecture of the deep learning model. The architecture has a $t \times 3$ input matrix, where t is the variable number of data samples, and the 3 represents the three types of time series data (i.e., fDOM, turbidity, and stage). As different peaks occur over varying sample lengths, we make use of PyTorch's pad_sequence function, which pads a list of variable length tensors with a given padding value. Specifically, we use a padding value of 0. We believe this is the least intrusive value possible, which is important as we do not want to give the classifier any extra bias from the padded values. The core idea behind the ResNet model is to use residual blocks that have shortcut connections between blocks to calculate the residual function, which eases learning as compared to much deeper convolutional neural networks (Hong et al. 2020 [23]).

5 Performance Evaluation

5.1 Experiment Setup

The anomaly detection framework used is multiclass classification. In the knowledge engineering approach, there is one binary classifier run for each anomaly type; the anomaly detection algorithm runs the multiple classifiers sequentially (not in parallel) to monitor individual time series, and, for each peak, looks at every classifier's response and determines the anomaly class. When the multiple classifiers detect different anomaly types, the precedence rule is applied to choose one. In the deep-learning approach, the three time-series -- stage, turbidity, and fDOM – are treated as one tri-variate time-series, as mentioned in Sect. 4.2.

Data Augmentation for Class Balancing. The dataset collected from the research watershed is severely skewed in the anomaly class distribution, with the non-anomalous peak (NAP) class accounting for 93% of the fDOM peaks and 73% of the turbidity peaks within the seven-year period of data between 2012 and 2019 (see Fig. 8(a) and (c)). Such a severe class imbalance would drive the classifier to focus on correctly detecting the far more numerous non-anomalous peaks rather than the far fewer anomalous peaks during training, as a result not trained adequately to detect anomalous peaks. So, we augmented the dataset to keep the class sizes better balanced (see Fig. 8(b) and (d)).

The augmentation scheme alters randomly selected real peaks in both the peak base widths and the peak amplitude to a degree randomly selected within a predefined range. This range varies by the peak type. The peak amplitudes were multiplied by a uniformly generated number in the range of 1.1 to 3 for flat plateaus, 0.2 to 3 for flat sinks, and 0.8 to 1.2 for the other peak types. To produce a balanced peak distribution, the augmentation algorithm tracks the current distribution of peaks, and samples a new peak based on the current distribution. In addition, test-time augmentation was used for statistical significance of the result.

Training, Validation, and Testing Scheme. We used pre-quential evaluation (as opposed to the conventional cross-validation) to consider the effect of temporal ordering inherent in time series. Basically, each new batch of data is first used as test data and then appended to the existing training data. Thus, the training data size keeps increasing, and so does the training time (see Fig. 9). Our prequential evaluation is a "growing window" version adopted from the empirical study done by Cerqueira et al. 2020 [25]. Each time series data was split into 90% for training/validation and 10% for testing. The batch size was set to 32 samples.

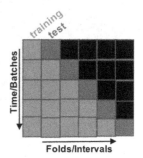

Fig. 9. Prequential evaluation (source: Cerqueira et al. [25]).

Knowledge Engineering Threshold Parameter Tuning. For each anomaly type, the random search approach was used to select parameter values in the parameter space defined by the threshold parameters belonging to the anomalous peak type. The set of parameter values that maximizes the anomaly detection performance was found using a random search iterated 1,000 times for each batch of data (added in the prequential evaluation). 1,000 iterations are more than enough, and it gives 99.996% probability of achieving near optimum within 1% of the true optimum. (A random search of n iterations has $1 - (1 - \varepsilon)^n$ probability of finding parameter values achieving near-optimum within the error ε from the true optimum (Firebug 2016 [26]).)

Deep Learning Model Parameter Tuning. Given the ResNet-50 used as the core model, the Adam optimizer was used, alongside a batch size of 32 samples, with 50 epochs and a learning rate of $1 \times e^{-3}$. Learning rate decay was added, with the learning rate decreasing by 0.1 every ten epochs. Early stopping was implemented as well, with a patience of five epochs. If the validation score did not change after five epochs, the algorithm stops training.

Performance metrics are the accuracy of peak anomaly detection and, additionally, computing resources (time and memory) consumed for the anomaly detection.

Computing Platform. All experiments were performed on a local desktop, equipped with an i7 quad-core 4790k CPU clocked at 4.0 GHz, 16 GB of DDR3 RAM, a GeForce GTX 1080 GPU, and 750 GB of SSD storage.

5.2   Experiment Results

Accuracy Results. Figure 10 and Fig. 11 show the confusion matrices of peak anomaly detection accuracy achieved by the knowledge engineering and the deep learning approaches for fDOM and turbidity time series, respectively.

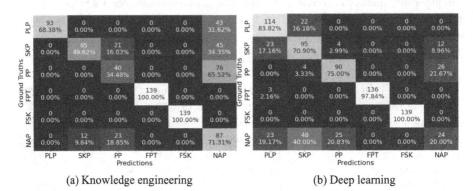

(a) Knowledge engineering   (b) Deep learning

Fig. 10. Confusion matrix of fDOM peak anomaly detection (PLP = plummeting; SKP = skyrocketing; PHP = phantom; FPT = flat plateau; FSK = flat sink; NAP = non-anomalous).

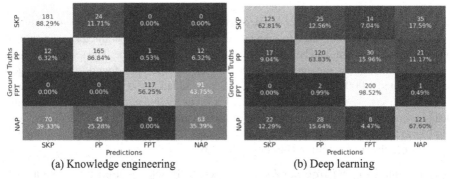

(a) Knowledge engineering   (b) Deep learning

Fig. 11. Confusion matrix turbidity peak anomaly detection (SKP = skyrocketing; PHP = phantom; FPT = flat plateau; NAP = non-anomalous).

Table 1 compares the accuracy achieved by the knowledge engineering approach and the deep learning approach (compiled from Fig. 10 and Fig. 11) for each applicable peak type of fDOM and turbidity.[2]

Additionally, Table 2 shows the composite accuracy (i.e., balanced accuracy and F1-score) achieved for fDOM and turbidity.

Computing Costs. Table 3 shows the computing costs of each approach in terms of the training time and memory usage. The computation time was clock time measured using

---

[2] Note that anomalous peaks are positive instances, and non-anomalous peaks are negative instances in this anomaly detection problem.

Table 1. Comparison of accuracy between knowledge engineering and deep learning for fDOM (left) and turbidity (right).

fDOM	KE (%)	DL (%)	DL/KE ratio	KE/DL ratio
PLP	70.59	83.82	1.19	0.84
SKP	50.00	70.90	1.42	0.71
PHP	33.62	75.00	2.23	0.45
FPT	100.00	97.84	0.98	1.02
FSK	100.00	100.00	1.00	1.00
NAP	70.83	20.00	0.28	3.54

Turbidity	KE (%)	DL (%)	DL/KE ratio	KE/DL ratio
SKP	88.29	62.81	0.71	1.41
PHP	86.84	63.83	0.74	1.36
FPT	56.75	98.52	1.74	0.58
NAP	35.39	67.60	1.91	0.52

Table 2. Composite accuracies achieved.

Approach	fDOM		Turbidity	
	Balanced accuracy (%)	F1-score (%)	Balanced accuracy (%)	F1-score (%)
Knowledge engineering	69.86%	67.74%	66.87%	66.01%
Deep learning	74.66%	72.05%	73.19%	71.23%

a Python's built-in time package called "datetime". The clock was started upon initiation of the split 1 and was stopped upon completion of the split 5. Memory usage tracking was done using a Python's built-in memory tracker called "tracemalloc" for CPU memory in knowledge engineering and the PyTorch CUDA memory summary function for GPU memory in deep learning. The memory usage tracking started and stopped at the same clock points as the computation time tracking.

Table 3. Computing resources consumed. The average memory usage was calculated over the entire run time.

Approach	Training time	Average memory usage	Peak memory usage
Knowledge engineering	1.03 h	1.39 MB	3.81 MB
Deep learning	4.08 h	2001.34 MB	3015.57 MB

5.3 Discussion

The knowledge engineering approach and the deep learning approach had different anomaly detection accuracies depending on the peak type (Table 1), while the deep learning did a bit better than the knowledge engineering overall (see Table 2). The knowledge engineering approach was computationally a lot more efficient (consuming less computation time and memory) than the deep learning (see Table 3). Let us share below some further observations made.

Accuracy. Summarizing the confusion matrices (Fig. 10 and Fig. 11) gives interesting contrasts in the peak anomaly detection accuracy between fDOM and turbidity (see Table 1).

- For fDOM, deep learning outperformed knowledge engineering for PLP (by 1.23 times), SKP (1.43 times), and PHP (2.18 times) while comparable for FPT and FSK. On the other hand, knowledge engineering outperformed deep learning for NAP (i.e., normal peaks) by 3.57 times.
- For turbidity, the results are different and somewhat reversed. Knowledge engineering outperformed deep learning for SKP (by 1.41 times) and for PHP (1.36 times) whereas underperformed for FPT (1.74 times) and NAP (1.91 times).

It is particularly noticeable that the deep learning did worse with NAP for fDOM while better with NAP for turbidity. We speculate this difference is due to their being more anomaly types for fDOM (five) than for turbidity (three), and therefore when being trained for fDOM the deep learning "paid more attention" to correctly detecting anomalous peaks at the expense of detecting non-anomalous peaks incorrectly.

Additionally, for turbidity, there was a large gap in accuracy for FPT between deep learning and knowledge engineering. We speculate the underlying cause is an excessive sparsity of FPT instances in the dataset. The original turbidity dataset has only one labeled FPT instance, and this single instance does not seem as steep (along the rising and falling edges of the plateau) as the knowledge engineering approach was looking for. Although during the peak augmentation (see Sect. 5.1) some of the FPT instances may have been made steep enough, not all of them would have been; and, as a result, the limited number of parameters for knowledge engineering caused the approach to miss the overall shape of the plateau, something that ResNet was extremely successful at (note that the accuracies for FPT and FSK in *fDOM* were quite high).

Computing Resources. As shown in Table 3, the knowledge engineering approach used much less computation time (25%) and memory (0.36% on average, 0.13% peak) for the threshold parameter tuning than the deep learning approach for the model train-ing (i.e., model parameter tuning). This is expected given the large difference in the number of parameters needed in the two approaches—that is, a few threshold param-eters per anomaly type in the knowledge engineering as opposed to over 25 million parameters (see Table 8 in Zagorukyo and Komodakis, 2016 [27]) in the deep learning. Note that the amount of computing resources used by the knowledge engineering is within the control of the "knowledge engineers" doing the parameter tuning and, spe-cifically, depends on the number of random search points tried during the tuning; the results in Table 3 are for 1,000 random search points.

Combining Knowledge Engineering and Deep Learning. Given the differences in accu-racies observed for the knowledge engineering and the deep learning for different peak types, combining the two approaches toward improving the accuracy would be a natural next step. One straightforward way is to use both approaches, and for each peak type, choose the approach that had the higher accuracy in the test results. For example, with fDOM, we would choose the deep learning approach for all peak types except for NAP, for which we would choose the knowledge engineering approach. Ultimately, integrating the two approaches into a single classifier would achieve the best accuracy, and we defer this to the future work.

6   Conclusion

This paper presented a study conducted to detect peak anomalies from hydrological time series data collected from a watershed in Vermont, U.S.A. We identified a set of peak anomaly types important to the hydrological and geochemical study of the watershed and implemented two different computational approaches, knowledge engineering and deep learning. We then assessed performance between the two approaches with respect to the anomaly detection accuracy and the computational resources (time and memory). The differences between knowledge engineering and deep learning for fDOM and turbidity were quite interesting. For fDOM, we believe that the lower detection accuracy on non-anomalous peaks can be attributed to dealing with a larger number (five) of anomalous peak type classes, as compared with three in turbidity. This difference caused the fDOM deep learning classifier to be worse at detecting non-anomalous peaks.

There are a number of future works in the plan. First, we will further improve the computational tuning/training by breaking the time series data by season and model each season separately. The breakdown can be by the calendar, such as winter (December – March), spring (April – May), summer (June – September), and fall (October—November), or can be adaptive to the actual data by incorporating a time series change point detection algorithm (e.g., BEAST (Bayesian Estimator for Abrupt Seasonal and Trend change) (Kaiguang 2022 [28])). Second, we will generalize the study to include multiple additional watersheds, and extend the work toward automated machine learning which selects the best model (tuned parameters) based on precompiled characteristics of the input time series data (Chatterjee et al. [29]). Having more data from different geographical areas would also lead to a more generalized classifier, as different watersheds may exhibit peak instances of different shapes for the same anomaly type. Third, we will develop a mechanism involving some form of merged classifier that trains using both the deep learning approach and the knowledge engineering approach. A model could learn to rely upon one or the other for a given peak type, using confidence values or some other form of measurement, and train using this method. This could lead to higher accuracies in detecting anomalies in different peak classes.

Acknowledgments. This material is based upon work supported by the National Science Foundation under Grant No. EAR 2012123. Any opinions, findings, and conclusions or recommendations expressed in this material are those of the author(s) and do not necessarily reflect the views of the National Science Foundation. Any use of trade, firm, or product names is for descriptive purposes only and does not imply endorsement by the U.S. Government. The work was also supported by the University of Vermont College of Engineering and Mathematical Sciences through the REU program.

The authors would like to thank the US Geological Survey (USGS) for offering the domain expertise that was crucial to identify the peak anomaly types that are of practical importance.

References

1. Cook, A., Mısırlı, G., Fan, Z.: Anomaly detection for IoT time-series data: a survey. IEEE Internet Things **7**(7), 6481–6494 (2020)
2. Sgueglia, A., Di Sorbo, A., Visaggio, C., Canfora, G.: A systematic literature review of IoT time series anomaly detection solutions. Futur. Gener. Comput. Syst. **134**, 170–186 (2022)
3. Hill, D.J., Minsker, B.S.: Anomaly detection in streaming environmental sensor data: a data-driven modeling approach. Environ. Model. Softw. **25**(9), 1014(2010)
4. Kim, J.-M., Cho, Y.W., Kim, D.-H.: Anomaly detection of environmental sensor data using recurrent neural network at the edge device. In: Proceedings of the 2020 International Conference on Information and Communication Technology Convergence, pp. 1624–1628. IEEE (2020)
5. Conde, E.: Environmental Sensor Anomaly Detection Using Learning Machines. MS Thesis. Utah State University (2011)
6. Hayes, M., Capretz, M.: Contextual anomaly detection in big sensor data. In: Proceedings of the 2014 IEEE International Congress on Big Data, pp. 64–71. Anchorage, AK, USA (2014)
7. Hill, D.J. and Minsker, B.S.: Automated fault detection for in-situ environmental sensors. In: Proceedings of the 7th International Conference on Hydroinformatics. Nice, France (2006)
8. Russo, S., Lürig, M., Hao, W., Matthews, B., Villez, K.: Active learning for anomaly detection in environmental data. Environ. Model. Softw. (134), 104869 (2020)
9. Jones, A.S., Jones, T.L., Horsburgh, J.S.: Toward automating post processing of aquatic sensor data. Environ. Model. Softw. (151), 105364 (2022)
10. Lai, K., et al.: Tods: an automated time series outlier detection system. In: Proceedings of the AAAI conference on artificial intelligence, vol. 35. no. 18, pp. 16060–16062 (2021)
11. Chandola, V., Banerjee, A., Kumar, V.: Anomaly detection: a survey. ACM Comput. Surv. (CSUR) **41**(3), 1–58 (2009)
12. Cho, H., Fryzlewicz, P.: Multiple-change-point detection for high dimensional time series via sparsified binary segmentation. J. Royal Statist. Soc. 475–507 (2015)
13. Enikeeva, F., Harchaoui, Z.: High-dimensional change-point detection under sparse alternatives. Ann. Statist. 2051–2079 (2019)
14. Fearnhead, P., Rigaill, G.: Changepoint detection in the presence of outliers. J. Am. Statist. Assoc. 169–183 (2019)
15. Fryzlewicz, P.: Wild binary segmentation for multiple change-point detection. Ann. Statist. 2243–2281 (2014)
16. Tveten, M., Eckley, I.A., Fearnhead, P.: Scalable change-point and anomaly detection in cross-correlated data with an application to condition monitoring. Ann. Appl. Statist. 721–743 (2022)
17. Pang, G., Shen, C., Cao, L. Hengel, A.V.D.: Deep learning for anomaly detection: a review. ACM Comput. Surv. 1–38 (2021)
18. Yu, Y., Wan, D., Zhao, Q., Liu, H.: Detecting pattern anomalies in hydrological time series with weighted probabilistic suffix trees. Water 1464 (2020)
19. Sun, J., Lou, Y., Ye, F.: Research on anomaly pattern detection in hydrological time series. In: 14th Web Information Systems and Applications Conference (WISA), pp. 38–43 IEEE (2017)

20. Qin, Y., Lou, Y.: Hydrological time series anomaly pattern detection based on isolation forest. In: IEEE 3rd Information Technology, Networking, Electronic and Automation Control Conference (ITNEC), pp. 1706–1710. IEEE (2019)
21. Lin, Y., Lee, B., Lustgarten, D.: Continuous detection of abnormal heartbeats from ECG using online outlier detection. In: Lossio-Ventura, J., Muñante, D., Alatrista-Salas, H. (eds.) Information Management and Big Data. SIMBig 2018. Communications in Computer and Information Science, vol. 898. Springer, Cham (2018). https://doi.org/10.1007/978-3-030-11680-4_33
22. Li, H., Boulanger, P.: A survey of heart anomaly detection using ambulatory Electrocardiogram (ECG). Sensors 1461 (2020)
23. Hong, S., et al.: Holmes: Health online model ensemble serving for deep learning models in intensive care units. In: Proceedings of the 26th ACM SIGKDD International Conference on Knowledge Discovery & Data Mining, pp. 1614–1624. ACM, New York, USA (2020)
24. Ismail Fawaz, H., Forestier, G., Weber, J., Idoumghar, L., Muller, P.-A.: Deep learning for time series classification: a review. Data Min. Knowl. Disc. **33**(4), 917–963 (2019). https://doi.org/10.1007/s10618-019-00619-1
25. Cerqueira, V., Torgo, L, Mozeti˘c, I.: Evaluating time series forecasting models: an empirical study on performance estimation methods. Mach. Learn. 109, 1997–2028 (2020)
26. Firebug: Practical hyperparameter optimization: random vs. grid search (2016). https://stats.stackexchange.com/q/209409
27. Zagorukyo, S., Komodakis, N.: Wide Residual Networks. In: Proceedings of the British Machine Vision Conference, p. 87.1–87.12. BMVA Press (2016)
28. Kaiguang: Bayesian Changepoint Detection & Time Series Decomposition. MathWorks (2022). https://www.mathworks.com/matlabcentral/fileexchange/72515-bayesian-changepoint-detection-time-series-decomposition
29. Chatterjee, S., Bopardikar, R., Guerard, M., Thakore, U., Jiang, X.: MOSPAT: AutoML based Model Selection and Parameter Tuning for Time Series Anomaly Detection. arXiv preprint arXiv:2205.11755 (2022)

Gas Sensors and Machine Learning for Quality Evaluation of Grape Spirits (Pisco)

Renzo Bolivar[1] , Edgar Sarmiento-Calisaya[1(✉)] ,
and Guina Sotomayor Alzamora[2]

[1] Universidad Nacional de San Agustín de Arequipa, Arequipa, Peru
{rbolivarv,esarmientoca}@unsa.edu.pe
[2] Universidad Nacional del Altiplano, Puno, Peru
gsotomayor@unap.edu.pe

Abstract. Pisco is Peru's national drink (The Peruvian state has the "Appellation of Origin"). It is distilled from grapes grown only in the regions of Lima, Ica, Arequipa, Moquegua or Tacna, and using methods that preserve the traditional principles of quality. Peru currently exports pisco to large-market countries (e.g. the European Union, the United States, Mexico, Canada, Australia, etc.); however, according to ADEX (The Peruvian Exporters Association), despite the fact that exports grow annually, losses have increased, mainly due to penalties and taxes for adulterated pisco. The adulterated pisco contains a high concentration of methanol and other types of alcohols, which are harmful to human health, and consequently it damages the economics of the beverage industry in Peru. This work addresses the design and development of a prototype tool to classify pisco and adulterated pisco, which is based on i) a gas sensor matrix that allows the identification of volatile compounds and congeners of pisco, ii) a data acquisition module based on a low-cost ARM (Advanced RISC Machine) micro-controller (Arduino), and iii) a classification model based on machine learning techniques. In the evaluation, pisco samples were used; and the results showed 97.29% of accuracy for the problem of classification and 7.43 s for the problem of training time. Therefore, it provides insights that the prototype is useful, low-cost, easy to use and fast. Thus, its development continues.

Keywords: distillate · grape spirits · pisco · classification · machine learning · PCA · sensors · aroma

1 Introduction

Pisco is the distilled drink most consumed and exported among alcoholic beverages in Peru. It is a special type of beverage produced from grapes grown only in the regions of Lima, Ica, Arequipa, Moquegua or Tacna (The Peruvian state has the "Appellation of Origin"). Its differential is the use of a preserved traditional knowledge in the aging process. That is, its process of preparation through

J. A. Lossio-Ventura et al. (Eds.): SIMBig 2022, CCIS 1837, pp. 158–174, 2023.
https://doi.org/10.1007/978-3-031-35445-8_12

fermentation and distillation is very particular if compared with other alcoholic beverages in the world, since only the fresh must of pisco grapes are used, which allows its originality by becoming a brandy of unique and exceptional purity[1].

According to ADEX (The Peruvian Exporters Association)[2], the exportation of pisco to large-market countries (e.g. the European Union, the United States, Mexico, Canada, Australia, etc.) has grown annually. However, the losses have increased, mainly due to penalties and taxes for adulterated pisco. An adulterated pisco contains high concentrations of methanol and other types of alcohols, which are harmful to human health.

In recent years, food and beverage safety have become a topic of interest because a contaminated or adulterated product (by chemical and biological contaminants) can negatively affect human health, and consequently it damages the economics of the beverage industry. Although different methods based on gas chromatography (determine the composition of a mixture of chemicals) [35], mass spectrometry (determine the distribution of the molecules of a substance as a function of its mass) [20], or other techniques are available for quality assessment of beverages, consumers are not motivated to adopt them due to complexity drawbacks in configuration, excessive number of steps for analysis, excessive processing time and costs, and lack of portability [6].

More recently, the development of analysis approaches based on electronic noses (e-nose) or electronic tongues (e-tongue) [25] have become more attractive tools for the food industry [29], beverages [22] and in other fields [18].

According to [29], an e-nose or e-tongue is a set of gas sensors or chemical sensors that mimic the human nose or human tongue. Both e-nose and e-tongue have shown great promise and usefulness in improving the analysis of beverage quality characteristics, compared to traditional detection methods. Most of the existing proposals are based on the aroma (odor) classification [19] by using neural networks, genetic algorithms or statistical techniques. E-tongue based methods are invasive, which can make them difficult to use in beverage analysis. Therefore, designing less complex, low-cost and easy-to-use tool for rapid analysis has become essential in beverage industry.

In this context, it is necessary to develop technological solutions of low cost and rapid analysis for detecting adulterated pisco, which should take into account the volatile and congener components of Pisco [13], i.e., the aroma. Several approaches based on aroma (reported in [12, 14, 16]) were proposed for the classification of other types of beverages such as wine, beer or cachaça (Brazil). Thus, aroma analysis allows the detection of anomalies in a rapid and timely way.

Therefore, this paper addresses the design and development of a prototype tool to classify pisco and adulterated pisco, which is based on i) a gas sensor matrix that allows the identification of volatile components and congeners of samples of pisco through chemical analysis; ii) a data acquisition module based on a low-cost ARM (Advanced RISC Machine) micro-controller (Arduino) connected to the gas sensors; and iii) a classification model based on algorithms of

---

[1] CONAPISCO https://bit.ly/3kQHt91.
[2] ADEX https://bit.ly/3gbMF8w.

signal processing, principal component analysis (PCA) and Back-Propagation neural networks performed on data obtained from samples of pisco. In the evaluation, pisco samples were used, and the results showed 97.29% of accuracy for the problem of classification and 7.43 s for the problem of training time. Therefore, it provides insights that the prototype is useful, low-cost, easy to use and fast. Thus, its development continues.

2   Related Work

Several approaches based on e-nose and machine learning algorithms have been proposed to classify or predict different parameters related to the quality of alcoholic beverages, mainly for the classification or quality analysis of wine, beer or distilled beverages. Consequently, there are different review studies [12,14,16] that compare or validate existing proposals.

Methods based on machine learning along with other technologies such as sensors and robotics have been proposed to classify beer or wine samples into different categories or to determine their quality. These are based on the analysis of aromas (foreign or adulterated) acquired by e-noses [11,15,22,27,34].

Santos and Lozano [27] used an e-nose, which consists of a device with a gas sensors matrix (metal oxide or polymer semiconductors) capable of emulating the olfactory system to analyze the two main odors of beer, acetaldehyde and ethyl acetate. They used the e-nose output values as input to develop a probabilistic neural network model to predict whether those compounds fell above a threshold (the presence of defects in the beer) with 94% accuracy at the validation phase.

Gonzalez Viejo et al. [15,34] developed methods based on artificial neural networks and e-nose for beer analysis, for instance, defect detection, classification of hops, barley, yeast and types of beer. The sensors are calibrated to measure volatile compounds such as carbon dioxide, ethanol, methane, diacetyl, hydrogen, hydrogen sulfide, carbon monoxide, ammonia, and benzene, which can affect beer quality. The proposed models reached an accuracy higher than 95% and the developed device is easy to use and portable.

Rodriguez et al. [11] developed a portable and compact e-nose based on thin-film semiconductor (SnO2) sensors and trained with a deep multilayer perceptron neural network approach for early detection of wine spoilage (Brazilian wines), whose results are delivered in less than three seconds. The accuracy achieved in the validation phase was 96.34%.

Liu et al. [22] developed a portable e-nose prototype using sensors (oxide semiconductor - MOS) to detect odors from different wines. Odor detection makes it easy the distinction of wines with different properties, including production areas, vintage years, fermentation processes and varietals. Four common machine learning algorithms were used for classification tasks, being the "Support Vector Machine" (SVM) and Back Propagation Neural Network (BPNN) algorithms the ones that achieved the best accuracy: 92.5% and 60.5%, respectively. The results demonstrate the efficacy of the developed e-nose, which could be used to distinguish different wines based on their properties after selecting an optimal algorithm. Insufficient samples or sensors may have affected the performance of the algorithms used.

Table 1 compares the most relevant proposals based on the following characteristics: Types of Sensors, Objective (Type of Beverage), Algorithms used for data processing and classification, Response Time, Cost, Portability and Size, Dataset Availability and Accuracy.

Table 1. Comparison of the most relevant e-nose-based beverage analysis approaches.

Approach	Santos and Lozano [27]	Gonzalez Viejo et al. [15,34]	Rodríguez et al. [11]	Liu et al. [22]
Sensor Type	Commercial microsensor of SILSENS (MGS 4000)	9 Gas sensors (MQ Sensors)	Thin film semiconductor (SnO2) sensors	Metal oxide semiconductor (MOS) sensors
Objective	Beer Quality	Beer Quality	Wine Quality	Wine Quality
Algoritmh	PCA, PNN	ANNOVA, ANN	PCA, Deep MLP	PCA, SVM, BPNN
Response Time	–	–	$<3\,$s	Real Time
Cost	Low	$<\$100$	Low	–
Portability	Small	15 cm	–	Portable
Dataset	–	–	–	–
Accuracy	94%	95%	96.34%	92,5%

Relevant existing approaches based on e-nose highlight the following challenges: i) sample preparation is challenging due to the amount of volatiles released from beverage depends on many factors such as temperature, pressure and humidity; ii) an insufficient number of data samples or sensors may affect the performance of the algorithms used; and iii) the dimensionality reduction can reduce the accuracy of classifiers.

Therefore, it is a challenging task to use e-noses in real environments or mobile detection. However, most of the proposed approaches can be extended to be used in other contexts, e.g. pisco.

Finally, it was difficult to find any proposal for the analysis of Peruvian pisco or any type of similar beverage. Therefore, we consider it important to develop a low-cost and portable prototype for the analysis or detection of adulterated pisco.

3   Materials and Methods

The main objective of this work is to develop a low cost prototype for quality analysis of pisco with a limited sample size [31] of pure and adulterated pisco (with high concentrations of methanol). In our approach, an array of MQ sensors is responsible for collecting gas data from pisco samples, then, it is analogically connected to a data acquisition board (based on an Arduino Nano micro-controller), which sends the data to a computer via Bluetooth. Finally,

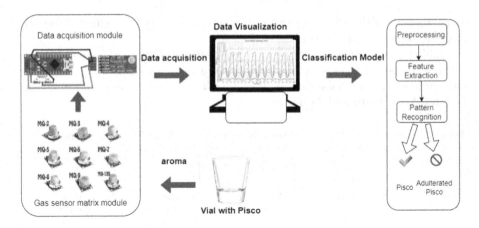

Fig. 1. Illustration of the pisco classification approach

the data processing and pisco classification will be performed by signal processing, principal component analysis (PCA) and neural networks algorithms on a computer. Figure 1 depicts the proposed approach.

3.1 E-Nose Prototype

The prototype is composed of two modules interacting in the following way: the sensor matrix module (Fig. 2a) in the bottom side that will reach the vial with the sample of pisco, and the data acquisition module (Fig. 2b) in the upper side connected to its power supply. The e-nose prototype is depicted in Fig. 2c.

The measurement begins with the e-nose prototype (see Fig. 2c) at the top of the elevation system, after 20 s, the prototype lowers to the height of the vial containing pisco or adulterated pisco, after 60 s, the prototype moves back to the top and initial state for a period of 40 s; then the cycle repeats going down for 60 s and going up for 40 s until completing 1000 s seconds. Finally, the acquired data is sent via Bluetooth to a computer, where the streamed data is displayed in real time. The data visualization is essential for sampling, because it allows the researcher to monitor in real time the acquisition of samples.

Sensor Matrix. According to the Peruvian Technical Standard (NTP 211.001. 2002), three distinct types of pisco were designated: Puro (pure), Mosto Verde (Green Must) and Acholado (Multivarietal). Likewise, it classifies the pisco grapes into aromatic (Italia, Moscatel, Albilla and Torontel) and non-aromatic (Quebranta, Mollar, Negra, Corriente and Uvina). Thus, pisco consists of a wide variety of volatile compounds, such as terpenes, higher alcohols, esters, methanol, acetaldehyde, acetic acid and furfural [17].

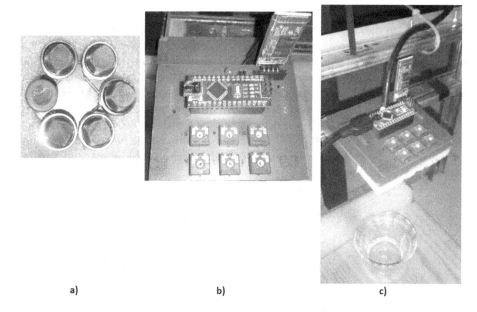

a)   b)   c)

Fig. 2. MQ sensors (a), data acquisition board (b), and e-nose prototype (c).

According to Garrido et al. [13], pisco contains nineteen different chemical compounds. This composition changes according to the type of pisco, as shown in Table 2.

Table 2. Pisco composition [13].

Compound	ITA	QUEB	TOR	MOSC	ALB	MOL	UVI
Methanol	Yes	Yes	Yes	Yes	Yes	Yes	Yes
Ethanol	Yes	Yes	Yes	Yes	Yes	Yes	Yes
Propan-1-ol	Yes	Yes	Yes	Yes	Yes	Yes	Yes
Isobutanol	Yes	Yes	Yes	Yes	Yes	Yes	Yes
3 - Metil Butan-1-ol	Yes	Yes	Yes	Yes	Yes	Yes	No
2 - Metil Butan-1-ol	Yes	Yes	Yes	Yes	Yes	Yes	No
Diethyl Acetal	Yes	Yes	Yes	Yes	No	Yes	Yes
Ethyl Acetate	Yes	Yes	Yes	Yes	Yes	Yes	No

In order to detect adulterated pisco, an e-nose must analyze the excess of methanol, because it impacts negatively the human health. Then, in this work, the sensors matrix was composed of MQ gas sensors because they present a high sensitivity to compounds derived from alcohol. Since not all these sensors are focused on alcohol, a careful selection of six sensors ($MQ-2$, $MQ-3$, $MQ-6$, $MQ-7$, $MQ-8$ and the $MQ-135$) [1,7] were made.

The MQ family of sensors has a sensitive layer made up of a metal oxide, in this case tin dioxide ($SnO2$). In the presence of a gas, the metal oxide causes the dissociation of the gas into ions, triggering an electron transfer and variation in the conductivity of the layer. Since this process depends on temperature, the sensor contains a heater to equilibrate the temperature of the pisco with the air in the vial [24]. Each sensor has different characteristics to identify the odor and taste of gas. The $MQ - 2$ sensor detects the presence of $H2$, alcohol, LPG, and $CH4$ [23]; while Sensor $MQ - 3$ detects the presence of alcohol, $CH4$ and CO [28]. Both $MQ - 2$ and $MQ - 3$ detect the presence of alcohol, however they have a different level of sensitivity. Table 3 shows the types of gas that can be detected by each sensor.

Table 3. Sensor array in e-nose prototype.

Sensor	Gas	Compound
MQ-2	Propane	H2, LPG, CH4, CO, Alcohol, Smoke, Propane, air
MQ-3	Ethanol	LPG, CH4, CO, Alcohol, Benzene, Hexane, air
MQ-6	Methane (CH4)	H2, LPG, CH4, CO, Alcohol, air
MQ-7	Alcohol	H2, LPG, CH4, CO, Alcohol, air
MQ-8	Methane (CH4)	H2, LPG, CH4, CO, Alcohol, air MQ-135 Alcohol, NH4, CO2, air
MQ-135	Acetone	Alcohol, NH4, CO2, air

Figure 3 displays the readings of the MQ sensors. Each response curve represents the voltage variation of each sensor with time when piscos' volatiles reached the measurement chamber. More details about the sensors matrix (see Fig. 2a) design and implementation can be found in [4].

Microprocessor and Peripheral Modules. An Arduino Nano microcontroller was used for the prototype and algorithm. The embedded software has three main functions: i) acquiring sensors' response, ii) processing data and iii) communicating with the computer via Bluetooth.

The design of the e-nose acquisition module was carried out in the *Eagle* tool. On the left side of Fig. 4, the six MQ sensors matrix is shown; on the right side (bottom), the six potentiometers matrix is shown, which are connected to the Arduino Nano $JP2$ (It presents 2 serial and wireless outputs) connector. On the upper right side, we have the $JP1$ (with the pins of the $CH - 05$ module for *Bluetooth*) and $S1$ (the serial output to connect to the power supply via USB) connectors.

Finally, a program in *C language* was embedded in the Arduino Nano for the acquisition of data from the MQ sensors (see Fig. 2b). Details about the design and implementation of the data acquisition board can be found in [4].

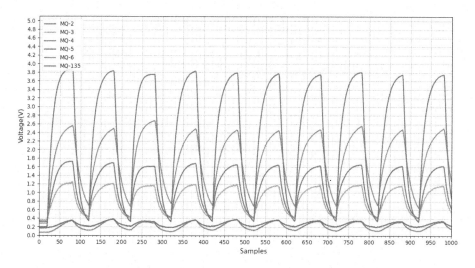

Fig. 3. Visualization of acquired data from MQ sensors.

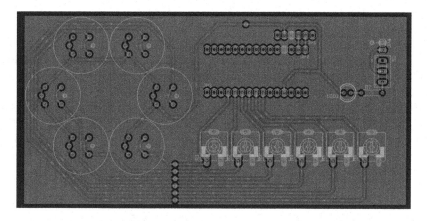

Fig. 4. Design of the e-nose acquisition module.

3.2   Pisco Samples

Samples of bottles of pisco (pisco and adulterated pisco) were used to analyze their properties. For each bottle of pisco, 1000 samples were taken; furthermore, 80% were used for model training, the remaining samples were used for testing.

For each bottle, as shown in Fig. 2c, 50 ml of pisco was put into a vial (100 ml) and was allowed to equilibrate the temperature with the air in the vial. The workflow of the e-nose prototype is depicted in Fig. 1.

The structure of the data acquired by the sensors is described by *8 columns* and *1000 rows* (1000 samples). Thus, the first 6 columns are the readings of the *MQ sensors*, and the last 2 columns are *sample date* and *sample enumeration*. Figure 5 shows the data after cleaning.

	MQ2	MQ3	MQ4	MQ5	MQ6	MQ135
0	0.32	0.42	0.08	0.22	0.16	0.26
1	0.32	0.42	0.08	0.22	0.16	0.26
2	0.32	0.42	0.08	0.22	0.16	0.26
3	0.32	0.42	0.08	0.22	0.16	0.26
4	0.32	0.41	0.08	0.22	0.16	0.26
...	...	...	...	...	...	...
995	0.73	0.60	0.18	0.24	1.36	1.20
996	0.70	0.59	0.17	0.24	1.30	1.11
997	0.67	0.56	0.17	0.23	1.25	1.03
998	0.64	0.54	0.16	0.23	1.21	0.96
999	0.62	0.52	0.16	0.22	1.16	0.89

1000 rows × 6 columns

Fig. 5. Data acquired from pisco samples

3.3   Pisco Classification

Preprocessing. Before training and testing, sensors' response data is cleaned - *Data Cleaning*, that is, the columns are labeled with their respective *MQ* sensor, the date and enumeration columns are removed (as in Fig. 5).

Then, a *Pearson Correlation Analysis* [3] on the data shows that the correlation between the variables of the *MQ* sensors is close to 1 (as in Fig. 6), which statistically indicates direct relationship among them, then, statistical analysis of regression and prediction can be carried out [30].

	MQ2	MQ3	MQ4	MQ5	MQ6	MQ135
MQ2	1.000000	0.994072	0.820174	0.835512	0.956327	0.997032
MQ3	0.994072	1.000000	0.810586	0.855832	0.934869	0.990906
MQ4	0.820174	0.810586	1.000000	0.947992	0.902927	0.796981
MQ5	0.835512	0.855832	0.947992	1.000000	0.852295	0.818456
MQ6	0.956327	0.934869	0.902927	0.852295	1.000000	0.945190
MQ135	0.997032	0.990906	0.796981	0.818456	0.945190	1.000000

Fig. 6. Pearson correlation analysis on the acquired data.

As a next step, response signals of the sensors (see Fig. 3) - *curves* have to be transformed into a format of features, in order to be carried out by pattern analysis and recognition algorithms.

Feature Extraction. Feature extraction[3] [8, 21] consists in transforming raw data, such as text, signals or images, into numerical features usable for machine learning, while preserving the information in the original data set. Feature extraction is related to Dimensionality Reduction [32] or Feature selection.

Research proposed in [10, 29] developed techniques to extract statistical values from a typical gas sensor matrix output signals (as in Fig. 3). Therefore, in this work was used a *sliding window* [5] technique to extract features. Several kinds of features (e.g., stable value - SV, mean-differential coefficient value, and response area value) can be used in pattern recognition algorithms.

Thus, our data is transformed into 32 columns with temporal features (see Fig. 7 and 8):

> '0_ECDF Percentile Count_0', '0_ECDF Percentile Count_1',
> '0_ECDF Percentile_0', '0_ECDF Percentile_1', '0_ECDF_0',
> '0_ECDF_1', '0_ECDF_2', '0_ECDF_3', '0_ECDF_4',
> '0_ECDF_5', '0_Histogram_0', '0_Histogram_1',
> '0_Histogram_2', '0_Histogram_3', '0_Histogram_4',
> '0_Histogram_5', '0_Histogram_6', '0_Histogram_7',
> '0_Histogram_8', '0_Histogram_9', '0_Interquartile range',
> '0_Kurtosis', '0_Max', '0_Mean',
> '0_Mean absolute deviation', '0_Median',

The feature extraction procedure was developed using Python language and the Time Series Feature Extraction Library - TSFEL [2] module (It computes over 60 different features extracted across temporal, statistical and spectral domains). Details about the formulas and the feature extraction transformations are available in [4].

	0_ECDF Percentile Count_0	0_ECDF Percentile Count_1	0_ECDF Percentile_0	0_ECDF Percentile_1	0_ECDF_0	0_ECDF_1	0_ECDF_2	0_ECDF_3	0_ECDF_4	0_ECDF_5	...	0
0	1.0	4.0	0.08	0.26	0.166667	0.333333	0.5	0.666667	0.833333	1.0	...	
1	1.0	4.0	0.08	0.26	0.166667	0.333333	0.5	0.666667	0.833333	1.0	...	
2	1.0	4.0	0.08	0.26	0.166667	0.333333	0.5	0.666667	0.833333	1.0	...	
3	1.0	4.0	0.08	0.26	0.166667	0.333333	0.5	0.666667	0.833333	1.0	...	
4	1.0	4.0	0.08	0.26	0.166667	0.333333	0.5	0.666667	0.833333	1.0	...	
...	...	...	...	...	...	...	...	...	...	...	...	
995	1.0	4.0	0.18	0.73	0.166667	0.333333	0.5	0.666667	0.833333	1.0	...	
996	1.0	4.0	0.17	0.70	0.166667	0.333333	0.5	0.666667	0.833333	1.0	...	
997	1.0	4.0	0.17	0.67	0.166667	0.333333	0.5	0.666667	0.833333	1.0	...	
998	1.0	4.0	0.16	0.64	0.166667	0.333333	0.5	0.666667	0.833333	1.0	...	
999	1.0	4.0	0.16	0.62	0.166667	0.333333	0.5	0.666667	0.833333	1.0	...	

1000 rows × 32 columns

Fig. 7. Features extracted from curves - part 1.

---

[3] SCIKIT https://bit.ly/3eM5Pl2.

ECDF_4	0_ECDF_5	...	0_Max	0_Mean	0_Mean absolute deviation	0_Median	0_Median absolute deviation	0_Min	0_Root mean square	0_Skewness	0_Standard deviation	0_Variance
0.833333	1.0	...	0.42	0.243333	0.090000	0.240	0.080	0.08	0.266708	0.130648	0.109189	0.011922
0.833333	1.0	...	0.42	0.243333	0.090000	0.240	0.080	0.08	0.266708	0.130648	0.109189	0.011922
0.833333	1.0	...	0.42	0.243333	0.090000	0.240	0.080	0.08	0.266708	0.130648	0.109189	0.011922
0.833333	1.0	...	0.42	0.243333	0.090000	0.240	0.080	0.08	0.266708	0.130648	0.109189	0.011922
0.833333	1.0	...	0.41	0.241667	0.088333	0.240	0.080	0.08	0.264102	0.065709	0.106523	0.011347
...	...	...	...	...	...	...	...	...	...	...	...	...
0.833333	1.0	...	1.36	0.718333	0.378333	0.665	0.455	0.18	0.843850	0.208914	0.442810	0.196081
0.833333	1.0	...	1.30	0.685000	0.351667	0.645	0.435	0.17	0.800698	0.195998	0.414598	0.171892
0.833333	1.0	...	1.25	0.651667	0.331667	0.615	0.400	0.17	0.760230	0.224605	0.391511	0.153281
0.833333	1.0	...	1.21	0.623333	0.313333	0.590	0.365	0.16	0.726338	0.254596	0.372857	0.139022
0.833333	1.0	...	1.16	0.595000	0.295000	0.570	0.335	0.16	0.691195	0.270303	0.351746	0.123725

Fig. 8. Features extracted from curves - part 2.

This procedure was carried out for both the pisco and adulterated pisco samples, and at this stage, we labeled the data by adding a last column with: 0 for *adulterated pisco* and 1 for *pisco*.

The resulting dataset (pisco + adulterated pisco) used for our experiment was expressed as a 2000 × 33 (32 extracted features + 1 label for pisco or adulterated pisco) matrix. Taking as an input this initial dataset, our Back-Propagation Neural Network model produced results with 20% of accuracy. In order to improve this result, we reduced the dimentionality of our dataset.

Dimensionality Reduction Dimensionality reduction [9,32] is the transformation of high-dimensional data into a meaningful representation of reduced dimensionality, i.e., reduce the number of features in a dataset by creating new features from the existing ones. Ideally, the reduced representation should have a dimensionality that corresponds to the intrinsic dimensionality of the data. Principal Components Analysis - PCA [33] is one of the most used linear dimensionality reduction technique.

In order to improve the accuracy of our experiment, we applied PCA, reducing the dimension from 32 (first) features to 14 principal components. In general, first few principal components whose cumulative variance contribution exceeds 95% are considered dimensionality-reduced data and often contain nearly all information from the original data [22].

Pattern Recognition. In this work, a Back-Propagation Neural Network (BPNN) was used to classify pisco and adulterated pisco. This technique uses supervised learning type. A multilayer perceptron neural network (MLP) with 4 neurons in the hidden layer was used. The training algorithm used was Back-Propagation. The pipeline of the classification approach is depicted in Fig. 1

Data Preparation: Data is divided into two subsets: input (14 principal components from PCA) and outcome (2 classes representing *adulterated pisco* and *pisco*).

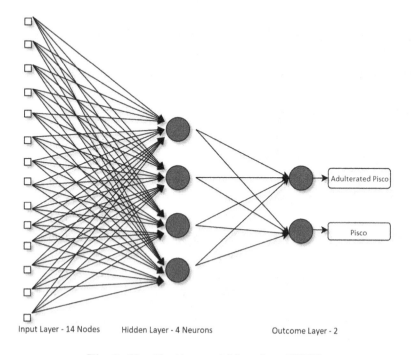

Fig. 9. Classification model based on BPNN.

Training the BPNN: In BPNN training, several neurons in the hidden layer were explored. The final model has 14 nodes in the input layer, 4 neurons in the hidden layer and 2 neurons in the output layer (See Fig. 9).

The initialization of the *hyperparameters* is very important for the accuracy and performance of neural networks. We started with *learning rate* = 0.01, a *ReLu* activation function in the hidden layer, and a *softmax* activation function in the outcome layer. This program was developed using the Python language and the *Keras*[4] module. In *Keras*, *accuracy* is used as metric for classification models; for *loss* argument we used *categorical cross entropy* and the *Adam* optimizer. In order to get a good time performance for training, we explored several values for *batchsize* and *epochs*, so our data was divided into a *batch size* of 32, and the number of *epochs* was determined to be 150.

---

[4] KERAS https://keras.io/.

Table 4 shows that the best accuracy and a good training time are obtained when we reduce the number of *epochs*, hidden layer *neurons*. Bold row indicates the best results.

Table 4. Accuracy values in training.

num. of principal components	neurons	epochs	batch_size	accuracy	time
2	16	500	32	68.80%	42.26 s
4	16	500	32	84.35%	27.03 s
6	16	500	32	91.50%	25.77 s
6	12	500	32	90.89%	23.27 s
6	12	300	32	89.95%	15.59 s
6	8	300	32	87.74%	13.88 s
8	8	300	32	91.54%	13.89 s
10	8	300	32	96.85%	14.00 s
10	4	300	32	82.95%	14.04 s
12	4	300	32	86.90%	14.08 s
13	4	300	32	93.19%	13.87 s
13	4	150	32	93.84%	7.57 s
14	**4**	**150**	**32**	**97.29%**	**7.43 s**
16	4	150	32	99.99%	7.71 s
18	4	150	32	100.00%	7.71 s

Validation: Cross-Validation [26] is a common solution when the available datasets are limited. Instead of training a fixed model only once as in Train/Test split, iteratively several models are developed on different portions of the data. K-Fold is a common cross-validation (CV) approach [31]. Table 5 shows the results obtained after applying *cross-validation* to our dataset. Bold row indicates the best results.

Again, the best accuracy results are obtained with 14 components, 97.20% and 96.00% for accuracy in training (accuracy_t) and validation (accuracy_v) data, respectively. Given, the accuracy values closely follow the training results, it validates the Pisco quality classification model with a BPNN.

4   Results and Discussion

The resulting model is a BPNN, with 3 activation layers, and a performance of 97.29% for accuracy (Tables 4 and 5):

– **Input layer**: The best accuracy is between 2 and *14 principal components*.
– **Hidden layer**: *4 neurons* for the shortest training time and high accuracy.
– **Output layer**: *2 neurons*, for pisco and adulterated pisco.

Table 5. Accuracy values in validation.

num. of principal components	neurons	epochs	batch_size	accuracy_t	accuracy_v	time
2	16	500	32	68.76%	67.10%	44.16 s
4	16	500	32	84.30%	83.05%	29.00 s
6	16	500	32	91.44%	89.62%	27.47 s
6	12	500	32	90.69%	88.99%	25.11 s
6	12	300	32	89.90%	90.12%	18.02 s
6	8	300	32	87.54%	85.92%	15.68 s
8	8	300	32	91.47%	90.09%	15.98 s
10	8	300	32	96.77%	94.43%	16.70 s
10	4	300	32	82.76%	81.01%	16.40 s
12	4	300	32	86.69%	84.33%	16.11 s
13	4	300	32	93.09%	91.65%	15.67 s
13	4	150	32	93.61%	94.79%	9.77 s
14	**4**	**150**	**32**	**97.20%**	**96.00%**	**9.21 s**
16	4	150	32	100.00%	99.99%	9.91 s
18	4	150	32	100.00%	100.00%	9.96 s

In Table 4, we observe that few components lead to high number of hidden neurons and high hyperparameters, i.e., high processing time and a low accuracy. On the other hand, when the number of components increase, we see that accuracy and training times improve. Thus, the **optimal number was determined to be 14 components**, since a higher number tends to overfitting, and a smaller number tends to take longer and lower accuracy.

Table 5 shows that accuracy and validation times improve for 14 components. Figures 10a and 10b depict the *accuracy* and *loss* values obtained for training and validation, respectively.

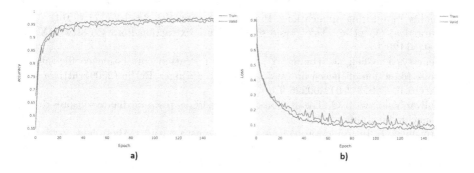

Fig. 10. Accuracy and loss in training and validation.

Testing in Production. Tests were carried out with samples of several bottles of pisco and adulterated pisco. Results have shown a high accuracy (100%) of the model and a low response time (Overall, 1018.10 ms = approximately 16.96 min):

– Sampling: 1000 ms = 16.6 min for collecting data from samples.
– Processing: 15.10 s for feature extraction and dimension reduction.
– Classification: 3.00 s.

5   Conclusion

An e-nose prototype was developed for pisco quality analysis, which is based on Gas Sensors, Principal Component Analysis and Back-Propagation Neural Networks. This prototype takes as an input the odors - aromas of pisco to detect adulterated pisco.

In general the prototype performed the classification problem with a high **accuracy (97.29%)** and in a low training time (**7.43 s**).

In order to validate the model, the data was divided into 80% for training and 20% for testing, the **validation accuracy was 96.00%**. It was used a **cross-validation** technique with a total training time of **9.21 s**.

The main limitation of this research is the limited sample size. In order to reduce this threat, we applied an approach for validation with a limited sample size proposed in [31]. Other limitation is the procedure to acquire the aromas from the samples, given that it is carried out in an open environment, the performance may have been affected.

As future work we intend: i) to develop a more portable prototype, which can be designed in an acrylic box where the aromas are more concentrated; ii) to extend the evaluation using several bottles of pisco and their types; iii) to adjust the accuracy of the prototype by analyzing other properties like grape variety, aging time, production areas and grape origin; and iv) to extend the research for analysis of other types of beverages.

References

1. Abraham, S., Li, X.: A cost-effective wireless sensor network system for indoor air quality monitoring applications. Procedia Comput. Sci. **34**, 165–171 (2014)
2. Barandas, M., et al.: Tsfel: time series feature extraction library. SoftwareX **11**, 100456 (2020)
3. Benesty, J., Chen, J., Huang, Y., Cohen, I.: Pearson correlation coefficient. In: Noise reduction in speech processing, pp. 1–4. Springer, Berlin (2009). https://doi.org/10.1007/978-3-642-00296-0_5
4. Bolivar Valdivia, R.G.: Evaluación de la calidad del pisco mediante sensores de gas y machine learning (2021)
5. Brownlee, J.: Introduction to time series forecasting with python: how to prepare data and develop models to predict the future. Machine Learning Mastery (2017)
6. Brudzewski, K., Osowski, S., Golembiecka, A.: Differential electronic nose and support vector machine for fast recognition of tobacco. Expert Syst. Appl. **39**(10), 9886–9891 (2012)

7. Carrillo-Amado, Y.R., Califa-Urquiza, M.A., Ramón-Valencia, J.A.: Calibration and standardization of air quality measurements using mq sensors. Respuestas **25**(1), 70–77 (2020)
8. Dara, S., Tumma, P.: Feature extraction by using deep learning: a survey. In: 2018 Second International Conference on Electronics, Communication and Aerospace Technology (ICECA), pp. 1795–1801. IEEE (2018)
9. Deng, L., Yu, D., et al.: Deep learning: methods and applications. Foundations and trends® in signal processing **7**(3–4), 197–387 (2014)
10. Fu, J., Li, G., Qin, Y., Freeman, W.J.: A pattern recognition method for electronic noses based on an olfactory neural network. Sens. Actuators, B Chem. **125**(2), 489–497 (2007)
11. Gamboa, J.C.R., da Silva, A.J., de Andrade Lima, L.L., Ferreira, T.A., et al.: Wine quality rapid detection using a compact electronic nose system: application focused on spoilage thresholds by acetic acid. Lwt 108, 377–384 (2019)
12. Gamboa, J.C.R., da Silva, A.J., Araujo, I.C., et al.: Validation of the rapid detection approach for enhancing the electronic nose systems performance, using different deep learning models and support vector machines. Sens. Actuators, B Chem. **327**, 128921 (2021)
13. Garrido, A., Linares, T., Cárdenas, L.: Estudio de la composición del pisco de diferentes variedades de uvas pisqueras desde el mosto hasta el producto (parte ii-el pisco). Revista Peruana de Química e Ingeniería Química **11**(2), 58–60 (2008)
14. Geană, E.I., Ciucure, C.T., Apetrei, C.: Electrochemical sensors coupled with multivariate statistical analysis as screening tools for wine authentication issues: A review. Chemosensors **8**(3), 59 (2020)
15. Gonzalez Viejo, C., Fuentes, S., Hernandez-Brenes, C.: Smart detection of faults in beers using near-infrared spectroscopy, a low-cost electronic nose and artificial intelligence. Fermentation **7**(3), 117 (2021)
16. Gonzalez Viejo, C., Torrico, D.D., Dunshea, F.R., Fuentes, S.: Emerging technologies based on artificial intelligence to assess the quality and consumer preference of beverages. Beverages **5**(4), 62 (2019)
17. Hatta, B., Domenech, A., Palma, J.: Influencia de la fermentación con orujos en los componentes volátiles mayoritarios del pisco de uva italia (vitis vinifera l. var. italia). In: XIII Congreso Nacional de Biotecnología y Bioingeniería y VII Simposio Internacional de Producción de Alcoholes y Levaduras, pp. 21–26 (2009)
18. Hsieh, Y.C., Yao, D.J.: Intelligent gas-sensing systems and their applications. J. Micromech. Microeng. **28**(9), 093001 (2018)
19. Jong, G.J., Wang, Z.H., Hsieh, K.S., Horng, G.J., et al.: A novel feature extraction method an electronic nose for aroma classification. IEEE Sens. J. **19**(22), 10796–10803 (2019)
20. Kaufmann, A.: The current role of high-resolution mass spectrometry in food analysis. Anal. Bioanal. Chem. **403**(5), 1233–1249 (2012)
21. Liu, H., Motoda, H.: Feature Extraction, Construction and Selection: A Data Mining Perspective, vol. 453. Springer Science & Business Media, Berlin (1998)
22. Liu, H., Li, Q., Yan, B., Zhang, L., Gu, Y.: Bionic electronic nose based on MOS sensors array and machine learning algorithms used for wine properties detection. Sensors **19**(1), 45 (2019)
23. Mouser: Mouser MQ-2 Technical Data. https://bit.ly/3AHF1bl, Accessed Aug 2021
24. Nagy, A.S., Polanco Risquet, A., Martínez de la Cotera, O.L., Carralero Ibargollen, O.: Medición simultánea de gases con sensores mq. Ingeniería Electrónica, Automática y Comunicaciones **41**(1), 34–43 (2020)

25. Orlandi, G., Calvini, R., Foca, G., Pigani, L., Simone, G.V., Ulrici, A.: Data fusion of electronic eye and electronic tongue signals to monitor grape ripening. Talanta **195**, 181–189 (2019)
26. Refaeilzadeh, P., Tang, L., Liu, H.: Encyclopedia of database systems. Cross-validation **5**, 532–538 (2009)
27. Santos, J.P., Lozano, J.: Real time detection of beer defects with a hand held electronic nose. In: 2015 10th Spanish Conference on Electron Devices (CDE), pp. 1–4. IEEE (2015)
28. Sparkfun: Sparkfun mq-3 technical data. https://bit.ly/3zG0SyK. Accessed Aug 2021
29. Tan, J., Xu, J.: Applications of electronic nose (e-nose) and electronic tongue (e-tongue) in food quality-related properties determination: A review. artificial Intelligence in Agriculture (2020)
30. Tukey, J.W., et al.: Exploratory Data Analysis, vol. 2. Reading, MA (1977)
31. Vabalas, A., Gowen, E., Poliakoff, E., Casson, A.J.: Machine learning algorithm validation with a limited sample size. PLoS ONE **14**(11), e0224365 (2019)
32. Van Der Maaten, L., Postma, E., Van den Herik, J., et al.: Dimensionality reduction: a comparative. J. Mach. Learn. Res. **10**(66–71), 13 (2009)
33. Vidal, R., Ma, Y., Sastry, S.: Generalized principal component analysis (GPCA). IEEE Trans. Pattern Anal. Mach. Intell. **27**(12), 1945–1959 (2005)
34. Viejo, C.G., Fuentes, S., Godbole, A., Widdicombe, B., Unnithan, R.R.: Development of a low-cost e-nose to assess aroma profiles: an artificial intelligence application to assess beer quality. Sens. Actuators, B Chem. **308**, 127688 (2020)
35. Yu, H., Dai, X., Yao, G., Xiao, Z.: Application of gas chromatography-based electronic nose for classification of Chinese rice wine by wine age. Food Anal. Methods **7**(7), 1489–1497 (2014)

Optimal Layer Selection on Deep Convolutional Neural Networks Using Backward Freezing and Binary Search

Henry Miguel Herrera Del Aguila$^{(\boxtimes)}$ (iD) and José Alfredo Herrera Quispe (iD)

Universidad Nacional Mayor de San Marcos, Cercado de Lima 15081, Peru
{henry.herrera2,jherreraqu}@unmsm.edu.pe

Abstract. Transfer Learning in Deep Convolutional Neural Networks is a highly used method for image classification, the performance depends on the selection of the layers to be frozen; the search for the optimal layer where the backward freezing will be applied becomes increasingly complicated as the number of layers increases. We found an approximation of the optimal layer to apply backward freezing using a modified Binary Search method. We experimented with InceptionV3, Xception, DenseNet121, NasNetMobile, and ResNet50; the case of study is the classification of melanomas of benign and malignant class from Kaggle. We use partitions with four-folds and measure the performance with the ROC AUC score. Our results show an improvement in the ROC AUC score for ResNet50 and no significant change for InceptionV3.
Code: https://www.kaggle.com/code/hherrera007/binary-search.

Keywords: Transfer learning · Deep Convolutional Neural Network · Optimal layer selection · Image Classification · Freezing

1 Introduction

Since the CNNs creation, various researchers have been responsible for building models called Deep Convolutional Neural Networks (DCNN) [13], this type of convolutional neural network has demonstrated its ability to solve image classification problems through a hierarchical model with millions of parameters and large databases [12]. Its use has been successfully implemented in the industry and commerce fields, and has had a great impact on the field of medicine [2].

These DCNN combined with transfer learning give us better results due to the reuse of the acquired knowledge. Transfer learning develops models based on historical data for tasks with low data availability, and new types of classification models are inferred [8]. DCNN with transfer learning frozen layers increases the classification accuracy. One of the problems is to determine which layers are optimal to freeze. This problem grows as the architectures grow and as the number of layers grows. In order to provide a solution, Nagae [11] proposes the use of genetic algorithms for which he initializes a number of genotypes that will increase the number of evaluations and generations to detect the layers

© The Author(s), under exclusive license to Springer Nature Switzerland AG 2023
J. A. Lossio-Ventura et al. (Eds.): SIMBig 2022, CCIS 1837, pp. 175–190, 2023.
https://doi.org/10.1007/978-3-031-35445-8_13

to be frozen. The main problem with this approach is the high variance of its results, which does not generate consistent accuracy, as well as the high number of iterations and its associated computational cost. In this work, we propose a modified binary search method, which achieves low variance results and reduces the number of iterations for the determination of the optimal layer by applying backward freezing.

2   Related Works

Although transfer learning is already an accepted method in current DCNN models, one of the problems this method faces is knowing from which layer it should be trained again and from which it should not. This can become a complicated process as current DCNN models deal with a large number of layers [11]; applying genetic algorithms for layer detection in the CIFAR-100 dataset can increase accuracy level by 12% to 15% [11]. Another work implements genetic algorithms to freeze selected layers to improve the accuracy in the classification of pneumonia increasing the accuracy level by 2% [9]. Both works [9,11] use genetic algorithms to improve the level of accuracy.

3   Materials and Methods

3.1   Dataset

For the experiment, we will classify 3,297 dermatoscopic images related to 2 melanoma classes (benign and malignant) divided into:

– 1,800 benign dermatoscopic images
– 1,497 malignant dermatoscopic images

For the training, we will use:

– 1,440 benign dermatoscopic images
– 1,197 malignant dermatoscopic images

For the validation, we will use:

– 360 benign dermatoscopic images
– 300 malignant dermatoscopic images

The dataset was provided by Kaggle[1] based on the images of the ISIC (International Skin Imaging Collaboration), all the images were resized to 224 × 224 pixels.

---

[1] https://www.kaggle.com/datasets/fanconic/skin-cancer-malignant-vs-benign.

3.2 Modified Binary Search

The modified binary search is shown in Algorithm 1, is very similar to the binary search algorithm, with some differences in the evaluation process as we are using a *delta*.

Algorithm 1. Modified binary search for layer selection

---

procedure BINARY_SEARCH($model, layers, folds, delta, data$)

    $LB \leftarrow 0$

    $UB \leftarrow layers$ ▷ DCNN layers embebbed in the model.

    $IB \leftarrow \lfloor \frac{LB+UB}{2} \rfloor$ ▷ First intermediate bound.

    $LB\_score \leftarrow train\_and\_evaluate(model, data, backward = LB, folds)$

    $IB\_score \leftarrow train\_and\_evaluate(model, data, backward = IB, folds)$

    $UB\_score \leftarrow train\_and\_evaluate(model, data, backward = UB, folds)$

    $iterations \leftarrow \lfloor \log_2(layers) \rfloor$

    for iteration in iterations do

        $min\_score \leftarrow min(LB\_Score, UB\_Score)$

        if $IB\_score + delta \geq min\_score$ **then**

            if $min\_score = LB\_Score$ **then**

                $LB \leftarrow IB$ ▷ New lower bound.

                $LB \leftarrow IB\_score$ ▷ New lower score.

            else

                $UB \leftarrow IB$ ▷ New upper bound.

                $UB \leftarrow IB\_score$ ▷ New upper score.

            end if

        else

            break   ▷ Stopping iterations.

        end if

        $IB \leftarrow \lfloor \frac{LB+UB}{2} \rfloor$ ▷ New intermediate bound.

        if $IB = LB$ **or** $IB = UB$ **then**

            break   ▷ Stopping iterations.

        end if

        $IB\_score \leftarrow train\_and\_evaluate(model, data, backward = IB, folds)$

    end for

    $best\_layer \leftarrow 0$

    $best\_score \leftarrow max(LB\_score, IB\_score, UB\_score)$

    if $best\_score = LB\_score$ **then**

        $best\_layer \leftarrow LB$

    else if $best\_score = IB\_score$ **then**

        $best\_layer \leftarrow IB$

    else

        $best\_layer \leftarrow UB$

    end if

    return $best\_layer$

end procedure

Binary search expects an ordered list of elements [3], in our case we are using deep convolutional neural networks, and one of the problems related to neural networks is randomness, changing the weights in the classification tasks can produce quite different results [4], and is possible that in the experiments the final values are very close, thus we will consider a *delta* to evaluate the scores obtained from the evaluation of the models.

Based on this algorithm the maximum number of iterations and evaluations are:

$$Iterations = \lfloor \log_2(layers) + 1 \rfloor \tag{1}$$

$$Evaluations = 2 + \lfloor \log_2(layers) + 1 \rfloor \tag{2}$$

3.3 DCNN Models

The DCNN models and the number of layers to be evaluated are the following:

- InceptionV3: 311 layers
- Xception: 132 layers
- DenseNet121: 427 layers
- NasNetMobile: 769 layers
- ResNet50: 175 layers

3.4 Evaluation

The models will be evaluated using the ROC AUC score, since we are working with medical images, the ROC AUC score can generate better results when we are assessing medical conditions [10]. We are using transfer learning for the DCNN models, the initial weights are provided by IMAGENET through transfer learning. We will use the best ROC AUC score among the 4 kfolds per layer to determine the value to evaluate as upper bound, lower bound, and intermediate bound. The number of kfolds was chosen based on previous works with CNN [7,15], we are adding a table indicating all the scores to determine their average, maximum, minimum, median, variance, standard deviation, and the box plot to compare our scores between the freezing in layer 0 (no freezing), the optimal layer, in case if such layer is found, and for all the frozen layers, we are setting our *delta* value to 0.01. Finally, we are going to compare our results to the ones produced by the genetic algorithms.

4 Experimental Evaluation and Discussion

4.1 InceptionV3 Evaluation

As shown in Table 1, our results are based on InceptionV3 with 311 layers and 8 iterations. Table 2 shows the details related to the ROC AUC score per Fold and Layer that was applied the backward freezing.

Table 1. InceptionV3 Experimental Results per Iteration.

Iteration/Layer	1	2	3	4	5	6	7	8
0	**0.895**	**0.895**	**0.895**	**0.895**	**0.895**	**0.895**	**0.895**	0.895
1								**0.8978**
2							0.8856	0.8856
4						0.89	0.89	
9					0.8525	0.8525		
19				0.8464	0.8464			
38			0.8369	0.8369				
77		0.8328	0.8328					
155	0.8222	0.8222						
311	0.8083							

In these iterations we are applying the modified binary search to find the optimal layer to apply the backward freezing, increasing the ROC AUC score from 0.8083 to 0.8978.

For iteration 7: We are applying the *delta* because the intermediate score is less than the minimum bound (0.8856 vs. 0.89), but the difference was not greater than 0.01. Had the *delta* not been applied, the iteration would have ended at this point, but we would not have gotten the best result (freezing layer 1).

Table 2. InceptionV3 Experimental Results per Fold and Layer.

Layer	0	1	2	4	9	19	38	77	155	311
Fold 1	0.895	0.891	0.886	0.890	0.843	0.838	0.804	0.833	0.811	0.781
Fold 2	0.876	0.894	0.880	0.882	0.826	0.846	0.837	0.822	0.798	0.808
Fold 3	0.883	0.891	0.873	0.872	0.853	0.824	0.814	0.819	0.804	0.769
Fold 4	0.875	0.898	0.882	0.885	0.833	0.808	0.822	0.808	0.822	0.741
Avg	0.882	0.894	0.880	0.882	0.839	0.829	0.819	0.820	0.809	0.775
Min	0.875	0.891	0.873	0.872	0.826	0.808	0.804	0.808	0.798	0.741
Max	0.895	0.898	0.886	0.890	0.853	0.846	0.837	0.833	0.822	0.808
Mdn	0.879	0.893	0.881	0.883	0.838	0.831	0.818	0.820	0.808	0.775
Var	8.6E-5	1.0E-05	2.7E-05	5.8E-05	1.3E-04	2.9E-04	1.9E-04	1.0E-04	1E-04	7E-04
SD	2.6E-04	3.0E-05	8.0E-05	1.8E-04	4.0E-04	8.6E-04	5.6E-04	3.0E-04	3E-04	2E-03

As shown in the box plot (Fig. 1) the optimal layer has a better value when the freeze was applied, and their values do not overlap, this could means that applying the freezing in layer 1 would be the optimal layer, in addition, its average value exceeds the one in the model that does not apply freeze.

Finally, the Inception model was designed to decouple its layers to achieve a better result [14]. Based on that fact, we can infer that freezing can be applied in the first layer because the layers are decoupled. We can also deduce that unfreezing all the layers produces a good ROC AUC score, but freezing the first layer slightly improves the ROC AUC score.

Fig. 1. ROC AUC comparison for the best layer in InceptionV3.

4.2   Xception Evaluation

As shown in Table 3, our results are based on Xception with 132 layers and 7 iterations. Table 4 shows the details related to the ROC AUC score per Fold and Layer that was applied the backward freezing.

Table 3. Xception Experimental Results per Iteration.

Iteration / layer	1	2	3	4	5	6	7
0	**0.8794**	**0.8794**	**0.8794**	**0.8794**	0.8794		
4					0.8875	0.8875	
6						**0.8939**	**0.8939**
7							0.86833
8				**0.8919**	**0.8919**	0.8919	0.8919
16			0.8655	0.8655			
33		0.8236	0.8236				
66	0.8336	0.8336					
132	0.7972						

In these iterations we are applying the binary search to find the optimal layer to apply the backward freezing, increasing the ROC AUC score from 0.7972 to 0.8939.

For iteration 2: We are applying the *delta* because the intermediate score is less than the minimum bound (0.8236 vs. 0.8336), but the difference was not greater than 0.01. Had the *delta* not been applied, the iteration would have ended at this point, but we would not have gotten the best result (backward freezing until layer 6).

Table 4. Xception Experimental Results per Fold and Layer.

Layer	0	4	6	7	8	16	33	66	132
Fold 1	0.868	0.873	0.879	0.868	0.881	0.836	0.824	0.806	0.797
Fold 2	0.865	0.888	0.880	0.864	0.881	0.866	0.791	0.834	0.775
Fold 3	0.879	0.872	0.894	0.873	0.892	0.857	0.810	0.813	0.796
Fold 4	0.876	0.880	0.850	0.867	0.871	0.864	0.822	0.833	0.762
Avg	0.872	0.878	0.876	0.868	0.881	0.855	0.812	0.822	0.782
Min	0.865	0.872	0.850	0.864	0.871	0.836	0.791	0.806	0.762
Max	0.879	0.888	0.894	0.873	0.892	0.866	0.824	0.834	0.797
Mdn	0.872	0.877	0.879	0.868	0.881	0.860	0.816	0.823	0.785
Var	4.3E–05	5.3E–05	3.3E–04	1.5E–05	7.0E–05	1.9E–04	2.2E–04	1.9E–04	2.9E–04
SD	1.3E–04	1.6E–04	1.0E–03	4.4E–05	2.1E–04	5.6E–04	6.7E–04	5.8E–04	8.7E–04

As shown in the associated box plot (Fig. 2) the optimal layer has a better value when the freeze was applied, but their values overlap, this could mean that applying the backward freeze in layer 6 would not be the optimal layer, but its average and median value slightly exceed the model that does not apply freeze.

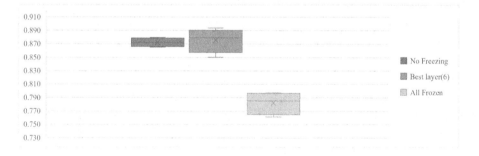

Fig. 2. ROC AUC comparison for the best layer in Xception.

Analyzing the Xception architecture, this is based on "Extreme" Inception, therefore we will find similarities with the Inception architecture. The key of Xception architecture is the depth wise separable convolution layers [1], based on that we can infer that the freezing can be applied in the firsts layers because the rest of the layers are decoupled, which leads to the conclusion that by unfreezing all the layers we have a good ROC AUC score, but when freezing the first 6 layers we have a better ROC AUC score.

4.3 DenseNet121 Evaluation

As shown in Table 5, our results are based on DenseNet121 with 427 layers and 5 iterations. Table 6 shows the details related to the ROC AUC score per Fold and Layer that was applied the backward freezing.

Table 5. DenseNet121 Experimental Results per Iteration.

Iteration/Layer	1	2	3	4	5
0	**0.8944**	0.8944	0.8944		
53			0.8958	0.8958	
79				0.8908	0.8908
92					0.8777
106		**0.9031**	**0.9031**	**0.9031**	**0.9031**
213	0.865	0.865			
427	0.8678				

In these iterations we are applying the binary search to find the optimal layer to apply the backward freezing, increasing the ROC AUC score from 0.8678 to 0.9181.

For iterations 1 and 4: We are applying the *delta* because the intermediate score is less than the minimum bound (0.865 vs. 0.8678 for iteration 1, 0.8908 vs 0.8958 for iteration 4), but the difference was not greater than 0.01. Had the *delta* not been applied, the iteration would have ended at these points, but we would not have gotten the best result (backward freezing until layer 106).

Finally, we are stopping the iteration in step 5 because the difference between the intermediate score and the minor score is greater than the *delta* (0.01).

Table 6. DenseNet121 Experimental Results per Fold and Layer.

Layer	0	53	79	92	106	213	427
Fold 1	0.894	0.896	0.889	0.873	0.889	0.861	0.868
Fold 2	0.889	0.880	0.888	0.878	0.903	0.856	0.844
Fold 3	0.896	0.896	0.891	0.870	0.889	0.851	0.861
Fold 4	0.884	0.876	0.884	0.870	0.884	0.865	0.849
Avg	0.891	0.887	0.888	0.873	0.891	0.858	0.856
Min	0.884	0.876	0.884	0.870	0.884	0.851	0.844
Max	0.896	0.896	0.891	0.878	0.903	0.865	0.868
Mdn	0.892	0.888	0.888	0.872	0.889	0.858	0.855
Var	3.4E–05	1.1E–04	7.1E–06	1.4E–05	6.8E–05	3.6E–05	1.2E–04
SD	1.0E–04	3.4E–04	2.1E–05	4.3E–05	2.0E–04	1.1E–04	3.5E–04

As shown in the associated box plot (Fig. 3) the optimal layer has a better value when the freeze was applied, but their values overlap, this could mean that applying the freeze in layer 106 would not be the optimal layer, but its average value slightly exceeds the model that does not apply the freeze without exceeding its median.

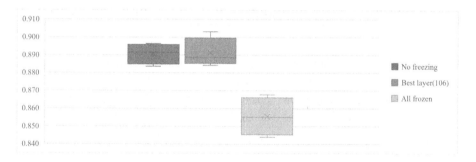

Fig. 3. ROC AUC comparison for the best layer in DenseNet121.

By analyzing the results, we notice that the fact that we are choosing layer 106 to apply the backward freezing could be related to the nature of the DenseNet architecture since the DenseNet layers depend on the previous layers to apply a composite operation [6]. Therefore, in the experiments, the first 106 layers with the knowledge acquired from transfer learning contain the essence that we need to maintain to obtain betters results and left the other 321 layers to retrain, but we modified the layers with the initial weights from transfer learning.

4.4   NasNetMobile Evaluation

As shown in Table 7, our results are based on NasNetMobile with 769 layers and 2 iterations. Table 8 shows the details related to the ROC AUC score per Fold and Layer that was applied the backward freezing.

Table 7. NasNetMobile Experimental Results per Iteration.

Iteration/Layer	1	2
0	**0.8961**	**0.8961**
192		0.6086
384	0.7614	0.7614
769	0.7653	

In these iterations, we are applying the binary search to find the optimal layer to apply the backward freezing, increasing the ROC AUC score from 0.7653 to 0.8961.

For iteration 1: We are applying the *delta* because the intermediate score is less than the minimum bound (0.7614 vs. 0.7653), but the difference was not greater than 0.01.

Finally, we are stopping the iteration in step 2 because the difference between the intermediate score and the minor score is greater than the *delta* (0.01).

Table 8. NasNetMobile Experimental Results per Fold and Layer.

Layer	0	192	384	769
Fold 1	0.888	0.609	0.563	0.765
Fold 2	0.862	0.595	0.761	0.738
Fold 3	0.896	0.564	0.610	0.729
Fold 4	0.884	0.562	0.600	0.760
Avg	0.883	0.582	0.633	0.748
Min	0.862	0.562	0.563	0.729
Max	0.896	0.609	0.761	0.765
Mdn	0.886	0.579	0.605	0.749
Var	2.1E-04	5.4E-04	7.7E-03	3.0E-04
SD	6.4E-04	1.6E-03	2.3E-02	9.0E-04

As shown in the associated box plot (Fig. 4) that not applying freeze has a better value than applying freeze and their values do not overlap.

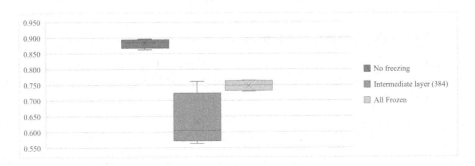

Fig. 4. ROC AUC comparison for the intermediate layer in NasNetMobile.

By analyzing these results, we can conclude that the use of a binary search shouldn't apply for this kind of network (the NasNets) because the best result is to unfreeze all the layers, the NasNet works with Recurrent Neural Networks(RNN), this kind of neural network use feedback in its processing [16], hence, the backward freezing disrupts the feedback and we have this drop in the score.

4.5   ResNet50 Evaluation

As shown in Table 9, our results are based on ResNet50 with 175 layers and 7 iterations. Table 10 shows the details related to the ROC AUC score per Fold and Layer that was applied the backward freezing.

Table 9. ResNet50 Experimental Results per Iteration.

Iteration/Layer	1	2	3	4	5	6	7
0	0.8881	0.8881					
43		0.8908	0.8908				
65			**0.9047**	**0.9047**	**0.9047**	0.9047	0.9047
66							**0.9181**
67						**0.9103**	0.9103
70					0.8986	0.8986	
76				0.8917	0.8917		
87	**0.8958**	**0.8958**	0.8958	0.8958			
175	0.8564						

In these iterations, we are applying the binary search to find the optimal layer to apply the backward freezing, giving us an increase in the ROC AUC score from 0.8564 to 0.9181.

For iteration 4: We are applying the *delta* because the intermediate score is less than the minimum bound (0.8917 vs. 0.8958), but the difference was not greater than 0.01. Had the *delta* not been applied, the iteration would have ended at this point, but we would not have gotten the best result (backward freezing until layer 66).

Table 10. ResNet50 Experimental Results per Fold and Layer.

Layer	0	43	65	66	67	70	76	87	175
Fold 1	0.881	0.890	0.905	0.918	0.873	0.899	0.873	0.894	0.850
Fold 2	0.869	0.890	0.885	0.903	0.910	0.885	0.879	0.896	0.842
Fold 3	0.888	0.891	0.892	0.885	0.899	0.884	0.878	0.885	0.850
Fold 4	0.875	0.877	0.903	0.898	0.877	0.893	0.892	0.896	0.856
Avg	0.878	0.887	0.896	0.901	0.890	0.890	0.881	0.893	0.850
Min	0.869	0.877	0.885	0.885	0.873	0.884	0.873	0.885	0.842
Max	0.888	0.891	0.905	0.918	0.910	0.899	0.892	0.896	0.856
Mdn	0.878	0.890	0.897	0.900	0.888	0.889	0.879	0.895	0.850
Var	6.9E-05	4.7E-05	8.6E-05	1.9E-04	3.2E-04	4.8E-05	6.2E-05	2.7E-05	3.4E-05
SD	2.1E-04	1.4E-04	2.6E-04	5.7E-04	9.7E-04	1.4E-04	1.9E-04	8.0E-05	1.0E-04

As shown in the associated box plot (Fig. 5) the optimal layer has a better value when the freezing was applied and their values do not overlap. This could mean that applying the backward freeze until layer 66 would be the optimal layer. In addition, its average and median values exceed the model that does not apply freeze.

Therefore, in the experiments, the first 66 layers with the knowledge acquired from transfer learning contain the essence that we need to maintain to obtain betters results, avoiding the backpropagation for those gradients in these frozen layers [5], and leaving the other 109 layers to retraining, but modifying the layers with the initial weights from IMAGENET.

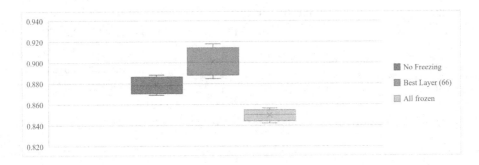

Fig. 5. ROC AUC comparison for the best layer in ResNet50.

4.6   Comparison with Genetic Algorithms

We have repeated the same models, data, and folds to apply the genetic algorithms, in this case, we chose 8 genotypes and the initialization is based on the current state of the art [11], for the experiments we chose the Elite selection method. As shown in Table 11 we have close values, but the binary search is better comparing the average and the median (except DenseNet121). A particular case is the evaluation of NasNetMobile. By using the binary search, the best result is to unfreeze all layers in 4 evaluations and 2 iterations. By using genetic algorithms, we have a lesser score and apply more evaluations.

Finally, Table 12 consists of a summary with the comparison of the average, median, variance, and standard deviation for each DCNN model. In all models, we can observe an increase in the ROC AUC score compared with the case of freezing all layers, proving that freezing specific layers improves the results using the binary search or genetic algorithms, except for NasNetMobile.

Table 11. Comparison between binary search vs. genetic algorithm.

| | InceptionV3 | | Xception | | DenseNet121 | | NasNetMobile | | ResNet50 | |
	Bin. search	Gen. alg	Bin. search	Gen. alg	binary search	Gen. alg	Bin. search	Gen. alg	Bin search	Gen. alg
Fold 1	0.8911	0.87472	0.8786	0.8831	0.8886	0.8936	0.8881	0.8650	0.9181	0.8719
Fold 2	0.8942	0.87972	0.88	0.8528	0.9031	0.8736	0.8619	0.8772	0.9028	0.8908
Fold 3	0.8911	0.87611	0.8939	0.8708	0.8889	0.8906	0.8961	0.8631	0.8847	0.8883
Fold 4	0.8978	0.90944	0.8503	0.8692	0.8842	0.8914	0.8842	0.8381	0.8981	0.8953
Avg,	0.8936	0.8850	0.8757	0.8690	0.8912	0.8873	0.8826	0.8608	0.9009	0.8866
Min	0.8911	0.87472	0.8503	0.8528	0.8842	0.8736	0.8619	0.8381	0.8847	0.8719
Max	0.8978	0.90944	0.8939	0.8831	0.9031	0.8936	0.8961	0.8772	0.9181	0.8953
Mdn	0.8927	0.8779	0.8793	0.8700	0.8888	0.8910	0.8862	0.8640	0.9005	0.8896
Var	1.02E-05	2.70E-04	3.34E-04	1.55E-04	6.76E-05	8.48E-05	2.15E-04	2.70E-04	1.90E-04	1.04E-04
SD	3.19E-05	1.64E-02	1.83E-02	1.24E-02	8.22E-03	9.21E-03	1.46E-02	1.64E-02	1.38E-02	1.02E-02

Table 12. Comparison summary between binary search vs. genetic algorithm.

	InceptionV3		Xception		DenseNet121		NasNetMobile		ResNet50	
	Bin. search	Gen. alg	Bin. search	Gen. alg	Bin. search	Gen. alg	Bin. search	Gen. alg	Bin. search	Gen. alg
Avg	✓		✓		✓		✓		✓	
Mdn	✓		✓			✓	✓		✓	
Var	✓			✓	✓			✓		✓
SD	✓			✓	✓			✓		✓

5   Conclusions

Based on these experiments, we conclude that binary search for transfer learning optimal layer selection has a better ROC AUC score for InceptionV3 and ResNet50. These results are consistent with the variance in all validation stages. Additionally, using this method, we discovered that just relying on the weights provided by IMAGENET does not guarantee the best score, therefore finding the layers to freeze increases the ROC AUC score, and the iterations reduce the execution time to find it logarithmically. It was found that binary search would not apply to all DCNN architecture types, as we observed in the NasNetMobile experiment that using RNN would not apply and maybe the best thing to do is unfreeze all its layers. Also, we can see an overlap (despite the fact that we had an improvement in the average) in Xception and DenseNet121, thus we can suggest repeating the experiments using other datasets. The use of genetic algorithms can improve our results but compare with the binary search method for this dataset, we were able to prove that the binary search has better results in terms of average and median (except for DenseNet121) and the number of evaluations is lesser in the binary search.

Finally, the optimal layer is not necessarily the one found in these experiments. Therefore, this value may vary depending on the dataset. Below is shown in Table 13 and Table 14 a summary of the DCNN experimental features and the improvements obtained when using this method.

Table 13. Summary Experimental Features.

Model	Layers	Max. Iterations	Experiment Iterations
InceptionV3	311	9	8
Xception	132	8	7
DenseNet121	427	9	5
NasNetMobile	769	10	2
ResNet50	175	8	7

Table 14. Summary Experimental Results (ROC AUC score).

Model	Optimal Layer	Optimal Layer score	All Frozen	No freezing	Overlap
InceptionV3	1	0.8978	0.8083	0.895	No
Xception	6	0.8939	0.7972	0.8794	Yes
DenseNet121	106	0.9031	0.8678	0.8944	Yes
NasNetMobile	0	0.8961	0.7653	0.8961	No
ResNet50	66	0.9181	0.8564	0.8881	No

Additionally, we are showing a comparison chart with the experimental results for non-overlapped results (Fig. 6) and Fig. 7 for overlapped results, excluding NasNetMobile.

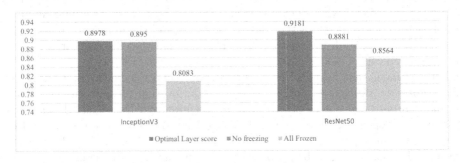

Fig. 6. Comparative ROC UAC score chart for InceptionV3 and ResNet50 (non-overlapped results).

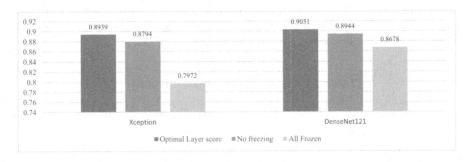

Fig. 7. Comparative ROC UAC score chart for Xception and DenseNet (overlapped results).

6   Future Works

In the field of DCNNs, the methods for selecting layers to improve accuracy in classification tasks are relatively new. Therefore, for any future work, we recommend trying new methods for the selection of the layers to be frozen, in addition to implementing genetic algorithms or the modified binary search method used in this article. It is also recommended to carry out this optimization work using other datasets. Finally, we suggest researching the layers inside the DCNN architectures to explain the improvements that can be obtained by applying the freezing using the binary search or any other genetic algorithms.

Acknowledgements. We would like to thank the postgraduate unit of the Faculty of Systems Engineering and Informatics at UNMSM, as well as Kaggle for promoting the study of data science and artificial intelligence in all its branches.

Finally, a special thanks to Charbel Elkhoury, Ph.D. in Information Technology Management, Capella University, for proofreading the article.

Conflicts of interest. The authors declare that there is no conflict of interest.

References

1. Chollet, F.: Xception: deep learning with depthwise separable convolutions. In: Proceedings of the IEEE Conference on Computer Vision and Pattern Recognition, pp. 1251–1258 (2017)
2. Cifuentes, A., Mendoza, E., Lizcano, M., Santrich, A., Moreno-Trillos, S.: Development of a convolutional neural network to recognize patterns in images. Investigación y desarrollo en TIC **10**(2), 7–17 (2019)
3. Cormen, T.H., Leiserson, C.E., Rivest, R.L., Stein, C.: Introduction to Algorithms. MIT Press, Cambridge (2009)
4. Dietterich, T.G.: Ensemble methods in machine learning. In: International Workshop on Multiple Classifier Systems, pp. 1–15. Springer (2000). https://doi.org/10.1007/3-540-45014-9_1
5. He, K., Zhang, X., Ren, S., Sun, J.: Deep residual learning for image recognition. In: Proceedings of the IEEE Conference on Computer Vision and Pattern Recognition, pp. 770–778 (2016)
6. Huang, G., Liu, Z., Van Der Maaten, L., Weinberger, K.Q.: Densely connected convolutional networks. In: Proceedings of the IEEE Conference on Computer Vision and Pattern Recognition, pp. 4700–4708 (2017)
7. Kawasaki, Yusuke, Uga, Hiroyuki, Kagiwada, Satoshi, Iyatomi, Hitoshi: Basic study of automated diagnosis of viral plant diseases using convolutional neural networks. In: Bebis, G., et al. (eds.) ISVC 2015. LNCS, vol. 9475, pp. 638–645. Springer, Cham (2015). https://doi.org/10.1007/978-3-319-27863-6_59
8. Li, B., Rangarajan, S.: A conceptual study of transfer learning with linear models for data-driven property prediction. Comput. Chem. Eng. **157**, 107599 (2022). https://doi.org/10.1016/j.compchemeng.2021.107599
9. de Lima Mendes, R., da Silva Alves, A.H., de Souza Gomes, M., Bertarini, P.L.L., do Amaral, L.R.: Many layer transfer learning genetic algorithm (MLTLGA): a new evolutionary transfer learning approach applied to pneumonia classification. In: 2021 IEEE Congress on Evolutionary Computation (CEC), pp. 2476–2482. IEEE (2021)
10. Mandrekar, J.N.: Receiver operating characteristic curve in diagnostic test assessment. J. Thorac. Oncol. **5**(9), 1315–1316 (2010). https://doi.org/10.1097/jto.0b013e3181ec173d

11. Nagae, S., Kawai, S., Nobuhara, H.: Transfer learning layer selection using genetic algorithm. In: 2020 IEEE Congress on Evolutionary Computation (CEC), pp. 1–6. IEEE (2020). https://doi.org/10.1109/cec48606.2020.9185501
12. Picazo, O., Baumela, L.: Deep convolutional neural networks for emotion recognition in images (2018)
13. Shanmugamani, R.: Deep Learning for Computer Vision: Expert Techniques to Train Advanced Neural Networks Using TensorFlow and Keras. Packt Publishing Ltd, Birmingham (2018)
14. Szegedy, C., Vanhoucke, V., Ioffe, S., Shlens, J., Wojna, Z.: Rethinking the inception architecture for computer vision. In: Proceedings of the IEEE Conference on Computer Vision and Pattern Recognition, pp. 2818–2826 (2016)
15. Wada, A., et al.: Differentiating Alzheimer's disease from dementia with Lewy bodies using a deep learning technique based on structural brain connectivity. Magn. Reson. Med. Sci. **18**(3), 219 (2019)
16. Zoph, B., Vasudevan, V., Shlens, J., Le, Q.V.: Learning transferable architectures for scalable image recognition. In: Proceedings of the IEEE Conference on Computer Vision and Pattern Recognition, pp. 8697–8710 (2018)

Profiling Public Service Accessibility Based on the Public Transport Infrastructure

Leibnitz Rojas-Bustamante[1] ⓘ, Crayla Alfaro[2] ⓘ, Ivan Molero[2] ⓘ,
Dennis Aparicio[3], and Miguel Nunez-del-Prado[2(✉)] ⓘ

[1] Pontificia Universidad Catolica del Perú, Lima, Peru
leibnitz.rojas@pucp.edu.pe
[2] Instituto de Investigación de la Universidad Andina del Cusco, Cusco, Peru
{calfaro,imolero}@uandina.edu.pe,
miguel.nunezdelprado@vrin.uandina.edu.pe
[3] Smartbus Peru, Cusco, Peru
daparicioceo@smartbus.pe

Abstract. Public services are essential to satisfy the needs of healthcare, education, justice, *Etc.* in citizens' daily life. Thus, individuals need these services in a certain proximity to their homes. Nonetheless, in big cities, some public services are not close enough. This is especially true for poor individuals who need public transportation to reach such services. To assess the accessibility of individuals to public services using the public transportation system, we propose a methodology to compute profile districts based on the accessibility to different services. We apply our methodology to Lima and Cusco cities in Peru, showing the tool's utility while being simple to understand. We profile fifty different districts in four groups, allowing policymakers and urban planners to observe the lack of public services to understand the urban dynamics and social exclusion.

Keywords: Public Service · Index Computation · Unsupervised Learning · Accessibility

1 Introduction

In recent decades, the influence of accessibility has been studied in different domains, like transport system access [18], public services access [19], parks access [23], jobs access [1], health access [21], food access [9], access to Covid-19 services [11], location selection for public service facilities [28], and even housing prices based on accessibility to public services [29]. The accessibility metrics are vital for understanding urban dynamics. Correspondingly, low accessibility to the public transportation system leads to social exclusion [24].

The work of Levinson and Wu [14] generalizes the concept of accessibility and details different aspects about where the trip starts; the impedance function in

J. A. Lossio-Ventura et al. (Eds.): SIMBig 2022, CCIS 1837, pp. 191–206, 2023.
https://doi.org/10.1007/978-3-031-35445-8_14

terms of time, distance, and economical cost; how to assess direct access, when the travel begins; the travel purpose; the transportation mode; and the access for whom. The authors focus on all the elements intervening in the accessibility and methodology that can be applied to all public services. Stewart [25] defines different accessibility metrics based on utility, space-time, or integral.

However, accessing relevant information limits measuring accessibility in a different context. Thus, accessibility metrics demand precise information about origins, destinations, infrastructure, and paths, which is not trivial to access. This is especially true for developing countries, which need this analysis, but the information sometimes does not even exist. Accordingly, one way to gather information for accessibility is to profit from a pervasive system present in smart cities [30]. In the last decades, cities have expanded the use of technology in order to improve various sectors [16]. Smart cities direct their services to analysis platforms to improve the quality and functioning of built environments, often conditioned to previously established urban patterns. There is an application work area oriented to intelligent public transport systems [4, 16]. Solutions leading to smart public transport in cities provide an efficient and safe practice for the user of these services, as well as sustainability and optimization of resources in city administration [26].

There are various methods to generate the matrix of origin and destination of the trips that are some essential inputs to start studies of the conditions of public transport in the cities. Trip chain methods under various patterns are essential strategies for estimating the destination of trips, especially for identifying unlinked trips, which are often a persistent problem [12]. Another study addresses the data from automated data collection systems, which exposes the feasibility of applying trip chaining to infer the origin-destination of the bus passenger from the automatic location of the vehicles. With the same probabilities, it is possible to estimate the times of descent of the passengers and the stages of travel in the public bus to link them subsequently [27]. In this context, many cities worldwide are concentrating on collecting urban traffic data to identify and monitor traffic patterns, in most cases multimodal, to have a structured, organic and scientific perspective in decision-making related to traffic. City and its equipment, as well as the support of the use of technology for more accessible and inclusive urban planning and mobility decision-making [13].

In the current effort, we propose a methodology to assess accessibility in terms of spatial access to public service amenities using the public transport system as infrastructure. The data used for this work is from open data and a pervasive system like the GPS to gather public transportation routes. The rest of the paper is organized as follows. Section 2 presents the related works. Section 3 introduces the proposed methodology, while Sect. 4 details the results of applying the described methodology to Lima and Cusco cities in Peru. Finally, Sects. 5 and 6 present the discussion, conclusion, and new research avenues, respectively.

2   Related Works

In the present section, we describe the different works quantifying accessibility in the literature. In our context, accessibility is a metric for quantifying the difficulty of accessing public services through the public transport network.

For instance, Atiullah *et al.* [24] made a literature review about public transport accessibility. They define accessibility as physical access to goods, services, and destinations. It allows accessing specific areas and measures the advantage of certain zones compared to others. Thus, good accessibility of public transport also improves the accessibility to other (public) services. Conversely, the low accessibility to public transportation systems leads to social exclusion. Therefore, the authors analyze the public transport accessibility relates to public health, employment, social exclusion, mobility, sustainability, economic, spatial, and temporal efficiency.

Fransen *et al.* [5] studies time gaps in accessibility for public transport due to its importance in providing poor population segments, especially those without private vehicles, the possibility to participate in society's daily basis activities. The study area was the Flanders region in the north of Belgium, with 6.4 million inhabitants in an area of 13 597 km^2 divided into 308 districts. The authors used three datasets: segmented socio-economic factors, facility locations, and transport networks. To quantify the gap between public transport demande and public transport provision, the methodology takes the difference between the index of public transport provision (IPTP) and the index of public transport gaps (IPTG). The former use socio-economical groups' distribution of computing an index of public transport needs for each district. Then, a statistical approach based on factor analysis was employed; as a result, a temporally reliable picture of accessibility by public transport was constructed. The latter builds a cost origin-destination matrix taking the shortest path between the district's centroids and some amenities (*e.g.*, jobs, schools, healthcare facilities, Etc.) for different three hours time windows. Finally, they take the difference between both indexes to quantify the gap.

Boisjoly *et al.* [2] study the healthcare accessibility of eight cities in Canada using the 2SFCA model with a temporal threshold of 45 min. The authors focused their study on accessibility using only public transport. Therefore, the data from travel time was gathered from public transport operators, hospital capacity from the CIHI hospital inventory, and trips from census tracts to hospitals, as well as population density from Statistics Canada Census 2016. Authors find that vulnerable census tracts have less healthcare access compared to other census tracts. Another work from Chen *et al.* [3] uses accessibility metrics to quantify disparities in Nanjing, Jiangsu Province, China. Authors propose an accessibility metric integrating the times of different modes in a trip, including the following parts: access to the initial bus/metro stop/station or a transfer by walking, the in-vehicle transport time, making interchanges or transfers between modes, and exiting the vehicle and walking to the final destination. The proposed metric is flexible and handles large amounts of timetable data for measuring accessibility disparities in urban areas. Besides, this model is not limited by the transportation type. Authors claim that their method could be used to analyze real estate, health care, education, retail, Etc. sectors.

Finally, Jeon *et al.* [8] analyze the accessibility to public services in rural areas using the public transportation system in Chungju-si, South Korea, as infrastructure. The objective of their research was to asses the accessibility of public facilities using public transportation from rural areas where the opportunity to reach public services is weaker than in urban areas. To quantify accessibility, they compute the elapsed time from departing from the community centre to the nearest bus stop by walking, riding the bus, and waiting time for transfer to the closest public service. The authors found that walking time from the community centre to the nearest bus stop takes ten minutes or more; the bus's average speed is 21.9 km/h. The accessibility time from the community centre to public services facilities is 15.43 min, to the emergency centre 35.15 min, to the medical centre 8.7 min, to elementary school 9.7 min, to middle school 16.26 min, to high school 22.61 min. Finally, the authors observed that traffic accessibility using bus vehicles in the East and South is lower than in areas in the West and North in the Chungju-si region. In the same spirit, we propose in the next section a methodology to quantify accessibility in the urban context to public service facilities based on open data, extending the methodology proposed by Nunez-del-Prado and Rojas-Bustamante [22]. The basic idea is to provide a tool for policymakers to evaluate public service delivery in terms of accessibility, for public policy making, to initiate cross-sectoral investments, or to assess urban planning.

3   Methodology

In the current section, we describe the proposed methodology to assess the accessibility metric in terms of distance to different public services relying on the public transport infrastructure as illustrated in Fig. 1.

The first step of the methodology is the road network or transport network acquisition. The graph G of the *transport network* models the streets as edges and the intersections as nodes for a given city where the vehicles, both public and private, circulate (*c.f.* Fig. 1A). To extract this graph, we rely on the Open-StreetMaps service[1], which can be query using the *OSMnx* Python Library[2]. The second step builds the graph G_T to represent the *public transportation network*. Thus, the spatial representation of the public transport routes is intersected with the *transport network* G to obtain G_T, which is a subgraph of G (*c.f.* Fig. 1B). The most common form to represent this information is using a geospatial vector data format generated by a geographic information system (GIS) software known as a shapefile or in a set of latitude and longitude coordinates in a comma-separated file. Once the *transport network* G and the *public transportation network* G_T are built, both graphs are intersected with the level

---

[1] OpenStreetMap: www.openstreetmap.org.

[2] OSMnx Python package https://github.com/gboeing/osmnx.

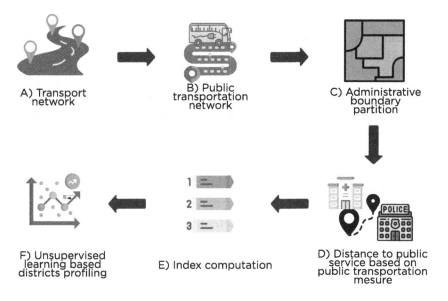

Fig. 1. Methodology schema.

three administrative boundaries *i.e.*, district i D_i (*c.f.* Fig. 1C). Thus, each *analysis area A_i* is establish using Eq. 1.

$$A_i = G \cap G_T \cap D_i \qquad (1)$$

where i is a given district.

Consequently, for each *analysis area A_i*, the minimal distance in the graph G_T to reach a given public service based on public transport infrastructure is measured (*c.f.* Fig. 1D). Accordingly, the minimal distance from the nodes in the subgraph G_i to the amenities snapped in G_i is computed using the Dijkstra algorithm[3] implemented in NetworkX [6] weighted by the street distance. Without loss of generality, the considered public services are financial services, justice, health, food, security, education, and higher education. These public services are represented by the bank, courthouse, hospital, marketplace, police, school, and university amenities.

The next step is the *index computation* that considers the set of amenities, namely hospitals, schools, universities, and marketplaces, among overs representing different public services. Hence, the distance expressed as a vector $v \in \mathbb{R}^n$ of average distances from all nodes in street network G through the public transportation network G_T to a set of amenities in a given administrative area A_i, where n is the number of evaluated public services presence. Finally, to have a single comprehensible metric, the average of the distance in the vector v was computed. Hence, the metric is simple to understand, not only for policymakers but for citizens. This metric aims to quantify the public services presence in

---

[3] Python recipe: https://code.activestate.com/recipes/119466/.

terms of distance as proposed in [1]. Thus, the spatial distance is easy to understand, simplifying more abstract models such as principal component analysis
(c.f. Fig. 1E). It is important to note that other amenities could be added to
enrich the index.

Finally, for profiling the analysis area A i.e., districts, the unsupervised learning k-Means algorithm [15] is used. This algorithm groups administrative areas
sharing a similar index vector (i.e., profile) in k groups. The clustering algorithm
takes as input the distance vectors v to output groups of districts sharing the
same public service access level.

4   Results

In this section, we describe the obtained results by applying the before-described
methodology. In the following paragraphs, we detail the attained outcomes of
Lima and Cusco cities in Peru.

4.1   Lima Study Case

Lima is the economical and political capital of Peru. It is the biggest capital
city in South America with about 10.6 million inhabitants [7]. Lima metropolis
is composed of Lima and Callao provinces, which are physically next to each
other. Thus, Lima province is composed of 43 districts (i.e., administrative level
3) where Lima district is the seat of the national government, and Callao con-
stitutional province is composed of seven districts where the major port and
airport, in the country, are located.

To model Lima with the 50 districts, we gathered the road network graph,
consisting of 14 207 nodes and 17 930 edges. Also, we obtained amenities locations from *OpenStreetMaps*. The public transportation network was provided by
the Urban Transportation Authority for Lima and Callao (ATU)[4].

Based on the collected information, we first built the graph for public transportation and then for each one of the 50 districts we calculate the average
distance to all the amenities taken for this study: bank, courthouse, hospital,
marketplace, police, school, and university. Thus, we built an origin-destination
matrix M_{OD}^i, for each district i in Lima as follow:

$$M_{OD} = \begin{array}{c} node_1 \\ node_2 \\ \\ node_n \end{array} \begin{pmatrix} \overset{p}{2.4} \ \overset{h}{1.3} \ \overset{b}{0.7} \ \overset{c}{1.2} \ \overset{s}{3.7} \ \overset{u}{4} \ \overset{m}{0.8} \\ 1.4 \ 2.3 \ 1.7 \ 0.2 \ 2.7 \ 2 \ 1.8 \\ \cdots \\ 2.1 \ 0.3 \ 4.3 \ 2.3 \ 1.3 \ 1.2 \ 2.2 \end{pmatrix}$$

----

[4] ATU: https://portal.atu.gob.pe.

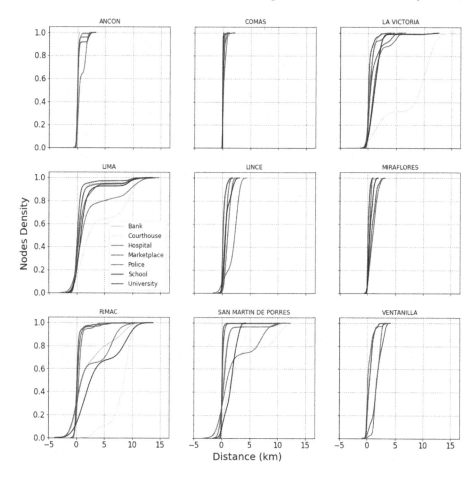

Fig. 2. Results Lima.

Where in the columns we have the shortest distance to police (p), hospital (h), bank (b), courthouse (c), school (s), university (u), and marketplace (m) amenities from $node_n$. It is important to notice that this distance corresponds to the public transportation graph. Thus, it represents the shortest distance to commute from one place to another inside a district through public transportation. To achieve this results, we used GostNets[5] and NetworkX libraries, which implement Dijkstra's algorithm weighted by the street distance to consider spatial distance instead of the number of hops.

Once the distance matrix M_{OD}^i for each district i was built, we can have the density distribution of served nodes depending on the distance. Figure 2 shows the per cent of nodes reaching a given amenity, representing public services,

---

[5] GostNets: https://github.com/worldbank/GOSTnets.

within a certain distance. For instance, we observe that in Lima, more than 60% of the inhabitants must travel more than 5km to access a healthcare facility.

Fig. 3. Accessibility to Lima's Public services.

In order to compare distances among all districts, we introduce the average distance to reach all amenities from all nodes of each district graph. It is worth noting that missing values are replaced with the maximum value of each amenity distance to penalize the absence of public service. We compute the accessibility index metric considering the average distances of all amenities per district as follows in Eq. 2:

$$index_j = \frac{\sum d_i}{n} \tag{2}$$

Where i corresponds to each amenity $amenity = \{p, h, b, c, s, u, m\}$ and j represents each district from Lima. Furthermore, if d_i is unavailable, we take the maximum distance on the amenity over all districts. We obtained how far or how close public services are located in each district. Finally, the higher the index is the less presence of government public services we have. Figure 3 shows the heatmap of the average distances to all the amenities considered for this study as well as the index previously calculated for Lima-Callao.

The last part of our methodology was about clustering districts into groups with similar accessibility characteristics in terms of distances to public services.

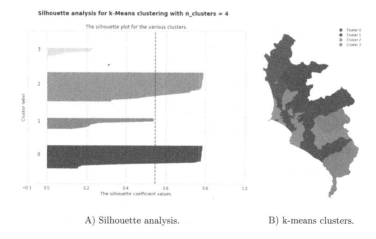

A) Silhouette analysis.   B) k-means clusters.

Fig. 4. District accessibility profiles.

For this aim, we used k-means algorithm [10,30] and the silhouette technique to find the optimal number k of districts profiles. As illustrated in Fig. 4A, the silhouette analysis indicates that the optimal number of profiles is $k = 4$. The output of the k-means algorithm is depicted in Fig. 4B. To obtain this result, the clustering algorithm takes as input the average distances vectors for all districts, as follows :

$$\begin{array}{c} \\ district_1 \\ district_2 \\ \\ district_n \end{array} \begin{array}{ccccccc} p & h & b & c & s & u & m \end{array} \\ \left(\begin{array}{ccccccc} 4.4 & 3.1 & 5.7 & 8.2 & 13.7 & 11 & 9.8 \\ 11.4 & 7.3 & 8.7 & 7.2 & 8.7 & 9 & 7.8 \\ \multicolumn{7}{c}{\cdots} \\ 12.1 & 15.3 & 14.3 & 2.3 & 6.3 & 8.2 & 5.2 \end{array}\right)$$

To describe each accessibility profile, we utilized a radial graph for district profiling visualisation as depicted in Fig. 5. Each radial graph contains seven axes representing the amenities' distance. Where each amenity provides a public service to the given district. Then, inner circles symbolize the distance in kilometers. Hence, we observe, in each radial graph, different profiles belonging to grouped districts. For instance, *Cluster 0* shows that justice, financial, higher education security and marketplace services are difficult to access. The districts belonging to this accessibility profile are *Ancon, Carmen de la Legua Reynoso, La Perla, Puente Piedra, Santa Rosa*, and *Ventanilla*. Regarding *Cluster 1*, the present accessibility profile evinces a complicated access to higher education services represented by the university. This profile is composed of *Ate, Breña, Carabayllo, Chaclacayo, Independencia, Jesús Maria, La Molina, Lima, Lince, Lurigancho, Lurín, Miraflores, Pueblo Libre, Santa Anita, San Isidro, San Juan de Lurigancho, San Martín de Porres, Surquillo, Villa el Salvador*, and *Villa María del Triunfo* districts. Concerning *Cluster 2*, we note the low accessibility to courthouses, marketplaces and police services. This profile is formed by

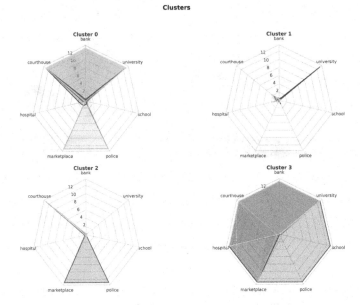

Fig. 5. Radial district profiling based on distance in *Km*.

Barranco, Bellavista, Callao, Chorrillos, Comas, El Agustino, La Victoria, Los Olivos, Magdalena del Mar, Pachacamac, Rimac, Santiago de Surco, San Borja, San Juan de Miraflores, San Luis and *San Miguel.* Finally, *Cluster 3* groups *Cieneguilla, La Punta, Mi Perú, Pucusana, Punta Hermosa, Punta Negra, Santa María del Mar* and *San Bartolo* districts, which are far away from most of the public services.

4.2 Cusco Study Case

Cusco city is the country's main tourist attraction due to Machu-Picchu, a modern wonder of the world, with 1.35 million inhabitants and eight districts.

The first step for analysing the accessibility to public services is to build the public transport network over the road network and district division. Therefore, to gather information from public transport, we have used the Smartbus ^{TM}solution from the Peruvian company Smart Innovation Group[6]. This solution allows gathering geolocated information using GPS technology on smartphones.

Once the public transportation network was built over the graph extracted from OSM service, the minimal distance from all nodes to the amenities representing public services is calculated. Figure 6 shows the proportion of nodes in each district having access to public services. The results in Cusco are pretty different from those obtained in Lima, as demonstrated in Fig. 6. In almost all

---

[6] Smartbus: https://smartbus.pe/.

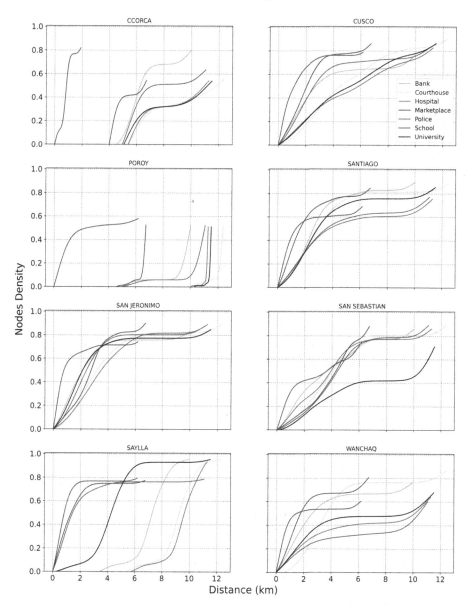

Fig. 6. Results Cusco.

districts, more than 60% of persons have to travel for more than 4km to reach health services.

The heatmap in Fig. 7 shows the average distances to all the amenities considered for this study in Cusco. We note that Ccorca and Poroy are the districts with less accessibility. Conversely, the district profiling process was only applied

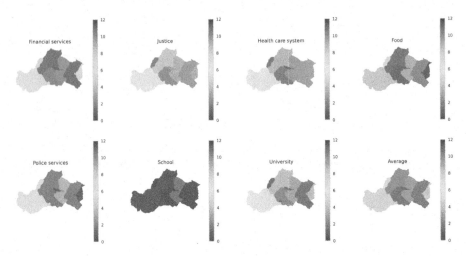

Fig. 7. Accessibility in Cusco Public Services.

to Lima-Callao since Cusco has only eight districts, and it is straightforward to analyze each district individually.

Consequently, the index proposed in this research is a tool for policymakers, urban planners, and citizens to understand and quantify access to public services through distance using the public transportation system.

5   Discussion

The findings of this analysis warn that two cities in Peru, specific cases of Lima and Cusco, present differences in accessibility to public services, having differentiated geography and some diverse districts. The common denominator is that both enjoy historical centrality. Thus, in both cases, the accessibility to its historical areas is much more viable than in the peripheral districts. Bearing in mind that although these have geographically lost their centrality, they still maintain the administrative and service centrality of the contemporary city.

An extension of this study considers how it has been identified that accessibility is aligned with the distributions of travel distance and route that must be carried out to reach certain public services so that the analysis of accessibility in transport can underestimate the benefits to users. Favored groups and overestimated the benefits provided to disadvantaged groups, creating a harmful bias.

The construction of the origin and destination matrix for each of the cities analyzed has made it possible to calculate the average distance of accessibility to them. Thus, a comparison of the advantage of connectivity in specific areas compared to others shows urban inequality concerning specific basic services. For example, the distance to travel to access health services between Lima and Cusco is an average of 4 km to 5 km.

The study also identifies and quantifies the relationship between accessibility and the distance that must be travelled to reach different public services. It is essential to clarify that the distances correspond to those travelling by public transport. The distance matrix shows us that there are districts served whose accessibility to services such as police, hospital, banking, justice, school, university, and the market are shorter in relation to others whose accessibility represents long interdistrict routes.

The multidimensional character is reflected in the social segregation of neighborhoods and the distribution of public services based on basic infrastructure. The heat maps presented demonstrate this character, which is expressed at the red level the more segregated the district is in services, thus generating urban inequalities resulting mainly from the absence of health and safety services. While accessibility measures have a long history in siting decisions of, for example, health facilities, travel times are generally taken as a static input, with little regard to actual transport provision or associated constraints [17].

It is essential to highlight the territorial groupings identified by the study that share similar accessibility indices, which have been oriented to the analysis of the city of Lima, chosen for the extension of the districts that form it, unlike Cusco, whose sample methodologically does not require such a grouping.

Under the proposed methodology, different generated profiles have been contrasted, which show the fragmentation of the city versus peripheral areas. For example, areas with a concentration of services such as those of justice located mainly in downtown Lima, on the other hand, health coverage, in general, requires a long distance to travel to the sectors with the highest population density, such as the extreme urban cones of the north and south. We observe that the accessibility to markets in the zone is less compared to the central zone. Besides, accessibility to police infrastructure is evenly distributed in all districts except in the southern part of the city. Secondly, there is no higher education coverage in the extreme north and south of the city [20].

It is essential to highlight that despite the limited number of public transportation routes 14 out of 18, we are able to provide an accessibility analysis for Cusco. Besides, our metric is only spatial, but we show the pertinence and simplicity of the metric to quantify accessibility to public services at different city scales.

The analysis demonstrated quantitatively the accessibility metric to public services. In addition, it referenced in the spatial planimetry a perspective of socio-spatial organization of the public sphere of cities that, following the academic postulates of the most relevant multilevel models, must incorporate individual attributes, instrumental variables and spatial regimes for political decision-making.

6   Conclusion

The present study proposes a methodology to quantify accessibility to public services using as infrastructure the public transportation system. As a study case, we have applied the accessibility metrics in various districts of Lima and Cusco from access to basic public services. The results show different distances in the various coverages that must provide quality of life to citizens, thus generating urban inequalities directly related to the level of facilities in cities at a spatial level. This is especially true for the lowest socio-economic sectors that need public transportation to reach public services.

It is essential to generate statistical information and increase installed institutional capacities to proceed to diagnose the various forms of segregation and inequalities around access to opportunities in the different Peruvian and Latin American districts. The indicators by districts analyzed from the clusters and profiles in both cities identify those that lack one or two public services, this being a necessary input for making decisions on urban and land policies, as well as transport networks, both keys to the role of government with the aim of contributing to building more accessible, equitable and democratic cities.

Accessibility planning must recognize the potential value in which people can reach different places in a city, controlling travel times and in optimal transport conditions. If the accessibility metrics presented are more significantly aligned with the resilience of citizens, they could be the basis for future research, promoting more meaningful participation and a fair process, recognizing the importance of the study to pay attention to the problems of gentrification and displacement.

Finally, the use of unsupervised learning to profile public service accessibility based on the Public Transport Infrastructure has shown that the public dimension of services in both cities is highly fragmented. As a result of the diagnosis of the structure of the urban order with the main police services, hospital, bank, courthouse, school, and university, which must be understood that the actions are unrelated to governments. Thus, the generated data are vital for decision-makers in cities for planning and promoting equal opportunities for citizens in all the studied districts.

As new research avenues, we plan to introduce the time in the accessibility metric to extend it to a space-time metric. Besides, we want to extend the analysis to a national level to study accessibility in urban and rural environments.

Acknowledgement. The authors thank *Smart Innovation Group S.R.L.*, the company that helped us to gather public transportation routes in Cusco using their Smartbus solution.

Data availability The code for the experiments is available at https://github.com/leiparov/intercon-simbig-2021.git. The dataset for public transportation in Cusco are publish in https://data.mendeley.com/v1/datasets/2rbs4pc894/draft?preview=1. The public transportation network for Lima is available upon request at https://soluciones.atu.gob.pe/saip_portal/.

References

1. Barboza, M.H., Carneiro, M.S., Falavigna, C., Luz, G., Orrico, R.: Balancing time: using a new accessibility measure in Rio de Janeiro. J. Transp. Geogr. **90**, 102924 (2021)

2. Boisjoly, G., et al.: Measuring accessibility to hospitals by public transport: an assessment of eight canadian metropolitan regions. J. Transp. Health **18**, 100916 (2020)

3. Chen, J., Ni, J., Xi, C., Li, S., Wang, J.: Determining intra-urban spatial accessibility disparities in multimodal public transport networks. J. Transp. Geogr. **65**, 123–133 (2017)

4. Chen, Z.: Application of environmental ecological strategy in smart city space architecture planning. Environ. Technol. Innov. **23**, 101684 (2021)

5. Fransen, K., Neutens, T., Farber, S., De Maeyer, P., Deruyter, G., Witlox, F.: Identifying public transport gaps using time-dependent accessibility levels. J. Transp. Geogr. **48**, 176–187 (2015)

6. Hagberg, A., Conway, D.: Networkx: network analysis with python

7. Instituto Nacional de Estadística e Informática - INEI: Estado de la población peruana 2020. https://www.inei.gob.pe/media/MenuRecursivo/publicaciones_digitales/Est/Lib1743/Libro.pdf (2020). Accessed 18 Aug 2022

8. Jeon, J., Kim, S., Suh, K., Park, M., Choi, J., Yoon, S.: Accessibility to public service facilities in rural area by public transportation system. J. Korean Soc. Rural Plan. **22**(4), 1–11 (2016)

9. Jiao, J., Moudon, A.V., Ulmer, J., Hurvitz, P.M., Drewnowski, A.: How to identify food deserts: measuring physical and economic access to supermarkets in king county, Washington. Am. J. Public Health **102**(10), e32–e39 (2012)

10. Jin, X., Han, J.: K-Means Clustering, pp. 563–564. Springer, Boston (2010)

11. Kang, J.Y., et al.: Rapidly measuring spatial accessibility of COVID-19 healthcare resources: a case study of Illinois, USA. Int. J. Health Geogr. **19**(1), 1–17 (2020)

12. Lee, I., Cho, S.H., Kim, K., Kho, S.Y., Kim, D.K.: Travel pattern-based bus trip origin-destination estimation using smart card data. PLoS ONE **17**(6), e0270346 (2022)

13. Lemonde, C., Arsenio, E., Henriques, R.: Integrative analysis of multimodal traffic data: addressing open challenges using big data analytics in the city of Lisbon. Eur. Transp. Res. Rev. **13**(1), 1–22 (2021)

14. Levinson, D., Wu, H.: Towards a general theory of access. J. Transp. Land Use **13**(1), 129–158 (2020)

15. Likas, A., Vlassis, N., Verbeek, J.J.: The global k-means clustering algorithm. Pattern Recogn. **36**(2), 451–461 (2003)

16. Ma, C.: Smart city and cyber-security; technologies used, leading challenges and future recommendations. Energy Rep. **7**, 7999–8012 (2021)

17. Neutens, T.: Accessibility, equity and health care: review and research directions for transport geographers. J. Transp. Geogr. **43**, 14–27 (2015)

18. Neutens, T.: Accessibility, in transportation planning. In: International Encyclopedia of Geography: People, the Earth, Environment and Technology: People, the Earth, Environment and Technology, pp. 1–4 (2016)

19. Neutens, T., Delafontaine, M., Scott, D.M., De Maeyer, P.: A GIS-based method to identify spatiotemporal gaps in public service delivery. Appl. Geogr. **32**(2), 253–264 (2012)

20. Nunez-del-Prado, M., Barrera, J.: Analysis of the health network of metropolitan lima against large-scale earthquakes. In: Lossio-Ventura, J.A., Valverde-Rebaza, J.C., Díaz, E., Alatrista-Salas, H. (eds.) SIMBig 2020. CCIS, vol. 1410, pp. 445–459. Springer, Cham (2021). https://doi.org/10.1007/978-3-030-76228-5_32

21. Nunez-del Prado, M., Barrera, J.: Analysis of the health network of metropolitanlima against large-scale earthquakes. In: 7th Annual International Conference SIMBig 2020 (2020)

22. Nunez-del Prado, M., Rojas-Bustamante, L.: Government public services presence index based on open data. In: Annual International Conference on Information Management and Big Data, pp. 50–63. Springer, Cham (2022). https://doi.org/10.1007/978-3-031-04447-2_4

23. Qin, J., Liu, Y., Yi, D., Sun, S., Zhang, J.: Spatial accessibility analysis of parks with multiple entrances based on real-time travel: The case study in Beijing. Sustainability 12(18), 7618 (2020)

24. Saif, M.A., Zefreh, M.M., Torok, A.: Public transport accessibility: a literature review. Period. Polytech. Transp. Eng. 47(1), 36–43 (2019)

25. Stewart, A.F.: Advancing accessibility: public transport and urban space. Ph.D. thesis, Massachusetts Institute of Technology (2017)

26. Strielkowski, W., Zenchenko, S., Tarasova, A., Radyukova, Y.: Management of smart and sustainable cities in the post-COVID-19 era: lessons and implications. Sustainability 14(12), 7267 (2022)

27. Wang, W., Attanucci, J.P., Wilson, N.H.: Bus passenger origin-destination estimation and related analyses using automated data collection systems. J. Public Transp. 14(4), 7 (2011)

28. Wang, W., Zhou, Z., Chen, J., Cheng, W., Chen, J.: Analysis of location selection of public service facilities based on urban land accessibility. Int. J. Environ. Res. Public Health 18(2), 516 (2021)

29. Yang, L., Zhang, S., Guan, M., Cao, J., Zhang, B.: An assessment of the accessibility of multiple public service facilities and its correlation with housing prices using an improved 2sfca method-a case study of Jinan city, china. ISPRS Int. J. Geo Inf. 11(7), 414 (2022)

30. Yeturu, K.: Machine learning algorithms, applications, and practices in data science. Handbook of Statistics, 43, 81–206 (2020)

Multiple Scale Comparative Analysis of Classical, Dynamic and Intelligent Edge Detection Schemes

Zhengmao Ye[1]([⊠]) [iD], Hang Yin[1] [iD], and Yongmao Ye[2] [iD]

[1] College of Science and Engineering, Southern University, Baton Rouge, LA 70813, USA
{zhengmao_ye,hang_yin}@subr.edu
[2] Broadcasting Department, Liaoning Radio and Television Station, Shenyang 110000, China

Abstract. Edge detection acts as a fundamental segmentation technique in the fields of remote sensing, computer vision and pattern recognition. It locates significant discontinuities and variations of digital images so as to identify intrinsic edge information involved. Various edge detection schemes have been implemented in numerous cases of science and engineering successfully, such as the classical edge detection (e.g. Canny, Sobel, Laplacian), dynamic edge detection (e.g. Gabor, Curvelets), and intelligent edge detection (e.g. Ant Colony Optimization, Particle Swarm Optimization, Genetic Algorithm) based on computational intelligence. However, there is still a lack of a systematic approach to analyze merits and drawbacks of the existing edge detection schemes from both qualitative and quantitative points of view. In fact, features of detected edges or contours can be represented at multiple scales, such as the 24-bit RGB scale, 8-bit gray scale and single bit binary scale. In this article, some typical edge detection techniques of Canny edge detection, Gabor edge detection and ACO edge detection are used to illustrate classical, dynamic and intelligent edge detection schemes, respectively. Several complex skyline digital images are selected in case studies. Qualitative analysis is conducted to examine visual appeals of detection outcomes based on three schemes at the RGB scale; while quantitative analysis will be conducted to compare edge detection outcomes based on three schemes at the gray and binary scales instead, in the frequency domain and spatial domain, respectively. It provides a comprehensive approach to thoroughly evaluate the overall quality of edge detection schemes.

Keywords: Canny Edge Detection · Gabor Edge Detection · Ant Colony Optimization (ACO) Edge Detection · Qualitative Analysis · Quantitative Analysis

1 Introduction

Edge detection is broadly applied to capture edge pixels and recognize object contours via search-based or zero-crossing based methods. For instance, remote sensing images are characterized by the spectral, temporal, spatial and radiometric resolutions. Edge detection has various remote sensing applications such as soil salinity detection, water

J. A. Lossio-Ventura et al. (Eds.): SIMBig 2022, CCIS 1837, pp. 207–221, 2023.
https://doi.org/10.1007/978-3-031-35445-8_15

body identification and ecological monitoring. However edge detection is sensitive to illumination, background, artifacts, noises, surface orientation, object geometry and so on. There is no unique way to overcome all uncertainties in feature detection processes to reach the ground truth and capture the perfect edges, thus numerous edge detection schemes have been proposed and successfully applied. Some classical edge detection approaches (e.g., Canny operator, Prewitt operator, Sobel operator) adopt the 1st-order gradient magnitudes or 2nd-order Laplacian of the Gaussian filter to identify edges. The dynamic edge detection approaches (e.g. Gabor filters, Curvelet filters) uses spatiotemporal information for dynamic recognition of textures and edges. Intelligent edge detection approaches (e.g. Ant Colony Optimization, Particle Swarm Optimization, Genetic Algorithm edge detection) are based on evolutionary optimization instead [1–3].

Canny edge detection searches for the edges via a Gaussian filter to reach the local intensity gradient minima of the intensity gradient. In practice, Canny edge detection employs bilinear interpolation and trilinear interpolation to switch between square and hexagonal structures. It improves the efficiency and accuracy to estimate the pixel edge strength [4, 5]. The ACO scheme is a statistical method to simulate real world issues when ants randomly seek for a path between food sources and the colony. The exploration scope is constrained while an optimal path will be followed by all ants via positive feedback at the end. The fuzzy-rule-based systems with continuous ACO are proposed, which use the online-rule-generation to identify the number of rules and initial parameters, in order to reach all the free parameter optimization via continuous ACO with higher learning accuracy. ACO is also applied to solve combinatorial optimization. ACO is relevant to regulator circuits with discrete components. It looks for optimal continuous values of inductors to optimize power electronic circuit design via the orthogonal approach. Furthermore, ACO has been successfully used for edge detection of typical landmarks. Integration of ACO and adaptive contour tracking provides strengthens the accuracy of edge detection [6–10]. The Gabor filter could also perform edge detection, even though it is not an orthonormal wavelet transform. Edge detection and contour tracing can be carried out together when Gabor wavelet transform and adaptive contrast stretching are integrated for true color RGB images. To capture surface topography features, the Gabor filter and pyramid decompositions of wavelets are applied to multiple texture characterization cases and topography partitioning. The Gabor filter has been used for biometric feature identification as well. It captures the ear features via the Gabor operator. The local features and global features can both be optimized via Genetic Algorithms. Quantitative comparisons between the Gabor edge detection and fuzzy C-means region detection are made in both spatial and frequency domains [11–13].

The notion of spatiotemporal characteristics is also applied in obtaining the spatiotemporal image descriptors so as to better represent the dynamic textures using the directional number transitional graph [14]. In practice, spatial-temporal patterns could be extracted automatically via the first-order statistics and Genetic Algorithms. It has been well applied for inductive thermography imaging, where a quantitative index F-score is used to objectively compare performance of several segmentation schemes [15]. In this research, three typical edge detection algorithms will be thoroughly analyzed. Both the qualitative and quantitative comparisons among diverse edge detection schemes will be made. Qualitative analysis will be conducted on detected edges at the RGB scales.

Selected information metrics of the discrete entropy, relative entropy, mutual information, Accuracy and F-Score will be used in quantitative comparisons at the gray scale and binary scale, respectively.

2   RGB Scale, Gray Scale and Binary Scale

From the trichromatic theory of additive color vision, each specific color represents a mixture of Red, Green, and Blue (RGB) components in the 3D Cartesian coordinate. The RGB model generates nonlinear visual perception. Inside the RGB color cube, the Red, Green and Blue are 3 primary color axes within [0, 255] (8 bits). The whole RGB color representation covers 24 bits or 6 hexadecimal bits. Black and white are located at two ends of the main diagonal. Any projection of the RGB components onto the main diagonal results in the gray scale within [0, 255] (8 bits). The dimensions of the RGB true color and gray scale images are (M × N × 3) and (M × N), respectively. When the binarization process is introduced via thresholding to generate two components of black and white in each pixel, the single-bit binary scale images are produced. The outcomes at the RGB color scale, gray scale and binary scale are all able to manifest the feature information from multiple aspects.

3   Classical Canny Edge Detection

Canny edge detection identifies edges at zero-crossings of the 2nd order directional derivatives of the digital images. The Canny operator utilizes Gaussian convolution with an optimal smoothing filter against noises as being shown as (1). The digital image could then be smoothed via Gaussian convolution as (2). The presence of Gaussian smoothing filter leads to noise removing in the digital image.

$$G(x,y,\sigma) = \frac{1}{2\psi^2}\exp\left(-\frac{x^2 + y^2}{2\psi^2}\right) \tag{1}$$

$$H(x, y) = I(x, y) * G(x, y) \tag{2}$$

where I denotes the intensity of the source image; H denotes the intensity of the smoothed image; G is the Gaussian smoothing filter; * stands for convolution.

The magnitude and phase of the 2D spatial gradient indicate the edge strength and edge direction. The local optima of the 1st order derivatives of the smoothed image H(x, y) is used to locate the edge in the direction of the gradient magnitude. It shows the zero-crossing point of the 2nd order derivative. The edge direction belongs to one out of eight $\pi/4$ degree evenly distributed angles $[0, 2\pi]$ to represent vertical, horizontal and diagonal directions. Edge thinning is applied next via non-maximal suppression. The edge direction can trace edges and suppress non-edge pixels. Adaptive edge tracing is applied afterwards via the Chain Code criterion, which can enhance the edge thinning. The 8-connectivity Chain Code can be applied to every pixels surrounding the testing node so as to illustrate the pixel thin line trajectory. Thresholding with hysteresis (upper and lower thresholds) is performed at last for better edge tracing and marking to avoid broken edges. The strong and weak edges are located using these two thresholds. The starting pixel of an edge is based on the upper threshold while path tracing is applied to detect true weak edges above the lower threshold.

4 Intelligent ACO Edge Detection

The application of ACO edge detection turns out to be an optimization issue of searching paths over the weighted graph, where the artificial ants track down solutions of the combinatorial optimization problem across a connected construction graph. The goal is to increase pheromone intensities relevant to good solutions and to decrease those intensities relevant to bad solutions through reinforcement and evaporation processes. It will expand the diversity and avoid stagnation. In ACO, the shortest path is made up of multiple segments. All ants tend to follow the actual pheromone trails to available food sources traversed by other ants when returning to the colony. The ants are able to mark best solutions and to use past markings for optimization. Prior information of food foraging is provided in decision making as well via positive feedback. ACO is formulated in two separate stages: Edge Selection and Pheromone Update.

In the first stage, an ant can move from node i to node j with certain probability. The path visibility η is defined as the ratio between the highest variation of intensity and the highest intensity. Edge pixels are preferred to have relatively larger values of visibility. The selection rule is formulated as (3).

$$P_{i,j} = \frac{(\tau_{i,j})^\alpha (\eta_{i,j})^\beta}{\sum (\tau_{i,j})^\alpha (\eta_{i,j})^\beta} \tag{3}$$

where α is a parameter to adjust the impact of $\tau_{i,j}$, β is a parameter to adjust the impact of $\eta_{i,j}$, $\tau_{i,j}$ is the pheromone intensity on edge between i and j, $\eta_{i,j}$ is the path visibility of between i and j. The maximal intensity variation is expressed as (4) to enhance the accuracy of edge detection.

$$\eta_{i,j} = \frac{\displaystyle \max_{[m,n] = (i-1, j-1)}^{(i+1, j+1)} |I(m,n) - I(i,j)|}{I_{MAX}} \tag{4}$$

where, I represents the pixel intensity and I_{MAX} is the maximal intensity. The higher the pheromone intensity variation (path visibility) is, the larger the chance an ant chooses that particular edge.

In the second stage, the pheromone intensity is subject to reinforcement when foods exist once again. Pheromone also evaporates over time so as not to be convergent to the local optima. The pheromone intensities are reduced by evaporation but enhanced by depositing pheromone. The pheromone density function relies on two processes of reinforcement and evaporation. It produces a self-organized indirect coordination system where all ants are able to exchange useful information indirectly by depositing their pheromones. The updating rule is shown as (5).

$$\tau_{i,j} = (1 - \rho)\tau_{i,j} + \Delta\tau_{i,j} \tag{5}$$

where ρ is the pheromone evaporation rate $(0 < \rho < 1)$, $\tau_{i,j}$ is the pheromone amount between i and j on the edge, $\Delta\tau_{i,j}$ is the deposited amount of pheromone, $\Delta\tau_{i,j} = \eta_{i,j}$ if the ant travels on the edge between i and j.

Each pixel is assumed to be connected with 8-neighborhood pixels. The ants start from strong endpoints and extend the search region so as to capture compensation segments for the fragmented edges. Thresholding is applied to detect pixel locations and then to make a binary decision if it lies in edge or not, as well as to overcome structural variation.

5 Dynamic Gabor Edge Detection

The 2D Gabor filter h(x,y) has been described as Gaussian kernel function modulated by the complex sinusoid, with varied orientations and diverse frequencies to catch edges dynamically and effectively without necessary fragment connecting. In the spatial domain, the 2D Gabor function is simply the product of the Gaussian envelope g(x,y) and complex sinusoid carrier c(x,y) as (6). In (7–8), σ_x and σ_y denote the standard deviations in x and y directions, u_0 and v_0 denote the central frequencies.

$$h(x, y) = c(x, y)g(x, y) \tag{6}$$

$$c(x, y) = e^{-j2\pi(u_0 x + v_0 y)} \tag{7}$$

$$g(x, y) = \frac{1}{2\psi_x\sigma_y}e^{-\left(\frac{x^2}{2\sigma_x^2}+\frac{y^2}{2\sigma_y^2}\right)} \tag{8}$$

The 2D Gabor filter is simply defined as (9). The high frequency edges are related to high output values when the Gabor filter is applied.

$$h(x,y) = c(x,y)g(x,y) = \frac{1}{2\psi_x\sigma_y}e^{-\left(\frac{x^2}{2\sigma_x^2}+\frac{y^2}{2\sigma_y^2}\right)}e^{-j2\pi(u_0 x + v_0 y)} \tag{9}$$

In the frequency domain, frequency shifts occur in both the u axis and v axis.

$$H(u, v) = G(u - u_0, v - v_0) \tag{10}$$

Via convolution, H(u, v) is derived to be (11):

$$H(u, v) = \frac{e^{-\left[\frac{(u-u_0)^2}{2\sigma_u^2}+\frac{(v-v_0)^2}{2\sigma_v^2}\right]}}{2\psi_x\sigma_y} = 2\psi_u\sigma_v e^{-2\pi^2\left[(u-u_0)^2\sigma_u^2 + (v-v_0)^2\sigma_v^2\right]} \tag{11}$$

where σ_u and σ_v denote standard deviations in the u and v axes.

$$\sigma_x = 2\psi_u; \sigma_y = 2\psi_v \tag{12}$$

2D Gabor wavelets are introduced the next to perform dilation and rotation operations on the Gabor function, using both scaling and phase factors.

$$g_{mn}(x, y) = g(x_0, y_0)/\alpha^m \tag{13}$$

where the scaling factor $s = \alpha^{(-m)}$ ($\alpha = 2$; $m = 0, 1,..., M - 1$) and phase factor $\theta_n = n\pi$ /N ($n = 0, 1,..., N - 1$). M and N indicate the total number of scales and orientations. x_0 and y_0 are formulated in (14–15).

$$x_0 = x\, \cos\theta_n + y\, \sin\theta_n \tag{14}$$

$$y_0 = -x\, \sin\theta_n + y\, \cos\theta_n \tag{15}$$

Since α is selected as 2 at each level of discrete wavelet transform in context, it will produce the 2×2 quadrant blocks with 4 subbands. Gabor filters can also be further expanded to optimal Gabor filters and Gabor pyramids.

6 Qualitative Comparisons at RGB Scale

The skyline is the scene viewed near the horizon. A skyline image can show features covering important information in both the natural and inspiring ways. It illustrates an comprehensive vision of the city environment with the dense spatial composition of complex physical structures, such as high-rise skyscrapers, iconic (towers, monuments and statues), peaks and ridges of mountains, blue (oceans, rivers, lakes, bays), sandy beaches and harbors, curves of bridges, green (parks, trees, landscape, vegetation), man-made structures (plazas, streets, walkways, sports fields and stadiums), as well as modern people and civilizations (aircrafts, vehicles, boats), etc.

Thus case studies are to be made using several typical digital images with diverse information complexity, including the skylines of Istanbul and Bosphorus Bridge, Yoko-hama and Landmark Tower, as well as Miami and Miami Beach. The source images together with the detected features using classical Canny edge detection, intelligent ACO edge detection and dynamic Gabor edge detection are depicted in Figs. 1, 2 and 3, respectively. Qualitative assessment can be directly made via visual appeals. At the full color RGB scale, edge detection is conducted at each of red, green and blue color channels individually. Then combination of information in three primary color channels gives rise to outcomes stem from diverse edge detection schemes.

Even though the information conveyed from three skyline images varies significantly, it is readily to make similar conclusions when 3 detection schemes are compared with each other. Canny edge detection produces good localization and response with thin and clean edges, which is also robust against noises. But it is time consuming since additional adaptive tracking is made along high values and maximal gradients in a 3 by 3 neighborhood pixels of output images. It can also generate broken segments due to faint outcomes generated. ACO edge detection can produce thin edges as well, while it is also efficient in compensating for broken edges. To reach optimal contour and edge detection, ACO edge detection applies a pheromone matrix to show image information by capturing pixel position and intensity of edges. It covers pixel-wise edge information on all routes dispatched by ants on the image. Thus missing edges can be easily recovered when indirect useful information exchange occurs to avoid information loss in its self-organization system. Fine details can be well collected by ACO edge detection. Dynamic Gabor filter edge detection has the high efficiency via

Fig. 1. Skyline of Istanbul and Bosphorus Bridge at RGB Scale (Source, Canny; ACO, Gabor)

Fig. 2. Skyline of Yokohama and Landmark Tower at RGB Scale (Source,Canny; ACO,Gabor)

multi-resolution analysis. It generates high edge detection accuracy and noise robustness. However Gabor edge detection produces relatively thick and blurry edges. Gabor edge detection highlights the essential edges in tradeoff with some extra excessive information.

For performance comparisons to be more convincing, corresponding quantitative analysis must be carried out as well. It will be applied to the comparative studies at both the gray scale and binary scale.

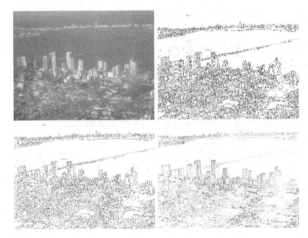

Fig. 3. Skyline of Miami and Miami Beach at RGB Scale (Source, Canny; ACO, Gabor)

7 Quantitative Analysis at Gray Scale in Frequency Domain

For quantitative analysis at the gray scale, there are numerous information metrics to choose from. In context, discrete entropy, relative entropy and mutual information are selected. Three gray scale source images and corresponding gray scale features using classical Canny edge detection, intelligent ACO edge detection, and dynamic Gabor edge detection are shown in Figs. 4, 5 and 6, respectively.

7.1 Discrete Entropy

The discrete entropy is to measure the average information content to show the uncertainty of information source. It leads to expected amount of conveyed information, which is defined as the sum of products of the outcome probability and the log function of its own inverse as shown in (16), taking into account every possible outcome $\{1, 2, ..., n\}$ in the event $\{x_1, x_2, ..., x_n\}$, $p(i)$ is the probability distribution, for all the histogram counts. In context it shows the average information conveyed from any digital image.

$$H(x) = \sum_{i=1}^{n} p(i)\log_2 \frac{1}{p(i)} = -\sum_{i=1}^{n} p(i)\log_2 p(i) \tag{16}$$

Being a statistical measure of randomness, the maximal entropy occurs in case all possible outcomes are equal with uniform probability distribution. For $n = 256$, discrete entropy can be derived as $\log_2(n) = 8$ bits. Instead the minimal entropy occurs when the outcome is certainty, which is equal to zero.

7.2 Relative Entropy

Relative entropy indicates how one probability distribution of the histogram differ from another probability distribution. Given two discrete probability distribution functions p and q. The relative entropy of p in terms of q is defined as (17). Relative entropy is nonnegative. When two distributions have equal quantities of information, the relative entropy reaches its minima of zero.

$$d = \sum_{i=1}^{n} p(i)\log_2\frac{p(i)}{q(i)} \tag{17}$$

7.3 Mutual Information

The mutual information is used to measure the uncertainty reduction of one random variable based on existing knowledge of another. The mutual information is the symmetric function, formulated as (18). It intuitively indicates that information Y could tell on X is equal to the reduction of uncertainty of X owing to the existence of Y. In case X and Y are independent, the mutual information is zero. The larger the I(X,Y), the more information will be shared by X and Y.

$$I(X;Y) = H(X) - H(X\,|Y) = \sum_{X,Y} p_{XY}(X,Y)\log_2\frac{p_{XY}(X,Y)}{p_X(X)p_Y(Y)}$$

$$= -\sum_{X} p_X(X)\log_2 p_X(X) + \sum_{X,Y} p_{XY}(X,Y)\log_2\frac{p_{XY}(X,Y)}{p_Y(Y)} \tag{18}$$

where I(X; Y) denotes the mutual information; H(X) and H(X|Y) denote the discrete entropy and conditional entropy, respectively.

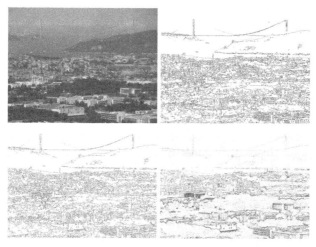

Fig. 4. Skyline of Istanbul and Bosphorus Bridge at Gray Scale (Source, Canny; ACO, Gabor)

In Tables 1, 2 and 3, the discrete entropies, relative entropies and mutual information of source images and detected features at the gray scale based on three schemes have

Fig. 5. Skyline of Yokohama and Landmark Tower at Gray Scale (Source,Canny; ACO,Gabor)

Fig. 6. Skyline of Miami and Miami Beach at Gray Scale (Source, Canny; ACO, Gabor)

been listed. Source images contain the complete information with the largest discrete entropies with no doubt. The classical Canny edge detection generates the feature of the smallest discrete entropy with the least amount of information, followed by intelligent ACO edge detection, and dynamic Gabor edge detection in order. More information has been retained by ACO edge detection and Gabor edge detection than Canny edge detection with faint edges. Conversely, in ACO edge detection, prior information is provided in decision making via positive feedback to enhance the edge detection; in Gabor edge detection, multiple resolution analysis produces high efficiency and detail information recovery.

When source images are used as references, relative entropies computed based on features extracted from Canny edge detection are much larger than those from ACO edge detection and Gabor edge detection, it shows the high level of dissimilarity with the source images occur when Canny edge detection is applied. It matches the qualitative analysis result where edges detected by Canny scheme are faint with merely thin edges captured exclusively. For mutual information between the source images and features extracted from three schemes, the features extracted from Canny edge detection lead to the largest mutual information, followed by those from ACO edge detection and Gabor edge detection. It indicates that the highest dependency on source images features exists in Canny edge detection, followed by ACO edge detection and Gabor edge detection. Gabor edge detection always generates the smallest amount of mutual information, because edges generated by the Gabor filter could sometimes be over-decorated, when wavelet functions are involved to generate the high resolutions in both spatial and frequency domains. Gabor filters are able to locate edges with the high efficiency and high robustness. However the extra information captured could even result in blurry edges. As an alternative, Gabor filters can be further expanded to optimal Gabor filters and Gabor pyramids.

Table 1. Metrics in Skyline of Istanbul at Gray Scale

Istanbul Skyline	Discrete Entropy	Relative Entropy	Mutual Information
Source Image	7.0514		
Canny Edge Detection	4.6047	4.6239	2.4466
ACO Edge Detection	5.2255	3.8287	1.8258
Gabor Edge Detection	5.8465	4.0402	1.2049

Table 2. Metrics in Skyline of Yokohama at Gray Scale

Yokohama Skyline	Discrete Entropy	Relative Entropy	Mutual Information
Source Image	6.5007		
Canny Edge Detection	3.6370	6.0594	2.8637
ACO Edge Detection	4.6641	4.2249	1.8366
Gabor Edge Detection	5.0157	3.756	1.4851

Table 3. Metrics in Skyline of Miami at Gray Scale

Miami Skyline	Discrete Entropy	Relative Entropy	Mutual Information
Source Image	6.2955		
Canny Edge Detection	3.6870	6.0709	2.6085
ACO Edge Detection	4.4768	5.9128	1.8187
Gabor Edge Detection	5.5257	4.3258	0.7698

8   Quantitative Analysis at Binary Scale in Spatial Domain

For quantitative analysis at the binary scale, still there are many information metrics to choose from. In context, the Accuracy and F-Score are selected. Three binary scale features via classical Canny edge detection, intelligent ACO edge detection, and dynamic Gabor edge detection are extracted by binarization using thresholding, whose edges are manifested in Fig. 7.

Fig. 7. Edge Detection of Skylines at Binary Scale (Canny; ACO; Gabor)

Neither the true binary edge information nor the ground truth is available in reality. Now the analysis is conducted in alternative ways. As both the intelligent ACO edge detection and dynamic Gabor edge detection will produce slightly better results than the classical Canny edge detection. Two assumptions can be made respectively: either the binary feature from intelligent ACO edge detection serves as ground truth; or the binary feature from dynamic Gabor edge detection serves as ground truth, then comparisons can be made easily. At last, the binary feature from intelligent ACO edge detection and the binary feature from dynamic Gabor edge detection are compared with each other.

The Accuracy and F-Score are defined in (19–20) whose results are listed in Table 4.

$$Accuracy = \frac{TP + TN}{FN + FP + TP + TN} \tag{19}$$

$$F\text{-}Score = \frac{2*TP}{FN + FP + 2*TP} \tag{20}$$

where the number of positives is defined as the total number of pixels that have intensity one on the reference binary image while the number of negatives is defined as the total number of pixels that have intensity zero on the reference binary image. Also if A is the ground truth image, then the number of true positives (TP) is defined as the total number of pixels which have the value one in both images A and B; the number of false positives (FP) is defined as the number of pixels whose intensities appear as one in B but zero in A; the number of true negatives (TN) is defined as the total number of pixels which have the value zero in both images A and B; the number of false negatives (FN) is defined as the number of pixels which appear as zero in B but one in A. Accuracy is adopted with correctly classified observations in case the True Positive and True Negatives are more important. For those imbalanced class distributions, though, F1-Score is the better measure to express the accuracy.

Table 4. Measures of Skyline Features at Binary Scale

Istanbul Skyline	Canny v.s.ACO	Canny v.s. Gabor	Gabor v.s. ACO
Accuracy	0.9237	0.7989	0.7987
F-Score	0.9561	0.8035	0.8274
Yokohama Skyline	Canny v.s. ACO	Canny v.s. Gabor	Gabor v.s.ACO
Accuracy	0.9486	0.7912	0.8116
F-Score	0.9708	0.8738	0.8824
Miami Skyline	Canny v.s. ACO	Canny v.s. Gabor	Gabor v.s.ACO
Accuracy	0.9502	0.8126	0.8301
F-Score	0.9723	0.8902	0.8975

Whichever is assumed to be the ground truth, it shows in Table 4 that the accuracy ranges from 0.79 to 0.95 while the F-Score ranges from 0.80 to 0.97 in all cases. It indicates that all three powerful edge detection schemes are able to generate cogent outcomes. Among 3 schemes from Table 4, classical Canny edge detection and intelligent ACO edge detection will produce outcomes with high similarities; while classical Canny edge detection and dynamic Gabor edge detection will produce outcomes with low similarities, showing the significant difference between the over-decorated (Gabor detection) and under-represented cases (Canny detection). In summary, Canny edge detection can provide clear thin edges with good connectivity at the expense of the potential broken edges and high structural variations. ACO edge detection covers more detail information to compensate for the thin edges with better connectivity, which is more accurate than Canny edge detection but it still contains structural variation. Gabor edge detection covers multiple resolution information with high efficiency and robustness as well as the least structural variation but it could be subject to blurry and magnified outcomes.

9 Conclusions

Comparative studies on 3 typical edge detection schemes are presented: Canny edge detection, ACO edge detection and Gabor edge detection, to represent classical, dynamic and intelligent edge detection approaches. The comprehensive comparisons are made from both subjective and objective points of view, where merits and drawbacks of each approach have been examined accordingly. In qualitative analysis, detected RGB scale features are selected. In quantitative analysis, detected gray scale and binary scale features are selected. A set of information metrics are also introduced to evaluate the quality of edge detection. Both the ACO edge detection and Gabor edge detection generate slightly better outcomes than Canny edge detection. If true edge detection and sharp detail information are major concerns, then ACO edge detection is the best among three typical edge detection schemes. If high efficiency and robustness as well as multiple resolutions are the major concerns, then Gabor edge detection is the best among three typical edge detection schemes.

References

1. Gonzalez, R., Woods, R.: Digital Image Processing, 2nd Edn. Prentice-Hall (2002)
2. Engelbrecht, A.: Computational Intelligence: An Introduction, 2nd Edn. Wiley (2000)
3. MacKay, D.: Information Theory, Inference and Learning Algorithms. University of Cambridge Press (2005)
4. Ye, Z., Cao, H., Iyengar, S., Mohamadian, H.: Medical and Biometric System Identification for Pattern Recognition and Data Fusion with Quantitative Measuring, Systems Engineering Approach to Medical Automation, Chapter 6, Artech House Publishers, pp. 91–112, Oct 2008
5. He, X., Jia, W., Wu, Q.: An approach of canny edge detection with virtual hexagonal image structure. In: 2008 10th International Conference on Control, Automation, Robotics and Vision. Hanoi, Vietnam, 17–20 Dec 2008
6. Lee, T.: Image representation using 2D gabor wavelets. IEEE Trans. Pattern Anal. Mach. Intell. **18**(10) (1996)
7. Senin, N., Leach, R., Pini, S., Blunt, L.: Texture-based segmentation with gabor filters, wavelet and pyramid decompositions for extracting individual surface features from areal surface topography maps. Measure. Sci. Technol. **26**(9) (2015)
8. Sajadi, S., Fathi, A.: Genetic algorithm based local and global spectral features extraction for ear recognition. Expert Syst. Appl. **159**(30) (2020)
9. Baterina, A., Oppus, C.: Image edge detection using ant colony optimization. Int. J. Circuit Syst. Sign. Process. **4**(2), 26–33 (2010)
10. Ye, Z., Mohamadian, H.: Strengthen accuracy of feature recognition via integration of ant colony detection and adaptive contour tracking. In: Proceedings of 2011 IEEE Congress on Evolutionary Computation, pp. 1799–1804, 5–8 June 2011, New Orleans, USA (2011)
11. Ye, Z., Mohamadian, H., Yin, Ye, Y.: Practical contour tracing via integration of adaptive contrast stretching and gabor wavelet transform. In: Proceedings of 2014 Second International Conference on Advances in Computing, Electronics and Communication, pp. 93–97, 25–26 Oct 2014, Zurich, Switzerland (2014)

12. Ye, Z.: Artificial-intelligence approach for biomedical sample characterization using raman spectroscopy. IEEE Trans. Autom. Sci. Eng. **2**(1), 67–73 (2005)
13. Ye, Z.: Quantitative comparisons of edge based and region based feature detection in digital aerial imagery analysis. In: 2021 International Conference on Electrical Engineering, Computing Science and Automatic Control. Mexico City, Mexico.10–12 Nov 2021
14. Rivera, A., Chae, O.: Spatiotemporal directional number transitional graph for dynamic texture recognition. IEEE Trans. Pattern Anal. Mach. Intell. **37**(10), 2146–2152 (2015)
15. Gao, B., Li, X., Woo, W., Tian, G.: Physics-based image segmentation using first order statistical properties and genetic algorithm for inductive thermography imaging. IEEE Trans. Image Process. **27**(5), 2160–2175 (2018)

Soil Organic Carbon Prediction Using Digital Color Sensor in Peru

Elida Montero[1] , Alex Vásquez[1] , Laura Alayo[1] , Pedro Gutiérrez[2] ,
and Carlos Mestanza[2]([⊠])

[1] Círculo de Investigación en Suelos - Universidad Nacional Agraria La Molina,
Lima, Peru
[2] Departamento Académico de Suelos - Universidad Nacional Agraria La Molina,
Lima, Peru
cmestanza@lamolina.edu.pe

Abstract. Soil organic carbon traditional analysis methods have a high
economic, environmental and time-consuming cost. General efforts are
focused on developing new low-cost and environmentally friendly alternatives. The aim was to evaluate the prediction of soil organic carbon
using machine learning for local conditions of Peru. A total of 351 dry
topsoil samples were analyzed to obtain soil organic carbon and color
measurements. The models used were multiple linear regression, generalized additive models, regression tree cubist, random forest, K-nearest
neighbors and neural networks. The results show that the simplest models were competitive with complex models, suggesting to incorporate
other predictor variables to improve the models performance.

Keywords: Soil color · Pedometrics · Machine-Learning

1 Introduction

Soil organic carbon is essential for weather regulation and keeping soil stability,
plant nutrient availability, water retention capacity and soil biodiversity, since it
is the main habitat of soil organism [27]. The most common methods for quantifying soil organic carbon are visible and near-infrared reflectance spectroscopy
[1], Walkley and Black [49], Heanes, Loss on ignition and Dumas combustion
by LECO [8], different methods will require different infrastructure, operational
cost, economic efficiency, time and precision [33]. In Peru Walkley and Black
is the principal method used in laboratories [24,36], nevertheless [37] reports
that this methodology has serious drawbacks and generates toxic acid waste [41]
containing reduced chromium (Cr^{3+}) and possibly oxidized chromium (Cr^{6+}),
besides being time consuming and expensive. [29] explains that the Cr^{6+} has
carcinogenic and non-carcinogenic effects, and in the Cr^{6+} exposed workers, all
parameters of pulmonary function had decreased. [22] inquires about an urgent
need to develop rapid and inexpensive soil characterization techniques to support
many important applications, such as precision agriculture.

© The Author(s), under exclusive license to Springer Nature Switzerland AG 2023
J. A. Lossio-Ventura et al. (Eds.): SIMBig 2022, CCIS 1837, pp. 222–233, 2023.
https://doi.org/10.1007/978-3-031-35445-8_16

A relationship between soil organic carbon and soil color is acknowledged, albeit not a direct one [31]. The traditional view of soil science believes that soil organic matters are mainly composed of humic substances [32]. The main soil pigments are humus providing a dark color, and hematite or hydroxides coloring the soil red and yellow [46]. Humic acid has extremely low reflectance throughout the visible range, suggesting a very dark color, while fulvic acid had a higher reflectance, particularly in the green and red spectral regions [40]. The relationship between soil color and soil carbonate components suggests that it is possible to estimate soil organic carbon from soil color. Different authors sought to obtain equations to estimate organic carbon using soil color [25,51], however the results are not encouraging or are only reproducible under local conditions. Therefore, the aim was to evaluate the prediction of soil organic carbon using machine learning for local conditions of Peru.

2   Related Work

The use of hand-held color sensors based on spectrometry is a rapid, inexpensive and non-destructive alternative for soil organic carbon estimation [18]. Sensors to measure soil organic carbon work at different wavelengths, such as portable X-ray fluorescence [14,28], ultraviolet to visible light [53], near-infrared [10], mid-infrared [15,47], visible to near-infrared [17] or hyperspectral wavelength sensors [9,54]. Low-cost spectrometers measure visible spectrum and are currently use to measure soil organic carbon [30] such as Konica Minolta [19,42] and Nix color sensors [45], this devices classify color into different color systems. The soil color is measured with Munsell system [38] conventionally, other system such as CIE, CIELab, XYZ, RGB or CMYK can be used. The color space of CIELab is composed of planes of constant lightness L (values from 0 to 100) with a net of lines parallel to the a and b axes (values from -100 to +100) [16]. RGB

Table 1. Research background of Nix color sensor use to predict soil organic carbon. Country, number of samples (N), minimum and maximum soil organic carbon values (SOC), metrics reported (R^2 and RMSE), color system (CS) [RGB (a), CIELab (b) and CMYK (c)], equation reported (EQT), best model (BM) [Multiple Linear Regression (MLR), Generalized Additive Models (GAM), Random Forest (RF), Support Vector Machine (SVM)] and reference (Ref).

Country	N	SOC	R^2	RMSE	CS	EQT	BM	Ref
Russia	21	[1.26,4.16]	0.86	—	b	No	MLR	[23]
USA	31	[0.20,3.60]	0.80	0.42	b	Yes	MLR	[43]
India	200	[1.27,3.96]	0.58	4.10	b	No	GAM	[26]
India	371	[0.08,2.26]	0.70	0.27	abc	No	RF	[44]
USA	134	[0.34,4.11]	0.60	0.50	abc	Yes	MLR	[39]
Brasil	705	[0.46,10.56]	0.34	1.75	abc	No	SVM	[12]

color space values vary from 0 to 255 in red, green, and blue color space [11]. There is not much research about soil organic prediction using the Nix Color sensor,existing results suggest potential in this technology. However, there are a few equations published that can be used in another contexts (Table 1).

Recent applications suggest a combination of remote sensing and field data with Nix [3] and the use of digital cameras to identify color and predict organic carbon content [9,13]. A not much researched area in the use of color sensors comes when processing data. A common issue between color data sets is the predictors high dimensionality and multicollinearity. [52] scouted different methods to reduce dimensionality before modeling and [35] proposed supervised and unsupervised models that incorporate dimensionality reduction.

3   Methodology

3.1   Soil Samples

A total of 483 topsoil samples were collected from all Peru regions, in exception of Tacna and Tumbes, inventoried by the Soils Department of the Universidad Nacional Agraria La Molina. The samples were air dried under shade and sieves (2 mm) to obtain fine earth air dried (FEAD), and the soil organic carbon (SOC) on % was quantified with the Walkley and Black method. Ten grams of soil were located in a white background, making sure the sample was distributed homogeneously and had not any white spots that could be detected by the Nix lector. The color was quantified in color systems RGB and CIELab using a pocket-size device Nix mini color sensor ^{TM} version 1.5. This device plugs in with smartphones through the Nix digital app in order to obtain RGB and CIELab values, each sample was measured three times and finally averaged.

3.2   Pre-processing

The initial dataset had 483 instances, 132 were eliminated for having higher SOC content than 2 %, following carbon upper limits for arable topsoils [4],resulting in 351 datasets. Before data calibration, scatter-plot were used to detect empty areas found when plotting the relationship between SOC and R, G, B, L, a, b variables. Thirteen values were removed following this procedure. Imputation of the predictors was done with the predictive mean matching method in the Mice library [6]. Data were transformed with the min-max method considering the maximum and minimum theoretical values of each one (Fig. 1).

3.3   Modelling and Validation

Data analysis and modeling were done using R language version 4.2.1 [34]. The color systems selected from the systems provided by Nix device readings were RGB and CIELab; these variables were used as the predictors. The validation method worked under the retention method, 70 % of the data was used for the

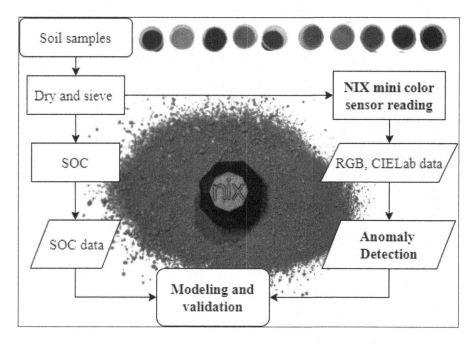

Fig. 1. Soil samples processing description, color readings, and SOC measurement for modeling and model validation.

statistical model and the other 30 % was used for validation. The implemented models were multiple linear regression (MLR), linear generalized additive models (GAM), regression trees (cubist), random forest (RF), k-nearest neighbors (KNN) and neural networks (NN). Variables for MLR and GAM under their significance inside the model and expert selection, for the other models all variables were used. The hyperparameters required to model RF were determined by 10-fold cross-validation looking for the best number of variables randomly sampled at each split and number of trees. The models KNN and NN require normalizing the predictors by mean and standard deviation. The KNN was tested by 10-fold cross validation from two to a hundred neighbors. Three neural networks of one, two and three hidden layers were adjusted with 32, 16 and 8 neurons in each layer, activation function for each layer was the rectilinear unit (RELU) and linear for out layer. The libraries used were caret [20], cubist [21], and Keras [7] implemented in R.

4   Results and Discussion

Some remarkable aspects during data collection were making sure the angle between the soil sample and the device lector in every reading was the same, considering we worked with such a wide range of soil samples from different regions and expected having an even wider range of textures. In clay soils with fine particles the device tended to sink because of its own weight inducing a null measurement, in these cases, we had to lift the device approximately 1cm from the sample to avoid the lector getting completely covered by the fine particles. It would have been appropriate to have the Powder Adapter provided by Nix Sensor ^{TM}, that helped us keep the same distance of 0.5 mm from the device to the sample in every lecture. Table 2 shows high variability in the dataset (CV greater than 20 %), the application of the models is restricted to the range of the soil organic carbon used.

Table 2. Estimated parameters for predictor and response variables. Mean, standard deviation (SD), median (Q2), minimum value (Min), maximum value (Max), and coefficient of variability in percentage (CV) were calculated.

Variable	Mean	SD	Q2	Min	Max	CV
SOC	0.62	0.55	0.44	0.01	1.98	89
L	44.94	7.99	45	18	63	18
a	5.64	4.01	6	-5	17	71
b	19.92	4.28	20	7	31	21
R	124.12	24.83	124	41	192	20
G	102.72	18.39	102	44	149	18
B	73.42	17.24	72	17	123	23.44

4.1   Models Description

A high correlation among predictors (color systems variables) was found, this violates the assumption of independence of the regression. [20] remarks that multiple linear regression will become unstable with high variability with predictors correlation. Which led us to select only the predictor most related to dark colors. The two most significant predictor variables were lightning (L) and the interaction between R:G:B, because they can tell about soil darkness. As [5] mentions, organic matter tends to cover mineral particles, darkening and masking the brighter colors of the minerals themselves as the organic matter increases. In order to acquire a more simple dataset, we worked with a square root transformation of the predictor. Table 3 shows a significant inverse relationship between organic carbon and square root RGB interaction or L values. Figure 2 depicts a better adjustment with RGB interaction, it is supported with a smaller RMSE value and higher R^2. Nevertheless, for each case a non-homogeneity of variances is remarkable, in addition, the Anderson-Darling test [2] indicates there is a non-existing residuals normality ($p < 0.0001$), which is a qualification for linear regressions.

   A scale-location GAM model was adjusted in order to correct the not normal distribution problem and the heterogeneity of variances. Table 4 displays

Table 3. Linear regression parameters of proposed models. Estimate coefficient (EST) and standard error (SE) were calculated by least-squares, t-value was used to test null hypothesis of existence of estimated coefficient.

Coefficient	EST±SE	t-value (p-value)
Model 1		
Intercept	1.3276 ± 0.1120	11.85(< 0.0001)
R:G:B	-2.9469 ± 0.4492	-6.56(< 0.0001)
Model 2		
Intercept	1.7396 ± 0.1742	9.985(< 0.0001)
L	-2.4918 ± 0.3819	-6.524(< 0.0001)

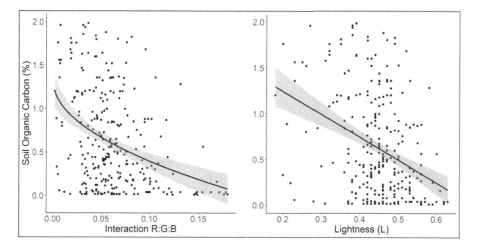

Fig. 2. Scatter-Plot of multiple linear regression proposed.

a significant no lineal relation among L and RGB interaction that can adjust the dataset variability into its linear form. The scale intercept (1/variance) z value was higher than the traditional intercept, indicating that modeling the variance separately was adequate. Also, Fig. 3 summarizes the result of a no linear form and a non-homogeneous variance with L predictor. Dark soils (low L) present greater variance than light-colored soils (intermediate and high L) and the prediction tends to become constant toward darker colors. This suggests a limitation in the prediction of soil carbon, the SOC can continue increasing but it cannot get darker to the human eye and the device itself, so for RGB and for L this critical point is 0.3.

Optimal performance in the random forest model was obtained with 2 randomly sampled variables in each split and from 300 trees the RMSE remained constant, the value was set at 500, default parameters were left for the cubist model. Both models resulted in a lower predictive power than linear models. The

Table 4. Generalized Additive Model parameters for proposed model. Estimate coefficient (EST) and standard error (SE) were calculated by least-squares, Z value was used to test null hypothesis of existence of estimated coefficient. Effective degree of freedoom (edf) reflects the non-linearity of predictor (edf > 1), Chi test was used to test null hypothesis of correct edf.

Intercept	EST±SE	Z (p-value)
Parametric Coefficients		
Intercept	-0.5472 ± 0.0620	-8.8240(< 0.0001)
Scale Intercept	7.0606 ± 0.0739	95.4600(< 0.0001)
Variable	**edf**	χ^2 **(p-value)**
Spline Smooth Coefficients		
L	2.549	34.162(< 0.0001)
Scale-RGB$^{0.5}$	1.000	3.843(0.05)

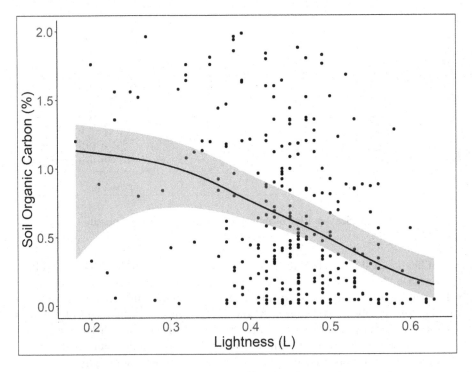

Fig. 3. Scatter-Plot of Generalized additive model proposed.

most important predictors for RF were the colors R, G, B, and for cubist the R color and b of CIELab. The best number of neighbors found for the KNN was 27 and the best neural network was the two layers network.

4.2   General Comparison

Table 5 shows that the simplest models (MLR and KNN) resulted in the best predictive power and fit to the data. Nevertheless, objectively the difference between metrics is way too small to consider it a different result. Complex models had poor performance compared to the simple models, showing that the prediction capacity is limited to using few parameters. The work of [23, 39, 43] got determination coefficients higher than 0.60, although these values were taken from homogeneous landforms or just with one soil class. Our work includes samples from a wide range of landforms from all over the country, the high variability explains the low determination coefficients in our models. [12] was also performed under an extensive region with different landforms and low values of soil organic carbon. Their results are close to us in variability (R^2) but with less predictive power (RMSE), possibly because we work with a small range of soil organic carbon.

Table 5. Metrics comparison between existing models and proposed models, the two best values of each metric were bold.

Model	RMSE	R^2
MLR 1	**0.5175**	**0.0465**
MLR 2	0.5239	0.0287
GAM	0.5251	0.0270
Cubist	0.5333	0.0400
RF	0.5726	0.0014
KNN	**0.5162**	**0.0412**
NN 1	0.5323	0.0243
NN 2	0.5349	0.0150
NN 3	0.5400	0.0202

The poor performance of machine learning models can be related to a problem of underfitting, what occurs when an algorithm lacks sufficient model capacity or sufficient training to fully learn the true relationship [48]. Different sources of error can accumulate in the data to bring it underfitting, inadequate predictors, the device precision, or lack of data. [33] comments that a disadvantage of using the RGB color system is that the three bands are highly correlated and determine illumination intensity jointly and suggest that CIELab is a better predictor of SOC, however, adds that the correlation is not reasonably high. The research commented in the section on related works were carried out using Nix Pro equipment, our research was done with a low-cost Nix mini. [50] indicates that Nix mini does not work with the precision required to be implemented in an industry setting, which is reflected in our results. We cannot attribute the underfitting problem to the amount of data since previous works [38] had less than 300 instances.

Despite this, our model prediction errors are very close to those reported by different authors, with the difference that our proposal may be applicable on a national scale. Models could be improved by incorporating other low-cost soil variables or by replicating the study with more accurate color sensors. Additionally, it is pending to extend the study to soils with organic carbon contents higher than ours.

5   Conclusions

Soil organic carbon can be predicted based on soil color with low-cost equipment such as the Nix mini color sensor. Simpler models like the multiple linear regression and k-nearest neighbors have a slight advantage in their predictive power over complex models. The main modeling problem was underfitting, so it is suggested to incorporate other low-cost variables to improve predictive capabilities.

6   Supplementary Files

Soil organic carbon and color measurements, R code, and figures were stored in Figshare https://doi.org/10.6084/m9.figshare.20410653

Acknowledgments. This work was supported by the laboratory for analysis of soils, plants, water, and fertilizers (LASPAF) of the Universidad Nacional Agraria La Molina (UNALM). Special thanks to William Ernesto Curi Guzman and Deysi Vanessa Villarroel Claudio cooperation during the samples selection and organization are appreciated.

References

1. Allory, V., et al.: Quantification of soil organic carbon stock in urban soils using visible and near infrared reflectance spectroscopy (VNIRS) in situ or in laboratory conditions. Sci. Total Environ. **686**, 764–773 (2019). https://doi.org/10.1016/j.scitotenv.2019.05.192
2. Anderson, T.W., Darling, D.A.: Asymptotic theory of certain "goodness of fit" criteria based on stochastic processes. Ann. Math. Stat. **23**(2), 193–212 (1952). https://doi.org/10.1214/aoms/1177729437
3. Barbetti, R.: Low-cost digital mapping of soil organic carbon using optical spectrophotometer and sentinel-2 image. EQA - Int. J. Environ. Qual. **44**, 1–8 (2021). https://doi.org/10.6092/issn.2281-4485/12071, https://eqa.unibo.it/article/view/12071
4. Blume, H.-P., et al.: Scheffer/Schachtschabel Soil Science. Springer, Heidelberg (2016). https://doi.org/10.1007/978-3-642-30942-7
5. Brady, N.C., Weil, R.R.: The Nature and Properties of Soils, p. 1104. 15th Global Edition. [Main author]
6. Buuren, S.V., Groothuis-Oudshoorn, K.: mice: Multivariate imputation by chained equations in R. J. Stat. Softw. **45**(3), 1–67 (2011). https://doi.org/10.18637/jss.v045.i03
7. Chollet, F., et al.: Keras (2015). https://github.com/fchollet/keras

8. Conyers, M.K., Poile, G.J., Oates, A.A., Waters, D., Chan, K.Y.: Comparison of three carbon determination methods on naturally occurring substrates and the implication for the quantification of 'soil carbon'. Soil Res. **49**(1), 27–33 (2011). https://doi.org/10.1071/sr10103

9. Dhawale, N.M., Adamchuk, V.I., Prasher, S.O., Rossel, R.A.V., Ismail, A.A.: Evaluation of two portable hyperspectral-sensor-based instruments to predict key soil properties in Canadian soils. Sensors **22**(7), 2556 (2022). https://doi.org/10.3390/s22072556

10. Di Iorio, E., et al.: Comparison of natural and technogenic soils developed on volcanic ash by vis-NIR spectroscopy. Catena **216**, 106369 (2022). https://doi.org/10.1016/j.catena.2022.106369

11. Dutta, S., Chaudhuri, B.B.: A color edge detection algorithm in RGB color space (2009). https://doi.org/10.1109/ARTCom.2009.72

12. de Faria, A.J.G., et al.: Prediction of soil organic matter content by combining data from Nix ProTM color sensor and portable X-ray fluorescence spectrometry in tropical soils. Geoderma Reg. **28**, e00461 (2022). https://doi.org/10.1016/j.geodrs.2021.e00461

13. Gorthi, S., et al.: Soil organic matter prediction using smartphone-captured digital images: use of reflectance image and image perturbation. Biosys. Eng. **209**, 154–169 (2021). https://doi.org/10.1016/j.biosystemseng.2021.06.018

14. Gozukara, G., Zhang, Y., Hartemink, A.E.: Using PXRF and vis-NIR spectra for predicting properties of soils developed in loess. Pedosphere **32**(4), 602–615 (2022). https://doi.org/10.1016/s1002-0160(21)60092-9

15. Greenberg, I., Seidel, M., Vohland, M., Koch, H.J., Ludwig, B.: Performance of in situ vs laboratory mid-infrared soil spectroscopy using local and regional calibration strategies. Geoderma **409**, 115614 (2022). https://doi.org/10.1016/j.geoderma.2021.115614

16. Hill, B., Roger, T., Vorhagen, F.W.: Comparative analysis of the quantization of color spaces on the basis of the CIELAB color-difference formula. ACM Trans. Graph. **16**(2), 109–154 (1997). https://doi.org/10.1145/248210.248212

17. Islam, K., Singh, B., McBratney, A.: Simultaneous estimation of several soil properties by ultra-violet, visible, and near-infrared reflectance spectroscopy. Soil Res. **41**(6), 1101–1114 (2003). https://doi.org/10.1071/sr02137

18. Johns, T.J., Angove, M.J., Wilkens, S.: Measuring soil organic carbon: which technique and where to from here? Soil Res. **53**(7), 717–736 (2015). https://doi.org/10.1071/sr14339

19. Konen, M.E., Burras, C.L., Sandor, J.A.: Organic carbon, texture, and quantitative color measurement relationships for cultivated soils in north central Iowa. Soil Sci. Soc. Am. J. **67**(6), 1823–1830 (2003). https://doi.org/10.2136/sssaj2003.1823

20. Kuhn, M.: Building predictive models in R using the caret package. J. Stat. Softw. **28**(5), 1–26 (2008). https://doi.org/10.18637/jss.v028.i05

21. Kuhn, M., Johnson, K.: Applied Predictive Modeling. Springer, Berlin (2014)

22. Madugundu, R., et al.: Estimation of soil organic carbon in agricultural fields: a remote sensing approach. J. Environ. Biol. **43**(1), 73–84 (2022). https://doi.org/10.22438/jeb/43/1/MRN-1873

23. Mikhailova, E.A., Stiglitz, R.Y., Post, C.J., Schlautman, M.A., Sharp, J.L., Gerard, P.D.: Predicting soil organic carbon and total nitrogen in the Russian chernozem from depth and wireless color sensor measurements. Eurasian Soil Sci. **50**(12), 1414–1419 (2018). https://doi.org/10.1134/s106422931713004x

24. Ministerio de Agricultura: Decreto Supremo 013-2010-AG: Aprueban reglamento para la ejecución de levantamiento de suelos (2010)

25. Moritsuka, N., Matsuoka, K., Katsura, K., Sano, S., Yanai, J.: Soil color analysis for statistically estimating total carbon, total nitrogen and active iron contents in Japanese agricultural soils. Soil Sci. Plant Nutr. **60**(4), 475–485 (2014). https://doi.org/10.1080/00380768.2014.906295

26. Mukhopadhyay, S., Chakraborty, S.: Use of diffuse reflectance spectroscopy and nix pro color sensor in combination for rapid prediction of soil organic carbon. Comput. Electron. Agric. **176**, 105630 (2020). https://doi.org/10.1016/j.compag.2020.105630

27. Muñoz-Rojas, M.: Soil quality indicators: critical tools in ecosystem restoration. Curr. Opin. Environ. Sci. Health **5**, 47–52 (2018). https://doi.org/10.1016/j.coesh.2018.04.007

28. Naimi, S., Ayoubi, S., Di Raimo, L.A.D.L., Dematte, J.A.M.: Quantification of some intrinsic soil properties using proximal sensing in arid lands: application of Vis-NIR, MIR, and pXRF spectroscopy. Geoderma Reg. **28**, e00484 (2022). https://doi.org/10.1016/j.geodrs.2022.e00484

29. Nasirzadeh, N., Mohammadian, Y., Dehgan, G.: Health risk assessment of occupational exposure to hexavalent chromium in Iranian workplaces: a meta-analysis study. Biol. Trace Elem. Res. **200**(4), 1551–1560 (2021). https://doi.org/10.1007/s12011-021-02789-w

30. Nocita, M., Stevens, A., Toth, G., Panagos, P., van Wesemael, B., Montanarella, L.: Prediction of soil organic carbon content by diffuse reflectance spectroscopy using a local partial least square regression approach. Soil Biol. Biochem. **68**, 337–347 (2014). https://doi.org/10.1016/j.soilbio.2013.10.022

31. Pretorius, M.L., Van Huyssteen, C.W., Brown, L.R.: Soil color indicates carbon and wetlands: developing a color-proxy for soil organic carbon and wetland boundaries on sandy coastal plains in South Africa. Environ. Monit. Assess. **189**(11), 1–18 (2017). https://doi.org/10.1007/s10661-017-6249-z

32. Qu, C., Ren, W., Li, X., Cai, P., Chen, W., Huang, Q.: Revisit soil organic matter. Chin. Sci. Bull. (2022). https://doi.org/10.1360/tb-2021-0704

33. Qureshi, A., Badola, R., Hussain, S.A.: A review of protocols used for assessment of carbon stock in forested landscapes. Environ. Sci. Policy **16**, 81–89 (2012). https://doi.org/10.1016/j.envsci.2011.11.001

34. R-Core-Team: R: A language and environment for statistical computing (2021). https://www.R-project.org/

35. Ribeiro, S.G., et al.: Soil organic carbon content prediction using soil-reflected spectra: a comparison of two regression methods. Remote Sens. **13**(23), 4752 (2021). https://doi.org/10.3390/rs13234752

36. Ruiz, C., Ubillas, C., Pretell, V., Ramos, W., Rodriguez, J.: Evaluación de los parámetros cinéticos por análisis termogravimétrico del esquisto en la formación muerto, Talara-Perú (2020). https://doi.org/10.18687/laccei2020.1.1.70

37. de Santana, F.B., de Souza, A.M., Poppi, R.J.: Green methodology for soil organic matter analysis using a national near infrared spectral library in tandem with learning machine. Sci. Total Environ. **658**, 895–900 (2019). https://doi.org/10.1016/j.scitotenv.2018.12.263

38. Schmidt, S.A., Ahn, C.: A comparative review of methods of using soil colors and their patterns for wetland ecology and management. Commun. Soil Sci. Plant Anal. **50**(11), 1293–1309 (2019). https://doi.org/10.1080/00103624.2019.1604737

39. Schmidt, S.A., Ahn, C.: Predicting forested wetland soil carbon using quantitative color sensor measurements in the region of northern Virginia, USA. J. Environ. Manage. **300**, 113823 (2021). https://doi.org/10.1016/j.jenvman.2021.113823

40. Schulze, D.G., Nagel, J.L., Van Scoyoc, G.E., Henderson, T.L., Baumgardner, M.F., Stott, D.E.: Significance of organic matter in determining soil colors. In: Soil Color, pp. 71–90 (1993). Proceedings of the symposium, San Antonio, 1990
41. Shamrikova, E.V., et al.: Transferability between soil organic matter measurement methods for database harmonization. Geoderma **412**, 115547 (2022). https://doi.org/10.1016/j.geoderma.2021.115547
42. Stiglitz, R., Mikhailova, E., Post, C., Schlautman, M., Sharp, J.: Evaluation of an inexpensive sensor to measure soil color. Comput. Electron. Agric. **121**, 141–148 (2016). https://doi.org/10.1016/j.compag.2015.11.014
43. Stiglitz, R., Mikhailova, E., Post, C., Schlautman, M., Sharp, J.: Using an inexpensive color sensor for rapid assessment of soil organic carbon. Geoderma **286**, 98–103 (2017). https://doi.org/10.1016/j.geoderma.2016.10.027
44. Swetha, R.K., Chakraborty, S.: Combination of soil texture with nix color sensor can improve soil organic carbon prediction. Geoderma **382**, 114775 (2021). https://doi.org/10.1016/j.geoderma.2020.114775
45. Swetha, R.K., Chakraborty, S., Dasgupta, S., Li, B., Weindorf, D.C., Mancini, M., Silva, S.H.G., Ribeiro, B.T., Curi, N., Ray, D.P.: Using nix color sensor and Munsell soil color variables to classify contrasting soil types and predict soil organic carbon in eastern India. SSRN Electron. J. (2022). https://doi.org/10.2139/ssrn.4082866
46. Vodyanitskii, Y.N., Kirillova, N.P.: Application of the CIE-L*a*b* system to characterize soil color. Eurasian Soil Sci. **49**(11), 1259–1268 (2016). https://doi.org/10.1134/s1064229316110107
47. Vohland, M., Ludwig, B., Seidel, M., Hutengs, C.: Quantification of soil organic carbon at regional scale: benefits of fusing vis-NIR and MIR diffuse reflectance data are greater for in situ than for laboratory-based modelling approaches. Geoderma **405**, 115426 (2022). https://doi.org/10.1016/j.geoderma.2021.115426
48. Walkley, A., Black, A.: An examination of the Degtjareff method for determining soil organic matter, and a proposed modification of the chromic acid titration method. Soil Sci. **37**(1), 29–38 (1934)
49. Walkley, A.: A critical examination of a rapid method for determining organic carbon in soils-effect of variations in digestion conditions and of inorganic soil constituents. Soil Sci. **63**(4), 251–264 (1947). https://doi.org/10.1097/00010694-194704000-00001
50. Wheeler, B.: Analysis of Low-Cost Color Sensor Device Performance as Compared to Standardized Spectrophotometers. Thesis (2022)
51. Wills, S.A., Burras, C.L., Sandor, J.A.: Prediction of soil organic carbon content using field and laboratory measurements of soil color. Soil Sci. Soc. Am. J. **71**(2), 380–388 (2007). https://doi.org/10.2136/sssaj2005.0384
52. Xie, S., Ding, F., Chen, S., Wang, X., Li, Y., Ma, K.: Prediction of soil organic matter content based on characteristic band selection method. Spectrochim. Acta Part A: Mol. Biomol. Spectrosc. **273**, 120949 (2022). https://doi.org/10.1016/j.saa.2022.120949
53. Zhang, Y., Hartemink, A.E.: Data fusion of vis-NIR and pXRF spectra to predict soil physical and chemical properties. Eur. J. Soil Sci. **71**(3), 316–333 (2020). https://doi.org/10.1111/ejss.12875
54. Šestak, I., Boltek, L.M., Mesić, M., Zgorelec, Ž, Perčin, A.: Hyperspectral sensing of soil pH, total carbon and total nitrogen content based on linear and non-linear calibration methods. J. Cent. Eur. Agric. **20**(1), 504–523 (2019). https://doi.org/10.5513/jcea01/20.1.2158

Ideation of Computational Thinking Programs by Assembling Code Snippets from the Web

Hasan M. Jamil[✉] [iD]

Department of Computer Science,
University of Idaho,
Moscow, ID, USA
jamil@uidaho.edu

Abstract. The emergence of Github Copilot, IBM's CodeNet, and Amazon's CodeWhisperer challenges the conventional wisdom of code development by expert developers. These machine learning based platforms aim to mine a large compendium of existing code bases, learning and refining their coding skills over time. Despite their promises, research show that these systems have a long way to go before being considered a proper development platform. For now, they probably will serve well as a programming aid and a promising research opportunity. In this paper, we introduce the idea of open-source code scavenging from the web toward constructing an executable programming solution for computational thinking exercises. We present a model and an architecture of *CodeMapper* that aims to scour the internet to find code segments to stitch together a target program fully autonomously.

Keywords: Computational thinking · Program synthesis · Program dependence graphs · Graph matching · Crowd sourcing · Programming in pseudocode

1 Introduction

Novice programmers often face difficulties in framing their computational thinking [27] solutions into a sequence of coherent conceptual steps. The challenges they face could potentially be at any level of the pseudocode, algorithm and computer program continuum. In an increasingly popular and feasible e-learning environment where one-on-one human mentoring is absent, persistent cognitive gaps in this continuum need to be removed by a smart learning environment using tool support. Systems such as Flowgorithm [4] and TryPL [14] try to reduce cognitive gaps by allowing novice learners to think in terms of visual or textual algorithms respectively as opposed to coding in full textual syntax of a programming language such as C++, Java or Python. While numerous tools are available to help master textual programming [5,17,18,23], not many are available to help programming in pseudocode [2]. Despite this array of tools, challenges novice programmers in general face are numerous [26], online novice programmers in particular [8].

© The Author(s), under exclusive license to Springer Nature Switzerland AG 2023
J. A. Lossio-Ventura et al. (Eds.): SIMBig 2022, CCIS 1837, pp. 234–245, 2023.
https://doi.org/10.1007/978-3-031-35445-8_17

Recent research on learners' approach to coding [22] suggest that auto grading and feedback [11,23], code comprehension support [26], solution tools [5], early identification of difficulties and personalized feedback [1,19], etc. can play a significant role in alleviating learning difficulties. One powerful technique, early validation of conceptual grasps of a computational thinking problem [20], to remove cognitive gaps however, has not received adequate attention. Thus, until recently there has been a dearth of tools or techniques to address it.

We believe that in ways similar to early feedback on assignments and assessment of progress, removing misconceptions and conceptual errors early could increase novice learners' confidence and subsequently, accelerate their progress [7,23,25] using tools such as PCDIT [15], COSPEX [10] or PAAM [18]. However, none of these tools allow the learner to simply explore if their solution will work without even beginning to code. We believe that novice programmers must be allowed to program in pseudocode in ways similar to MaBL [2]. We also believe that technologies similar to Amazon's CodeWhisperer, Github Copilot and IBM CodeNet could significantly revolutionize pseudcode based programming to help novice programmers learn better coding.

In this paper, we introduce the model of a tool, called Code*Mapper*, for a pseudocode based programming. Code*Mapper* allows novice programmers to use a graphical tool to construct a pseudocode using conceptual terms such as *sort* or *order, swap, largest* or *smallest, search* or *locate, compute average*, etc. Learners develop pseudocode by appropriately and meaningfully sequencing these concepts that lead to a computational thinking solution. Since pseudocodes will have to be mapped to an executable program to test the correctness or validity of the solution, Code*Mapper* scours online sites such as StackOverflow, GitHub, SourceForge, Bitbucket, GitLab, etc. for code snippets or program modules not available in CondHunter repository. Once all the components are identified, standardized, and unified, an executable program is synthesized for execution, and the executed results are presented for learners' review and validation.

In the remainder of the paper, we present the model on which Code*Mapper* is based. Then we discuss the design and functions of each of its major components. We highlight the novel features of Code*Mapper* in relation to contemporary systems and discuss its strengths and weakness. Finally, we also discuss its planned usage as a community coding tool for novice programmers.

2   Code*Mapper* Model

The goal of Code*Mapper* is to help learners organize their thoughts into a coherent sequence of modules toward a solution. There are no artificial limits on the choice or characteristics of these modules. They can be as simple and elementary as *"swap the two values"* to as broad, abstract or high-level as *"find all subgraph isomorphs of graph G"*. The model assumes that learners will be able to find codes corresponding to such instructions in Code*Mapper*s codebase. Once the codes are found, identified and selected, the fragments are *"aligned"* to match type declarations, variable names and scopes, and so on, and a complete program is synthesized for compilation. If the compilation is successful, the results are presented to the user for review or consumption.

Formally, a Code*Mapper* database $\mathcal{D}$ is a tuple of the form $\langle \Pi, \Xi, \Sigma, \Omega, \Upsilon, \Lambda \rangle$ where Π is a set of code fragments or snippets, Ξ is a program synthesizer that analyses the pseudocode, and develops a construction plan for synthesizing a program P given a pseudocode C, Σ is a search and recommendation function to help identify candidate code fragments in Π, Υ is a unification function that makes the code fragments chosen as part of a synthesized program P congruent in terms variables and types, and finally, Λ is a set of compilers, one for each language to compile and execute a synthesized program P.

2.1   Concept Hierarchy of Code Snippets

Code fragments or snippets π in the set $\Pi \in \mathcal{D}$ are the main ingredients of $\mathcal{D}$. These code snippets are of the form $\langle \nu, \delta, \beta, \phi, \varphi, \iota \lambda \rangle$ where 1) β is the body of the code snippet, ϕ is a binary switch indicating if the code snippet is a compilable program (a function or a complete program), or not, 2) φ is the complete set of variables and their types in the snippet, 3) $\iota \subseteq \varphi$ are the variables receiving values from another snippet (formal parameters or connecting values), and finally, 4) λ is the language of the body of the code snippet (C++, Java or Python). These code snippets are placed as the leaf nodes in a partial order of group membership relation $\preceq$ in the concept hierarchy Ω, e.g., $m_i \preceq m_j$ where m_i, m_js are distinct concepts and means that m_j is a broader concept than m_i and the reverse does not hold, i.e., $m_j \npreceq m_i$. This also means that every code snippet belonging to one concept (denoted $\pi_i \in m$ as opposed to $\pi_i \preceq m$ which is used to denote concept hierarchy) behaves identically to another code snippet $\pi_j \in m$, or $\pi_j \in m'$ such that $m \preceq m'$ holds or $m \preceq m''$ and $m' \preceq m''$ holds, i.e., $\pi_i \equiv \pi_j$ holds as they are functionally equivalent and belong to the same broader group. For example, bubble sort and selection sort are members of quadratic-sort group, while heap sort and merge sort are logn-sort group[1], yet all are sorting algorithms. Finally, ν and δ are the snippet's identifying name and a description that characterizes the code snippet for human consumption.

2.2   Program Synthesizer

The synthesizer function Ξ is implemented both as a graphical and text interface in Code*Mapper*. It functions in conjunction with the search and find function Σ, and the code snippet unifier function Υ. While the outcomes of its two interface modes are likely the same, they function slightly differently. In text mode, it accepts complete pseudocode and synthesizes a target program in a compiler mode returning either a success or failure status, and executing the code if the synthesis is successful. In the process, it looks for code snippets in the database Ω to match, and leaves an order for the search function Σ to hunt for a code on

---

[1] Worst-case complexity for both groups.

sites such as StackOverflow or SourceForge that matches the missing requests, sanitizes the discovered snippet and includes it in Ω for future use, and abandons the synthesis, largely because the discovery process is likely offline.

In its graphical interface incarnation, it supports both a compile mode and an interactive interpreter mode. In the compiler mode, the interface presents the Ω database partial order to the user to choose code segments on a drag and drop canvas (see Figs. 1(a) and 1(b)), and string them together in a sequence that reflects her imagination of a solution (see Fig. 1(c)), and compiles it with the press of a button (see Fig. 1(d)). In this mode, it can only use the code snippets available in Ω and is unable to find or request new code segments using Σ. The advantage of this mode is that synthesis of a program is certain because Ξ is able to stitch up the code segments.

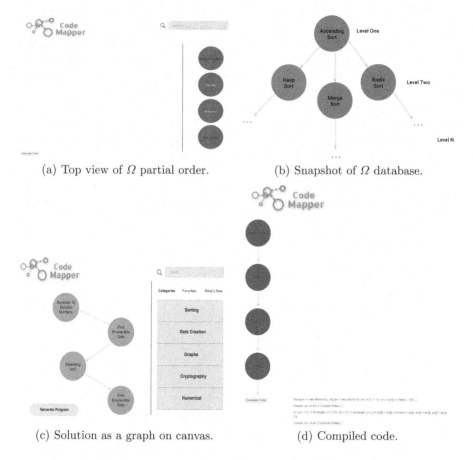

(a) Top view of Ω partial order.   (b) Snapshot of Ω database.

(c) Solution as a graph on canvas.   (d) Compiled code.

Fig. 1. Program development using Code*Mapper* compile mode.

In contrast, the interpreter mode is interactive and functions in a more user friendly way. It has a type ahead search bar that is able to look through the database descriptions to find the code snippets with maximal match, and shows the search in a dynamic, visually synchronized graph, matching the type-ahead text, i.e., in text type-ahead search bars, the matching text is shown, in Code*Mapper*, and the graph nodes that match are shown relative to the texts typed. With a click of a mouse, CodeHunter then drops the node on the canvas for the user, so that it can be connected with other nodes, as shown in Fig. 1(c). In this mode too, Code*Mapper* can only use snippets in the Ω database. However, the description can now be used to search the internet, as in the text mode, for a code snippet should the database search fail.

2.3 Search, Find and Annotate with Σ

Code snippet discovery requests from the internet can be made manually as shown in Fig. 2(a), or left for the Code*Mapper* system to process automatically, using the same search engine. Once a code snippet is found, a crowd curation request is set for public annotation of the code snippet using the form in Fig. 2(b) before the snippet is placed in Ω in a searchable and editable index as shown in Fig. 3, and used in the graphical view as shown in Fig. 1(b). Indexing the code snippets has been found to be useful for efficient program synthesis [16]. Crowd annotation is adopted because research has shown [28] that automated program synthesis systems such as Copilot and CodeWhisperer are prone to suggesting buggy codes that also pose security risks [3,6], necessitating significant cleaning [21] before they can be safely used. A detailed discussion on code snippet indexing follows in Sect. 3.

Fig. 2. Search, Find and Annotate with Σ.

2.4 Code Snippet Unification Using Υ

It is highly likely that the code snippets assembled and indexed in Ω are authored by a wide number of people having distinct coding styles, heterogeneous variable

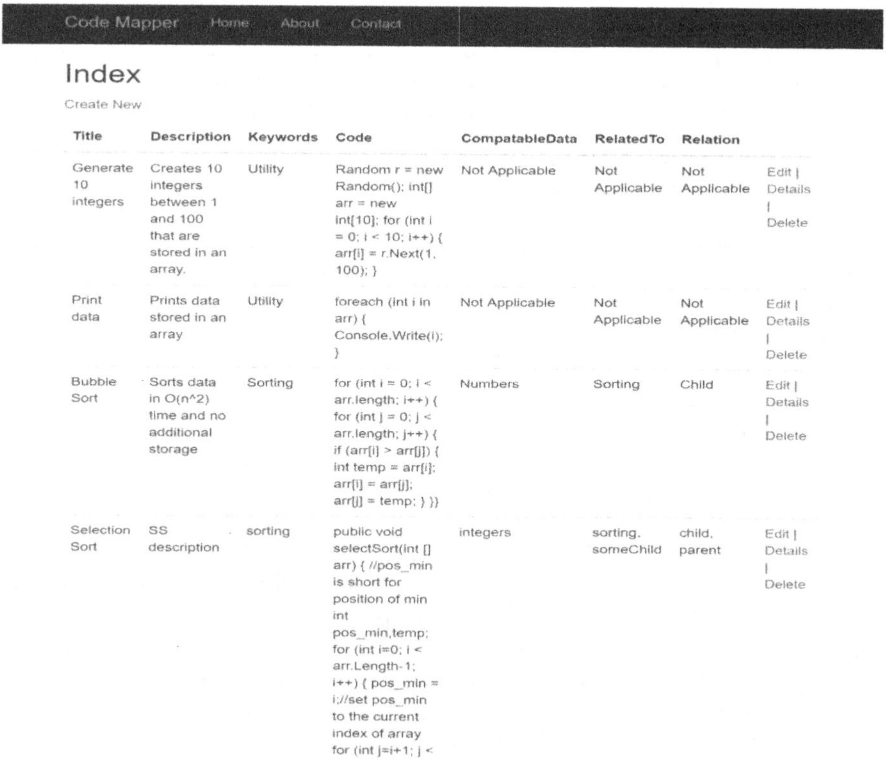

Code Mapper Home About Contact

Index

Create New

<table>
<tr><th>Title</th><th>Description</th><th>Keywords</th><th>Code</th><th>CompatableData</th><th>RelatedTo</th><th>Relation</th><th></th></tr>
<tr><td>Generate 10 integers</td><td>Creates 10 integers between 1 and 100 that are stored in an array.</td><td>Utility</td><td>Random r = new Random(); int[] arr = new int[10]; for (int i = 0; i < 10; i++) { arr[i] = r.Next(1, 100); }</td><td>Not Applicable</td><td>Not Applicable</td><td>Not Applicable</td><td>Edit | Details | Delete</td></tr>
<tr><td>Print data</td><td>Prints data stored in an array</td><td>Utility</td><td>foreach (int i in arr) { Console.Write(i); }</td><td>Not Applicable</td><td>Not Applicable</td><td>Not Applicable</td><td>Edit | Details | Delete</td></tr>
<tr><td>Bubble Sort</td><td>Sorts data in O(n^2) time and no additional storage</td><td>Sorting</td><td>for (int i = 0; i < arr.length; i++) { for (int j = 0; j < arr.length; j++) { if (arr[i] > arr[j]) { int temp = arr[i]; arr[i] = arr[j]; arr[j] = temp; } }}</td><td>Numbers</td><td>Sorting</td><td>Child</td><td>Edit | Details | Delete</td></tr>
<tr><td>Selection Sort</td><td>SS description</td><td>sorting</td><td>public void selectSort(int [] arr) { //pos_min is short for position of min int pos_min,temp; for (int i=0; i < arr.Length-1; i++) { pos_min = i;//set pos_min to the current index of array for (int j=i+1; j <</td><td>integers</td><td>sorting, someChild</td><td>child, parent</td><td>Edit | Details | Delete</td></tr>
</table>

Fig. 3. Detail database view of the code snippets.

names, and types. Therefore, it is highly unlikely that two code snippets chosen by a learner or the synthesizer Ξ to string together will match entirely. It is, therefore, essential that we align these code segments in terms of their variable names, types and scopes. If the snippet is a compilable function or a program (i.e., $\phi = True$), then the only remaining issue is to determine how to send values to its formal parameters. However, if it is not, then it needs to be assembled either into a function, or as part of the previous code segment by unifying the variables using a data flow analysis and adding all missing type information.

For example, consider the three code fragments f_1 through f_3 below, respectively. How these fragments are indexed and selected, will determine how they will be processed by Ξ. Assuming that the pseudocode included the two instructions – 1) pick a list of five numbers, and 2) arrange the list in ascending order. The synthesizer essentially has two choices – pick the pair f_1 and f_2, or the pair f_1 and f_3 requiring diametrically different synthesis strategies.

```
//f1:
int values[] = {5, 1, 4, 2, 8};

//f2:
```

```
void bubbleSort(int arr[], int n)
{ int i, j;
  for (i = 0; i < n - 1; i++)
    for (j = 0; j < n - i - 1; j++)
      if (arr[j] > arr[j + 1])
        swap(arr[j], arr[j + 1]);
}


//f3:
for (k = 0; k < last - 1; k++)
  for (j = 0; j < last - k - 1; j++)
    if (v[j] > v[j + 1])
    {
      t = v[j];
      v[j] = v[j+1];
      v[j+1] = t;
    };
```

The choice of the pair f_1 and f_2 will result in the following program. In this construction, Code*Mapper* follows two principles – minimal editing, and no code writing. Based on these principles, the pair f_1 and f_2 are preferred over the pair f_1 and f_3. For the former pair, the synthesizer only needs to add the last two lines in the main() and link the function with a function call to bubbleSort() by creating a dependency graph of function calls. However, the program will not execute until a function for swap() is not made available in Ω. Note that, in this instance, no unification was necessary since the interaction of the variables are entirely through the function call. The snippet description for the fragment f_2 includes the formal parameters array arr, and size n, while the formal description of fragment f_1 includes only the array variable values.

```
void bubbleSort(int arr[], int n)
{ int i, j;
  for (i = 0; i < n - 1; i++)
    for (j = 0; j < n - i - 1; j++)
      if (arr[j] > arr[j + 1])
        swap(arr[j], arr[j + 1]);
}

void main()
{ int values[] = {5, 1, 4, 2, 8};
  int n = 5;

  bubbleSort(values, n);
}
```

Since the size of the array values can be taken from the pseudocode, it is initialized as the statement int n = 5; as the minimum editing possible and not considered coding although the size is missing in this code snippet. However, if the bubbleSort function was not available, the synthesizer would be forced to choose the f_1 and f_3 pair. In this case, the construction of the program will be as follows. Note that in this case, Code*Mapper* again added the missing types for the variables in the fragment f_3, and unified the variable names values and using a data flow analysis based on fragment descriptions.

```
void main()
{ int values[] = {5, 1, 4, 2, 8};
  int last = 5, j, k, t;

  for (k = 0; k < last - 1; k++)
    for (j = 0; j < last - k - 1; j++)
      if (values[j] > values[j + 1])
        {
          t = values[j];
          values[j] = values[j+1];
          values[j+1] = t;
        };
}
```

3   Code Snippet Database Powered by Crowd Sourcing

Every code segment associated with a terminal concept (code snippet π) can be represented using a graph, called the program dependence graph (PDG) [9]. Clustering of these graph structures helps organize them in the concept hierarchy into functionally similar nodes as structurally similar graphs exhibit similar execution behaviors. However, structurally dissimilar graphs can also be functionally identical. For example, though the PDGs corresponding to insertion sort and quick sort are structurally different, they are functionally identical – sorting. It therefore becomes necessary that we engage the crowd to annotate each concept node, and manually establish their functional similarity. Figure 3 shows the annotated information available for each of the concepts entered using the form in Fig. 2(b). Furthermore, the granularity of concepts could also be varied. For example, it need not be a complete procedure. We could also have a concept called *counter loop*, specialization of which could be a *for counter loop* and a *while counter loop* with respective *for* and *while* statement incarnations.

Manual curation by crowd is also necessary since concepts can be aggregations of simple concepts (called terminal, not defined in terms of other concepts), or complex concepts (concepts defined using other simple or complex concepts recursively). Most complex concepts that represent similar functions cannot be clustered using PDG. For example, the node structure in Fig. 1(b) is created or curated by the crowd to show heap, merge and radix sorts each to be a special type of ascending sort. Clearly, merge sort is a complex concept, and so is quick sort. While it is conceivable that most merge sort and quick sort PDGs are group wise similar, it is unlikely for the merge sort and quick sort PDGs to be similar, although they function similarly. The annotations and their position in the concept hierarchy thus becomes important in Code*Mapper*, allowing the system to use the specificity and referencing (aggregations) relationships among concepts to make smart decisions in synthesizing high quality programs. From this perspective, concepts and their realization in Code*Mapper* have strong similarity with those of knowledge representation of ontologies and the semantic web, and we envision Code*Mapper* to be similar to sites such as StackOverflow or Github, in which crowd sourcing fuels its success.

4   Open Source Implementation of Code*Mapper*

We have developed Code*Mapper* as an open source system so that it can be developed as a community project and leverage combined ideas. The source code of Code*Mapper* project is publicly available at [24]. It is therefore open to contributions and will soon be under the MIT license. We plan to create a suggestions page to solicit ideas about desired features and implementation strategies to facilitate its continuous development.

4.1   Software Tools and Operating Platform

Code*Mapper* is built with Microsoft's new platform ASP.NET Core 2.0 with Facebook's front end library React. The choice of the .NET platform was motivated by its flexibility and easy extensibility. This platform allows flexible addition and removal of functionality as needed, and thus supports incremental design while focusing on the end goal. Facebook's React was utilized due to the need for dynamic user experience and user interface operations, and for leveraging React's ability to allow for building reusable components. Several command line tools node package manager, .NET common line tools, and yarn package manager were also used. For back-end system development, we have used either a yarn or npm development server, and the IIS Express along with the .NET command line servers.

4.2   Hardware and Operating System

The current implementation was on MacBook Pro running macOS High Sierra version 10.13.1. The computer is equipped with a 2.8 Ghz Intel Core i7 processor, 16 GB 2133 MHz MHz LPDDR3, Radeon Pro 555 2 GB Intel HD Graphics 630 1536 MB. Much of the development was done on a virtual machine utilizing Parallels software. Code*Mapper* is compliant with most widely used browsers such as Google Chrome, Microsoft Edge, Internet Explorer, Safari, and Fire Fox. We tested the software on different machines of varying configurations and did not experience any performance related glitches to date.

4.3   Online Code Harvesting

In order to make Code*Mapper* a truly powerful tool, users should be able to scour the internet for code snippets to be used in node creation. It supports the search and find interface shown in Fig. 2(a) for this purpose. In this interface, search for codes can be initiated using a brief description of target code. Code*Mapper* then initiates search using the APIs provided by sites such as GitHub, SourceForge, GitBucket, etc. The APIs are then interrogated using NLP techniques to pick out specific terms. Once the results are returned in a list as shown, users pick and choose snippets of code as needed to create nodes. Users are able to copy the code snippets into the system database for cataloging in ways discussed in Sect. 3.

5   Conclusion and Future Research

Being crowd reliant, Code*Mapper* inherits typical drawbacks of this paradigm, yet being a community system, it also has some serious responsibility. For example, annotation accuracy is largely curator dependent and a weak, incompetent or malicious curator may jeopardize the system, and thus, a user's ability to construct meaningful and useful programs. One of two possible solutions appears appropriate. The standard approach practiced in similar circumstances such as GitHub is to accept only administrator curated annotations, and allow local overriding by any user on their own without affecting the community annotation. The second approach is to use an inaccurate model where the reliability of an annotation is dependent upon the combined credibility of all the curators who contributed to the annotation, an approach adopted in CrowdCure system [13].

The focus of this paper has been to articulate a novel idea of softening the transition cost of novice programmers and K-12 STEM learners from block-based languages to text-based imperative languages and foster their computational thinking. Code*Mapper* stands in significant contrast to systems such as Flowgorithm or TryPL that are still at the algorithm level. Code*Mapper* is more coarse grained, and abstract. It encourages novice programmers to think in conceptual terms or concepts, and modules, small or large without any focus on the finer logical details (at the sentence level). It is thus squarely geared toward prototyping and conceptual validation of a computational thinking solutions. Although the Code*Mapper* system is at the prototype stage, most of its core components have been developed and tested, but its integration with the sister system Mind*Reader* [12] remains as a future research. We believe that though Code*Mapper* is a part of the overall Mind*Reader* system, it stands on its own as an intelligent web application that has significant potential to help impart quality computational thinking education.

Acknowledgement. This publication was partially made possible by an Institutional Development Award (IDeA) from the National Institute of General Medical Sciences of the National Institutes of Health under Grant #P20GM103408. The author wishes to acknowledge that Patrick Vanvorce implemented an initial edition of CodeMapper as part of an undergraduate class research project.

References

1. Ahadi, A.: Early identification of novice programmers' challenges in coding using machine learning techniques. In: Sheard, J., Tenenberg, J., Chinn, D., Dorn, B., (eds.), Proceedings of the 2016 ACM Conference on International Computing Education Research, ICER 2016, Melbourne, VIC, Australia, 8–12 September 2016, pp. 263–264. ACM (2016)
2. Albin-Clark, A.: Mabl: a tool for mapping pseudocode to multiple implementation languages. In: Hughes, J.M., Peiris, D.R., Tymann, P.T., (eds.), Proceedings of the 12th Annual SIGCSE Conference on Innovation and Technology in Computer Science Education, ITiCSE 2007, Dundee, Scotland, UK, 25–27 June 2007, pp. 315. ACM (2007)
3. Asare, O., Nagappan, M., Asokan, N.: Is github's copilot as bad as humans at introducing vulnerabilities in code? CoRR, abs/2204.04741 (2022)
4. Cook, D.: Flowgorithm. http://www.flowgorithm.org/. Accessed 17 June 2022
5. Corno, F., Russis, L.D. , Sáenz, J.P.: Textcode: a tool to support problem solving among novice programmers. In: Harms, K.J., Cunha, J., Oney, S., Kelleher, C., (eds.) IEEE Symposium on Visual Languages and Human-Centric Computing, VL/HCC 2021, St Louis, MO, USA, 10–13 October 2021, pp. 1–5. IEEE (2021)
6. Dakhel, A.M., et al.: Github copilot AI pair programmer: asset or liability? CoRR, abs/2206.15331 (2022)
7. Denny, P., Whalley, J., Leinonen, J.: Promoting early engagement with programming assignments using scheduled automated feedback. In: Szabo, C., Sheard, J., (eds.) ACE'21: 23rd Australasian Computing Education Conference, Auckland, New Zealand (and virtually), 2–5 February 2021, pp. 88–95. ACM (2021)
8. Fabito, B.S., Trillanes, A.O., Sarmiento, J.R.: Barriers and challenges of computing students in an online learning environment: Insights from one private university in the Philippines. CoRR, abs/2012.02121 (2020)
9. Ferrante, J., Ottenstein, K.J., Warren, J.D.: The program dependence graph and its use in optimization. ACM Trans. Program. Lang. Syst. **9**(3), 319–349 (1987)
10. Gupta, N., Rajput, A., Chimalakonda, S.: COSPEX: a program comprehension tool for novice programmers. In: 44th 2022 IEEE/ACM International Conference on Software Engineering: Companion Proceedings, ICSE Companion 2022, Pittsburgh, PA, USA, 22–24 May 2022, pp. 41–45. IEEE (2022)
11. Hogg, C., Jump, M.: Designing autograders for novice programmers. In: Merkle, L., Doyle, M., Sheard, J., Soh, L., Dorn, B., (eds.) SIGCSE 2022: The 53rd ACM Technical Symposium on Computer Science Education, Providence, RI, USA, 3–5 March 2022, Vol. 2, pp. 1200. ACM (2022)
12. Jamil, H., Mou, X.: Automated feedback and authentic assessment in online computational thinking tutoring systems. In: 22nd IEEE International Conference on Advanced Learning Technologies (ICALT 2022), Bucharest, Romania. 1–4 July 2022, pp. 53–55. IEEE Computer Society (2022)
13. Jamil, H.M., Sadri, F.: Crowd enabled curation and querying of large and noisy text mined protein interaction data. Distrib. Parallel Databases **36**(1), 9–45 (2018)
14. Keene, J., Jamil, H.: Natural language programming with trypl. In: 22nd IEEE International Conference on Advanced Learning Technologies (ICALT 2022), Bucharest, Romania. 1–4 July 2022, pp. 38–40. IEEE Computer Society (2022)
15. Kurniawan, O., Jégourel, C., Lee, N.T.S., Mari, M.D., Poskitt, C.M.: Steps before syntax: helping novice programmers solve problems using the PCDIT framework. In: 55th Hawaii International Conference on System Sciences, HICSS 2022, Virtual Event / Maui, Hawaii, USA, 4–7 January 2022, pp. 1–10. ScholarSpace (2022)

16. Lorenzen, T., Mondshein, L., Sattar, A., Jung, S.: A code snippet library for CS1. Inroads **3**(1), 41–45 (2012)

17. Luxton-Reilly, A., McMillan, E., Stevenson, E., Tempero, E.D., Denny, P.: Ladebug: an online tool to help novice programmers improve their debugging skills. In: Polycarpou, I., Read, J.C., Andreou, P., Armoni, M., (eds.) Proceedings of the 23rd Annual ACM Conference on Innovation and Technology in Computer Science Education, ITiCSE 2018, Larnaca, Cyprus, 02–04 July 2018, pp. 159–164. ACM (2018)

18. Malik, S.I., Mathew, R., Al-Sideiri, A., Jabbar, J., Al-Nuaimi, R., Tawafak, R.M.: Enhancing problem-solving skills of novice programmers in an introductory programming course. Comput. Appl. Eng. Educ. **30**(1), 174–194 (2022)

19. Marwan, S., Gao, G., Fisk, S.R., Price, T.W., Barnes, T.: Adaptive immediate feedback can improve novice programming engagement and intention to persist in computer science. In: Robins, A.V., Moskal, A., Ko, A.J., McCauley, R., (eds.) ICER 2020: International Computing Education Research Conference, Virtual Event, New Zealand, 10–12 August 2020, pp. 194–203. ACM (2020)

20. Nirgude, M.: Debugger tool to improve conceptual understanding of programming language of novice learners. In: Kinshuk, Iyer, S., (eds.), 2013 IEEE Fifth International Conference on Technology for Education, T4E 2013, Kharagpur, India, 18–20 December 2013, pp. 69–72. IEEE Computer Society (2013)

21. Reid, B., Treude, C., Wagner, M.: Optimising the fit of stack overflow code snippets into existing code. In: Coello, C.A.C. (ed.) GECCO'20: Genetic and Evolutionary Computation Conference, Companion Volume, Cancún, Mexico, 8–12 July 2020, pp. 1945–1953. ACM (2020)

22. Sáenz, J.P., Russis, L.D.: On how novices approach programming exercises before and during coding. In: Barbosa, S.D.J., Lampe, C., Appert, C., Shamma, D.A., (eds.), CHI '22: CHI Conference on Human Factors in Computing Systems, New Orleans, LA, USA, 29 April 2022–5 May 2022, Extended Abstracts, pp. 361:1–361:6. ACM (2022)

23. Thangaraj, J.: Automated assessment & feedback system for novice programmers. In: Schulte, C., Becker, B.A., Divitini, M., Barendsen, E., (eds.), ITiCSE 2021: 26th ACM Conference on Innovation and Technology in Computer Science Education, Virtual Event, Germany, 26 June- 1 July 2021 - Working Group Reports, pp. 672–673. ACM (2021)

24. Vanvorce, P., Jamil, H.: Codemapper source code in github. https://github.com/maholeycowdevelopment/code-mapper-react (2018). Accessed 8 July 2022

25. Veerasamy, A.K., D'Souza, D.J., Apiola, M., Laakso, M., Salakoski, T.: Using early assessment performance as early warning signs to identify at-risk students in programming courses. In: IEEE Frontiers in Education Conference, FIE 2020, Uppsala, Sweden, 21–24 October 2020, pp. 1–9. IEEE (2020)

26. Wang, W.: Novices' learning barriers when using code examples in open-ended programming. In: Schulte, C., Becker, B.A., Divitini, M., Barendsen, E., (eds.) ITiCSE 2021: 26th ACM Conference on Innovation and Technology in Computer Science Education, Virtual Event, Germany, 26 June-1 July 2021, pp. 394–400. ACM (2021)

27. Wing, J.M.: Computational thinking, 10 years later. https://tinyurl.com/yapf5zas. (2016). Accessed 31 August 2017

28. Yang, D., Hussain, A., Lopes, C.V.: From query to usable code: an analysis of stack overflow code snippets. In: Kim, M., Robbes, R., Bird, C., (eds.) Proceedings of the 13th International Conference on Mining Software Repositories, MSR 2016, Austin, TX, USA, 14–22 May 2016, pp. 391–402. ACM (2016)

Smart Doorbell with Telegram Notification for Multifamily Dwellings

Gianfranco Perez-Aquise[1]([⊠]) [iD] and Frank Edmundo Escobedo-Bailón[2] [iD]

[1] Facultad de Ingeniería de Sistemas e Informática, Universidad Nacional Mayor de San Marcos, Lima, Perú
gianfranco.perez@unmsm.edu.pe
[2] Facultad de Ingeniería y Gestión, Universidad Nacional Tecnológica de Lima Sur, Lima, Perú
fescobedo@untels.edu.pe

Abstract. Currently, Peru's population has a great sense of insecurity. According to INEI surveys, 85% of the population has this perception of insecurity, being burglary in homes one of the criminal acts that affect this perception, also according to INEI data, due to the lack of information that the victims have about the perpetrator, they do not report the case. That is why the present work aims to design and implement a smart doorbell for multifamily dwellings, in order to be able to register and identify people who visit the home through the Telegram messaging application. This ensures that vulnerable people in the home cannot let in unknown or dangerous people by being able to identify the visitor at the door of the home, when the person in charge is not present. This system is achieved by using a Raspberry Pi to connect all the devices used and send all the data collected to the respective people, according to a list of identifiers for each group of people living in the building.

Keywords: Smart doorbell · Telegram · Home burglary · Home security · Internet of things

1 Introduction

In Peru, there has been a strong sense of insecurity among the population for several years, provoked by the various reported cases of criminal acts such as crimes against property, life, body and health. According to the survey conducted in [1], 21.1% of the population aged 15 and over have been victims of some type of crime and 85% have a perception of insecurity within the next 12 months. This perception of insecurity comes from the fear of being a victim of some type of crime, being one of the reasons why people implement security practices in order to feel safe [2].

Related to this, in [1] it is also indicated that in the last six months of the data collected, 9.5% of urban dwellings have been affected by burglary or attempted burglary. In addition, it was also found that the three main reasons why people do not report these incidents are because they consider it to be: a waste of time, the act was not consummated, and they do not know the offender.

J. A. Lossio-Ventura et al. (Eds.): SIMBig 2022, CCIS 1837, pp. 246–256, 2023.
https://doi.org/10.1007/978-3-031-35445-8_18

In addition, according to other studies on this type of crime, it is noted that alarms, dogs or other forms of surveillance used in the home do not generate the desired deterrent effect; however, many of these criminals always look for a time when no one is in the house, and even knock on the door to make sure of this [3, 4]. Therefore, having a system that can register the people who visit the home would help to safeguard the integrity of the home and its family, and could avoid exposing vulnerable people in the home to dangerous people when they are alone at home.

Therefore, this paper presents a smart doorbell based on the Internet of Things (IoT), which can be used to notify the residents of the house through messages in the Telegram application. This system allows to specifically notify a group of people living in the same building, preserving their privacy, in addition to being able to respond to visitors from a distance.

2 Literature Review

There are several works on intelligent doorbells, being the technologies used one of the main differences between them. In [5], the focus is on the safety of elderly people. Due to the fact that many of these people have certain reduced capacities and therefore need assistance. Therefore, they develop a solution using facial recognition, relying on Microsoft's Project Oxford for facial recognition, and a Raspberry Pi 2 to communicate the doorbell and camera used. The process begins when a person presses the doorbell, capturing an image of his face and identifying himself, based on an inclusion or exclusion list, to finally inform through a mobile application to the elderly person in the home, being able to choose the option to inform his caregiver or not so that he can help him according to the situation, in case it is a person from the exclusion list the caregiver would be informed without the elderly person having to do it.

Another similar work is [6], which differs from the previous one in that it is more focused on people in general and on maintaining the tranquility of the home. This is done based on the facial recognition result, to determine whether to trigger the usual doorbell sound or to send a notification to the user's application with the data obtained from the image. In these two works, an own Android application is developed to be able to use such a system.

Other works were also found using external applications to communicate with the user, as in the case of [7], where an intelligent doorbell is developed using Gmail to receive notifications. In this way, they seek that the owners of the house can know about the visitor even when he is not in the house. For the development of this solution, a NodeMCU is used that will connect to the doorbell and will connect through the Internet to a web server which will be responsible for sending the respective mail. Similarly, [8] develops a home security system with the help of the Thingspeak IoT platform, which will send all the data collected by various sensors (PIR, smoke, vibration and temperature), in addition to a pi camera, notifying the user via Gmail of the anomalies detected, and if required contacting the emergency services.

The use of more means to notify the user has also been addressed in other research, such as in [9], detecting whether a person is present at the door by means of a PIR sensor and taking pictures or recording a video of this, notifying via SMS and Gmail the user about this if he/she presses the doorbell within a given time frame or otherwise triggering an alarm. Another similar work is found in [10], where the image taken will be used to perform facial recognition, if it is recognized the door will be unlocked otherwise it will activate the sound of the doorbell or notify the owner of the house, in addition to activating the alarm if the person tries to break the door.

Another way to communicate with the end user is found in [11], which develops an alert system for deaf or hard of hearing people. In this solution, SMS messages are used to receive notifications and also a vibrator to alert the hearing impaired person. Thus, every time the button is pressed, a photo of the person's face is taken and stored on a server, and at the same time the SMS message is sent to the mobile device and the vibrator, which the person will be wearing, is activated by means of a Bluetooth connection. In addition, it should be mentioned that an Rs232 Modem is used to send the SMS, as well as a Raspberry Pi and a Bluetooth HC-05, necessary to connect the vibrator via Bluetooth.

In addition, several works using the Telegram application are also found in the literature. According to [12], among the end-user communication applications, Telegram is the best option for these IoT systems, due to the fact that it presents a high level of security and speed, in addition to allowing two-way communication, compared to other alternatives such as E-mail, Twitter and WhatsApp. It should also be noted the ease of handling Bots in Telegram and the tools available for this purpose.

With this in mind, some of the IoT work using the Telegram application is as follows. In [13], smart spaces were developed to facilitate access to certain devices within the employees' workspace by sending commands to a Telegram Bot. In case of [14, 15], a security system is designed for door access with facial recognition, in case the person is in the database the door will be opened, otherwise the person or persons in charge will be notified to authorize the entry via Telegram with the collected image, if they authorize the entry by sending a message to the Telegram Bot the door will be opened. In [16], a surveillance system is designed, in which it will take an image capture when a human face is detected and store it in a database, which via Telegram can be consulted. In a similar way, [17] develops a security application, but performing the notification whenever any body movement is detected within the range of the camera. And finally, in the case of [18–20], home security systems are developed using cameras and other devices, such as a PIR sensor for data collection at the door of the home, in addition to a Raspberry Pi to connect these devices and send data or receive orders from the user by sending commands within the Telegram application to a Bot created for this purpose.

3   Methodology

In order to design and implement the proposed system of this work, we will continue with the architecture for this system and the identified use cases. However, before continuing with these points, it is necessary to specify the terms Visitor and Inhabitant used in these, in order to improve the understanding of the system:

- Inhabitant: Person or group of persons residing inside an apartment of the building.
- Visitor: Person or group of persons visiting or seeking to meet with an Inhabitant.

3.1 System Architecture

The architecture for this smart doorbell system was developed based on a 4-layer Internet of Things architecture, as seen in Fig. 1.

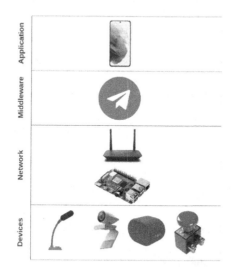

Fig. 1. 4-layer system architecture

The hardware components in the Device layer are a microphone, a webcam, a speaker and two buttons. In the Network layer, a Raspberry Pi 3B+ will be used to communicate all the components of the Devices layer, and will be connected to a router in the building to be able to communicate with the Telegram messaging application. Within the Middleware layer, there is the Telegram application in which the Inhabitant will be able to interact with the system. Finally, in the Application layer, there is a mobile device through which the User can make use of the Telegram application.

The connections from the Devices layer to the Network layer are made through the available ports on the Raspberry Pi, in the case of the speaker it can be connected via Bluetooth. For the connection between the router and the Raspberry Pi, it is done through an ethernet cable or Wi Fi. The connection between the Network layer and the Middleware layer is done through the HTTP protocol, because a Telegram Bot will be used, which is controlled by the API that the Telegram company provides within its services. It is also worth mentioning that the Telegram application uses MTProto for its instant messaging services.

3.2 Use Case Diagram

Taking into account the aforementioned architecture, the use cases identified for the development of this system are shown in Fig. 2.

Following these use cases, the process performed by the proposed system can be described as follows:

1. Visitor presses the external button at the entrance.

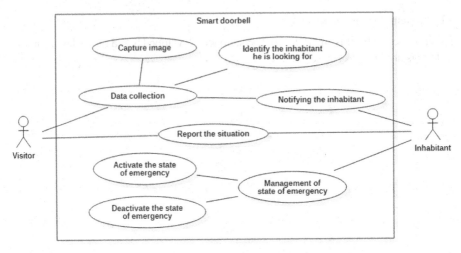

Fig. 2. System use case diagram

2. System asks him/her about the person he/she is looking for and about his/her information.
3. Visitor answers the questions.
4. System identifies the Inhabitant he is looking for.
5. System captures an image of the Visitor's face.
6. System notifies the Inhabitant with the collected data via Telegram.

From the latter, optionally, the Inhabitant can send a voice message via Telegram to the system, to play it on the speaker at the entrance. In addition, he/she can press the internal button at the entrance, when opening the door, in case he/she considers that he/she is in danger when opening the door, causing the alarm sound to be emitted and notifying the other inhabitants of the building (see Fig. 3).

3.3 Software Requirements

For the realization of this system, it is necessary to use the following software:

– Raspberry Pi OS: This is the official operating system for Raspberry Pi boards, provided by the Raspberry Pi Foundation itself.
– Python: It is one of the most popular programming languages, in which a wide variety of applications can be developed.
– SpeechRecognition: It is a Python library for speech recognition.
– pyTelegramBotAPI: It is a Python implementation of Telegram Bot API.
– gTTS: It is a Python library to interact with the Google Translate's text-to-speech API.
– OpenCV: A programming library focused on real-time computer vision.
– pydub: A Python module for audio manipulation.

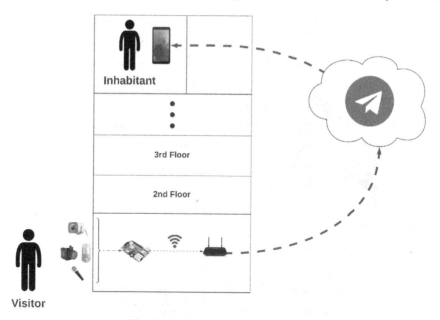

Fig. 3. Layout of system components

4 Experimental Results

For this section a prototype of the proposed system was made, using all the necessary hardware components mentioned above and a Protoboard to connect the Raspberry Pi with the buttons to be used, in the case of the microphone, this is built into the webcam used (see Fig. 4). Also, 2 Telegram chat groups were created in order to test the correct functioning of the system, which have as name "Floor 2" and "Floor 4", in them will be added to the Telegram Bot created with all permissions enabled. The code of the system was made in Python, inside it there is also the Telegram Bot handler, and it will be executed by the Raspberry Pi.

To identify each Inhabitant a single JSON file is used that stores the names to identify to which Telegram group to send the collected data using the group ID (see Fig. 5).

When the Visitor mentions a stored name, the system recognizes the ID of the Telegram group to send the collected data to. Once notified about the visit, a time limit is set to send a voice message to the group to be played on the system's speakers, which will inform the Visitor if the Inhabitant is not at home or any other situation (See Fig. 6). In addition to this, the correct functioning of the emergency system was verified, which is activated by pressing the respective button three times and deactivated only once, reproducing the alarm sound and sending the alert messages to all the inhabitants of the building (See Fig. 7).

However, it should be mentioned that the Inhabitant that the Visitor is looking for is not always correctly recognized, this is caused by the fact that the library still has problems in distinguishing certain proper names, for example, in the case of names like "Juan" it is recognized correctly, but in the case of "Gianfranco", it sometimes recognizes

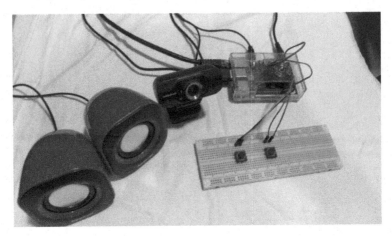

Fig. 4. Realized prototype of the system

```
[
    {
        "Names": [
            "Floor 2",
            "Juan Pérez"
        ],
        "ID_Telegram": -1001658500393
    },
    {
        "Names": [
            "Floor 4",
            "Andrea Fernández"
        ],
        "ID_Telegram": -1001634714745
    }
]
```

Fig. 5. Example of a JSON file of identifiers

it as "yan Franco". This is also affected by the visitor's pronunciation or ambient noise. One way to minimize these errors is to opt for an easy-to-pronounce alias such as a floor or apartment number, or to add these other results in the corresponding name section of the JSON file.

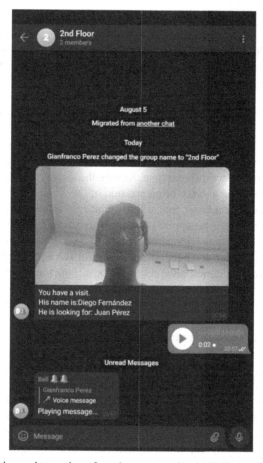

Fig. 6. Notification and reception of a voice message by the Telegram bot implemented.

Fig. 7. Alert message sent by the Bot

5 Discussion

In this paper we propose a prototype of an intelligent doorbell that by means of questions asked by the system, it can recognize and record the visitor's answers in order to make an accurate decision based on these data. In the literature, one of the technologies frequently used in intelligent doorbells is facial recognition [5, 6, 10, 14, 15], a very useful technology to be able to recognize the Visitor, however, this requires a previous training to have a good accuracy in recognizing people, which usually will be people that are known by the Inhabitant. However, in many cases, the Visitors will be unknown to the

Inhabitant, so it is not enough to be able to identify if the person is someone unknown or not, it is necessary to be able to extract as much information from the Visitor (Who is he looking for?, Why is he looking for him?, etc.) to make a correct decision in order to safeguard the security of the home. Therefore, the implementation of technologies such as speech recognition and speech synthesis can help in this data collection, providing useful information to the Inhabitant about the Visitor.

It is worth mentioning that there are still some errors in the complete recognition of the words pronounced by the Visitor when answering the system, this happens mainly with proper names that are not common or originate from other countries, in these cases the system usually recognizes them as a word that generally will have some similarity, but sometimes returns a very different one. Among the factors that may influence in this case are the ambient noise and the pronunciation of the Visitor. For ambient noise, the library itself incorporates a basic function to reduce its influence. For the last factor, if the country where it will be applied is known in advance, the library used allows configuring certain languages with certain countries (when using the Google service), so it would achieve greater accuracy to the dialect differences, however, the problem still persists in the proper names, although it can be minimized by adding similar words in pronunciation in the JSON file is not very effective. It is worth mentioning that if the Visitor says the words slowly, there is a better chance of recognizing it, but this is not always the case.

Another aspect to mention for this developed system is the user interface, although it is not the main focus of this work, it is important to take into account this aspect, especially if among the Inhabitants there are elderly people who will use the system. For this prototype, the interface is simple, the Inhabitant receives the data from the Bot through a group chat in the Telegram application, allowing him/her to send a voice message through that chat, to be played to the Visitor, within a time limit after receiving the visit notification, in addition to receiving messages from the Bot about changes in the emergency status. In other research works such as [5, 6] mobile applications are created, thus facilitating the use of the system. In this case, the interface is limited to the features of Telegram, however, it should be mentioned that this application allows the creation of interactive menus that can help improve the usability of the system.

6 Conclusion

The smart doorbell developed in this work aims to provide an extra layer of security to visitors at home. To do this, it allows to notify about the presence of the visitor at the entrance even if the inhabitants are not present at home through the Telegram application via a developed Bot. Previously, it collects data about the visitor by capturing an image of his face and registering his answers to questions that the system asks him, sending them as part of the notification to the inhabitant. This is achieved thanks to the application of voice recognition and voice synthesis technologies.

Also, the system gives the inhabitant the possibility to send a voice message to the Bot so that the system can play it back to the visitor. In this way, the inhabitant can communicate any information to the visitor without being present in the home. In case the door is going to be opened, a button is placed inside the entrance which can be pressed to activate an alarm in case of danger situations, causing the Bot to notify the other inhabitants of the alert.

However, it should be mentioned that voice recognition still has problems identifying uncommon proper names, so it is preferable to opt for easy-to-pronounce aliases in order to recognize which inhabitant is being searched for.

7 Future Work

For future work, several new technologies can be applied to the context developed in this work, such as the application of voice biometric recognition as a means of authentication, apart from passwords or facial recognition, especially useful to add specific functionalities for the inhabitant, such as opening the entrance door remotely. On the other hand, machine learning models can be designed to detect suspicious behavior or risky situations outside the home by means of the camera, in order to warn the inhabitants or the respective authorities. And finally, the creation of intelligent chat Bots to improve the interaction of this type of systems with different users.

References

1. Instituto Nacional de Estadística e Informática. Informe Técnico - Estadísticas de Seguridad Ciudadana: Noviembre 2021 - Abril 2022, Lima. Accessed 14 July 2022. www.inei.gob.pe
2. Kanashiro, L.: Entre el miedo y la ira. Prácticas de seguridad en los sectores de menores recursos en Lima, Perú. Rev. Mex. Cienc. Polit. Soc. **66**(241), 317–345 (2020). https://doi.org/10.22201/fcpys.2448492xe.2020.241.69997
3. Ianole, D.I.: Los robos con fuerza en casa habitada en el municipio de Sant Cugat del Vallés, Universidad Pompeu Fabra (2019). http://hdl.handle.net/10230/43438
4. Agustina, J.R., Reales, F.: En la mente de un asaltante de viviendas: Estudio cualitativo de una muestra de autores de robo en casa habitada. Rev. Española Investig. Criminológica **11**, 1–30 (2013). https://doi.org/10.46381/reic.v11i0.73
5. Ennis, A., et al.: Doorstep: a doorbell security system for the prevention of doorstep crime. In: 2016 38th Annual International Conference of the IEEE Engineering in Medicine and Biology Society (EMBC), vol. 2016, pp. 5360–5363 (2016). https://doi.org/10.1109/EMBC.2016.7591938
6. Qian, M., Sun, Y., Zhang, F.: An intelligent Internet-of-Things (IoT) door bell system for smart notification alert. In: 8th International Conference on Natural Language Processing (NLP 2019), pp. 43–50 (2019). https://doi.org/10.5121/csit.2019.91205
7. Setiawan, A., Suprapto, Y., Fachrurrozi, M.I., Manab, K.R.N., Sasmita, N.R., Diyasa, G.S.M.: Real-time home bell notification using node-MCU through E-mail (base on the Internet of Things). J. Phys. Conf. Ser. **1845**(1), 012007 (2021). https://doi.org/10.1088/1742-6596/1845/1/012007
8. Madupu, P.K., Karthikeyan, B.: Automatic service request system for security in smart home using IoT. In: 2018 Second International Conference on Electronics, Communication and Aerospace Technology (ICECA), no. Iceca, pp. 1413–1418 (2018). https://doi.org/10.1109/ICECA.2018.8474684
9. Akter, S., Sima, R.A., Ullah, M.S., Hossain, S.A.: Smart security surveillance using IoT. In: 2018 7th International Conference on Reliability, Infocom Technologies and Optimization (Trends and Future Directions) (ICRITO), pp. 659–663 (2018). https://doi.org/10.1109/ICRITO.2018.8748703

10. Pawar, S., Kithani, V., Ahuja, S., Sahu, S.: Smart home security using IoT and face recognition. In: 2018 Fourth International Conference on Computing Communication Control and Automation (ICCUBEA), pp. 1–6 (2018). https://doi.org/10.1109/ICCUBEA.2018.8697695
11. Kumari, P., Goel, P., Reddy, S.R.N.: PiCam: IoT based wireless alert system for deaf and hard of hearing. In: Proceedings - 2015 21st Annual International Conference on Advanced Computing and Communications ADCOM 2015, pp. 39–44 (2016). https://doi.org/10.1109/ADCOM.2015.14
12. Anvekar, R.G., Banakar, R.M., Bhat, R.R.: Design alternatives for end user communication in IoT based system model. In: 2017 IEEE Technological Innovations in ICT for Agriculture and Rural Development (TIAR), pp. 121–125 (2017). https://doi.org/10.1109/TIAR.2017.8273698
13. Muslih, M., et al.: Developing smart workspace based IOT with artificial intelligence using telegram chatbot. In: 2018 International Conference on Computing, Engineering, and Design (ICCED), pp. 230–234 (2018). https://doi.org/10.1109/ICCED.2018.00052
14. Nag, A., Nikhilendra, J.N., Kalmath, M.: IOT based door access control using face recognition. In: 2018 3rd International Conference for Convergence in Technology (I2CT), pp. 1–3 (2018). https://doi.org/10.1109/I2CT.2018.8529749
15. Mahesh, D.S.S., Reddy, T.M., Yaswanth, A.S., Joshitha, C., Reddy, S.S.: Facial detection and recognition system on raspberry pi with enhanced security. In: 2020 International Conference on Emerging Trends in Information Technology and Engineering (ic-ETITE), pp. 1–5 (2020). https://doi.org/10.1109/ic-ETITE47903.2020.130
16. Vela-Medina, J.C., Guerrero-Sanchez, A.E., Rivas-Araiza, J.E., Rivas-Araiza, E.A.: Face detection for efficient video-surveillance IoT based embedded system. In: 2018 IEEE International Conference on Automation/XXIII Congress of the Chilean Association of Automatic Control (ICA-ACCA), pp. 1–6 (2018). https://doi.org/10.1109/ICA-ACCA.2018.8609835
17. Othman, N.A., Aydin, I.: A new IoT combined body detection of people by using computer vision for security application. In: 2017 9th International Conference on Computational Intelligence and Communication Networks (CICN), pp. 108–112 (2017). https://doi.org/10.1109/CICN.2017.8319366
18. Anvekar, R.G., Banakar, R.M.: IoT application development: Home security system. In: 2017 IEEE Technological Innovations in ICT for Agriculture and Rural Development (TIAR), no. Tiar 2017, pp. 68–72 (2017). https://doi.org/10.1109/TIAR.2017.8273688
19. Hema, N., Yadav, J.: Secure home entry using raspberry pi with notification via telegram. In: 2020 6th International Conference on Signal Processing and Communication (ICSC), pp. 211–215 (2020). https://doi.org/10.1109/ICSC48311.2020.9182778
20. Sharma, H.K., Sharma, M.: IoT based home security system with wireless sensors and telegram messenger. SSRN Electron J (2019). https://doi.org/10.2139/ssrn.3352452

Performance Analysis of Machine Learning for Food Fraud Prediction

Joshep Douglas Estrella Condor$^{(\boxtimes)}$ ⓘ and Félix Armando Fermín Pérez ⓘ

Universidad Nacional Mayor de San Marcos, Lima 15081, Peru
{joshep.estrella,fferminp}@unmsm.edu.pe

Abstract. Food fraud is the set of practices based on adulteration, intentional manipulation of food or counterfeiting, which are carried out to obtain an economic benefit. They are considered criminal actions, as they are punishable by law, are harmful to society and are morally reprehensible. One of the solutions to prevent the entry of fraudulent foods is their early detection. The study focuses on identifying two types of offenses, either the presence of improper sanitary certifications in a food or verifying whether the product belongs to an illegal or unauthorized import. To achieve this objective, the RASFF (Rapid Alert System for Food and Feed) data set will be used, which is a system where the European Union food and feed control authorities exchange information on the different risks that have been detected. The use of information from the RASFF model can be useful for predicting the type of fraud they are committing. Several techniques already implemented will be used to compare the results. Naive Bayes model, logistic regression, multilayer perceptron, decision tree, random forest and SVM. The best model was the multilayer perceptron.

Keywords: machine learning · fraud food · RASFF

1 Introduction

Over the past few years, there has been a significant increase in the number of documented cases of foodborne diseases reported by various countries across the globe. Worldwide, the number is estimated to be 600 million cases of foodborne illnesses annually, resulting in 420,000 deaths, with about 30% of the deaths recorded in children [19]. The Grocery Manufacturers' Association estimates that global food fraud costs between $10 billion and $15 billion per year; equating to an estimated 10% of all food products sold commercially. Others such as PricewaterhouseCoopers estimate much higher, $30 to $40 billion annually in 2017 [20]. Food fraud is carried out for financial gain. It is the fraudulent and intentional substitution or addition of a substance in a product to increase the apparent value of the product or reduce the cost of the product. Product to increase the apparent value of the product or reduce the cost of its production of its production [14,15]. Food fraud is committed when a food product is placed

© The Author(s), under exclusive license to Springer Nature Switzerland AG 2023
J. A. Lossio-Ventura et al. (Eds.): SIMBig 2022, CCIS 1837, pp. 257–269, 2023.
https://doi.org/10.1007/978-3-031-35445-8_19

on the market that, intentionally and in breach of the relevant legislation, is not
of the agreed or defined nature, thus constituting a deception of the consumer
or purchaser, with the aim of obtaining an economic benefit. Among the fraudulent practices employed are adulteration, counterfeiting, misleading labeling and
others related to the sale. And, their scope can range from loss of consumer confidence in the agrifood chain to a public health problem. The Rapid Alert System
for Food and Feed (RASFF) is the tool used by the authorities that control food
and feed, the network is composed of the Member States of the European Union,
the European Commission, EFSA, EFTA, In this way, when a member of the
network has information about a risk derived from feed and food, it immediately
notifies the European Commission through the RASFF, which in turn transmits
the notification to all the members of the network. The institution collects a lot
of information about the types of fraudulent products and report them, thanks to
this information we can use various machine learning models to predict the type
of fraud that could incur a product that is entering the European market and
thus prevent all the consequences explained above. Despite the relevance of predicting food safety risks, some authors [11] show that the problem of prediction
in food and feed safety has not yet been studied in depth. Few works approach
the problem within the RASFF framework or use the information stored in its
portal for this purpose and none of them fully exploit the huge amount of data
stored there. In addition, there are no studies on which is the best predictive
strategy or which of the available techniques, whether the more classical ML or
the more novel neural approaches, is more suitable for this problem [11]. In this
study, the food fraud notifications in RASFF range from the year 2000 to the
year 2020 and were used to develop several machine learning models for predicting the type of food fraud. To validate the model, Cross validation with 10
iterations with the KNIME software and the use of grid search to find the best
parameters. In addition, the objective of the article is based on the fact that the
data will have the same seed and therefore the same proportion of data for an
effective comparison [2]. A total of 1144 food reports are used which have the
data of year, product, country of origin, country of notification and type of fraud
[3].

2   Methodology

First we enter the data understanding phase, we use the collected data previously created by the RASFF organization, we understand the dataset and its
distribution, then we do data preparation. The tasks include selection of most
important data, elimination of empty data and finally conversion of categorical
data to numerical data using one hot encoding technique [10]. Then we move to
the stage of using algorithms, we use cross validation with 10 iterations for each
algorithm and compare the results. By using metrics such as accuracy, f1-score
and AUC we evaluate the results to finally propose the best model, which can
be seen graphically in Fig. 1 [12].

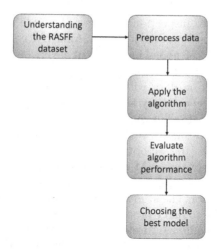

Fig. 1. Methodology

3   Related Work

Machine learning (ML) has proven to be a useful technology for data analysis and modeling in a wide variety of domains, including food science and engineering [16]. Food fraud can damage human health and erode consumer confidence, it is imperative that it is detected at an early stage [14,15]. Soon's study aimed to use Bayesian network to predict fraudulent food products originating from China. For this purpose, the RASFF database was used, where 1668 fraud-related notifications were included. Six categories of food and beverage, year, hazard/other, notification of both origin or route of distribution and action taken were used. The types of food fraud were divided into artificial enhancement (AE), adulteration, documentation, illegal trade, other and unauthorized activities. The BN model predicted the probability distribution for AE type food fraud (43.77%), other forms of fraud (20.20%), adulteration (15.95%), documentation (10.49), illegal trade (6.47%) and unauthorized activities (3.18%). The model correctly predicted 85% of the fraud [1]. Bouzembark's study aimed to predict the type of food fraud expected for imported foods. For this purpose, a Bayesian Network (BN) model was used, which was developed based on reports of adulteration/fraud (RASFF) in the period 2000 to 2013. In this period, 749 food fraud notifications were reported and categorized into 6 different types of fraud (i) improper, fraudulent, missing or non-existent health certificates, (ii) illegal importation, (iii) tampering, (iv) improper, expired, fraudulent or missing declarations common entry or import documents, (v) expiration date, (vi) mislabeling. The constructed BN model was validated using 88 food fraud notifications reported in RASFF in 2014. The proposed model correctly predicted 80 % of the food fraud types when the food fraud type, country and food category had been previously reported in RASFF. The model predicted 52% of the 88 types of food fraud correctly. The presented model can help the risk manager/controller in border inspection messages to decide which type of fraud to check for when importing products [14,15]. An ELM is a type of NN and, for that study, the number of nodes in the input layer, output layer, and hidden layers was set to 11, 3, and 20, respectively. The proposed model is used to analyze food safety inspection data with complex, discrete, high-dimensional and nonlinear properties. The accuracy and training time are verified using 10% randomly selected unused data. The model is validated using the unused half of the same data set, and the results reveal a network prediction accuracy level of 86 % for the ELM network [16]. To obtain the best classification results, however, several key parameters of the SVM model must be set correctly,and this is not easy. An study apply a parallel SVM model to explore a model of risk assessment for dairy production.The study is based on several data sources, including analytical data relating to dairy products, including the concentration of related factors (e.g., protein, sodium). Model prediction accuracy was as high as 90% [16]. Alberto's study describes how the use of different ML techniques can help solve the prediction problem in the field of food and feed safety and increase the chances of detecting specific products and/or contaminants that present a higher risk at a given time. The author has carried out a comparison between neural and non-neural ML models that have been used to predict three different problem features within the RASFF dataset. The author indicates that predictors are incoming alert notifications. For this purpose, the author used both neural models and non-neural machine learning methods combined with different strategies to categorize the data set. Among the neural models used were the multilayer perceptron and the convolutional neural network, using gridsearch to obtain the best parameters. The use of the Categorical Embeddings and the use of a multilayer perceptron obtained an accuracy of 86.81% in the prediction [11].

4   Materials and Methods

4.1   Dataset

The data contains information about food fraud. A total of 1,144 food fraud notifications for the period 2000-2020 were downloaded from the Rapid Alert System for Food and Feed (RASFF) database. Each record contains detailed information on the type of notification and the products and countries involved. Based on the description of each notification, we add a variable "type of food fraud" (that is, two different types of food fraud). This dataset can be used to analyze food fraud and a subset was used to train various machine learning models [3] (Table 1).

The Fraud column will be the data to be predicted, therefore we need a clearer view of the data. We will provide a table where we put the definitions of the variables (Table 2).

The data set has different distributions depending on the data type. In the first place we will show the number of instances per data in the type of fraud. It is observed that the largest number of frauds is given by the type HC as can be seen in Fig. 2.

Table 1. Table of variables

Variable	Description	Data
Year	Year of fraud notification	2001,2002...2020
Product	Product category	alcoholic, molluscs,..., wild
Notified	RASFF member country	RASFF member country
Origin	Country where the product was imported	United States, Japan,..., Brazil
Fraud	Type of fraud	HC, Illegal-importation

Table 2. Description of the target variable

Name	Description
HC	Inappropriate, Fraudulent, Missing or Non-existent Health Certificate (HC)
Illegal Information	Illegal or unauthorized import, trade or transit

4.2   Random Forest

Random Forest is a combination of predictive trees that is, a modification of Bagging, which works with a collection of trees uncorrelated and averages them in which each tree is held to depend of the values of a random sample vector independently and with the same distribution of all trees in the forest. generalization error for forests converges to a limit as the number of trees in the forest is great The generalization error of a forest of trees of classification depends on the strength of the individual trees in the forest and the correlation among them. Using a random selection of features to split each node produces error rates that compare favorably to the AdaBoost algorithm but are more robust with respect to noise (strong classifier). Internal estimates monitor for error, strength, and correlation. Also, these are used to show the response to increasing the number of features used in the split. Internal calculations are also used to measure the importance variable. The ideas are also applicable to regression.

The common element in all these procedures is that for the kth tree a random vector k is generated, independent of the last random vectors 1, ..., k-1 but with the same distribution; and a tree is developed using the set of training and of k, which results in a classifier where h(x, k) is a vector input. As noted above, the Random Forest method is based on a set of decision trees, that is, a sample enters the tree and is subjected to a series of binary tests at each node, called split, until you reach a leaf where you find the answer. This technique can be used to break down a complex problem into a set of simple problems. In the training stage, the algorithm tries to optimize the parameters of the split functions from the training samples [4].

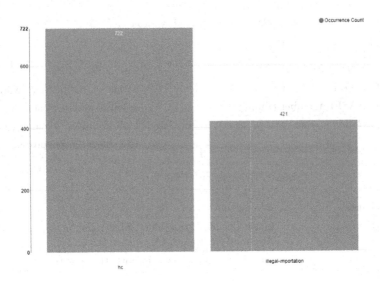

Fig. 2. Comparison of the amount of data from HC and Illegal importation

4.3 Decision Tree

A decision tree is a prediction model whose goal is main one is inductive learning from observations and logical constructions. They are very similar to systems rule-based prediction, which serve to represent and categorize a series of conditions that occur in a successively to solve a problem. constitute probably the most used and popular classification model. The knowledge gained during the learning process inductive is represented by a tree. a tree graphically it is represented by a set of nodes, leaves and branches. the node main or root is the attribute from which the process is started classification; internal nodes correspond to each of questions about the particular attribute of the problem. Each possible answer to the questions is represented through a child node. The branches coming out of each of these nodes are labeled with the possible values of attribute 2. The final nodes or leaf nodes correspond to a decision, which coincides with one of the class variables of the problem to solve This model is built from the description narrative of a problem, since it provides a graphic view of the decision making, specifying the variables that are evaluated, the actions to be taken and the order in which you take them decision will be made. Every time this type is executed model, only one path will be followed depending on the value value of the evaluated variable. The values they can take The variables for this type of models can be discrete or continuous.

A decision tree generation algorithm consists of 2 stages: the first corresponds to the induction of the tree and the second to the classification. In the first stage The decision tree is constructed from the set of training; commonly each internal node of the tree is consists of a test attribute and the portion of the set of training present in the node is divided according with the values that this attribute can take. construction of the tree starts by generating its root node, choosing an attribute from test and dividing the training set into two or more subsets; for each partition a new node is generated and so on successively. When in a node there are objects of more than a class generates an internal node; when it contains objects of only one class, a leaf is formed to which is assigned the class tag. In the second stage of the algorithm each new object is classified by the constructed tree; Later traverses the tree from the root node to a leaf, starting at which determines the membership of the object to some class. The path to follow in the tree is determined by the decisions taken at each internal node, according to the attribute of proof present in it [5].

4.4 Naive Bayes

Bayesian classification methods are based primarily on principally in Bayes's Theorem, then exposes this theorem and the naïve bayes classifier.

This refers to the calculation of the conditional probability of event A given that the event has occurred. event B, its general form is: If A1 , A2 ,...,An are events exhaustive and exclusive such that $P(Ai/B) > 0$, for all i=1,2,...n. ,..., let B be any known event conditional probabilities $P(B/Ai)$, the probability $P(Ai/B)$ is given by the expression

$$P(A_i|B) = \frac{P(B|A_i)P(A_i)}{P(B)} \tag{1}$$

Until now the discussion has derived from the model of independent charac- teristics, that is, the Naive Bayes probability model. The Naive Bayes classifier combines this model with a decision rule. The first common rule is to collect the most likely hypothesis, also known as the maximum posterior or MAP [6].

4.5 Logistic Regression

Logistic regression is one of the statistical models widely used in different disci- plines that is widely used in different disciplines that is used to predict a binary categorical binary categorical variable centered on several independent variables, either quantitative or independent variables, which can be quantitative or qual- itative. qualitative.

Performing a statistical model of this type allows to model the probability of a given event occurring as a function of these explanatory variables. these explanatory variables.

The likelihood-based inference approach is the most commonly used to make inferences (parameter estimation, parameter estimation used to make inferences (estimation of parameters, confidence intervals, hypothesis testing, prediction) in the logistic regression model. logistic regression model. This approach works well when there are large samples. However, this is not the when working with small samples, as this approach is based on asymptotic arguments. approach is based on asymptotic arguments.

The Multiple Logistic Regression Model allows us to study whether or not a binary response variable is dependent on other variables. a binary response variable is dependent or not on other independent variables. independent variables. That is, it statistically models a binary response in terms of a set of independent variables. independent variables. In this way, what distinguishes it from a linear regression model is from a linear regression model is fundamentally that the response variable in logistic response variable in logistic regression is binary or dichotomous [7].

4.6   Multilayer Perceptron

Artificial Neural Networks (ANNs), which is a form of artificial intelligence, that in its architecture tries to mimic the biology of the human brain and nervous system was used in this study. The important component of this simulation is the novel structure of the information processing system which consists of a huge amount of well-interconnected processing elements (neurons) focused on solving a particular problem. Just as it is the case in human beings, ANNs also learn by training. An ANN is developed for a distinct application. These applications include patterns recognition and data classification through a learning process. There are several types of ANNs with different applications, such as data association, data prediction, data classification, data conceptualization and data filtering. The most common type of ANN has three interconnected layers: input, hidden and output. Multi-layer networks make use several types of learning techniques [8]. Multilayer Perceptron (MLP) is a feedforward supervised neural network model. It consists of an input layer, an output layer, and an arbitrary number of hidden layers. The basic MLP has a single hidden layer. Neurons use nonlinear activation functions, either sigmoid, hyperbolic tangent, or Rectified Linear Unit (ReLU). Learning is carried out through backpropagation using the generalized delta rule to update the weights matrices [11].

4.7   SVM

A Support Vector Machine (SVM) learns the decision surface from two different kinds of input points. As a one-class classifier, the description given by the support vector data is able to form a decision boundary around the learning data domain with little or no knowledge of the data outside this boundary. The data is mapped by means of a Gaussian kernel or another type of kernel to a feature space in a higher dimensional space, where the maximum separation between classes is sought. This boundary function, when brought back to the input space, can separate the data into all the different classes, each forming a cluster [9].

5   Results and Discussions

There are some metrics that will help to better evaluate the models.

Accuracy helps us to get the percentage of observations that have been correctly classified, the closer its value is to 1, the better it will be [13].

$$\text{accuracy} = \frac{\text{TP} + \text{TN}}{\text{TP} + \text{FP} + \text{FN} + \text{TN}} \tag{2}$$

Precision measures the ability of a classifier not to label as positive a Observation to be considered as negative. The higher this value is, the better [11]. Its formula is:

$$\text{precision} = \frac{\text{TP}}{\text{TP} + \text{FP}} \tag{3}$$

Recall (sensitivity): It is a measure of the integrity of a classifier, it measures the actual observations that are labeled (predicted) correctly, that is, how many positive class observations are labeled correctly.

F-measure (measure F): It is a weighted average between precision and recall.

ROC curve: It is possible to compare the performance of one classifier with another using the area under the ROC curve. It is the most used evaluation metric. The ROC curve is formed plotting the true positive rate (sensitivity) and the false positive rate (specificity). The area under the curve (AUC) will be the best performance measure for evaluate the classifiers. This measure is the most recommended for unbalanced data, and It will be the main measure for decision making when choosing the models. Without However, it is emphasized that although ROC curves have been (and continue to be) widely used in the scientific literature, these should be complemented with other curves such as as the PRC curve (precision and sensitivity curve) [13].

5.1   Multilayer Perceptron Analysis

Neural networks have three variable components, the epochs, the number of layers, and the number of neurons per layer. The number of epochs will be constant for all comparisons, the number will be a thousand epochs because it is observed in Fig. 3 that the error decreases significantly at iteration 1000 and the same event was observed for all comparisons.

In this study, we used the ten fold cross-validation and gridsearch to determine appropriate parameters according to the average value of accuracy.Now, to determine the size of the hidden layer, we used the following steps [17]. First, for a single hidden layer, we set the initial number of nodes in the hidden layer to be 1 and the model was trained and tested and the average accuracy value was obtained. Then the number of nodes in the hidden layer was gradually increased (2 for each time until it reached 19). Second, on the premise of fixing the parameters of the previously hidden layers, we added neurons for each layer starting from 1 and then determined their optimal number of neurons with the first step. Third, we repeat the second step, but now it would be increased by 2 neurons per layer. Later, when the best model with maximum precision was found, the 10-fold cross-validation was used for training and testing the model to obtain the

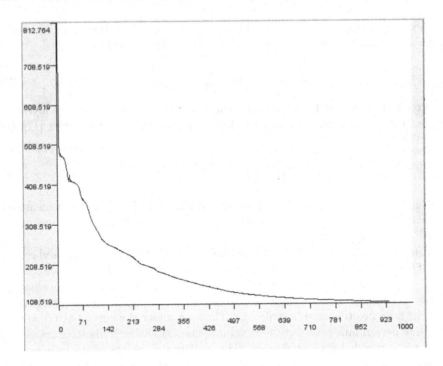

Fig. 3. Comparison of the error with the number of iterations of a neural network

best accuracy. As shown in Fig. 4, we find that the model has the best accuracy when the number of hidden layers is 1 and the number of neurons is 15.

Finally, we select the model with 1 hidden layer, whose number of nodes is 15 neurons per hidden layer. With these parameters, an accuracy of 0.829 is obtained [18].

5.2   Comparison of Algorithms

After applying the algorithms to the data set, the three algorithm evaluation metrics were used: Accuracy, AUC and F-measure. The three algorithms with the highest precision are the multilayer perceptron with 0.829 percent, the random forest with 0.818 percent ,the Decision tree with 0.761 . The three algorithms with the highest AUC are the multilayer perceptron with 0.859, the random forest with a value of 0.857 and the Decision Tree with 0.721 . The three algorithms with the highest F measure are the multilayer perceptron with 0.814,random forest with a value of 0.803, the Desicion tree with 0.824 (Table 3).

5.3   Discussions

The best algorithm seen in the experimental part was the multilayer perceptron with an accuracy of 0.829 outperforming the other machine learning models. It

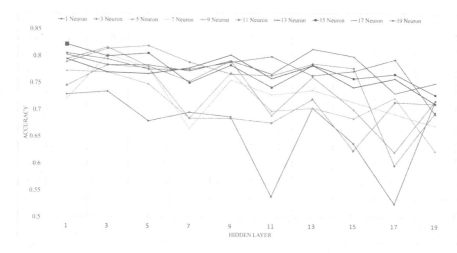

Fig. 4. Maximum precision with different numbers of layers and neurons per layer

Table 3. Table of results

N°	Algorithms	Accuracy	AUC	F-Measure
1	Multilayer Perceptron	0.829	0.859	0.814
2	Random Forest	0.818	0.857	0.803
3	Decision Tree	0.761	0.721	0.824
4	SVM	0.753	0.65	0.7255
5	Logistic Regression	0.681	0.718	0.636
6	Naive Bayes	0.613	0.5	0.5095

is shown that the use of a neural algorithm is better for the prediction of the case study as shown also by the analysis of Nogales in his article for the prediction of food safety risk and using the multilayer perceptron obtaining an accuracy of 86.81% using the categorical Embeddings technique and using the RASFF dataset [11]. Wang's paper that studied the application of machine learning algorithms for food safety prediction also suggests using neural algorithms. He suggested using neural models to analyze food inspection data with complex, high-dimensional and nonlinear properties. In his literature review he found that the use of an ELM model to predict food safety risks in dairy products obtained an accuracy of 0.86 [16].

6   Conclusion

Food fraud is a problem that affects the European Union, resulting in the deception of the authorities in order to obtain an economic benefit. The RASFF is a dataset that informs us about various types of products and the type of fraud they may have. The data used from the dataset were the year, the type of product, the notification, the country of import, the country of origin of the import, and the target variable which would be the type of fraud. The types of fraud were classified into two categories which were HC(Non-Existen Health Certificate in the product) and the presence of an illegal import of the analyzed product. Several algorithmic techniques were used including Naive Bayes model, Logistic Regression, Multilayer Perceptron , Decision Tree, Random Forest and SVM. The best performing model was the Multilayer Perceptron with an AUC of 0.859 and an Accuracy of 0.829 outperforming the other algorithms. It is recommended for future work to use more types of food fraud, i.e. to use expired-date type, tampering, no labelling, ced, non-existence of fraud, among others. In addition, it is recommended to use deep learning models such as convolutional neural networks to compare them with the models presented in the proposed work. As a continuation of the work, the model could be deployed in a Web application so that the authorities can verify imported food in real time and can detect in time the type of food fraud before it enters the country of destination.

References

1. Soon, J.M.: Application of Bayesian network modelling to predict food fraud products from China. Food Control **114**, 107232 (2020). https://doi.org/10.1016/j.foodcont.2020.10723
2. Takano, Y., Miyashiro, R.: Best subset selection via cross-validation criterion. TOP **28**(2), 475–488 (2020). https://doi.org/10.1007/s11750-020-00538-1
3. Hoenderdaal, W.: Food fraud data based on the European Rapid Alert System for Food and Feed (RASFF) [Data set]. Zenodo (2020). https://doi.org/10.5281/zenodo.4299495
4. Merino, R.F.M., Chacon, C.I.N.: Bosques aleatorios como extension de los arboles de clasificacion con los programas R y Python. Interfases **10**, 165–189 (2017)
5. Martınez, R.E.B., et al.: Arboles de decision como herramienta en el diagnostico medico. Rev. Med. Univ. Veracruzana **9**(2), 19–24 (2009)
6. Constantino, M. (s/f). Clasicadores bayesianos. El algoritmo Naıve Bayes. Nebrija.es. Recuperado el 5 de junio de 2022, de https://www.nebrija.es/cmalagon/inco/Apuntes/bayesianlearning.pdf
7. Corraltitlán, A.S.V., Olvera, L.G.S.: Propuesta de un modelo de regresión logística múltiple para el diagnóstico del cáncer de mama
8. Bunyamin, S.A., Ijimdiya, T.S., Eberemu, A.O., Osinubi, K.J.: Artificial neural networks prediction of compaction characteristics of black cotton soil stabilized with cement kiln dust. J. Soft Comput. Civil Eng. **2**(3), 50–71 (2018)
9. Betancourt, G.A.: Las m aquinas de soporte vectorial (SVMs). Sci. Tech. **1**(27) (2005). https://doi.org/10.22517/23447214.6895
10. Yu, L., Zhou, R., Chen, R., Lai, K.K.: Missing data preprocessing in credit classification: one-hot encoding or imputation? Emerg. Markets Finan. Trade **58**(2), 472–482 (2022). https://doi.org/10.1080/1540496x.2020.1825935
11. Nogales, A., Díaz-Morón, R., García-Tejedor, Á.J.: A comparison of neural and non-neural machine learning models for food safety risk prediction with European Union RASFF data. Food Control **134**, 108697 (2022). https://doi.org/10.1016/j.foodcont.2021.108697

12. Vadhwani, D., Thakor, D.: Predictive analysis of injury severity of person across angle crashes using machine learning models. Int. J. Crashworthiness (2022). https://doi.org/10.1080/13588265.2022.2109772

13. Rodrıguez, A.R.M.: Prediccion de fuga de clientes en una empresa de telefonıa utilizando el algoritmo Adaboost desbalanceado y la regresion logıstica asimetrica (2018)

14. Bouzembrak, Y., Marvin, H.J.P.: Prediction of food fraud type using data from Rapid Alert System for Food and Feed (RASFF) and Bayesian network modelling. Food Control **61**, 180–187 (2016). https://doi.org/10.1016/j.foodcont.2015.09.026

15. Marvin, H.J.P., Bouzembrak, Y., Janssen, E.M., van der Fels- Klerx, H.J., van Asselt, E.D., Kleter, G.A.: A holistic approach to food safety risks: Food fraud as an example. Food Res. Int. **89**, 463–470 (2016). https://doi.org/10.1016/j.foodres. 2016.08.028. (Sacar)

16. Wang, X., Bouzembrak, Y., Lansink, A.O., van der Fels-Klerx, H.J.: Application of machine learning to the monitoring and prediction of food safety: a review. Compr. Rev. Food Sci. Food Saf. **21**(1), 416–434 (2022)

17. Ruan, X., Zhu, Y., Li, J., Cheng, Y.: Predicting the citation counts of individual papers via a BP neural network. J. Inform. **14**(3), 101039 (2020). https://doi.org/10.1016/j.joi.2020.101039

18. Li, X., Tang, X., Cheng, Q.: Predicting the clinical citation count of biomedical papers using multilayer perceptron neural network. J. Informet. **16**(4), 101333 (2022). https://doi.org/10.1016/j.joi.2022.101333

19. Dada, A.C., et al.: Microbiological hazards associated with food products imported from the Asia-Pacific region based on analysis of the rapid alert system for food and feed (RASFF) notifications. Food Control **129**, 108243 (2021). https://doi.org/10.1016/j.foodcont.2021.10824

20. Robson, K., Dean, M., Brooks, S., Haughey, S., Elliott, C.: A 20-year analysis of reported food fraud in the global beef supply chain. Food Control **116**, 107310 (2020). https://doi.org/10.1016/j.foodcont.2020.10731

Author Index

J. A. Lossio-Ventura et al. (Eds.): SIMBig 2022, CCIS 1837, pp. 271–272, 2023.
https://doi.org/10.1007/978-3-031-35445-8

Printed in the United States
by Baker & Taylor Publisher Services